THE CANADIAN PRESS

STYLEBOOK

A GUIDE FOR WRITERS AND EDITORS

16th edition

Patti Tasko
Editor

THE CANADIAN PRESS

36 King St. East, Toronto, Ontario M5C 2L9
416-364-0321 www.thecanadianpress.com

Copyright © 2010 The Canadian Press
1st edition 1940
2nd edition 1947
3rd edition 1954
4th edition 1957
5th edition 1966
6th edition 1974
7th edition 1983
8th edition 1989
9th edition 1992
10th edition 1995
11th edition 1999
12th edition 2002
13th edition 2004
14th edition 2006
15th edition 2008
16th edition 2010

Library and Archives Canada Cataloguing in Publication

The Canadian Press stylebook : a guide for writers and editors /
Patti Tasko, editor. -- 16th ed.

Previous ed. under title: The Canadian Press stylebook : a guide for writing
and editing.

Includes bibliographical references and index.
ISBN 978-0-920009-46-8

1. Journalism--Style manuals. 2. Canadian Press--Handbooks, manuals, etc.
I. Tasko, Patti II. Canadian Press

PN4783.C35 2008   808'.06607   C2008-903633-6

Design and cover art by Sean Vokey, The Canadian Press.

Contents

Canadian Press policies

The working journalist

Legal

Tools and technical guides

The news report

Public relations and the media

Introduction

The Canadian Press Stylebook began life as a modest little pamphlet more than a half-century ago. It was a sort of operator's manual for staff at The Canadian Press, Canada's national news agency.

It has blossomed since then into a comprehensive reference work used in newsrooms and business offices across Canada. It is required reading in university and college media courses.

Through its many editions, the stylebook has increasingly taken on the concerns of a wide variety of editors and writers outside the news media who work with words and need a standard Canadian reference.

The stylebook has been organized into six main sections:

Canadian Press policies: The standards that guide the work of collecting and distributing news. Basic journalism ethics, but also specific help with sensitive areas like racism, sexism, misquotes and anonymous sources.

The working journalist: From creating audio to reporting from a war zone, a guide to working as a journalist. Organized alphabetically, with advice on specific areas such as business and sports, and on using different media such as video, photos and broadcast to tell stories. Down-to-earth tips on writing and editing, and lots of examples to illustrate each point. A how-to guide for access-to-information laws.

Legal: Libel. Copyright. Court coverage. Police searches of the newsroom. Contempt. The rights — and limitations — that govern the everyday work of reporters and editors.

Tools and technical guides: Organized alphabetically, this is the section that editors can consult for advice on punctuation, capitalization and other grammatical elements, as well as specific style guidance on every topic from Aboriginal Peoples to weather. Also includes a section on tricky words and a pronunciation guide for Canadian place names.

The news report: A how-to-read-the-wire guide. Sets out the news agency's procedures for advisories, updating stories, corrections and other important elements of the news report.

Public relations and media: Writing and editing pointers for those trying to make news.

White space is provided throughout for notes and observations — particularly helpful at publications that modify or expand on our style.

What's new

Increasingly, people are getting their news and information on the go, not while settled comfortably in front of a newspaper or television, and this 16th edition addresses the challenges of wireless communications. We have updated our advice in all chapters, when relevant, on how to effectively reach these on-the-move, distracted eyeballs. In particular, we expanded chapters that deal specifically with online news and its elements: headlines, video and graphics. We have also updating the chapter on polls to reflect the new reality of online polling.

In this edition you will find the following specific changes to style:

1. We now abbreviate the political titles **senator** and **representative** in front of names: **Sen. Nancy Greene, Rep. Chris Tucker**.

2. We now use **Somali**, not Somalian, as the adjective for all things from the African country.

3. To reflect usage, we accept **data** in both singular and plural uses.

4. To reflect its official name, it is **Yukon**, not *the* Yukon.

Our basic style changes cautiously: evolution, not revolution. While this edition contains changes of emphasis and detail, there are few departures from long-standing fundamentals. We continually assess our style to keep it up to date and sensible. Suggestions for improvement are always welcome.

Patti Tasko, Editor

patti.tasko@thecanadianpress.com

What is The Canadian Press?

There is probably no other organization that has made such an ongoing contribution to Canadian life and yet has such a low public profile. Since The Canadian Press was founded in 1917, the news agency has been instrumental in telling Canadians about themselves. It has shaped the way Canadians see the world. It has played a crucial role in the growth of the country's news industry.

Canadians who read a newspaper over morning coffee, listen to a radio newscast on the drive to work, check their BlackBerrys for news headlines at lunch, watch the TV news before bed and pick up weekend sports scores on the Internet would likely be surprised to discover a lot of that information came from The Canadian Press.

News from The Canadian Press is found everywhere in Canada. It is used by daily newspapers and hundreds of radio and television stations, from national all-news, sports and business channels to tiny stations in remote corners of the country. Canadian Press news, photos, interactive graphics and video reports appear on countless websites. Canadian Press headlines are on big screens in sports venues and small screens in elevators. Politicians and other newsmakers, who are well aware of the agency's reach, purchase a Canadian Press service that pushes stories to their mobile devices so they can keep up on the news minute by minute.

Some days the agency's reach is glaringly obvious. The day after the funeral of former prime minister Pierre Trudeau, readers in every major city in Canada saw a Canadian Press picture of his son Justin Trudeau, mourning beside his coffin, in their newspapers. Some days the reach creeps up on people. Average Canadians, quoted or photographed by the agency for a story, are often amazed to discover the number of places where their face or name will turn up.

Much of the agency's daily news report comes from the agency's own staff of reporters, editors and photographers who work in bureaus across the country. Their work is broadened with news contributions from newspapers and the many broadcast outlets that also contribute news tips, delivered in time for deadlines that span six time zones.

The result is a Canadian news report that is unmatched for its depth, breadth, timeliness and diversity. More often than not the first word on a major Canadian story, whether it comes from a tiny community in the mountains of British Columbia or a fishing village in Newfoundland, comes from The Canadian Press.

Our reach is not limited to Canada, but also includes full coverage from around the world. The bulk of the international report originates with The Associated Press. Canadian Press editors monitor a massive file of AP news every day, ensuring stories of particular interest to Canadians are relayed. (The Associated Press also relies on The Canadian Press to cover Canada for the world by transmitting Canadian Press stories and photos on its worldwide network.) A permanent Canadian Press bureau in Washington and a temporary bureau in Afghanistan, to cover the Canadian Armed Forces military action there, supplement this report. The agency's journalists also regularly travel outside the country to cover news of interest to Canadians.

The Canadian Press was created by newspaper publishers to provide a flow of news across the sparsely populated regions of the country. Before 1917, newspapers exchanged news within regional associations and received international news from The Associated Press on north-south telegraph circuits. But there was no ready means of sending news east and west across Canada.

Then the First World War came along, and publishers were desperate to receive news of Canada's troops in Europe. Part of the early financing of The Canadian Press was a $50,000 federal grant to pay for telegraph circuits linking the Maritimes to Quebec and Ontario and the Prairies to British Columbia. The government offered to help because of the organization's potential to serve the cause of national unity during the war.

That funding ended in 1924 by mutual agreement and the founding publishers of The Canadian Press voted never again to risk the appearance of compromise by accepting government money for any news purpose.

A French-language service was established in 1951. In addition to providing an important service to French-language clients, this service, based in Montreal, also serves as an important pipeline of news from Quebec. The best elements of this are translated into English for Canadian Press clients and the best elements of the English service are translated into French for Presse Canadienne clients. This ensures that Quebecers are not isolated by language from important news from English Canada and that newspapers, radio and TV broadcasters in English Canada, likewise, are not isolated from important stories and issues in Quebec.

Since the early days of public and private radio, The Canadian Press has served the broadcasting industry. An early task was preparing scripts for Lorne Greene and other well-known voices who read the latest dispatches from Second World War battlefronts over the fledgling Canadian Broadcasting Corp.

A separate broadcast division, Broadcast News, was formed in 1954. As the industry expanded, more and more stations turned to BN as a major source of news. In the 1960s, an audio component, featuring voice reports and sound bites of newsmakers, was added to the service. Network newscasts began in 1979. In 2006, as media convergence eliminated some of the boundaries between print and broadcast media, the BN signoff was replaced by The Canadian Press moniker to give the agency a consistent identity in all the media markets it serves. About the same time, The Canadian Press broadened its repertoire to include video reports, mainly for use online but also available to traditional broadcasters.

On the technical side, in 1973 The Canadian Press became the first news organization in Canada to make extensive use of word processors to write and edit stories. In the mid-1980s, the agency switched from land circuits to satellite for delivery of stories, photos and audio reports. In 1997 The Canadian Press started delivering news reports over the Internet. The following year a French-language service was added "en ligne" as well.

Past generations of Canadian Press journalists who practised their craft to the click of Morse code and the beat of teletype machines would find the modern newsroom a strange beast indeed. But some things would feel comfortably familiar. The Canadian Press continues to be an organization driven by a quest for first-rate journalism. Its mission hasn't changed. The goal is to keep Canadians informed and help them understand and experience their world more fully. The Canadian Press tells people the story of their country, every day, in all forms and from all corners of the land. In the 21st century of the global village the stories of our nation are a cornerstone of who we are and will become.

Eric Morrison
President

Notes

Why Canadian Press style is the way it is

Singer Taylor Swift, who has seven million Facebook friends and is known for sending tweets to her fans, will host a live chat to talk about a new album.

Several words in that sentence would have made no sense to an average reader a few years ago. Many of today's readers would find the phrasing normal in a news report.

That's one of the reasons why stylebooks are needed. When new terms are added to our ever-changing lexicon, capitalization and spelling should be consistent, whether the story appears in a lifestyles section or a business report. Otherwise, readers may be annoyed or even confused.

English is a fluid language, but it's bound by complicated rules of grammar. Working reporters and editors don't have time to research decisions on vocabulary and capitalization and grammar every time a problem arises. A stylebook presents such decisions in a logical, handy form.

Whimsy is found in every stylebook. But style decisions overall are based on sound reasons. Most are basic grammar and common sense, with the stylebook simply a reminder. Other decisions involve choosing from among a range of valid alternatives, and at that point a number of factors come into play.

Among the ones that have influenced Canadian Press style over the decades:

Preferences of Canadian newspapers

Newspapers were the main client of The Canadian Press for many decades and their preferences still come into play regularly. Many readers of newspapers are passionate about the English language and how it is used and provide constant feedback to newspapers, and the editor of the stylebook, on spelling and capitalization issues and what Canadians prefer. The majority preference becomes Canadian Press style.

For example, The Canadian Press became the first western news agency to drop the courtesy titles **Mr., Mrs., Miss** and **Ms.** from all copy. Over the years, the use of such titles had become erratic — sometimes used on news pages but not in sports sections, for instance. Most papers agreed the rules needed to change, and the soundest course was to drop all such titles. Some papers continue to use them, either throughout the paper or in particular sections.

More recently, The Canadian Press adopted the "our" spelling for words of more than one syllable in which the "u" is not pronounced. The Canadian Press had written with **color** and

rigor for 80 years, and felt the "or" spelling was an established Canadian option. But "our" was the spelling preferred by many readers and taught in most Canadian schools. A significant number of the agency's member newspapers had already adopted the "our" spelling. A survey showed that 77 per cent of newspapers wanted The Canadian Press to use this style as well. So we started writing with **colour** and **rigour**.

The complete list of "our" words can be found in the stylebook's companion volume, *Caps and Spelling*.

Consistency

A style that is full of exceptions is difficult to use. One goal of this stylebook is to keep exceptions to a minimum.

Maintaining consistency can be troublesome. New words crop up all the time, and often a certain style becomes commonplace — even if it is inconsistent with similar uses. That's why people write **T-shirt**, but **email**. Canadian Press style tries to maintain consistency as much as possible given the influence of common usage.

Popular usage

News reporting is meant to inform the public, not to score points with language purists. Outdated expressions can get in the way of that goal. Some of the changes in the meaning of words may not be for the better, but if most readers are led to believe that **presently** means **right now**, rather than **soon**, there's no point in using the word in a news story and risking misunderstanding.

The Canadian Press won't be the first to accept the misuse of a word, and occasionally we're a bit stubborn about changes that seem to debase the language. But eventually a misused form can take on a life of its own and we bow to the inevitable. We have reluctantly accepted the word **gender** to mean the difference between males and females, given its overwhelming usage this way, even though grammarians would tell you the word is traditionally used to distinguish between masculine, feminine and neuter words, not people.

Sensitivity

Today's perfectly normal word can be tomorrow's flagrant example of sexism, racism or other abuse. In particular, people who feel put upon by society are likely to reject labels that seem to limit their potential or lock them into hurtful self-images.

People who are identified by certain words (**cripple, housewife, Indian**) can easily believe that the language is insensitive and prefer another description (**disabled person, stay-at-home mom, aboriginal**). In time, those labels may also fall out of favour.

The Canadian Press believes that people's preferences should be respected when new forms are adopted by a significant number of those concerned and become familiar to the general public. But we don't want to be faddish, accepting words for routine use that are so *sensitive* that they have little clear meaning left — expressions like **developmentally challenged**. Nor will we go along casually with new labels that are politically controversial among the people most concerned.

Words like **spokesman, chairman** and alderman cause resentment, understandably, when applied to women. The Canadian Press uses **spokeswoman** and **chairwoman**, as well as such forms as **salesperson, chairperson** and **spokesperson** when the sex of the individual is unknown. Even better, we opt for a neutral word such as clerk, firefighter or councillor.

The goal at The Canadian Press is to carefully think out style decisions and come to a decision that is agreeable to both the public and those who use our stylebooks. However, our main influence is readers and what works for them. We don't expect everyone to agree with all of our style decisions, but we do welcome input and feedback from everyone.

Canadian Press policies

Principles

When The Canadian Press was founded in 1917, it was for one reason: to serve the newspapers that owned it, and through them, the Canadian public. For decades, the only contact The Canadian Press had with the public was through its member newspapers. But rapid changes in the communications industry have changed the way the news agency fulfils its mandate of keeping Canadians informed.

The Canadian Press serves many of the daily newspapers in Canada, providing reliable and relevant news, photos, video and graphics. But beyond the traditional printed word, its role in new media continues to expand. Regardless of whether Canadians are getting their news from the Internet, their BlackBerrys or all-news television channels, there's a good chance much of the information comes from The Canadian Press. It is truly Canada's No. 1 source for news — in French and English. Newsgathering is an imprecise science, but the depth of the agency's network makes its newsgathering reach unmatched: a dedicated staff in bureaus and correspondent points across the country; bureaus in Washington and Afghanistan; a working partnership with newspaper, TV and radio newsrooms; and an exclusive relationship with the Associated Press, the largest news agency in the world.

There's a difference between providing information and telling Canadians what is happening in their vast country — and how events beyond our borders affect them. Context and perspective are fundamental parts of the report of The Canadian Press. It's the goal of its reporters and editors to focus on real people — not just institutions — to show in human terms how events affect our lives. It's a busy world out there so every story needs to convince people that they should make time for it. If the news report doesn't strive to be interesting or tell the reader why they should care, Canadians will click to another website, turn the page or flip the channel.

Although our role continues to evolve, the principles that guide our work are unchanged. Everything that we do must be honest, unbiased and unflinchingly fair. We deal with facts that are demonstrable, supported by sources that are reliable and responsible. We pursue with equal vigour all sides of a story.

Accuracy is fundamental. Discovery of a mistake calls for immediate correction. Corrections to stories already published or broadcast must not be grudging or stingy. They must be written in a spirit of genuinely wanting to right a wrong in the fairest and fullest manner.

Our work is urgent. Speed must be a primary objective of a news service committed to round-the-clock deadlines. But being reliable is always more important than being fast.

Good taste is a constant consideration. Some essential news is essentially repellent. Its handling need not be.

Staff responsibility

Responsibility for upholding Canadian Press standards rests with our reporters, editors and supervisors. So much individuality is involved in reporting, writing and editing news that it is impossible to have precise rules covering every eventuality. Being guided by proven practices is the surest way of meeting the standards that Canadians have come to expect from its national news agency.

Among the most important of these practices:

1. Investigate fully before transmitting any story or identifying any individual in a story where there is the slightest reason for doubt. When in doubt cut it out. But never make this an excuse for ditching an angle without thorough checking. The doubt must be an honest doubt, arrived at after examination of all the facts.

Prime Minister Stephen Harper talks to reporters outside the House of Commons on Parliament Hill in 2007. Journalists have a point of view, but it must not get in the way of balanced reporting.

THE CANADIAN PRESS/Tom Hanson

2. Cite competent authorities and sources as the origin of any information open to question. Have proof available for publication in the event of a denial.

3. Be impartial when handling any news affecting parties or matters in controversy. Give fair representation to all sides at issue.

4. Stick to the facts without editorial opinion or comment. Reporters' opinions are not wanted in copy. Their observations are. So are accurate backgrounding and authoritative interpretation essential to the reader's understanding of complicated issues.

5. Admit errors promptly, frankly. Public distrust of the media is profound and troubling. The distrust is fed by inaccuracy, carelessness, indifference to public sentiment, automatic cynicism

about those in public life, perceived bias or unfairness and other sins suggesting arrogance.

6. The Canadian Press can help overcome such public attitudes through scrupulous care for facts and unwavering dedication to fairness. We must not be quick to dismiss criticism and complaints, a trait journalists refuse to accept in others.

7. The power of news stories to injure can reach both the ordinary citizen and the corporate giant. The Canadian Press's integrity and sensitivity demand that supervisors and staff respond sympathetically and quickly when an error has been made. It doesn't matter whether the complaint comes from a timid citizen acting alone or from a powerful figure's battery of lawyers.

8. Every story shown to be erroneous and involving a corrective must be drawn to the attention of supervisory staff.

Ethical behaviour

Part of our responsibility as journalists is to ensure we don't do anything that demeans the craft or weakens our credibility. Because we deliver the bad news about politicians who turn dirty, caregivers who abuse their trust and business people who discard ethics for gain, we must observe stringent ethical practices, and be seen to be doing so.

It is impossible to raise all potential ethical challenges in this book. But the following guiding principles are offered in the spirit of wanting to advance, not restrain, our work.

1. Pride in yourself and in the practice of journalism nourishes ethical behaviour.

2. The Canadian Press pays its own way. Staff should not accept anything that might compromise our integrity or credibility.

3. The Canadian Press does not pay newsmakers for interviews, to take their pictures or to film or record them.

4. Canadian Press reporters do not misrepresent themselves to get a story. They always identify themselves as journalists.

Impartiality

Impartiality is somewhat like exercise. You have to work out regularly to build tone and strength.

The best exercise for impartiality is to stop regularly and ask yourself: "Am I being as impartial, honest and fair as I can be?"

Some other guides to impartiality:

Parties in controversy, whether in politics or law or otherwise, receive fair consideration. Statements issued by conflicting interests merit equal prominence, whether combined in a single story or used at separate times.

But always try to get opposing sides for simultaneous publication.

If an attack by one group or person on another has been covered, any authoritative answer is also carried. If a proper source cannot be reached, say so, and keep trying.

When a comparative unknown expresses controversial views, question his or her expertise on the subject. If there is no expertise, or the individual does not have an official position that puts weight behind the views, consider carefully whether the report should be carried.

Quotations

Quotes are the lifeblood of any story. They put rosiness into the cheeks of the palest stories. They add credibility, immediacy and punch.

They can also bring grief to writers and editors who play loose with them. Some news organizations permit liberties with quotes. The Canadian Press takes a somewhat stern approach to any tampering with just what was said.

In general, we quote people verbatim and in standard English. We correct slips of grammar that are obvious slips and that would be needlessly embarrassing. We remove verbal mannerisms such as *ah*'s, routine vulgarities and meaningless repetitions. We fix careless spelling mistakes and other typos in emails and text messages. Otherwise we do not revise quotations.

While we don't routinely use abnormal spellings and grammar to indicate dialects or mispronunciations, they can have a place in helping to convey atmosphere.

Cleaning up or parphrasing this tweet from a teenage fan in a story about pop singer Justin Bieber's use of Twitter would have taken a revealing element out of the story:

"i wonder if @justinbieber ever sees my tweets, probably not, but im never gonna stop trying<3"

Quotes containing bafflegab are routinely paraphrased in plain English, no matter how eminent the speaker.

Other points to remember about handling quotes:

1. Whenever possible, interviews should be recorded. When there is risk that a quote is not exact, for whatever reason, a paraphrase is safest.

2. When exactness is essential — if it's one person's word against another's — quote verbatim.

3. When a speaker uses what is obviously a wrong word, check back when possible. When a quote does not make sense, check back with the speaker or ditch it.

4. Misquotes result not only from tampering or carelessness. Failure to place a quote in context can have the same eroding effect on credibility. For instance: **"If our tax revenues allow it, I'll repave all secondary highways"** should not be parlayed into the bare reported statement that the speaker promised to repave all secondary highways.

Similarly, failure to indicate tone can skew a quote. A speaker's jocular comment may need to be reported with an explanatory **she said with a smile. There are other occasions when the bare words benefit from addition of a brief description: "I'm not guilty," he said, glowering at the jury.**

5. When clear and concise, a full quote is preferred to a partial quote. But a partial quote can be useful for spicing a lead, setting off a controversial statement or giving the flavour of a speaker.

6. Make only cosmetic changes to quotations from a text: changing spelling and capitalization to Canadian Press style, for example, or fixing typos and other small errors in spelling and punctuation.

7. If words are left out of a text or middle of a quotation, show the omission with an ellipsis. Note: **Ellipses are best avoided. Prefer other devices, such as paraphrases or partial quotes.**

8. Long bracketed explanations and paraphrases should not be inserted at the beginning or end of a quote.

Not: "(The new program) is imaginative, realistic and worth the time and money invested," Scott said.

But: The new program "is imaginative, realistic and worth the time and money invested," Scott said.

9. Guard against attributing one person's quote to several speakers.

Not: Most retailers surveyed condemned the new tax, saying that "it will mean working half a day a week for the government."

10. Do not include in a quote words that the speaker could not have spoken.

Not: Davis said he "was delighted that the prize is going to the American."

But: Davis said he was "delighted that the prize is going to the American."

Davis's words were "I'm (not **was**) delighted."

➤ See **Slang**, page 398.

11. If the quotations are coming from an email, text message, chat room or some other online service where it is virtually impossible to verify the source, make that clear in the story. Always push for an interview in person or on the phone. Gathering comments this way should be a last resort. Anonymous quotes from a chat room are useless except to provide colour or humour.

12. Do not alter audio or video clips except to make sound clearer and reduce line noise. Within a clip, edit only to remove pauses and stumbles.

13. On rare occasions, audio and video is sometimes distorted to protect the identity of someone, such as a minor. This should only be done after consulting with a supervisor.

Language

A reminder to be careful with translations. We should not imply that someone is speaking English when he is not.

In interviews and speeches, make clear what language is being used unless it is obvious. At a news conference where both French and English are used, specify when French was the original language. When reporting the shouts of a crowd or the wording of protest signs that are in other languages, specify that a translation is involved.

Readers are entitled to know when a direct or indirect quote is based on translation rather than the exact words used.

Obscenity

Casual obscenity, blasphemy and vulgarity are not wanted in the news report. Four-letter words shouted from a crowd or muttered by an angry demonstrator add nothing useful to a story. Canadian Press news stories are used by a wide variety of media, and some, especially broadcasters who may rip and read a story, do not want obscenities in copy.

There are few exceptions. A prominent figure who uses obscene language in a public situation is one. An interview subject may use obscenities in such a way that leaving them out would paint a false picture. Or a quote that includes a vulgarity might be the most effective way to connote certain emotions. But these are the exceptions, not the rule. Always consider other ways of getting across this element of the story before resorting to the use of obscenities.

Obscenities or vulgar language should always be flagged in an Editors Note that contains the obscenity as well as the word **CAUTION** in all-caps:

CAUTION: Note language (fuck) in para 3.

Note: When such a note is required on Canadian Press copy moving to broadcasters, include it in the **Update** line so it appears on the broadcast wire.

When an obscenity or vulgarity must be reported, do not use the prissy device of replacing some letters of the offensive words with hyphens, or use an euphemism such as **effing** or **f-word**. Put the questionable language in a separate paragraph that can be readily deleted by editors who do not want to use it.

When the obscenity is part of an audio or video clip, discuss its handling with a supervisor. In most cases, we do not bleep highly profane words, although it may be possible to send two versions of the clip to subscribers, one that ends or begins before the obscene word. Any audio clip that includes an obscenity should include a **CAUTION: Note contents** warning beside the slug line that the language may be offensive to listeners.

Sensitive subjects

Potential for offence lurks in every news story. Age, race, sex, disabilities, religion — all are sometimes pertinent to the news but must be handled thoughtfully.

Use fairness, sensitivity and good taste when identifying age, colour, creed, nationality, personal appearance, religion, sex, sexual orientation and any other heading under which a person or group may feel slighted.

Aboriginal Peoples

In Canada, there are status (or reserve) Indians, non-status Indians (living outside reserves), Métis (people of mixed European and native origin) and Inuit. Collectively, they are known variously as Aboriginal Peoples, original peoples, aboriginals, indigenous peoples, the First Nations and other variations.

Some points concerning Aboriginal Peoples:

1. The Canadian Press uses uppercase for **Aboriginal Peoples**, which includes all Indian, Métis and Inuit people in Canada. **First Nations** is also uppercase. Other variations — **indigenous people, aboriginals** (except for Aboriginals of Australia), **native peoples** — are lowercase.

2. In all references, be guided by the preference of those concerned.

3. Use **Indian** with discretion. Some people object to it because it originated with the European explorers' misconception that they had landed in India. Others, especially status Indians, prefer it to be used.

4. Use **native** advisedly. **Aboriginal** and **First Nations** are more specific and are preferred by many in the community.

5. Where reasonable, prefer the actual name of the community — Cree, Mohawk, Blackfoot, Ojibwa — to a generality. For band names, use the spelling the band prefers, which is also the spelling used by the federal government.

6. The word tribe in its original sense was reserved for primitive peoples. Some natives use it casually and it need not be entirely avoided. But **community, people, nation, band, language group** are alternatives.

➤ See **Aboriginal Peoples**, page 260.

Age

Often age is relevant as part of a personal description or for identification. Ages also help readers to relate to people in news stories.

In general, give a person's age rather than imprecise and possibly derogatory terms such as **senior citizen, retiree, elderly** or **middle-aged.**

Put the age in the lead only when it is significant, such as in obituaries or when an 85-year-old is cycling across the country, or when a three-year-old child is missing. Guard against the formula lead — **a 30-year-old dentist; a 52-year-old fisherman; a 23-year-old convict** . . .

Writing **Mario Lalonde, 30,** is usually preferable to the more cumbersome **30-year-old Mario Lalonde.**

If age is unavailable for an obituary, give an indication of it from the person's activities, such as year of graduation or year of retirement.

Infant describes a baby that is no more than a few months old; a **baby** is a child who is not yet walking. **Toddler** describes a child around the age of two, while a **preschooler** is between the ages of three and five. Males up to 16 are called **boys** and females to that age are **girls.** Use a phrase like **young people** for those of both sexes who are somewhat older.

First names may be used in subsequent references for those under 18, except in sports stories.

Youth in general includes both sexes: **the youth of Canada.** Applied to individuals, it usually means males. Try to avoid the latter use.

Disabilities

Be accurate, clear and sensitive when describing a person with a disability, handicap, illness or disease. They are people first; their disability is only one part of their humanity and most would say it is the least important part.

Mention a disability only if it is pertinent. Never dismiss someone with an unqualified **disabled, crippled** or the like. Write **Romanov, whose hands are twisted with arthritis,** . . . And perhaps indicate to what extent a person has overcome a disability or how she copes with it: **Girushi uses a wheelchair once she leaves her studio.**

Be specific. **Afflicted with** suggests pain and suffering. It doesn't always apply. Nor does **suffering.** People who use wheelchairs are not necessarily **confined** to them. **Crippling** can be a temporary or permanent condition. People may be **deaf, slightly deaf** or **hard of hearing; blind** or have **poor eyesight.** A **patient** is someone under a doctor's care or in hospital. **Victim** connotes helplessness. A child who is **mentally handicapped** (slow) is not necessarily **mentally disturbed** (ill). Epileptics have **seizures,** not **fits.**

While it is important to be specific for clarity, there are also some terms that may be used in the scientific community that are not as acceptable in casual use. **Mentally retarded** is a valid clinical description often found in medical journals, yet many dislike it because of the schoolyard insults associated with the term. Use **mentally challenged** or **mentally handicapped** instead.

Don't define people by their disorders: **the disabled, the blind, the handicapped.** Writing **people with disabilities** emphasizes the human beings and not the disabilities.

Race and ethnicity

Canadian Press reporting should reflect the ethnic diversity of the country in a natural way, free of explicit or unconscious racism.

Identify a person by race, colour, national origin or immigration status only when it is truly pertinent. It is appropriate to report that a woman facing deportation is Polish. Similarly, the victim of hate mail may be referred to as a Jew. A full description, including but not limited to colour, may be used if a person wanted by police is at large.

The appearance of racial minorities in news reports should not be confined to accounts of cultural events, racial tension or crime. Comments on subjects that are a matter of public interests should come from a wide variety of people of different backgrounds.

Remember that what is obvious to a university-educated Christian whose parents were born in Britain might need explanation for persons from a variety of other backgrounds. It should not be taken for granted that a Muslim ceremony needs explanation while a Roman Catholic mass does not. Too often journalists — a profession that is only slowly starting to reflect the many faces of Canada — assume their readers share their WASP background. Watch the labels — labelling a fruit as "exotic" might make sense to someone raised in rural Saskatchewan but would not ring true to many foreign-born readers in Toronto who grew up eating it for breakfast.

Race and ethnicity are pertinent when it motivates an incident or when it helps explain the emotions of those in confrontation. Thus references to race or ethnic background are relevant in reports of racial controversy, immigration difficulties, language discussions and so on.

When an incident cuts across ethnic lines, say so, as when a sizable number of Canadian-born individuals join Chinese immigrants demonstrating against immigration procedures.

That a man found guilty of shoplifting is, say, an aboriginal is usually irrelevant and he should not be identified as such.

Race is pertinent in reporting an accomplishment unusual in a particular race: for example, if a Canadian of Chinese origin is named to the Canadian Football Hall of Fame.

Beware of playing up inflammatory statements at the expense of the main story. Be certain that a spokesman indeed speaks for a community or organization, and give a brief description of that organization, its aims and number of members.

Don't always turn to the same minority spokespeople and organizations for reaction. This can give unwarranted standing to groups that don't necessarily reflect the full range of views of their communities.

Arguing that humour was intended is no defence for a racial slur.

Use racially derogatory terms like **Paki** and **nigger** only when part of a direct quotation and when essential to the story. Flag such a story:

CAUTION: Note racial slur in para 15.

Names of races

1. Capitalize the proper names of nationalities, peoples, races and tribes.

Aboriginal Peoples, Arab, Caucasian, French-Canadian, Inuit, Jew, Latin, Negro, Asian, Cree

2. Note that **black** and **white** do not name races and are lowercase.

3. The term **black** is acceptable in all references in Canada and the United States. In the United States **African-American** is also used; in Canada **African-Canadian** is used by some people but not by others. In the United States there is a National Association for the Advancement of Colored People, usually identified as the NAACP.

4. There is usually no need to use hyphenated descriptions such as **Polish-Canadian** or **Jamaican-Canadian**, given they may put an inappropriate emphasis on the person's ethnic background. But these descriptions can be used if the individual prefers it and it is relevant.

Sexism

Treat the sexes equally and without stereotyping. A woman's marital or family status — single, married, divorced, grandmother — is pertinent only to explain a personal reference or to round out a profile. The test always is: Would this information be used if the subject were a man?

Referring to a woman gratuitously as **attractive, leggy** or **sexy** is as inappropriate as describing a man as **hot, well-muscled** or **having great buns**. But there are stories beyond the routine in which it is appropriate to describe someone's appearance.

Never assume that **a family of four** always consists of a man, a woman and their two children. Don't write as if every **married couple** consists of a man and a woman.

Shoppers (not **housewives**) are paying more.

When writing in general terms prefer **police officer** or **constable** to **policeman, firefighter** to **fireman, mail carrier** to **mailman, flight attendant** to **stewardess**.

But if sex is pertinent, masculine and feminine forms are proper: **postman, policewoman, air steward**.

Use only established feminine variants ending in **-woman**.

Write **businesswoman, Frenchwoman, spokeswoman** but not **journeywoman, linewoman, defencewoman**.

Avoid other feminine variants unless they are so well established that a substitute rings false.

Thus it is proper to describe a woman as a **hostess, masseuse, princess, seamstress** or as an **author, comedian, Jew, murderer, poet, sculptor. Actor** and **actress** are both acceptable.

Avoid cumbersome coinages like **alderperson. Chairperson, salesperson** and **spokesperson** are in general use and can be used.

There is not an entirely satisfactory substitute for **fisherman**, although **fisher, fish harvester, fish industry worker, fishing licensees** or the phrase **fishermen and women** are all possibilities.

Some readers find the use of **he (him, his)** as a word of common or indeterminate gender to be sexist. **His or her** and the like can be used but may prove awkward. In that case reword the sentence if possible. Instead of: **Whoever is promoted will have $50 added to his or her pay**, write: **Whoever is promoted will get a $50 raise**. As a last resort, **they (them, their)** is an increasingly acceptable alternative to **he (him, his)**.

Often a plural construction solves the sex problem:

Retired officers are not usually referred to by their former rank.

Not: A retired officer is not usually referred to by his or her former rank.

The generic **man** is regarded by some as excluding women. Instead of **man** or **mankind**, you can write **people, human beings, humanity, human race**. Alternatives to **manmade** include **artificial, constructed, manufactured, synthetic**. But don't get carried away. To write **human energy** or **human resources** to avoid **manpower**, or **person-eating tiger** to avoid **man-eating tiger** is being hypersensitive.

Lance Bateman places a ring on William Woods's finger during their wedding in Vancouver in 2003. The terms husband and wife can exclude some people.

THE CANADIAN PRESS/Richard Lam

Sexual orientation

A person's sexual orientation should be not mentioned unless relevant to the story.

Gay and **lesbian** are the preferred terms to describe people attracted to the same sex; **homosexual** is considered offensive by some. Avoid except in clinical contexts and quotations. **Lesbian woman** is redundant. Don't use **gay** as a noun. Although many gay people use the expression **queer**, avoid except in quotations as some readers might construe it as offensive.

Use **sexual orientation**, not **sexual preference**; sexuality is not an option. Don't refer to a gay **lifestyle** or suggest that the majority of gay men and lesbians routinely live unorthodox lives; most don't. Don't use **admitted homosexual** or similar, which suggests criminality; use **openly gay** or **openly lesbian**, but only if it is necessary to use a modifier for clarity.

Language is still evolving on what to call the individuals in a same-sex relationship or marriage. Follow their preference if it is known. **Boyfriend, girlfriend, partner, husband** and **wife** are all acceptable options depending on situation and preference.

While there is some dispute about the definitions of the terms, **transgender** is usually regarded as a general term under which more specific descriptions, such as cross dresser, transvestite, drag queen, shemale and transsexual, fall. **Transsexual** has a clinical definition as someone who identifies as a member of the sex opposite to that assigned at birth. Use a term the person in question uses (explain if necessary) and a pronoun consistent with how they live.

Derogatory terms such as **faggot** should only be used when part of a direct quotation and when essential to the story. Flag the story with a **Caution** note spelling out where in the story the slur is contained.

Abortion

Certain descriptives used in the abortion debate are considered loaded terms by many. While the terms **pro-life** and **pro-choice** are allowed if they are used by the person or group involved, for general references it is preferrable to use specific, neutral terms, such as **abortion rights advocates** or **opponents of abortion**.

Sources

Cultivating knowledgeable sources who can provide the background and insight necessary for delivering a complete story is the trademark of the excellent reporter.

Without good sources — be they the town clerk in the small northern mining town, or the fast-moving executive assistant to a cabinet minister — The Canadian Press cannot hope to craft a comprehensive daily picture of life in Canada and the world.

Getting and keeping good sources is hard work. It involves patient telephone work plus breaking free from our desks to get out and meet people.

Reporters, editors and supervisors are encouraged to pull back from the front lines occasionally to spend time with people who know what's happening in the world beyond our own limited horizons. Special efforts should be made to develop contacts in non-urban areas and other places beyond the bright spotlight of big-city journalism.

It is the job of journalists to meet a variety of people. We should all take a special interest in people and listen to what they have to say. Developing good sources is a way of living to the committed journalist.

When dealing with sources, remember that many people are not used to dealing with the media. Ensure they understand they are being quoted, and their words or picture may appear in many newspapers.

A cardinal rule with sources is to avoid close personal involvement. There is nothing wrong with social contact with sources, but close personal relationships can lead to conflicts of interest.

Unnamed sources

The public interest is best served when someone with facts or opinions to make public is identified by the press by name and qualifications. Readers need to see named sources to help them decide on the credibility and importance of the information.

Regular use of unnamed sources weakens our news reports. The Canadian Press firmly discourages the quoting of sources who want to hide their identities. Leaks, especially in government and business, are often designed to undermine new policies or to damage rivals.

There are of course many situations when people with information important to the public insist on concealing their identity for understandable reasons. The Canadian Press would be foolish, and in some cases irresponsible, never to grant anonymity in news copy, but it can show leadership in working to stop misuse of unnamed sources.

Some guidelines:

1. Push sources hard to understand that putting their names to what they say is important to freedom of information. This is especially important in dealings with public servants who demand anonymity in routine circumstances.

2. Beat reporters should regularly test the willingness of their sources to be named.

3. Information from unnamed sources should be confirmed whenever possible by one or two other sources (always respecting the original source's anonymity, of course). Try to get supporting documentation. One-source stories are rarely acceptable these days.

4. Reporters writing stories containing unnamed sources must be able to demonstrate: (a) The information is of genuine public interest; (b) The information can be verified by at least one other source, even if unnamed; (c) The source is known to them; (d) There is no real possibility that the source is using The Canadian Press for selfish purposes; (e) Normal standards of fairness and balance are followed.

5. Supervisors must be consulted before a story with unnamed sources is released. Names of sources will be given to Head Office when requested.

6. Direct quotes should be avoided unless the actual words have unusual significance. This is especially important when opinion is being expressed and the sources might be tempted to use bolder language than if they were being named.

7. If the source is presenting one side of a controversy, the opposing side's views must be sought and presented fairly in the original story.

8. Do not say a person declined comment if this person is also an unnamed source in the story.

We don't have to tie every bit of information to a named source. Naming the airline employee who hands out a list of dead and injured in a plane crash adds nothing to the story. The government official who provides routine background or uncontestable fact need not always be named.

But always note names, just in case. For confidential sources, don't put the name or other identifying information in a notebook used for the story and never put it in an email. Documents, including emails and notebooks, can be picked up in a search warrant. Emails, in particular, are a dangerous place to mention confidential sources as they can be accidentally forwarded to wrong addresses.

It is prudent to store notes and recordings in safekeeping for one year at least. In extremely important matters, notes and recordings should be kept indefinitely.

Government officials often insist on anonymity at information briefings, such as in the locked room where reporters write federal or provincial budget stories in advance of delivery. The Canadian Press abides by such restrictions if necessary, but will not go along with deliberate misrepresentation, such as when a cabinet minister wishes to pass as a civil servant.

Statements from such briefings should not be passed off as general knowledge or undisputed fact. The reader should be told as much as possible about the source and the circumstances should be described.

It is not unheard of for a source to give information confidentially, then deny it by name. If The Canadian Press feels obliged to carry such a denial, it will identify the original source as the person denying it, provided we are confident the original story accurately reflected the source's information. Consult Head Office before proceeding.

Ethics and sources

When we do promise anonymity we must scrupulously respect that pledge. But it cannot be absolute and it is only fair to tell potential sources so. The courts may require reporters to disclose sources.

Verbal contracts with sources are enforceable in court. Make sure both you and your source understand precisely what that agreement is before you get the information. Do not make promises you cannot keep.

For instance, you can promise not to identify the source in your story and to not willingly make the identity known beyond your employer. You cannot promise to protect the source from any damages that result if the name does become known, through accident or through court order.

The Canadian Press will not require or advise an employee to balk at the court's direction. It will provide counsel who can advise the employee and who will seek to persuade the court that the public interest does not require disclosure, or who will plead for a closed hearing.

Sources also should know that reporters must identify their sources to their supervisors. This could include anyone from a bureau News Editor to the President. This does not mean that everyone in the chain of command must know. A staffer in a delicate circumstance may go directly to the Editor-in-Chief or the President.

In extreme circumstances the President might have to inform the Chairman of the Board of a Canadian Press source because the member newspapers are legally responsible with the agency for the Canadian Press news they publish.

If a source must be disclosed beyond the level of the President, senior management will make a concerted effort to advise the originating staffer in advance.

There may be cases where 100 per cent confidentiality is essential on an extremely sensitive news tip and The Canadian Press is unable to confirm the information with other sources. In such a case senior management will consult the originating staffer. If the problem is insurmountable, we will not carry the material.

Good reporting dictates that readers be given as much information as possible about the unnamed source's background. This helps readers judge why the story is worth their attention. Qualifications ascribed to the unnamed source must never be misleading. A bit of thought should produce a description helpful to the reader yet protective of the source.

It may be necessary to consult the source about the wording of such a description so the story can inform the reader without revealing the identity.

Other details should be clarified with sources. May all material be used, or must some be treated as only for the reporter's information and guidance (called *background* or *deep background* in the jargon of officialdom)? Are direct quotes permissible or only paraphrases?

Some phrases like **off the record** can have different meanings to different people. Be sure everyone is operating under the same meanings. Consult Head Office when someone proposes unusual restraints.

Some informants may provide information that may be attributed by name, then insist on anonymity for additional information. Attributing this confidential information is tricky: it would be misleading to specify that it came from someone else (**another Finance Department official, who asked for anonymity, said**). Usually it is preferable to rely on phrasing such as **It was also learned**.

Other guides to dealing with unnamed sources:

1. Don't use the unnamed sources of others as if they were those of The Canadian Press. Unnamed sources in stories picked up from newspapers or broadcast should be specifically tied to the paper or broadcaster: **The News quoted an unidentified official in the Energy Department as saying . . .**

2. Stories should specify that the source requested anonymity and explain why.

3. Spokespeople and officials should not be confused. A spokesperson puts forward the position of others; an official actually helps formulate that position.

4. Where a fictitious name is being used — for instance, in the case of a juvenile in trouble or a family on welfare — or where a composite person is created to represent a variety of similar individuals, the artifice must be explained promptly. It is a device that cannot be used often without losing impact. A supervisor must be consulted before it is used.

Involving Head Office

Stories from unnamed sources pack much potential for harm against an individual or an institution. Thoughtless journalism damages careers, personal lives, companies and public faith in the media. It also can hurt The Canadian Press's reputation and its legal position in any suits that might arise.

Safeguards have been designed to help ensure that major stories with potential for harm get plenty of thoughtful evaluation before being rushed into print.

Bureaus with major news breaks involving unnamed sources and with legal and ethical implications must follow these steps:

1. In consultation with the Main Desk, have counsel review the story.

2. Consult with the Editor-in-Chief and a Main Desk editor to answer such questions as:

(a) Who are the sources? How credible are they? What motives exist for a leak of information? Can further verification be obtained?

(b) What public good will the story serve? What are the legal risks? What ethical considerations are involved?

3. Every opportunity to respond must be given to the person or institution involved. Where conscientious effort does not produce a response, the story must detail the attempts made and the reasons why no response was provided.

A final caution: The source who does not want to be named in copy will rarely be available to defend The Canadian Press in the event of court action. This could leave us with no defence and lacking any ability to prove what we distributed for public consumption.

Internet and social media sources

The Internet and social networking sites such as Facebook, where individuals can exchange information, have changed newsgathering. The Internet is usually the first stop for journalists looking for information. It is particularly effective in tracking down people who may have direct knowledge of a news event, identifying news tips or trends, finding new sources and confirming factual background.

The same principles used in vetting a source found any other way must be applied to online sources. But there are extra challenges online. How do you know for sure the person who is answering your emails is the defence minister or the defence minister's communications chief? Some rules to follow:

1. If the main source for your story refuses to do a personal interview, try to find someone else. Only agree to email

interviews as a last resort. Specify in your story that the quotes came from an email, text message or blog — otherwise you leave the impression that you talked to the source in person or by phone.

2. Never use unsolicited emails without checking their source.

3. If an Internet source claims to be an official spokesperson or representative of an organization, confirm that is the case by calling the organization.

4. It has become acceptable to use Facebook and Twitter to give a general sense of how people are reacting to a news event — a modern-day man-in-the-street interview, if you will. If a Facebook page is set up to gather reaction to a news event, then using comments from the page is acceptable.

5. Social media sites should not be used as the sole source of factual information. And since you cannot know for sure who is saying the words, it is best to try to establish direct contact by sending a message through the site and asking for a phone interview before reporting comments from someone claiming to have special knowledge of the story. For example, it is OK to quote general comments from a Facebook site set up to mourn someone who has been murdered, but beware of quoting someone purporting to be the mother of the victim. Ask for a direct interview. If such material must be used, make clear that it is from the site.

6. Information from Wikipedia, which describes itself as a site "anyone can edit," should be confirmed through another source, such as a government or professional website.

The same copyright rules apply to material from websites as print publications. Material must be fully credited when paraphrased and enclosed in quotation marks when carried word for word.

Material from websites must be fully credited. Stick to authoritative sites.

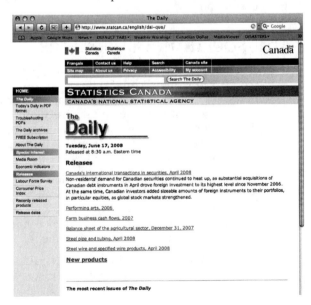

Guard against accidently cutting and pasting words that are not your own into copy with proper attribution.

➤ See **Video**, page 175.

Diverse sources

A balanced news report will provide a full range of voices and perspectives representing the diverse Canadian population. Comments from these groups should not be limited to particular "special interest" topics such as child care or multiculturalism, but also the economy, sports, science, the law and all other news areas.

Taste and tough calls

The media should do their work with compassion, good taste and respect for individual privacy. On the other hand, some media are only too happy to feed the appetite from some segments of the public for gore and salacious detail.

How far to go in informing the public is a dilemma faced every day.

Do we publish the photos of people jumping off the top floors of the burning World Trade Center? Some newspapers did, arguing that the dramatic illustrations made the enormity of the tragedy real on a human level. Others did not, arguing the pictures were just too horrific.

Some editors considered photos of people jumping off the World Trade Center on Sept. 11, 2001, too horrific to publish. Others used them as a graphic representation of the terror of those trapped in the towers.

(AP PHOTO)

Were the bounds of decency overstepped by publishing the photos of U.S. soldiers abusing Iraqi prisoners at the Abu Ghraib prison in Baghdad?

Was it offensive to publish pictures of the burned bodies of four foreigners hung from a bridge in Iraq? Was there any journalistic justification for carrying photos showing body parts strewn on the ground after the bombing of a train in Spain?

What about republishing an editorial cartoon that many Muslims consider an insult to their religion but that was also the catalyst for violent protests?

These are tough calls, with strongly felt opinions on each side.

At The Canadian Press we approach each tough call thoughtfully, relying on our experience, good taste and news judgment to help us make the right decision. We weigh carefully what the public needs to know and wants to know against what some might consider repugnant.

The Canadian Press acts as both retailer and wholesaler of news, and this can sometimes influence how such decisions are made. We reach the public directly through some of our services, such as our online news reports and national radio newscasts. Here, our decisions directly affect what is seen and heard and we must act accordingly. We also provide material to newspapers and broadcasters and expect that their staff will apply their own standards before deciding whether to publish it. We must not act as their censors, rejecting material based on standards that are more stringent than they, or their reading public, are willing to accept.

That said, it is our job to select and edit, and we must not abandon journalistic standards and principles on the premise that the final gatekeepers are other editors.

Some guidelines:

1. An individual's grief is private. The Canadian Press respects privacy and does not exploit grief to enhance the news.

2. Before covering any funeral, we must ask ourselves: What possible important information will we gain for the public by intruding on this intensely private event?

➤ See **Obituaries**, page 91.

3. Flag questionable stories and photos with a **Caution** note that the material might offend some readers.

CAUTION: Note contents in paras 5-8 may be considered offensive.

4. When dealing with grieving sources, be respectful and understanding. Don't push your way in. Most people are willing to share their thoughts in situations involving grief, provided there is legitimate public interest. Don't ask people how they feel about a loss.

5. Public interest must also be carefully weighed when deciding whether to publish the identity of a victim. Details of some crimes are so graphic that naming the victim can only cause more anguish to the innocent party. This can be especially harmful when publishing the victim's name serves no public purpose and adds nothing to the story.

Terrorism, hostage-takings

No news story is worth someone's life. Going for the scoop at any cost when lives are at stake belongs to a time long past.

A police officer and a paramedic assist a man held hostage in a store in Ottawa in June 2007. The Canadian Press has a clear policy on handling breaking news on hostage-takings.

THE CANADIAN PRESS/Jonathan Hayward

That's why we treat terrorist incidents and hostage-takings with extreme caution: They are life-and-death situations.

We have a responsibility to report the news but we have an even greater responsibility to ensure that our actions in news-gathering and reporting do not endanger human lives.

We do not want to become an open publicity line for lawbreakers or give unwitting support to destructive or violent causes.

Some guidelines:

1. Notify police immediately when you receive a phone call, fax or note about an unpublicized hostage-taking or other threatening act. Make all information available to police.

2. Do not move a story before checking with a senior editorial supervisor at Head Office.

3. If the story is approved, consult with Head Office before naming The Canadian Press as the news organization that received the information.

4. Never telephone the terrorists or their hostages without the approval of a senior editorial supervisor at Head Office. If approval is received, consult the same supervisor again before moving a story.

5. Do not detail police or security countermeasures or any other information that might aid the terrorists.

6. We will not tailor or distribute demands or platforms from organizations without Head Office approval. Head Office will not give approval without consulting police or government, or both.

7. Translate the language of terrorists and police for readers: use plain English such as **note** and **kill** for **communique** and **execute**.

8. Terrorism is an international phenomenon, and there can be pressure on The Canadian Press to match extensive coverage provided by American and other foreign networks or news agencies. Carefully weigh the need to inform the public against the risk of encouraging more such acts. Consult supervisors about the quantity of material moved, especially on services that go directly to the public, and the detail that should be provided.

9. Check with a Head Office supervisor before moving an initial story dealing with a Canadian kidnapped and held hostage abroad. Canadian Press supervisors need to evaluate the specifics of a particular case in the context of a number of complex considerations before deciding when to publish a story and what details to include. As with a domestic hostage-taking, the news service sometimes will know more than it chooses to publish while an incident is continuing. Extra thought and scrutiny is called for in regards to stories to be published while a person is held overseas for political demands or ransom, whether it is Day 1 or Day 50 of the hostage-taking.

10. Photo coverage from Canada and abroad should be monitored carefully to ensure that terrorists are not being glamorized, that victims are not being endangered and that the incidents are not being sensationalized.

11. News of ongoing hostage-taking or other terrorist incidents in Canada should not be transmitted on cable, broadcast or online services without the approval of a senior supervisor, to guard against the possibility that such reports are being monitored by those involved.

12. Keep newspapers and other clients informed through non-publishable advisories when these policy restraints affect coverage of an incident.

Defining terrorism

For decades the United Nations has been attempting to agree on what exactly the term should mean. The events of Sept. 11, 2001, put the issue on front pages. Slamming hijacked passenger jets into office towers seems to be accepted by almost everyone as terrorism. But there are often discrepancies in the way the media define and interpret other activities. Sometimes the word **terrorist** is used; other times **militant, guerrilla** or even **freedom fighter.** The perceptions of an activity can certainly be influenced by the choice of language — "One person's terrorist is another person's freedom fighter," as the saying goes.

Most definitions of terrorism incorporate the idea that it involves the use of violence or threat of violence to attain political, ideological or religious goals. Some specify that it is perpetuated against civilian, not military, targets. For journalists, the best advice is to be specific in the choice of terms used, and to guard against automatically labelling one side the terrorists, which makes the other side automatically the good guys. We do not shy away from the word **terrorist**, but we do use it with caution. There are always more neutral words available. Terms such as **bombers, gunmen** and **killers** also offer the advantage of being more specific.

Scare stories

The number of terror scare stories took a quantum leap after Sept. 11, 2001 — buildings evacuated, border points closed, flights cancelled, sometimes over such things as a package left unattended. Many of these incidents were not news.

Before treating such a story as news, ask:

1. Is there anything to the scare? If an office building is cleared for a suspicious package that turns out to be someone's forgotten lunch, then there is no story. If the suspicious package turns out to contain a dangerous substance, then there is likely a story. Wait to see which it is.

2. Is the reaction to a scare such as a bomb threat newsworthy in itself? A plant being evacuated for a short time is not news. An airport that is shut down for hours is.

Internet viruses

The reality of our wired world means Internet viruses, or even the threat of them, can cause widespread concern among Canadians who depend on computers to live their lives. News organizations can provide a valuable service in ensuring reports on new viruses are distributed quickly. This reporting should be done without glorifying the cyberterrorists who create these viruses. The same rules for reporting on other supposed threats apply to coverage of Internet viruses. Stories should only be carried if there is proof that a virus poses an unusual or significant threat.

The working journalist

Audio

Sound is integral to a good radio story; it adds colour and immediacy. A strong audio clip does for radio what dramatic footage does for television. It can also have a role in telling a story online, where sound can be packaged with stories and photos for a multi-media perspective on a news event.

There are many ways to present a radio story. Customarily, reporters use clips, voicers, wraps and voicealities.

Clips: A segment of audio from a newsmaker — a quote, a few sentences from a speech, the answer to a question posed by a reporter at a news conference, etc.

Voicers: A straight read of a report that includes no additional sound but has the reporter's signoff. It should never exceed 30 seconds.

Wraps: Short for wraparound. It is a voicer with a very short clip inserted into the body. Look for a piece of tape with pizzazz that says a lot in few words. Given the limited length of radio newscasts, a reporter should stick to the 35-second rule for a wrap.

Voicealities: A straight read, but is meant to sound more casual and could run anywhere from 15 to 25 seconds. It does not include a signoff.

For example, the newscaster reads an intro, such as **Bad news for Metro Air staff.** Correspondent Jane Doe reports a lot of pink slips are going out tomorrow. The reporter then says: **The airline says it will lay off 2,000 staffers — everyone from pilots to ticket agents will be affected. And Metro Air says this might just be the beginning. It says if conditions don't improve, more workers will lose their jobs.** Then comes a tag line from the newscaster: **Metro Air is reporting losses of $1.2 billion this quarter.**

Selecting clips

An audio clip should be a quick hit of your interview subject. Pick out something dramatic, an interesting turn of phrase, a touch of humour, or some hard-hitting words.

There are no hard and fast rules, but a good clip, depending on the subject, can run anywhere from two or three seconds to around 20 seconds. You wouldn't want to go much longer unless the tape is extraordinary, like a pilot pleading with a hijacker. Let a clip run if it tells the story better than words.

Modern technology makes it possible to file audio clips from an event back to the newsroom in seconds.

THE CANADIAN PRESS

Raw sound

Raw sound is a great scenesetter and pulls the listener into the story.

And it's easy to get. All you have to do is hold up your microphone. The sound of bombs dropping from a fighter jet, screaming protesters with police banging on shields, bullets being fired — they can all paint a picture better than words.

Writing around audio

When writing the script for a clip, your aim is to showcase the speaker and get the listener's attention. Explain what the story is about and who is speaking. Wrap it up with a one or two-sentence ending called a tag line.

Intro: Prime Minister Jones is fighting mad. He says the leader of the Opposition is implying that he's a liar.

Clip: "I have contacted my lawyers about suing the Opposition leader for libel. He called me a liar outside the house and doesn't have the protection of the House of Commons. Now let's see how tough he is."

Tag: The Opposition leader maintains his words were taken out of context and he would never call the leader of our country a liar.

Variety

To keep the reader's interest, vary the offerings on the same story. Two actuals, a voicer, and a voiceality can make the same story seem fresh and provide a reporter the chance to introduce different angles.

Recording audio

It may sound obvious, but one of the reasons many reporters fail to record an interview is that they forget to, or improperly, press the record button. Always make sure your recording device is on and recording before conducting an interview or gathering sound. You should also ensure record levels are correct, and not overmodulated or too low, by checking the sound level meter.

Audio levels

Just as distance is measured in metres, sound is measured in decibels, or Db. Audio is recorded using either microphone level or line level. Microphone level is basically an amplified line level, typically operating in a level range of -30 Db. Line level operates in the -8 to 0 Db frequency range. While a microphone is needed for conducting interviews or obtaining natural sound, line level is always cleaner and of better quality. Many news conferences where sound boards are made available offer a choice between microphone and line level. It is recommended that you use line level whenever possible to obtain the best-quality sound. An attenuator or attenuated cable can be used to reduce microphone level sound to line level when necessary.

Level meters

There are two types of meters in general use to determine audio levels. VU meters provide you with an average level that is usually set at 0 Db. A DB meter will give you peak value of the sound level at all times.

Microphone technique

Audio quality can be affected by the way a microphone is handled during an interview. Holding it too close to a person's mouth could cause distortion, while placing it too far away could muffle the sound or make it inaudible. To prevent distortion, your microphone should be held a few inches away from your interview subject. To avoid popping sounds in recorded audio, microphones can be outfitted with wind socks.

Using sound boards

Professional sound boards can be daunting to anyone using them for the first time. But they are an essential tool for recording audio from several sources. Most sound boards use straight-line slide controls, knobs, or a combination of both, to control volume levels. Desktop and portable units normally offer multiple line or microphone inputs, as well as line inputs. Each input can be assigned a specific task (TV, phone, etc.) Several microphone inputs can be used to mix from different microphone sources. You should only use one volume control at a time, unless you are mixing in sound from another source.

Business news

Business news is about companies, industry, trade, commerce, finance and the economy. But ultimately it concerns people — their jobs, mortgages, bank accounts, investments and long-term prosperity.

Changes in economic conditions affect people. And people's behaviour can influence the economy.

• The merger of two companies, for example, may combine their strengths and improve production efficiency. But it may also mean lost jobs.

• Consumers continuing to spend despite signs of an impending recession may temporarily delay the start of the downturn.

• Higher interest rates could mean a higher Canadian dollar, which benefits someone travelling abroad but hurts exporters. Closer to home, higher interest rates may mean a bigger monthly mortgage payment, but savings in the bank may earn a bit more interest.

Business news deals with fluctuations in financial markets. As much as possible, business stories should explain what the price movements indicate. To what extent do they reflect investors' perception of economic conditions or a company's prospects? How much of the change is affected by political events? By sheer speculation? Is there a herd mentality at work? How about the interplay of greed and fear?

Like other news, business news occurs within the context of society. Bottom lines can be affected by developments in areas not traditionally associated with business. Environmental concerns, new standards of ethics and morality, the spread of disease, an aging population — these are some of the factors that can affect a company's prospects.

Similarly, business news in Canada is affected by what goes on elsewhere. A war in the Middle East could improve the economic outlook of oil-producing western provinces. The discovery of a cheaper and better substitute overseas may hurt the prospects of Canadian producers of, say, lumber or steel. Eventually, people who work in these industries feel the effect.

Business reporting

There is a great appetite for timely business news among newspapers, broadcasters, Internet news services, so-called day traders on the stock market and the corporate world. There are many news sources and services, all competing to be first with their stories.

While there's a premium on getting the story first, accuracy must always be the top priority. The business community is the biggest rumour mill around, and a rumour picked up by a media outlet can have a great effect on stock prices. Be careful. Check reports with more than one source.

Discard the assumption that business writing has to be staid, uninteresting and faceless. Business stories are often dynamic and colourful, driven by compelling personalities making their way through a constantly changing economic landscape.

Business writers should keep in mind the two kinds of readers: general readers who want to keep up with what is happening in the business world; and business readers who want information on investments, the economy and developments in fields related to their own. But both audiences appreciate easy-to-read stories that are free of jargon.

A graphic can cover background or related information for which there is no room in a business story.

Canadian iPhone price plans

Rogers and Fido will begin selling the iPhone 3G on July 11. The phone will sell for $199 for the 8Gb model and $299 for the 16Gb model based on a three-year contract. Here are the monthly plans which will include unlimited Wi-Fi access at Rogers and Fido hotspots:

Price/month	Voice calling	Data
$60	150 minutes with unlimited evenings and weekends	400 MB
$75	300 minutes with unlimited evenings and weekends	750 MB
$100	600 minutes with unlimited evenings and weekends	1 GB
$115	800 minutes with unlimited evenings and weekends	2 GB

SOURCE: Rogers Wireless   THE CANADIAN PRESS

Common pitfalls

• Check all figures. One extra digit can throw a number off completely. A single letter turns million into billion.

• Watch accounting terms. Net operating income and net income, for example, can be quite different things.

• Watch percentages. A statement that a company's profit is up 50 per cent isn't helpful without the raw numbers: $150 is 50 per cent more than $100, and $1.5 million is 50 per cent more than $1 million. Include actual figures.

• Don't make readers do the math in stories that compare numbers such as unemployment reports or corporate earnings. Include the current figure, the percentage increase or decrease, and last year's figure.

- Be wary of corporate self-interest in all aspects of business reporting. Remember that securities analysts are not unbiased observers of a company or sector. They work in an industry whose main job is to promote stock trading.

- Companies often use polls to increase brand awareness and market new products. Ask yourself if the poll provides newsworthy information. Question statistics to ensure they are not being used selectively by companies and lobby groups to advance their interests.

- Don't get bogged down with numbers. Use numbers that tell the reader something, such as net profit or revenues or earnings per share. Don't load the story with secondary figures such as cash flow or capital spending unless they are important to the news peg.

- Verify corporate identities. Some companies have similar names but are not directly related, or one may be a subsidiary of another. Appliance-maker **Camco Inc.** and uranium producer **Cameco Corp.** are in entirely different lines of business.

- Keep up to date with corporate name changes; **Molson Inc.**, for example, now is **Molson-Coors Inc.** after its merger with the U.S. brewer. In stories, make a reference to what the company used to be called if the change was recent or the new name is not easily recognizable. Product names are also bought and sold — check with the company concerned.

- Be careful when using the term **bankruptcy**. A troubled company can ask a court for bankruptcy protection from creditors as it restructures and carries out business as usual. That doesn't mean it's bankrupt, although it can be called insolvent. If a court-monitored restructuring can't be done, creditors can petition the company into bankruptcy, which means its assets will be sold and the firm will go out of business.

Some suggestions

- Keep human faces high in the story whenever possible. It's a way of saying a corporate development affects people in real life. For example, if **Really Clean Inc.** announced a layoff of 150 employees, an effective approach to the story might be:

James Lee walked home from work to save bus fare. He and 140 of his co-workers at Really Clean received layoff notices Friday.

- Always ask how any development is likely to affect the reader. Some events, such as World Trade Organization negotiations, may have no immediate impact on readers but their long-term impact can be significant, affecting the Canadian economy and such things as food prices. Reforms in China may not directly affect Canada, but they may help boost the Chinese economy and lift demand for oil, lumber, minerals and other products imported from Canada.

• When doing stories about economic predictions — especially bank and corporate forecasts of the coming year — try to include the previous year's forecast and how accurate it was. That helps readers decide how much weight to give the report.

• Concepts such as unemployment are hard to define statistically and can be measured differently in Canada and other countries. In Canada, the jobless numbers released each month don't include part-time workers or discouraged workers — people who have given up looking for work. That means the true jobless rate may be higher than the official count.

• Keep long corporate names or unfamiliar acronyms out of the first paragraph. Instead, use a short name that may be readily recognized, or a quick explanation of the type of business. The full name can be included a bit later in the story.

• It sometimes helps to mention a company's best-known products. For example: **Kruger Products, the company that makes White Swan tissue** . . .

• Complex corporate relationships, company holdings or a corporate history might best be laid out in a sidebar, a chart or a QuickFacts box. This allows the story to deal with the impact of a development.

• Translate business jargon into plain English. If a technical term must be included, explain what it means. Even readers with a lot of business knowledge appreciate accessible writing.

• Business stories on interest rates, company shutdowns, expansions or big shifts in stock markets and the dollar frequently find their way on to general news pages. The Canadian Press moves such stories on both business and general wires with a note alerting editors: **Eds: Moves Business and General. Avoid duplication.**

• Stock symbols for companies listed on Canadian exchanges should be included in stories. Many readers and clients sort business news according to stock symbol.

• Good illustrations and video for business pages can be hard to come by and therefore are in great demand. Reporters should think about possibilities for a good graphic, photograph or video when they get their business-news assignment because it may take time to arrange. If a steel company is expected to report sharply lower year-end earnings in the next few days, alert the photo desk so a photographer can be sent out to get still photos and video of workers leaving the plant. This gives editors a livelier picture to work with than might otherwise be available on deadline. Annual meetings can be a good source of people pictures, whether of a reclusive chairman or an angry shareholder. Corporate websites can provide charts and other illustrations.

Business terms

Asset-backed security
A financial security backed by loans, leases, credit-card debt, royalties, a company's accounts receivables, etc.

Bonds, debentures
The buyer of **bonds** or **debentures** is a creditor who lends money to the company for a fixed term at an agreed interest rate.

Debentures are unsecured promises to repay the loan. Corporate **bonds** are ordinarily secured by fixed assets. Although government securities are often called bonds, they are actually debentures — guaranteed by the government but without assets being pledged. If a company goes out of business, secured creditors' claims on its assets have priority over claims of other creditors and preferred shareholders, who in turn are ahead of common shareholders.

Cash flow
Refers to a company's cash resources. Unlike earnings, cash flow includes interest, taxes, depreciation and amortization. Cash flow shows investors the company's ability to pay dividends and finance expansion.

Consolidated statement
A financial statement that includes the results of subsidiary companies. This is usually done when the parent company owns 50 per cent or more of a subsidiary.

Derivative
A contract whose value depends on the financial performance of its underlying assets, such as mortgages, stock or traded commodities.

Extraordinary items
Year-over-year comparisons of net profit can be distorted in a year when, for example, plants and equipment are sold or the value of investments or assets is written down because they have lost market value. A big layoff or restructuring will also dramatically affect a company's bottom line because of severance and restructuring costs. In general, focus on the figures that give a true picture of a company's performance. BCE Inc. might say it had an annual profit of $1.4 billion from operations but wrote off $2.9 billion in assets, posting a net loss of $1.5 billion. But that doesn't mean BCE is in trouble, since the writeoff was an accounting measure and not a loss of cash.

For a meaningful comparison from year to year, it is usually necessary to look as well at **net profit** before **extraordinary items,** generally referred to as operating profit or profit from operations. Whenever possible, try for longer-term comparisons such as a five-year range or average. Figures should be given for comparable earlier periods.

Financing

Equity financing means raising money through the sale of common shares. The buyer becomes a part-owner of the company.

Debt financing means raising money through bonds and debentures. The buyer lends money to the company, which promises to repay the amount in the future with interest.

Net profit, net income, net earnings

The three terms means the same thing — a company's profit (or loss) after all expenses and taxes have been paid. It is out of **net profit** that dividends are paid — first to preferred shareholders, then to common shareholders.

Net operating profit

Money earned from a company's operations — the sale of its products or services. It should not be confused with **net profit,** which includes both income from operations and non-operating sources like rents, interest and investments.

Net earnings per share

Obtained by deducting from net profit any amount paid to preferred shareholders, and dividing the resulting amount by the number of common shares outstanding. It is a key figure that investors, analysts and other players in the financial industry consider in determining the performance of a company. Companies often take a beating in the stock market when their earnings per share fall short of analysts' predictions.

Revenues

A company's overall sales and money earned from other sources. This should not be mistaken for profits. The cost of doing business, including wages, is subtracted to get profits.

Share, stock

A part-ownership of a company obtained by providing capital to the business. **Common shareholders** have the right to vote in the company. If the company performs well, shareholders benefit from the rise in the value of the shares. The term **a share** refers to a common share unless otherwise stated.

Preferred shares entitle the holder to a fixed dividend from net profit before common shareholders are paid. Preferred shares generally carry no voting privileges as long as promised dividends are paid.

Company meetings and reports

Some Canadian companies have played important roles in the country's economic development. Other firms have been the economic bedrock of their community. Some occupy pivotal positions in their sector of the economy. Others have high name recognition among consumers who use their products. The financial health and future plans of these businesses are often news of wide interest.

Company meetings and reports can provide information on how these companies are doing and where they are going financially. Company websites can supply many of these documents.

Stories based on company reports need not be dry recitals of statistics. Many companies explain in their reports why profits are small or sales have increased. This kind of information, along with background on the company and its products, can brighten the story and give it depth.

Securities commissions settlements

Allegations made against individuals by staff at Canada's securities commissions are sometimes settled without a formal hearing. These settlements often result in the individual paying a fine or facing other sanctions.

However — and this is where reporters can go wrong — agreeing to a penalty does not mean the individual has admitted the allegations are true or that there has been a finding of culpability. The wording of the settlement is the guide to what can be said about the case. Lawyers for the individual can be expected to take on the media if the characterizations and distinctions they fought to get into the settlement to benefit their client aren't reflected in news stories.

Precise figures

Precise figures are preferred in routine financial items but should be rounded off in business stories.

CALGARY – Liquidation World Inc., auctioneer and seller of discounted merchandise, says its first-quarter profit fell 31 per cent under pressure from the economic slowdown and pricing competition.

For the 13-week period ended Jan. 6, net profits fell to $1.56 million or 18 cents a share, from $2.28 million or 27 cents a share a year earlier. Sales slipped slightly to $48.7 million from $48.9 million.

Earnings
Canadian earnings declared Thursday
Canadian earnings declared Thursday:
Amica Mature Lifestyles Inc. (TSX:ACC): Three months ended Feb. 28, 2006, net income $0.10 a share; 2005; net loss $648,000, net loss $0.12 a share. Revenue: 2006, $9,592,000; 2005, $9,685,000.

Foreign currencies

In business stories from most parts of the world other than the United States it is best to convert amounts into Canadian dollars. (The daily item slugged **Tab-Foreign-Exchange** can be used to convert many foreign currencies into Canadian dollars.) Use phrases like **the equivalent of C$500** to avoid giving the impression that the deal was done in Canadian currency. The **C$** is usually necessary only on first reference.

Note: Keep the original currency amount in the story, especially in items concerning major takeovers and acquisitions. This makes it easier for editors using the story as background later to determine the exchange rate that was used.

Conversions are not done in the following cases:

1. U.S. dollar figures may be kept in copy with U.S. placelines. Specify the currency on first reference only:

> NEW YORK — Seagram Co. Ltd. said Monday it will spend more than US$10 billion to buy PolyGram, the world's biggest record company. The deal will also mean Seagram will put its juice division up for sale, for about $3 billion.

2. Most of the world's commodities — gold, oil, nickel, lumber and pulp and paper — are traded on world markets in U.S. dollars. In business copy and routine financial items it is acceptable to keep U.S. dollar prices. In broader stories, it may be desirable to include a Canadian dollar equivalent in one or two examples.

Note: In stories where U.S. and Canadian dollars are both used, add an Editors' Note: **EDs: The following figures are in Canadian dollars unless otherwise stated.**

BizFlashes

1. Canadian business news on The Canadian Press wire always begins with a BizFlash — a headline and a short summary of the news development. The goal is to get out the basic information as soon as possible to traders and other market watchers.

> **TD Bank wins takeover bid for VFC Inc.**
> **THE CANADIAN PRESS**
> TORONTO – TD Bank (TSX:TD) declares victory in $326-million takeover bid for user-car loan company VFC Inc. (TSX:VFC). About 90 per cent of shares tendered, rest to be taken up.

2. For minor news items, there may be no followup story. In those cases, the BizFlash should carry an Eds note saying that no story is planned.

Stock symbols

1. Stock symbols are used by many readers to search for news on companies they follow. All stories moving on the Business and Finance wires carry the stock symbol in brackets after the first mention of a company.

> TORONTO – The Royal Bank of Canada (TSX:RY) said Monday it is issuing $300 million in new preferred shares to strengthen its capital ratios.

Note: If two or more companies are mentioned in the lead of a story, the primary company's stock symbol goes in the lead and the other symbols are inserted after the second reference to the companies.

Editing for print

Few people grow up longing to edit someone else's writing. It's not glamorous work; it is invisible at best and resented at worst.

But some people who love the written language develop a passion for perfecting its use on the page. The best publications rely on such editors for success. The best editors strive for excellence in every story they handle.

Pride comes from turning around a mediocre or erroneous story. The trick is to do more than just catch mistakes but less than rewrite.

As the last ones to touch copy before it gets into the reader's hands, editors have a vital role. They are the watchdogs over clarity, good taste, balance and accuracy.

Editors should be the reader's best friend. They add background and perspective. They make a story relevant and fun. They don't challenge readers to get through a story — they dare them not to.

Principles

1. When time allows, read a story three times: once for content, once to edit and once to clean up.

2. If you don't understand the story, the reader certainly won't. When some-thing is unclear, either get it explained or chop it.

3. Generalities blur the picture; demand specifics for your readers. Make sure the story is animated by human beings.

4. Suggest improvements to the writer: revealing quotes, touches of colour, specific details, an example or anecdote.

5. Watch for holes and fill them. Ask the writer. Check reference works. Consult a supervisor.

6. Shorten the story — but not at the expense of human interest, significant detail, daubs of colour or meaty quotations.

7. Avoid overediting, which can reduce good writing to mediocrity or headline language.

8. Change copy if you have a good, explainable reason — not just because it's not the way you would have written it yourself. Leave extensive rewriting to the writer whenever possible.

How to do it

Look at the lead. The first sentence is supposed to lead the reader into the story. If it isn't interesting, why would the reader go any further? If readers aren't enticed by the first sentence or two, they're not going to stick around to be informed or educated or provoked.

1. Replace vague or complicated words with simple, specific ones.

2. Brighten the lead with descriptive verbs and the active voice.

Not: Two men are dead following an avalanche Tuesday on a popular ski slope in the Rocky Mountains.

Better: An avalanche thundered down Mount Norquay on Tuesday, crushing two men who had been learning to ski at the Rocky Mountain resort.

3. Take a scalpel to long leads. Aim for fewer than 30 words. Cut unwieldy phrases. Remove secondary information or unnecessary attribution from the lead and place it lower.

Not: Human Resources Minister Diane Finley announced Monday that after six months of study and $3 million in funding, the government has come up with new educational and job training guidelines that she predicts will make the Canadian labour force the most skilled in the world.

Better: After spending $3 million and six months studying education and job training, the federal government has a plan it predicts will make Canadians the most skilled labour force in the world.

4. Never assume the reader knows the subject as intimately as the writer does.

Not: Joy Medinski was found Thursday in Bienfait, apparently unharmed.

Better: A five-year-old girl who vanished from a family campsite in southeastern Saskatchewan last week was found two kilometres away on Monday, apparently unharmed.

5. Beware of the double-barrelled lead.

Not: Thousands of seniors angry over federal pension changes marched on Parliament Hill on Monday while their national spokesman condemned the Conservative government as the worst threat to seniors in Canadian history.

Pick the most interesting or important element, the seniors or the spokesman, and make that the lead. Put the other one in the second paragraph.

Tighten the story

1. Keep paragraphs short, usually no more than two or three sentences. Don't assault the reader's eyes with massive blocks of words.

2. Tighten sentences to clarify, inject life and save space. Be ruthless in cutting wordiness and secondary detail.

3. Replace cumbersome words with short, everyday words that convey the same meaning.

Not: The correctional facility workers voted in favour of a prolonged work stop-page.

But: The jail guards voted to strike.

4. Cut vague modifiers and qualifiers: **fairly, really, pretty, quite, very.**

5. Cut overattribution. Are all those *he said*s necessary?

Brighten the story

1. Prefer one or two interesting angles fully developed to a dull, bare-bones account that touches all bases regardless of merit.

2. Change passive voice to active where appropriate. **Police took no action** is better than **No action was taken by police.**

3. Change boring expressions to lively ones. Watch for participles ending in -*ing* or nouns ending in -*ion* — they may signal that a sentence can be punched up. Watch for the weak verb *to be.* Can it be replaced by an active verb?

Not: The government is planning to implement a program aiming for a reduction in the number of alcohol-related deaths this year.

Better: The government aims to cut alcohol-related deaths this year through a new program.

Best: Police will be able to seize the cars of drinking drivers on the spot under a government plan to cut alcohol-related deaths this year.

4. Translate or cut journalistic hype and jargon, the kind of language you would never use in ordinary speech. Prefer the specific to the general.

Not: Residents of this farming community were reeling in shock Thursday in the wake of the slaying of two respected schoolteachers.

Better: Flags flew at half-mast outside the Shoal Lake elementary school Thursday in tribute to two teachers killed in an apparently unprovoked attack.

Not: A twofold habitat mitigation program is in full swing at the Oldman River dam site.

Better: The provincial government is spending $2 million to preserve the environment for wildlife around the Oldman River dam and create new protected areas to replace those destroyed by the dam.

Best: Ducks will swim in new ponds and deer will munch on their favourite grasses under a $2-million program to preserve wildlife around the Oldman dam.

Check accuracy

1. Check proper names and unusual spellings. Make sure unusual surnames are spelled the same way throughout. Never guess at capitalization. Think of your reader again — few things are as annoying as misspelled names.

2. Check math. Make sure percentages are right. If portions of a total number are used, make sure they add up.

3. Check days and dates for obvious errors.

4. Watch closely for mistakes in the use of *not* in court cases and important judgments: *not guilty, not responsible.*

Check style

1. Strive to retain the writer's tone and choice of phrasing.

2. Fix errors in grammar, style and structure. Watch for mistakes in word order that mislead the reader.

Not: A Winnipeg police officer who shot a man with a toy gun has been cleared of any wrongdoing.

Better: A Winnipeg police officer who shot a man pointing a toy gun has been cleared of any wrongdoing.

3. Check that plural subjects are followed by plural verbs and pronouns, singular by singular. **The government announced its** (not **their**) **long-awaited social reform package Tuesday.**

4. Does punctuation mislead the reader? Fix it.

Not: She said the company is run by men, who have no ethics.

But: She said the company is run by men who have no ethics.

Make it clear

1. Lighten overloaded sentences by putting some of the facts into another sentence.

Not: The U.S. economy slid into recession in March but consumer spending has managed to hold up relatively well during the slump, due to low interest rates, free-financing offers, extra cash coming from a refinancing boom in home mortgages, heavily discounted merchandise and improved consumer confidence.

Better: The U.S. economy slid into recession in March but consumer spending has managed to hold up relatively well during the slump. Low interest rates, free-financing offers, extra cash coming from a refinancing boom in home mortgages and merchandise sales have induced people to spend. Consumer confidence also has improved.

2. Answer all pertinent questions. Make sure all unusual and technical terms are explained.

Wealthy Britons often buy private health insurance, just as they send their children to "public" schools, which in Britain means fee-paying, private and elite.

3. Move sentences or paragraphs to improve flow or strengthen emphasis.

Make it fair

1. Put both sides of a controversial issue high in the story.

2. Tone down or play up material wrongly treated by the writer. Guard against partial quotes that may create the wrong impression.

The woman was hired for her "talent," the premier said.

3. Watch for unintentional editorializing.

Not: The Opposition blamed the government for ruining the economy.

Better: The Opposition accused the government of ruining the economy.

4. Remove material that is potentially libellous or in bad taste.

Handle with care

1. When source material is sensitive or confidential, lock it safely away while the reporter works from a copy.

2. Make sure a supervisor is fully aware of the source material's contents and the source's reliability.

3. Before an investigative report is published, make every effort to give everyone who may be criticized an opportunity to reply.

4. Counsel must approve the final wording of any possibly dangerous material.

➤ See **Principles**, page 13.

Entertainment

Entertainment is a catch-all title covering a broad range of activities and interests. For so-called popular tastes, there are television and radio, pop music and movies, circuses and standup comedy. For the highbrows, there are books and plays, operas and concerts, museums and balls.

Each of these categories can produce a hard-news story on any given day — everything from a fundraising crisis at the art gallery to the arrest of a prominent actress. On other days, they'll merit a profile or feature.

Or they may be dealt with in a review or column.

News

It's often regarded as soft news, but basic principles of journalism apply to entertainment coverage.

1. **Look for hard news:** Ask the TV actor if and when he plans to move on from his current sitcom. When the tour of a controversial rap group is announced, ask police whether they'll have extra patrols when the musicians hit town. Ask the author of the new bestseller her opinion of sales taxes on books.

2. **Take the high road:** So much entertainment "news" today is actually celebrity gossip. Gossipy items about the lives and loves of celebrities, if properly sourced, are usually harmless. But beware of picking up items from tabloids and celebrity TV shows that are not adequately sourced — their focus is usually on entertaining, not news reporting. Consider the track record of the source. If the news is worthy of pursuit, try to confirm it independently.

3. **Strive for balanced coverage:** If a songwriter complains that music royalties in Canada are tiny, check copyright laws and how royalties compare with those in other countries. When an author trashes a celebrity in a book, get comment from the star or his representatives. In articles about the state of a particular art form in Canada, include representatives from across the country.

4. **Avoid single-source stories:** When the artistic director of a theatre announces a new stage season, some insightful comments may be provided by actors, directors or even academics and drama critics about the choices. In a profile of a sexually provocative singer, talk to others — his parents, perhaps? — about his image.

5. **Inject colour and personality:** If the popstar wears cocktail party attire to a court hearing on whether she should have custody of her children, describe her clothes: **Britney Spears arrived at the hearing wearing bright pink lipstick, sunglasses, shiny gold platform shoes and a very short black dress with a ruffled hem.** In reviews of new works,

describe the atmosphere in the hall and the reaction of the opening night audience. If a usually suave young actor trips and falls at your feet when you come to interview him, don't brush it off — include it in your article.

Think pictures and graphics. Nothing sells a story like a good illustration.

For newspapers, keep section deadlines in mind. Deliver a time-sensitive story well in advance of deadline to help editors making up pages. Keep editors advised of late-breaking or short-notice material they can expect soon.

Awards

Industry awards are among the highest profile entertainment events. There are so many of them, the challenge is to determine how much and what type of coverage to give each awards event and how to develop lively, interesting copy from it.

Performer Feist holds five Juno awards during the 2008 show in Calgary. Although self-serving, entertainment awards are popular with the public.

THE CANADIAN PRESS/Jonathan Hayward

Entertainment awards tend to be self-serving. Major events such as the Emmys, Grammys, Oscars, Junos, Geminis and Genies are of interest to the average reader and merit extensive coverage. Lesser-known events may warrant little or no coverage.

A little homework in advance can be valuable. For example, research may turn up that the director of a film on long-distance running suffered polio as a child.

Award ceremonies usually take place in the evening when newspaper deadlines are tight. Whenever possible, ask the organizers for an embargoed list of winners in advance and have the story prepared ahead of time. Colour and quotes can be added in Writethrus after the ceremony begins. Use the special **bargo** coding (See **Advances**, page 443) to ensure the copy isn't sent to other Canadian Press clients until the embargo is lifted.

Complete lists of winners are an important companion to stories on the event. The list should give the category first followed by a colon and the name of the winner.

Best songwriter: Alanis Morissette

Some category titles may have to be shortened to fit in a single column. **Outstanding Performance by a Lead Actor in a Drama Series** might be changed to **Best Actor — Drama**.

Embargoes and other conditions

Entertainment newsmakers are increasingly demanding embargoes and other restrictions before they will provide information or interviews.

Sometimes the request is reasonable: an embargo on an announcement of a major book prize winner, for instance, seems reasonable in return for getting the information early so a full story can be constructed. It also makes sense to agree to hold a story based on an interview with a singer or the star of a TV show until the singer's album is about to be released or the show is aired.

In other cases the newsmaker's motivation seems more self-serving: a TV network asks for an embargo on news about one of their shows until after they can announce it themselves on their own entertainment news show. Or an over-zealous PR agent might block an interview unless a reporter promises not to ask certain questions.

The news report should not be held hostage by such requests, which need to be considered on a case-by-case basis. Consult a supervisor before agreeing to any conditions.

In all cases, ask yourself if the request is reasonable, given the importance of the news. In many cases, it is not. For instance, if you are asked not to move a story until the release date of the singer's new CD, that is acceptable if it is understood that if the person says something timely, a spot story may move immediately, as well as the longer story later. And it is best to avoid agreeing not to ask about specific subjects, although it makes pragmatic sense to leave such questions until the end of the interview!

Features

Entertainment feature-writing generally allows more freedom to inject colour, personality and imaginative writing.

Colourful metaphors or similes can sometimes paint a vivid mental image. **Rock music on television is a lion in a cage. The BMW on Rodeo Drive glistened like a well-buffed Gucci loafer.**

Summing up a well-known person in a choice phrase can do two things: distil the subject's personality for the reader, plus set a tone for the article. **The artistic film director is a 32-year-old bundle of neuroses.**

While actors may make for identifiable hooks for a story, producers and directors are often more articulate about a project and can provide fresh insight. A good entertainment story often mixes the creative insights with the star quality of a Hollywood figure.

Reviews

In a world teeming with entertainment choices, the thoughtful review is especially important to help readers decide how to spend their leisure time.

Basically, a review gives the reader a synopsis of the work with some commentary on its artistic merit or entertainment value.

Full-time reviewers have more credibility and leeway than part-timers — who would do well to approach the assignment as a news event, describing it and getting audience comment or quoting newspaper reviewers.

Reviewers should avoid cheap shots or gush. While someone like George Bernard Shaw could get away with a demolishing review, readers can be turned off by harshness or apparent unfairness.

Commentary needs to be grounded in specific detail. Saying a rock band's show was atrocious means nothing. Rather: **The lead singer was off-key on three numbers, the lighting failed during another and people at the rear of the hall complained they couldn't hear the lyrics.**

Give readers a signpost: **The band conjures up the driving rhythm of the early Rolling Stones.**

When reviewing drama or books, reveal only as much of the plot as necessary to set the scene for the review. Readers will be annoyed to have the ending revealed by a thoughtless reviewer.

Feature newswriting

There are no hard and fast rules separating "hard" news and "features." The lines have blurred since the old newspaper days when softer, more descriptive material was relegated to the inside pages and the front-page stories contained just the facts. Today's 24-hour news day presents the challenge of providing a unique perspective beyond the headline that has already run on TV and other screens.

Although all stories should be written in a lively way with plenty of context and colour, many can benefit from a specific approach as well, emphasizing analysis, context or background that can help a reader better understand a development. Perhaps a virtual unknown has just been elected leader of a major political party. Or the price of oil has jumped by a third in two months. Or the anniversary of a major news event is on the horizon. In these situations, it is time to think about a special approach to coverage.

Analyses

A News Analysis tests the best qualities that reporters and editors can bring to the news report.

The writer must know the subject intimately to give the reader an informed, intelligent and reasoned assessment of the issues involved. Readers look an analysis for a clear and unbiased understanding of what has happened or may happen — and why.

An analysis cannot be done off the cuff. It demands careful forethought and discussion with a number of outside experts. Familiarity and comfort with the underlying issues is a must for the writer.

Most important: an analysis is not a soapbox. It can focus on a single perspective or point of view, but that perspective must be dispassionate and logical. Opposing views must not be neglected.

Some guidelines:

1. A strong analysis is usually built around a single thesis: the new tax will have little effect on consumer spending; the Opposition leader's staff is hurting her image. The thesis is supported by material marshalled in logical order. Objections can be noted, experts cited and secondary angles explored a bit. But the analysis should never lose sight of the main theme by jumbling it with distractions.

2. The analysis should open the reader's eyes, not belabour the obvious. Worthwhile analyses can be built on an unconventional viewpoint, a perspective that hasn't been explored much in the

past, a prediction that seems calm when others are confused or even hysterical.

3. The analysis should strike the right balance and tone in the first paragraph. It should not be cute or hyper. Get right to the point:

> **By Bruce Cheadle**
>
> OTTAWA — When it's raining abuse, maintain a sunny disposition.
>
> Conservative Leader Stephen Harper stuck to his playbook in Monday night's federal election debate, striking a world-wearing, good-natured pose under a barrage of criticism from Liberal Leader Paul Martin.
>
> In a spirited debate marked by sharp exchanges among all four party leaders, Harper was notable for his stubborn grin and calm demeanour.

4. Unlike a backgrounder, a news analysis focuses more on perspective than on factual background while the backgrounder leans more toward straight-ahead treatment of the major issues in a complex news story.

5. Analyses written for The Canadian Press do not float a writer's pet theory. They do not pass judgment. They do not offer the writer's solutions. The Canadian Press must be able to stand behind every word of every analysis. That means editorializing — or anything that can be construed as editorializing — is out.

Unacceptable: The question that Liberals asked, so ineffectually, during an eight-week campaign suddenly is now pertinent to every Canadian.

Acceptable: The question that Liberals asked during an eight-week campaign, only to have to dismissed at every turn, suddenly is now pertinent to every Canadian.

Never try to build a case with adjectival powder when mortar in the form of facts and thoughtful opinion is lacking. Keep digging or abandon the story as a lost cause.

6. Keep loaded phrases and words out of analyses. They can turn a sound argument into instant rhetoric — and send a reader away.

Unacceptable: The decision to cut the GST during an economic boom was based strictly on political considerations, but it will benefit government candidates in the next election. (Two errors: speculating on motivation and making a hard prediction.)

Acceptable: Opposition MPs see pure political strategy behind the decision to cut the GST two years before an election. Among government MPs, there is fear that by the time an election is called voters will have forgotten about the cut. (The information is the same, but the sources for it are people in a position to say.)

7. Many analyses lend themselves to human touches. In a piece dealing with a major corporate shakeup, for example, a reader might wonder what elements in a new chief executive officer's background particularly qualify her for the top job. Who are the political winners and losers in a federal throne speech? What is the likely impact of a cabinet shuffle on the new or shifted ministers' prospects in the next election?

8. The one-voice *analysis* has no place in The Canadian Press news report. Instead, analyses should attempt to synthesize opinion and be as well sourced as news stories. They should give the reader a sense of the sources who have been consulted, even if they must be unnamed. In an analysis on aboriginal issues, for example, it makes a big difference whether the issues are looked at through the eyes of academics or aboriginals themselves.

9. Avoid over-attribution — a constant **he said, she said**. It's important in analysis to communicate to the reader a sense that the writer has ownership of the material. Often a general line early in an analysis can help.

. . . **interviews with several senior Conservative party members.**

This gives the reader a sense that the writer has done his homework.

10. The writer's own observations and conclusions can be helpful in shaping some analyses. For example, a reporter who has covered a major environmental story from its beginnings to a key development months later should have the background and understanding to assess the situation fairly and from all perspectives. More often, however, the analysis flows from exhaustive research, an uncluttered understanding of the issues involved and solid contact with sources on all sides of those issues.

11. Analyses should be written as close as possible to the news event to maximize their impact and relevance to readers.

12. A writer assigned to an analysis on a fixed time event, such as an election night, should not be assigned other duties. He or she will require an uncluttered mind (and desk) to concentrate on the event and its meaning for readers.

In these cases, it should usually be possible to rough out a couple of potential analyses based on different outcomes. If, for example, it appears possible that a minority government could be elected, some obvious questions could be explored in advance. How will the leading party hold power? What alliances might be made? How will the minority status affect the ruling party's election promises? What has been the experience of other minority governments? Is another election likely soon?

13. Analyses should be reviewed by a senior supervisor before being transmitted.

14. Copy should carry the identifier **News Analysis** as part of the headline:

News Analysis: Tory minority set to start work on changing Canada's political culture

Backgrounders

When it's time to pull together a tangle of news threads or to stand back from a particularly confusing story, the backgrounder is the mechanism of choice — and a welcome friend to the reader.

Above all, a backgrounder gives the reader the answers to basic questions: What's really going on here? What does it mean to me and my families and my neighbours?

Backgrounders differ from analyses. Where the analysis builds a structure of interpretation upon a foundation of factual material, the backgrounder focuses on the foundation stones through an orderly assembly of factual detail and perspective.

The backgrounder provides historical context, sets out the whys and wherefores of a complicated issue in the news, explores legal questions or lists the pocketbook impact of the development under review.

Where appropriate, the backgrounder will also quote knowledgeable authorities — or everyday people with first-hand experience in similar circumstances — about future implications for the lives of readers.

A strong sense of a key player's human side is usually needed to give the reader an understanding of the personalities involved.

There is no practical limit to the kinds of situations that can be served by a well-thought-out backgrounder:

• How researchers are exploring Parkinson's disease after actor Michael J. Fox reveals he has it.

• How Prairie farmers are coping with a string of bad luck: drought, debt, coyotes and grasshoppers.

• How the premier has pulled her party together at the last minute to head into an election, with the story focusing on her persuasive personality and political savvy.

• Why some major corporations are lopping off subsidiaries after years of bigger-is-better thinking.

• What's behind a new NHL rule on face masks, reviewing a rash of facial injuries from a doctor's perspective.

Effective backgrounders can often be worked up on matters that might otherwise receive only passing attention in the spot news report.

An example:

Business interests, local residents and nature lovers are locked in a battle over a proposed tourism development in the North. What is at stake? Why are the various sides in conflict? How have the battle lines been drawn?

The story could include interesting sketches of people on each side of the dispute, description and history of the area being fought over and some sense of the values being promoted — a rare breeding ground for song birds versus jobs in a high unemployment area, for example.

The writing approach to such stories is as wide open as the imagination of the writer. It often helps to focus on a specific element in a many-sided situation or on a single human being directly involved. The story should not read like a spot news item — refer only briefly to the hard news angle that has provoked the backgrounder.

Be wary of the grab-bag lead that tries to gather in a large number of major components. It is an approach that rarely works.

Point form can be especially effective in setting out key issues or background to give the reader some fast and tidy context.

A backgrounder on the Atlantic provinces, for instance, could hit points like this high up in the story:

• The four provinces have 194 legislature members and 34,000 civil servants for a population of 2.2 million. Alberta, with a population of 2.4 million, has 83 legislature members and 12,000 civil servants.

• Newfoundland and Labrador gets 47 cents of every government dollar from the federal treasury; P.E.I. 46 cents; New Brunswick and Nova Scotia 39 cents each.

• The cap on federal transfer payments has already cut $400 million from the amount the region had been counting on, and more cuts seem certain.

Copy should carry the identifier **Backgrounder** as part of the headline:

Backgrounder: Scientists have found no test, no cure for Parkinson's disease

Flashbacks

The key to Flashbacks is to make clear why the events were important when they happened and why they deserve to be remembered now.

Readers are always interested in a nicely written historical piece on anything from Louis Riel to the October Crisis, especially one sprinkled with human touches and appealing anecdotes.

1. Flashbacks tied to anniversaries should note that connection somewhere in the first two or three paragraphs: **It was 60 years ago this week that** . . .

2. The successful Flashback starts with a strong idea, usually in one of these two categories:

a) Recognizable historical events like Prohibition and the October Crisis, tied to a specific anniversary, or an event like the Vietnam War that is tied to a veterans reunion.

b) All-but-forgotten happenings that can be successfully revived for today's reader — events like the Frank landslide of 1903 that killed at least 70 people in the territory that in 1905 became Alberta.

3. Flashbacks can also be tied to a specific anniversary as well (birth, death, special honour, etc.) — the 100th anniversary of the publication of *Anne of Green Gables,* for example.

Ordinary people who bore witness to history can often provide the most striking perspectives, and so can serve as excellent focal points for Flashbacks on major events — the security guard who was on duty the night the mine exploded; the woman whose car was lifted during the tornado.

4. Look for topics with some direct impact on people — then or now.

5. Try to find someone who was around at the time. That will be impossible in some cases, of course, so it will mean a trip to an archive or a library — public, university or newspaper — to search for contemporary accounts or comments on the incident being recalled.

6. Thorough research for a flashback story can often yield excellent colour. Sometimes personal scrapbooks or letters can be helpful. Quoting the flowery language of the day, perhaps from a newspaper or other primary source, can bring a dusty piece of history to life.

7. If the subject is controversial, check at least three different sources to ensure you're not quoting someone with an axe to grind.

Copy should carry the identifier **Flashback** as part of the headline:

Flashback: Story of red-haired Anne from P.E.I. celebrates its 100th birthday

Profiles and Newsmakers

Profiles and Newsmakers tell people about people. They put human beings into news stories.

Profiles usually deal with people who may not be in the public eye but whose lives, jobs, hobbies or thoughts are interesting and appealing. Similarly, Newsmakers are generally reserved for people who are making headlines, but who themselves might be unknown or lesser-known figures who need some introduction — the new leader of a national First Nations organization, the provincial cabinet minister whose public statements have caused a furor, the unlikely hero of a Stanley Cup championship game.

Except for the time element, or *peg*, Profiles and Newsmakers have much in common. At their best, they leave the reader with a sense of knowing the subjects as individuals — the next best thing to meeting them in person.

The Profile and Newsmaker must be fair and in good taste. They should never be a vehicle for cheap shots, sexist comments, irrelevant detail or clumsy description.

These stories should skilfully blend background, colour, personality touches and newsy tidbits about the subject. They should avoid logjams of detail and gratuitous information. Good quotes that convey the mood or personality of the subject are particularly important.

Stories such as Profiles and Newsmakers offer a great opportunity to take the reader where the TV camera can rarely go. Look for telling actions that would probably not take place before the cameras: a federal cabinet minister gets upset when he can't get into his hotel room because he's misplaced his key; a notoriously tough football coach spends his days off as a volunteer art instructor for inner city youngsters.

The keen-eyed reporter can also sketch things a TV viewer might miss: the politician's aide always wears red neckties and combs his hair exactly like his mentor; the baseball player warming up for the all-star game keeps a jealous eye on the television camera.

Profiles and Newsmakers should be tight and bright. They should tell readers something about who the subjects are, how they got where they are, a little about what makes them tick. Friends and colleagues can be helpful in providing perceptive insights and anecdotes. So can enemies, but only if they're named.

Did the subject grow up on a farm and save egg money to buy books? Did she run three newspaper routes at the same time to buy a bicycle? Does she read books for blind people at a nursing home?

Let the reader in on your subject's home surroundings, revealing his likes, dislikes and interests.

Look for the unexpected. Dennis O'Connor, the judge appointed to investigate the tainted water scandal in Walkerton, Ont., went to local hockey games while in the small town conducting hearings. Prime Minister Stephen Harper was a long-distance runner in high school.

Colour and description

1. Description should be fresh, imaginative and relevant. It should help the reader get a sense of the subject's appearance and personality or to feel what it was like to be at the news scene.

2. A string of generalized adjectives is usually less effective than active and specific words.

Not: Porn star Ron Jeremy was in the elaborately decorated lobby of a downtown hotel, enjoying a traditional English high tea.

But: It's tea time at a downtown hotel and the afternoon sunlight casts an amber hue on an unlikely sight — porn star Ron Jeremy perched on an opulent antique chair, ready to tuck into a plate of scones and raspberry preserves while sipping a cup of Darjeeling tea.

3. A basic description of physique or character should be provided when it is pertinent to the news event. The lined faces and baggy eyes of the jurors as they file into the courtroom after two weeks of deliberations are worth noting. But description should always serve a purpose. Too often, the clothing of female newsmakers is carefully described, while that of men is ignored. Inclusion of such details should be driven by relevance, not sex.

4. Examples will speak louder than adjectives. The anecdote about the Liberal MP moving her seat in the Commons out of the line of sight of her former boyfriend, a Conservative, is a telling detail.

5. Watch for chances to use a description that provides more information than a bald statement:

Not: The prime minister was angry.

But: The prime minister's face tightened with anger as he spun on his heel and strode quickly off the platform.

6. It sometimes helps to encourage subjects to talk about themselves. Ask lots of questions about childhood, hobbies, former jobs, dreams and hopes. Many people will be refreshingly open when given the chance.

7. Subjects who are naturally reserved and taciturn are particularly challenging. So is the individual who dislikes media attention. Look for body language from such people. Some of them convey a wealth of information even though their actual answers may be sparse or even gruff. Or ask someone close to the subject for revealing stories. When asked how her husband, UN envoy Stephen Lewis, stayed so energetic, Michelle Landsberg told a Canadian Press reporter: "I have no idea where he gets it. He leads the unhealthiest lifestyle. He doesn't exercise except for running for planes." That's not information her husband would have provided.

8. When it comes to effective use of colour and description, take pains to ensure it is weaved carefully into the copy to ensure it doesn't look forced. A paragraph devoted entirely to colour to the exclusion of news, quotes or anything else to inform the reader will seem distracting. Laborious descriptive clauses are also discouraging. Instead, use colour the way an artist would — sparingly, strategically and in a natural way:

The judge who will recommend how much time Albert Walker ought to spend in prison for murdering Ronald Platt denounced the convicted Canadian on Monday as a callous and ruthless man who used people for his own selfish ends.

> The judge who will recommend how much time Albert Walker ought to spend in prison for murdering Ronald Platt denounced the convicted Canadian on Monday as a callous and ruthless man who used people for his own selfish ends.
> Walker, 52, blinked twice when the foreman of the eight-woman, four-man jury announced the guilty verdict after two hours of deliberation.
> Later, as he was led down the stairs of the dock into the holding cells, the composure Walker maintained throughout the trial appeared on the verge of collapse. His eyes were reddening and his facial muscles seemed ready to give way.

9. Avoiding repetitive language is important, but take care not to fall into the trap of tediously substituting bits of background for the person's identity:

Para 1:   John Simpson said Tuesday . . .

Para 2:   . . . the former Vancouver engineer added.

Para 3:   The lanky, grey-haired bureaucrat insisted . . .

Instead, consider giving readers an early mental image that can stay with them as they read on:

> Simpson, lanky and grey-haired, is a former Vancouver engineer who in 1996 joined the federal Transport Department and rose quickly to the No. 2 spot. In that job he is now insisting that the harbour project be shelved.

10. The word **Profile** or **Newsmaker** is included in the slug and should also be included in the headline, which should be substantially different than the headline on any accompanying news story:

Harper-Newsmaker
Newsmaker: New PM Stephen Harper defies easy pigeonholing

Freedom of information laws

The federal government, provinces and territories currently have laws that give Canadian citizens, corporations and others the right to acquire government-controlled information.

The federal law, in effect since 1983, is called the Access to Information Act. Provinces generally use the phrase "freedom of information" in their statutes. The laws are intended to foster open, transparent and accountable government and are used primarily by businesses, lawyers, political parties and individual citizens.

Freedom of information laws can be effective tools for journalists looking for the story behind the headlines or for the untold story about issues not yet part of public debate. The process can also be lengthy, frustrating and costly, depending on the jurisdiction and the nature of the request.

Delays are common. Media requests for sensitive material normally take far longer than the 30-day deadline imposed by the federal law, for example, which also gives departments the right to claim time extensions. Even so, dated material can shed new light on key issues and developments and provide an opportunity to revisit important stories. Other information on issues never before in the public arena can still play as news, even though the audit, report or study may be months or years old. Typically, the released material has the added attraction of being exclusive to a reporter or newsroom.

Freedom of information requests are a supplement to, not a substitute for, informal requests for government information. A formal request has the advantage of clear rules and a system of appeals. But a reporter working a source effectively can often get more timely information. Consider using both approaches simultaneously when chasing a story.

The laws are generally inexpensive to use, despite horror stories about million-dollar fees for searching and photocopying. Most jurisdictions charge a fee for making an application, $5 under the federal law. A certain amount of free search time and photocopying is usually available, but costs can rise steeply after these thresholds are crossed.

Some tips

1. A well-focused request can avoid additional charges and speed the response time. Limit the time period covered; cite specific subject areas or issues; exclude newspaper clippings; ask for executive summaries only; break down large requests into smaller individual requests; ask for title pages, indices or lists of documents, then file second requests for specific documents.

2. Photocopy charges can be avoided by asking to view the records in a local office of the government department. Some

departments will provide records in digital formats, such as on a CD or in electronic files that can be emailed, thereby cutting costs for the requester.

3. Some categories of records are relatively fruitful sources of information: briefing notes, audits, program reviews, polls, expense claims, contracts, minutes, and accident investigation reports. Ask for draft versions if the final version is not yet complete.

4. Many governments routinely post some material on their websites. Do a thorough web search before making a request, but consider that governments may suppress controversial material by posting only abbreviated versions.

5. Requests for information can usually be sent by letter, though pre-printed forms are faster. Some departments and agencies accept requests electronically, with fees paid by credit card.

6. Use the word "record" when asking for federal material, as this term includes a broad range of formats, from photographs, audio tapes, videotapes and computer disks to printed reports, letters and memorandums. Governments are not required to create records in response to a request, only to release existing records.

7. Requests are sent directly to the person designated by a department, agency or ministry to handle freedom of information inquiries. This person can often be a good source of confidential advice about how to narrow requests. Always diligently follow up requests by telephone, email or letter to ensure deadlines and commitments are met. Busy freedom-of-information units tend to provide better service to those who demand it.

Some examples (federal law):

"All briefing notes provided to the defence minister since Jan. 1, 2008, on Hercules aircraft."

"Minutes of, records of decisions, agendas and materials distributed at or for the most recent meeting of the senior management committee of the Health Department, including any draft or interim versions if final versions not yet complete."

"Executive summary of the internal program review of the RCMP's aboriginal policing initiative."

Limitations

The statutes give governments the right to refuse disclosure of certain kinds of information. Cabinet confidences, police investigation records, material related to inter-government relations, legal advice, national security records, records impinging on the privacy of a person or business, can all be withheld legally. Some quasi-public bodies, such as Nav Canada, are exempt altogether. The laws are also typically restricted to government records, and do not extend to political records such as those held in a minister's office or a member of Parliament's office. Some officers of Parliament are covered, however, including the federal auditor general and the information commissioner. In 2007, many formerly exempt Crown corporations became subject to the Access to Information Act, including Canada Post, Via Rail and the CBC.

Complaints about delays or exemptions can be made to public officials whose job is to investigate alleged breaches of the law. At the federal level, the office of the Information Commissioner of Canada can take complaints to court at taxpayer's expense on behalf of a requester if moral suasion does not resolve disputes. Requesters can themselves take matters directly to court. Such cases can further delay release of material but may also heighten public interest. Requesters should attempt to resolve the dispute directly with the offending department, however, before making a formal complaint.

Keep trying

Freedom of information laws can be an exercise in frustration, but for tenacious reporters they can also unlock vital information about government operations and public policy. Despite their weaknesses, the laws remain effective tools for enterprising journalists. Freedom of information stories have become an important addition to investigative journalism as practised in Canada, providing readers and viewers with fresh perspectives on the actions, intentions and foibles of governments.

The future

The Access to Information Act has been reviewed numerous times, though no fundamental changes have been made since it was passed in 1983. Federal court decisions over the last two decades have generally broadened the scope and strengthened the provisions. The Federal Accountability Act (2006) made some important changes, including the addition of 70 government agencies to the purview of the Access to Information Act. The scope of provincial laws has also generally broadened, often to include municipal, hospital and university records, though fees have increased sharply in some jurisdictions. Canadian governments have also become more cautious about releasing any information touching on security, especially since the events of Sept. 11, 2001. User groups can be a source for information and advice, including the Canadian Access and Privacy Association. The Canadian Association of Journalists also regularly conducts FOI seminars at its annual conventions.

Websites

The federal government's main Access to Information Act website:

www.tbs-sct.gc.ca/gos-sog/atip-aiprp/index_e.asp

Information Commissioner of Canada website:

www.oic-ci.gc.ca/eng/

Graphics

Not every news story is best told in paragraphs. Graphics, whether designed for print, video or websites, can combine words, images, sounds and visuals in a way that explains complex stories in simple and engaging ways.

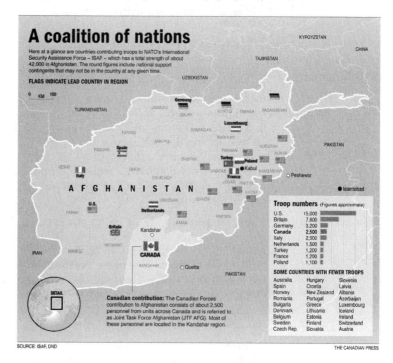

Graphic artists research, design and construct graphics that show readers the how, who, what, where, when and why of a story — or any combination thereof. The best graphics combine strong information, design and technology to present a story in a new way. They immediately attract a reader with strong images and catchy information, but also offer a reward — informative details and extra material — the longer the reader spends with the graphic.

A graphic can be a single one-column chart showing the day's closing stock numbers, or a full page of words and pictures organized around one topic, such as a major sporting event. It can be static — all of it is visible at once — or interactive, which requires viewers to click on elements for further information.

The online world presents many options for cleverly presenting information. Interactive graphics can front massive databases that allow viewers to select text, pictures, sound and animation, according to what interests them or what they would like to check out first. But both interactive and stationary graphics can contain a lot of information. One interactive graphic can have several elements and deep information: a text account of the story, an album of pictures, audio from newsmakers, maps and chronologies. But a well-designed stationary graphic can have an immediate visual impact on a reader and encourage him to dig through the presentation for more details.

Staffers everywhere should suggest ideas for graphics. They are often the best way to locate an event, explain a complicated statistical trend or compare products.

Information, please

The average news day is full of material that can be made into a graphic. The letterhead on an accreditation application might make a good standing logo for continuing stories on a coming sports tournament. The diagram in the back of the press release that helps reporters understand a new product might be just as helpful for readers. Audio of the Queen's first radio speech will make a memorable addition to an interactive graphic on her 90th birthday. A car company's website might have images of the car models it is eliminating. Give the graphics department a heads-up on what is available.

The best graphics result when writers and graphics artists work closely together to present a story in the most illuminating way possible. Reporters need to gather this detail in their contacts with news sources. If a plane crashed on takeoff, find out what runway it was using. How are the runways configured? How far did it go past the runway? Did it crash in trees or a field? What buildings are in the area? Reporters can get this information on the phone.

A business reporter who hears that a company's sales have been climbing steadily since 2005 can get a graphic going if the annual sales figures can be obtained. Specific numbers are required to produce a graphic, obliging sources to back up their statements with precise facts. The numbers might show that sales are up from 2005, but there have been a number of ups and downs in the period. The fact-digging needed for a graphic is often important in getting an accurate understanding of the story.

Graphics can effectively present a snapshot of a complex story with many elements.

The artist needs references. A graphic about the new offshore oil project requires a depiction of the rig as seen by the planners. The artist can't just dream something up. Details are important and are known by somebody familiar with the story. Find the person. That detail included in the graphic ensures accuracy and conveys a sense of heightened realism for readers.

Sometimes a photographer's pictures will help with detail, but many times graphics portray action that can't be seen by photographers, like the inside of a mine that's collapsed. Get it from an expert.

Email can get information to artists quickly. Information available in digital format is more easily incorporated into a graphic. Give the graphics desk details like street addresses, nearest intersections or GPS locations when available.

Graphics can effectively present a snapshot of a complex story with many elements.

Experts blame a variety of economic, social, political and environment factors for the skyrocketing prices of staples like wheat, corn, rice and soybeans. But they do agree on one point – it isn't simply because the world is running out of food.

PRICES ON THE RISE

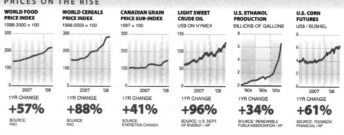

WORLD FOOD PRICE INDEX	WORLD CEREALS PRICE INDEX	CANADIAN GRAIN PRICE SUB-INDEX	LIGHT SWEET CRUDE OIL	U.S. ETHANOL PRODUCTION	U.S. CORN FUTURES
+57%	+88%	+41%	+96%	+34%	+61%

HARD HIT COUNTRIES

Grain prices have jumped around the world, especially in developing countries which tend to rely on food imports. Some examples:

Somalia: Price of wheat flour in northern areas has almost tripled in the last year.

Sudan: Price of wheat in the capital of Khartoum in February was 90 per cent higher than a year ago.

Uganda: Price of corn in March was up by 65 per cent from September 2007 levels.

Ethiopia: Wheat was 42 per cent higher in Addis Abbaba in March, double the cost of a year ago.

Philippines: Rice prices have increased 50 per cent in the past two months.

Sri Lanka: Rice prices in March were almost double those of a year ago.

Bangladesh: Rice prices increased by 66 per cent in the last year.

Tajikistan: Price of bread in February was twice the level of a year ago.

Armenia: Price of wheat flour has increased by one-third in a year.

Haiti: Food prices are 50 to 100 per cent higher than a year ago.

FOOD PRICE FACTORS

Soaring fuel prices Oil prices have almost doubled since the beginning of 2007. This makes it more expensive to ship food around the world and also increases grain production costs for things like fertilizer and tractor fuel.

Biofuels demand Corn, especially that grown in the United States, the world's largest corn exporter, is increasingly being used to produce a fuel called ethanol. This means less is available for food.

Weather woes Such phenomenon as droughts, heavy rain and heat waves have affected crop yields in several big grain-growing countries.

Trade restrictions Some countries, including big exporters like Russia and China, have added taxes or other restrictions to grain trade, pushing prices up.

Meat demand Economic development in large countries like China and India has increased demand for meat, which in turn increases demand for feed grain for animals.

SOURCES: Food and Agriculture Organization of the United Nations, AP, Statistics Canada

SEAN VOKEY / THE CANADIAN PRESS

Tips on creating graphics

1. Be sure to work closely with the reporter or editor on a story. The facts in the graphic must agree with the facts in the story.

2. The simpler, the better — focus on the central message and lose the extraneous material.

3. A clean, consistent design works better than a complex approach.

4. Break down complex information into easily understandable bite-sized pieces.

5. Colour is not just for decoration — use it to help the reader understand the data.

6. Not all readers can see colours, so don't rely on it alone for organization. Use shapes to flag details that go together.

7. The Internet is a valuable resource for information — but always be sure to use credible websites.

➤ See **Sources**, page 25.

Cautions

Although visual interest is important in a graphic, it comes second to accuracy. A few tips:

1. Do not project, surmise or estimate in a graphic. Only work with what you know.

2. Confirm the location before moving or posting a locator map.

3. Make sure the information is clear and concise. If you don't understand it, the reader won't.

4. Create charts in a perspective that gives an accurate representation of data. Do not skew or alter data to fit a visual need.

5. Credit sources on every graphic, including graphics for which Canadian Press journalists have created the data.

6. Graphics often combine various photographic elements, which necessarily means altering portions of each photograph. But there is a limit on what is allowed. The background of a photograph, for example, may be removed to leave the headshot of the newsmaker. This may then be combined with a logo representing the person's company or industry, and the two elements may be layered over a neutral background.

Such compositions must not misrepresent the facts and must not result in an image that looks like a photograph — it must clearly be a graphic.

Similarly, when photos are used in online graphics, the integrity of the image should be retained. Limit changes to cropping, masking and adding elements like logos.

Corrections

Graphics, like stories and pictures, must be corrected immediately. Any graphic being corrected must carry the word **FIX** in the slug and an explanation of the correction in the replacement graphic.

The incorrect graphic must be removed from the archives to prevent further use.

Headlines

General

Headlines are the hidden weapons of writers and editors. More than any other element, a strong headline can grab the attention of readers and lure them into a story. A good headline — specific, lively and concise — should tell readers everything they need to know about the story, but still make them want to read more.

Headline writing is a special art. Some editors seem to have a natural talent for it. Others have to work at it. It is kind of like solving a crossword puzzle — practice makes it easier because you learn the little tricks. But accuracy always comes before cleverness. Many readers stop at the headline; if it gives them a misleading impression of the story, they will take that with them. Headlines must face the same tests of accuracy and fairness as all other publishable copy. The headline can't say **Five Dead in Prison Riot** if this is based on unconfirmed TV reports quoting unnamed sources. Such information must be qualified in a headline the same way it would be in the body of the story. Headline style allows statements to be condensed but not by sacrificing accuracy on crucial points.

Canadian Press stories carry two headlines. There is a short headline of about six words (under 45 characters), used by websites and wireless services, that should intrigue readers into clicking into the story. A second headline, about double in length, may be carried on a headline-only service. It should give the reader the main details of the story, not leave him hanging since he has nowhere to go to get the details. Both headlines should be clearly written, eye-catching and, most importantly, accurate.

Headline-writing tips

1. **Think about what information must be included in the headline.** Imagine it on a flash card, all on its own. What are the key elements of the story? Will it need a locator? Sometimes it helps to draft a headline before you write or edit the story — afterwards you may be too familiar with it to recognize that the headline is incomplete or hard to understand.

2. **Now think specifics.** Are there any images or quotes in the story that could be worked into the headline to give it flavour? Try to improve the language in your working headline to make it more specific. Look at the words you have used. Can you create stronger images? How about a wordplay — not a bad pun, but a twist of phrasing? Techniques such as rhyming words and alliteration can brighten up a headline. On a story about a clerk

at a doughnut shop being fired for giving food to a baby, one headline read: **Much a Dough About Nothing: Tim Hortons Red-faced Over Free Timbit Firing**. On another story about the amount of junk in food aimed at kids, the headline was: **Sugar and spice and everything vice, study finds that's what kid food is made of.**

3. **Speak to the reader directly.** Personalize headlines. This headline on a routine story lifted it above the predictable: **Parents, Get Ready: 'American Idol' Summer Concert Tour Will Make 50 Stops.**

4. **A strong, active verb can help create a mental picture.** Put it in the present tense.

Not: Defence minister slated to make appearance in rugby game

But: Defence minister laces on rugby boots for Nova Scotia Keltics

5. **Make sure your headline encapsulates the central emotion or drama in the story.** In this headline, the emphasis is on the wrong group — the defence authorities:

Defence authorities revive plan to kill 400 kangaroos in Australian capital

Instead, put the kangaroos front and centre, and add a hint on why they are being killed:

400 grass-chomping kangaroos near Australian capital face death sentence

6. **Handle attribution with care.** Although it can sometimes work at the end of a sentence, avoid using a colon for attribution at the beginning, since this hampers immediate understanding:

Not: China state media: Some 26,000 people still buried in earthquake debris.

But: China quake death toll nears 15,000: state media

Even better: State media report China quake death toll nears 15,000.

7. **Watch for times when a description or title is better than a name.** While it is OK to refer to the prime minister only as Harper in a headline, don't use a name-only reference with people who are not well-known. Try to judge how immediately recognizable the names are across Canada.

Not: Pocklington pleads guilty to stay out of jail.

But: Ex-Oilers owner returns Stanley Cup rings

8. **Avoid long phrases.** They can be hard to absorb for the reader, especially if there is no other context.

9. **Avoid headlines that can be read two different ways** — Iraqi Head Seeks Arms.

10. **Have fun — on stories that are lighthearted or frivolous.** Here's a fun headline for a fun story: Livin' Evita loca: Ricky Martin to star in Broadway revival of 'Evita.'

But if the content is serious, keep it straight:

Not: Har, matey! 'Pirate' trundle bed recalled

But: Pirate-themed bed can trap toddlers' heads

11. **Think about what keywords people are likely to use in a search for a story.** Headlines are important to search engines, RSS feeds and other content aggregators online. Include keywords in the headline so the story is more likely to be picked up by search engines. Think people, places and things — the sorts of words that would be commonly searched for. If the story is about a hockey player appearing in court, for instance, then using the word hockey in the headline will help guarantee it pops up in a search. If the key facts of a story involve, say, a cat, a box of Band-Aids and a missing car, then getting those words into the headline will help readers track it down online. It's also another good reason to avoid abbreviations in headlines, because people usually spell out words in searches.

Updating headlines

Headlines must always be changed when a story changes. Otherwise online readers are not alerted that there is something new in the story. Even if it is only a straightforward update, like changing the number of victims killed in a disaster, make sure the headline carries the most recent information available.

Headline style

1. Only the first letter in the first word of the headline is uppercase. All other words in the headline follow normal Canadian Press style for capitalization. However, the principal words of headlines are capped when they are quoted within the body of a story (as they are in this chapter).

2. The usual rules on abbreviations also apply, with some additions. For Canadian provinces, it is OK to use **B.C., P.E.I., N.B., N.L., N.S.** and **N.W.T.** in all references (nouns and adjectives) in headlines. **Sask., Alta., Ont., Man. and Que.** can also be used. Use these abbreviations only if space constraints require it. Don't shorten **Yukon** and **Nunavut.** Do not load up a headline with numerous abbreviations — reading a headline should not be an exercise in decoding a foreign language.

3. Use numerals — **8** instead of **eight**, **1st** instead of **first**, etc. — for numbers under 10.

4. Use **%** instead of **per cent.**

5. It is OK to use **M**, capped, for **million** after a numeral: **$2M in funding.**

6. On business stories, business quarters can be represented as Q1, Q2, Q3 and Q4.

7. Use single, not double, quotation marks in headlines. This is the style most newspapers follow.

Headline glossary

More short synonyms can be found in the Plain Words chapter of *Caps and Spelling*.

Instead of	Use
abandon	quit, leave
abolish	end, scrap
acknowledge	admit
administer	direct, control
advise	tell
agreement	pact, deal
amalgamate	join
amendment	change
approves	OK's
arrest	bag, bust, nab
assist	aid
attempt	try
bargain	deal
cancel	nix
catch, apprehend	nab
celebrate	mark
child(ren)	kid(s)
collision	crash
company	firm
comparable	like
competitor	rival
conclude	end
Conservative	Tory
consult	ask
consume	eat, use up
currently	now
decrease	cut, drop, fall
explosion	blast
father	dad
federal government	Ottawa
former	ex-
frequently	often
friend	pal
fundamental	basic
guerrilla	rebel
implement	do, set up, begin
increase	boost, up, rise, grow
inform	tell
injunction	ban, order
inquire	ask
Liberal	Grit

looking for	seek
manufacture	make
marijuana	pot
mother	mom
numerous	many
obtain	get
occasion	event
offer	bid
oil and gas industry	oilpatch
persuade	coax, sway
physician	doctor
pickup truck	pickup
police	cops
position	job
prohibit	ban
promises	vows
proposal	plan
purchase	buy
prime minister	PM
principal	main, chief
procedure	way, method
project, proposal	plan
provide	give
reduce, lay off	cut
reduction	cut
replace	swap
rescue	save
resign, retire	quit
Statistics Canada	StatsCan
stop	nix
Toronto	T.O.
transport	ferry, tote
treaty	pact, deal
unemployment rate	jobless rate
versus	vs.
were supposed to be	slated

Interviewing

The basics

Know your subject. Read up on the newsmaker and the topics you're likely to talk about. A reporter who walks into an interview unprepared isn't likely to get a good story.

Rough out a list of questions. Use open-ended questions that cannot be answered yes or no. List them in a logical order so you don't jump from subject to subject. Don't hesitate to abandon your prepared questions if a more newsworthy angle pops up.

Microphones and video cameras often make people nervous. Too many taped interviews are ruined because the newsmaker is uncomfortable and the interviewer hasn't taken the time to make things right.

Often, all it takes is a friendly manner and some banter before the tape is turned on to put the person at ease. You can assure the subject they'll be fine and tell them the interview will be edited. If they think every sentence will be heard by large audiences, the words will be chosen with unnatural precision and result in stilted dialogue. If they know only brief segments are going to be used, it will help them loosen up.

Unless you are in a hurry, try leaving the toughest questions for the end. If you start with the hard ones, the subject is likely to go on the defensive and clam up. On the other hand, if your subject is experienced at dealing with the media, a tough question might be just what you need to put them off balance and shake them loose from the stock answers they've rehearsed. Think about which approach to take.

Make eye contact as much as you can. Look interested. Give an occasional nod when a point is made, but don't interrupt the answer. If the subject senses you're interested, they'll open up, giving you the information and vocal animation you want.

Know your questions well enough that you take only occasional glances at the paper they're written on. If you have to keep referring to your notes, the subject will be distracted and your interview disorganized.

Let the interview take on a life of its own and, above all, pay attention. Listen for answers you didn't expect and be prepared to follow up. Too often, the reporter is so busy thinking of what to ask next, he doesn't hear the answer to the previous question until he listens to the recording. By then it's too late.

If the newsmaker doesn't give you a straight answer, rephrase the question. If you still don't get a direct answer, try again. Interrupt if you have to — politely. Ask why the person is avoiding the question. You're conducting the interview — don't let the subject be evasive. The fact that someone won't talk about something suggests there may be something to hide.

As you listen to the answers, think of how they will sound on the air, in a video or in a story. Too often, a comment that would make a good actuality or quote is ruined by a longwinded or disjointed answer. Come back to it by rephrasing the question — even asking the person to sum up what's just been said.

When you've asked all your questions and followed up interesting points, ask if there's anything else your subject would like to talk about. Is there anything you've missed? You'd be surprised how often this produces an unexpected story.

Don't ignore what the subject says when your recording device is off. You're still interviewing her. It's best to make it clear that everything is on the record.

Take notes whenever possible — at a news conference, for example. Note where the key quotes or information are located on your recording device. This way, you can write a quick story based on your notes and quickly find the clip you want. If you can't make written notes, make mental ones. You'll save time.

Dialing for news

The phone is the lifeline of the newsroom.

It should be second nature to pick up a phone whenever a story needs filling out. If you get word, for example, of an alleged scandal involving a business executive and a cabinet minister, phone them both. You may only get a "no comment," but at least you tried to get both sides of the story. Then try someone else; the opposition will always comment when a cabinet minister is avoiding questions or may be in a scandal.

If a breakthrough in cancer treatment is announced in the United States, phone the cancer society here. Find out what they think. Maybe a Canadian researcher was in on the study.

When a popular NHL player is traded, call him at home.

Keep an updated list of contacts with work and home numbers. Call once in a while to chat. A familiar voice always gets the facts faster than an unfamiliar one.

Get to know the police and fire officials who handle media calls. That's where the bread-and-butter information comes from in an emergency, and if they know and trust you, you'll get the story before anyone else.

Before you begin an interview, get the person's title and have her spell out her name. Even if you don't quote her directly, at least you'll know whom to ask for if you need to call back.

Get the five Ws out of the way first. That way you'll have the vital details you need if the person on the other end has to break away quickly. Once you have the basics, poke around for the colour — anything that might make this story different.

You get the cold, hard facts from faceless officials. The human element comes from talking to ordinary people. If there's a five-alarm fire with people trapped inside a building and you can't get a reporter to the scene, use the Internet or a city directory to track down someone across the street. They can tell you how bad the fire is and describe the attempted rescue. It's dramatic. It brings the story to life. News is people.

Look for help. If you're not having any luck tracking down an out-of-city story, call a local radio station or newspaper. They may already know something or be able to provide the name and number of the right person to call. They may welcome getting a tip on a local story. You can offer to return the favour some day.

If you're running into dead ends because a number you need is unlisted or there's no answer, ask who else you can call to track this person down? An aide? A business partner? His mother? How about calling a neighbour?

In the heat of tracking down a story, take a moment to ask yourself: What do we know? What do we need to know? In the mad scramble of fighting deadlines, you sometimes lose sight of things that are important.

Don't forget, any time you tape a telephone conversation, you must get the person's permission up front to broadcast it on radio. It's the law.

➤ See **Quotations**, page 15; **World news**, page 186; **Legal**, page 215.

Being interviewed

Often reporters are called upon to be interviewed by broadcast media. It puts journalists on the other side of the microphone — not a comfortable experience for many!

Here are few simple guidelines to help make it a success:

Before you go on air, ask the host or producer how long the interview will be and what length of answers she's looking for. Is it a 45-second interview during a newscast where 10-second replies are needed? Or is it an hour-long call-in show where more elaborate answers are appropriate?

Once the show is underway, respond the way you'd like someone you're interviewing to respond to you. Brief, yet descriptive remarks are usually the best. Put some animation in your voice. If you're on TV, keep still. And remember to relax — you will be astonished at how quickly the time passes.

Lifestyles

Lifestyles coverage should be a mirror on how our society is changing — how we take care of ourselves, how we relate to each other, what we eat, wear, do for fun.

It is a broad field that includes health, fitness, medicine, food, fashion, leisure, human interest, gardening, homes, psychology, social affairs and science.

Lifestyles stories are not fluff. They are often tied to the day's news and can hit page 1 or the top of a newscast.

An inquest into the death of someone following liposuction, for example, calls out for an article outlining the procedure. The closing of a department store chain's fur salons could be accompanied by a story examining trappers who relied on the stores for their livelihoods. A piece on gardening trends could focus on concerns about pesticides.

In short, basic rules of journalism apply in lifestyles coverage: watch for the hard-news angle; keep copy tight; strive for balance; avoid single-source stories.

Aim for QuickQuotes, QuickFacts and graphics that can help an editor lay out a page attractively. Photos are essential. Accompanying video will make some stories more attractive to online editors.

On an ongoing topic, always seek a new angle or twist. A look at the dangers of suntanning may turn up an angle that some sunscreens do little to decrease the dangers of skin cancer.

Remember to include cross-sections of society — both sexes, various age and racial groups, geographical regions and income levels.

Avoid stereotypes. Most grandmothers are not silver-haired matrons in aprons.

Write in simple language. When technical terms must be used, explain them in plain English. Don't talk about **a fractured tibia** when most people are more likely to understand **a broken leg.**

Trends

While readers want to keep abreast of the latest trends, guard against inventing trends by exaggerating their scope. Two or three men seen wearing eye makeup doesn't mark a trend toward men wearing women's cosmetics.

On the other hand, keep an eye out for larger changes in society that narrowly focused writing may overlook. Changes in the family unit, living arrangements, family size and division of work are constant. These changes are worth writing about and should also influence writing on society as a whole.

Use personal observation as a tipoff, then seek out research material and Statistics Canada data to gauge how widespread a trend may be.

Promotion

Guard against promotion. Manufacturers and retailers have an outlet for promoting new goods and services — it's called advertising.

Be wary of the public relations practitioner's sales pitch. Some new products or services are newsworthy. Others are not. Be wary of claims for health treatments, parapsychology, the latest how-to books and so on. The litmus test is: Who will benefit from the story — the source or the reader? Always aim to include comments from outside sources.

Health and medical stories

Fiercely competitive pharmaceutical companies spend millions of dollars on research and development, and are always eager to be mentioned in the news. A positive report about a new drug can have far-reaching implications — it can improve the stock price for the manufacturer, cause patients to request the drug from their doctors and put pressure on provincial health plans to expand their coverage.

Drug manufacturers and health-care lobbyists hire public relations firms to deal with the media. Some of their favourite techniques include polls of Canadians on a particular health issue. A "study" may include the name of a doctor who is actually being paid by the drug manufacturer, and therefore can't be seen as an unbiased expert. The release of a new painkiller may be endorsed by a university or health centre, but did those institutes receive any funding from the firm? Hospitals, in desperate competition for scarce research dollars, may claim breakthroughs and medical firsts. Independent experts should validate those claims.

Reporters and editors who handle health stories should always have their antennae up. Question the source of all material. Be aware of news releases dressed up as something that serves no other purpose than to promote a new health-care product or drug. Find out whether doctors and other health professionals have a pecuniary interest in the story — if they do, let the reader know. Use outside sources to verify or challenge claims.

Some tips:

1. Stories from The Associated Press on drugs being approved or reviewed by the U.S. Food and Drug Administration or pulled from the market by a manufacturer usually require the addition of a line or two about the status of the drug in Canada. This can be obtained by calling Health Canada. If the story is important,

send the AP version immediately, then include the Canadian information in a Writethru.

2. When a press release concerns raising awareness of a certain disease, the first question should be "Who is paying to have this release disseminated?" Often, it will turn out to be a manufacturer trying to promote a certain drug or therapy. A story may still be written if the release is deemed to be of interest to readers, but it is essential to include information on who sponsored the release.

3. Reporters should be wary about reporting on a special "week" or "month" dedicated to a certain disease as health news because these are usually linked to fundraising.

4. Medical studies that have been published in a peer-reviewed journal have a stamp of approval in that experts in the field have already assessed the quality of the work and the findings. But often this work is funded by drug companies and interested parties, and their contributions should be noted in the story.

5. Academics and universities that are looking for attention and funding for their work are eager to have their names in the media. Always ask if the work has appeared in a peer-reviewed journal. If it hasn't, and the topic is still worth writing about, then the story should note that the study has not been published in a peer-reviewed journal, and should include comment from outside experts.

6. The Canadian Press typically does not write about clinical trials before they reach Phase 3, unless a drug or vaccine is considered to be a real breakthrough. For instance, results of a Phase 1 trial on a new statin drug would not be newsworthy since there are many statins on the market already.

7. Websites of reputable organizations can be a useful resource for definitions of various diseases and conditions. The websites for the Public Health Agency of Canada and the Centers for Disease Control and Prevention are considered reliable and official.

8. It is worth remembering that antibiotics are not effective against viruses. When in doubt, check whether a disease is caused by a virus or bacteria.

Obituaries

Readers are attracted to obituaries for many reasons. It may be simple curiosity or wanting to learn the secret of the person's success, happiness or failures, or wanting to know what kind of person society has lost.

Obituaries are stories about life — about recognizing a life for what it was and what it meant.

They should be portraits, with brush strokes provided by friends, family, colleagues or acquaintances who can provide insights into the person's personality and life. Sharp quotes add colour and depth.

But the portraits should be exact, with no attempt to brush out wrinkles and warts. Resist the tendency to canonize the departed; very few are true saints.

Some general guidelines:

1. Report deaths of newsworthy people. Don't limit obits to lawyers, politicians and other automatically prominent members of society. Be on the lookout for the deaths of average folk: the waitress who worked 30 years at the town's most popular diner to put seven foster children through university; the amateur philosopher who operated a downtown newsstand for many decades.

2. Often an obituary item of 200 to 250 words will suffice, but it should include a significant fact or two about the person and his or her life.

3. Unsavoury details may be pertinent as part of a life story but should be kept in perspective.

4. The spot story opens with the simple facts — the name, other identification, notable achievements, cause of death and particularly age — the first questions that a reader wants answered.

One of the world's finest voices has fallen silent. Canadian contralto Maureen Forrester has died at the age of 79. Her daughter, Gina said her mother ``quietly slipped away" Wednesday after her family had spent two days at her bedside.

5. After the lead paragraphs, details of the subject's life are given in inverted-pyramid style rather than chronologically. The early years and schooling are rarely as interesting as later accomplishments. By the same token, details on the death itself, unless it was unusual in some way, should not be the focus of the story.

6. For a next-day story, a featurish top may be the best approach in the absence of worthwhile developments.

A quarter-century hasn't dulled Richard Margison's memory of the first time he took the stage with Maureen Forrester.

It was 1986. Margison was 33 and in the fledgling stages of his career, while Forrester, who died Wednesday at the age of 79, was at the time already "in full stride."

7. The length of an obituary depends on the person's newsworthiness. In addition to the lead information, longer obituaries should include biographical facts, the names of survivors and funeral arrangements.

8. For unusually prominent public figures, as well as for people in the news business, include precise details of funeral arrangements.

9. At some point — but preferably not in the lead where it might confuse readers — include the full name of the subject: **Alexander Young Jackson** for the painter usually known as **A.Y. Jackson.**

10. The identifying feature in the first paragraph should be the one that best highlights the subject's life and career. Often it is something that happened years ago.

A.Y. Jackson, a father of modern Canadian painting and last survivor of the original Group of Seven artists, died today in a nursing home at age 91.

11. In reckoning age, take into account the birth month and day. A person born March 27, 1926, who died Jan. 10, 2010, was 83, not 84. To say **She was in her 84th year** is correct but confusing.

12. When the precise age is not available, give some indication of it from the person's activities, such as the year of graduation or the setting up of practice in law.

Cause of death

1. The cause of death should be given, except when the story makes plain that death resulted from the complications of old age. When the cause is not available, say so, and why.

2. Never speculate about the cause. If information doesn't come from someone clearly in a position to know, it is irresponsible to speculate.

3. When the cause of death of a publicly known figure is known to be suicide but the family has asked that it not be reported, their preference is usually outweighed by the public's right to know. If in doubt, consult Head Office.

4. In listing the cause of death, prefer a plain term to medical jargon: **heart attack** and **heart disease** rather than **coronary thrombosis** or **coronary occlusion.**

5. Explain unfamiliar scientific terms: **Hodgkin's disease — an uncommon disorder of the lymph nodes and spleen.**

6. Taste and redundancy often rule out detail when death resulted from violence.

Language

1. Write **die, bury, coffin** and **undertaker** or **funeral director** rather than **pass away, inter** or **laid to rest**. Do not use **resting** for the dead, or other euphemisms.

2. Write **die of**, not **from**, an illness.

3. Use **widow** and **widower**, but **wife** and **husband** until after the funeral. Guard against the redundant **widow of the late**. Write **wife of the late** or **widow of**.

4. Do not describe people as **late** when referring to something they did while alive. Not: **The late doctor fought the epidemic alone.**

5. In general, use **the late** only of a person who died recently. It is not needed, for instance, in **the late John Lennon**.

6. Beware of such common non sequiturs as **Born in Calgary, she was an ardent skier.** The two ideas are not linked by meaning and do not belong in the same sentence. Better: **She was born in Calgary. Six years later, the family moved to Collingwood, Ont., where she soon developed a taste for skiing.**

Prepared obits

1. When an obit shows up in The Canadian Press's inbox from a newspaper's electronic return news, it is wise to check with the paper by telephone. The story may be one prepared in advance.

2. Each bureau prepares biographical sketches of its most prominent citizens. These sketches should be reviewed periodically to make sure they are up to date and complete.

3. As with spot obituaries, prepared obits are made interesting by quotations and anecdotes bringing out the character of the subject.

4. To make an obit stand up for use at any time, avoid past tenses except when tied to a specific date or time. Include religious affiliations or activities if newsworthy.

Funerals

1. Funerals and memorial services are often public events, and arrangements are made for reporters and photographer to attend. In the case of private funerals, journalists should respect the wishes of the family. It is sometimes acceptable to cover the funeral from outside the church or funeral home. At both public and private funerals, do not intrude into the service or approach

the mourners unless it is evident that they are willing to talk to the media.

2. Never misrepresent yourself as a mourner.

3. In coverage, do not sentimentalize the dearly departed. Plain language is best, avoiding any attempt at tear-jerking.

4. Do not suggest that the remains are in any way the person.

Pierre Trudeau's family follow the coffin of the former prime minister as it is carried into Notre Dame Cathedral in Montreal. Funerals are often of great interest to readers.

THE CANADIAN PRESS/Paul Chiasson

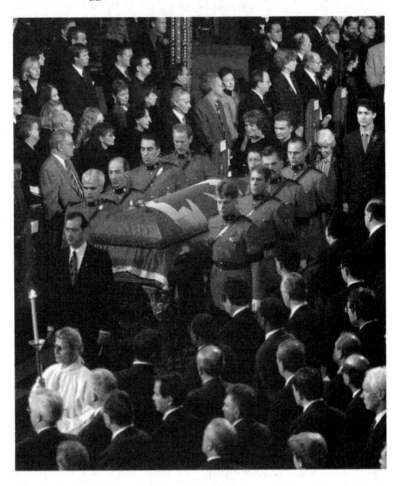

Online news

General

The Internet has quickly become a very popular way to get news and information. Readership is increasing all the time, especially on wireless devices that give people access to news anytime and anywhere they want. At the same time, many readers have reached the limit of their "human bandwidth." They can't handle any more information. Online editors and webmasters have to help them or they'll go away.

Many of these people are Canadians seeking out stories written and produced by The Canadian Press. The words, audio and pictures are seen several million times a day. The multimedia combination of stories, pictures, graphics, audio and video makes for ideal information packages. People come to our stories because we have something they need to know. Our credibility makes them come back.

Even though the Internet is the newest way to distribute news, the newsgathering techniques that wire service reporters have used for years are perfectly suited for a medium that can be updated anywhere, anytime. Advice from the 1940 stylebook still works: *It is the aim to keep the report up to the minute insofar as outstanding news is concerned. Quick action on spot news around the clock is essential because with five time zones, editions are almost invariably going to press at some points, regardless of the hour.*

The advice on reporting, writing, updating and correcting the news, found throughout this book, apply to the world of online news. This chapter focuses on the aspects of online news writing and editing that make it unique.

The audience

The term web surfer conjures up the image of someone moving from site to site, never stopping to engage long in a particular story or topic. While this is certainly true of many online news consumers, recent research also suggests that there are lots of readers who will stop and read an article thoroughly, perhaps even more thoroughly than they would in a newspaper.

The trick for online news editors is figuring out what makes them stop.

Playing to strengths

Online editors have many tools at their disposal and online news has many strengths not shared by traditional media. It's fast. It can be updated constantly. There is no limit to what can be included or linked to a news story, from photo galleries to other websites, from raw audio and transcripts to relevant databases and historical background.

While it is true there is no limit to what you can do, be selective. Readers will be confused and turned off is there is too much information to wade through, or if the signage on the coverage is confusing and difficult to navigate. One good photo, played prominently, is better than a photo gallery of 15 slightly out of focus ones.

The Internet is an unmonitored free-for-all of content of wildly varying value. The newsroom's traditional role of gatekeeping couldn't be more relevant.

Online writing

People reading news online are not necessarily focused on the screen alone. They are not sprawled on the couch with a newspaper or a big-screen television in front of them. They might be glancing at a BlackBerry while walking to work, or running several screens of software while also surfing websites. This can severely limit their appreciation of stories that beat around the bush. A 400-word story displayed on a tiny screen can seem endless. Get to the point. Quickly.

The traditional rules of newspaper writing — pyramid style, tight leads, strong quotes — also apply to online writing, as long as long passages are broken into chunks. A story that sums up its main elements in a paragraph or two at the top is effective, while one with a circle-back ending — a teaser in the first paragraph and the answer in the last paragraph — doesn't work as well.

Other techniques

1. Readers eat up quotes. Use them in stories and around stories as supporting material or to break up copy.

2. Highlight key words with boldface or colour to help the reader navigate through the material. But don't go overboard. Too much of this makes copy harder to read.

3. Short, clear headings are a must. Use bullets with subheads to organize key points. Bullets should be constructed in a consistent fashion. But don't turn your entire story into a list. The point is to break up copy, not turn copy into a repetitive list of bullets.

4. Your biggest hook is the headline, even bigger than a picture. Sometimes the simple, direct headline works well, yet most of the time you need to draw the reader into the story. For information on what makes a good headline, see **Headlines**, page 80.

5. Keep a light tone. The web is an informal setting, so there is lots of room for levity.

6. Don't put every story in pyramid style. Readers will quickly tire of such a formulaic approach. There is always room for a story with a beginning, middle and end if you engage readers' interest

throughout and help them through the piece with some of the other devices mentioned here. Profiles or histories can often be best told chronologically, with signposts highlighting turning points or key developments.

7. Some writers forgo brevity unless it is forced upon them by the demands of their medium. With the web, any length fits. This can lead to overwriting of the worst sort. Edit ruthlessly. Use simpler words. Watch run-on sentences. Don't repeat yourself — say it once, well.

8. Proof, proof and re-proof your copy. This shows your reader your site is credible.

➤ For further tips, see **Writing for print,** page 203.

Keep it current

1. The web is fast and live. Play to these strengths. Never sit on developments. A story can be updated many times and readers expect to get the latest. Make sure all elements, especially the headlines, are refreshed when the news changes.

2. But, as always, never sacrifice accuracy. It is virtually impossible to pull a mistake back from the Internet. Always confirm information before moving it.

Not just words

Sound and images are a huge plus in web journalism. Audio and video clips that explain the basic facts of a story have some value but the really crucial clip reveals mood and emotions. Especially strong are the voices of the newsmakers themselves — the figure skater tearfully thanking the crowd after she wins the gold medal; the Queen speaking for the first time publicly on the death of the Princess of Wales; the tornado survivor walking through her damaged house, looking for her wedding album.

Always think about how a package of online material will hold together. Each element may be prepared by different desks, but they should complement each other. Online readers might read the headline, then click on the video or check out an interactive graphic before finishing the story.

If the main story is focused on the defence minister's announcement of the purchase of new military helicopters, then the video should be focused on some other aspect — perhaps raw footage from the scrum afterwards, when he refused to answer a related question, or footage of the helicopter in action. A graphic can focus on yet another element — a diagram of how the new helicopters differ from the ones they are replacing. All together, these elements add up to a complete package that for readers has several entry points and appeals to different interests.

➤ For more details, see **Audio,** page 41; **Graphics,** page 75; **Video,** page 175.

Quality links

1. Following a reference to another page can be cumbersome with paper — think of footnotes — but natural on a screen. Links are useful for expanded material that is relevant but not essential, such as transcripts, court documents or reports that provide more information about the story.

2. Links can also sidetrack a reader to move off the story, so don't overdo them. Don't use a link just because it exists; make sure it will take the reader somewhere worthwhile that is directly related to the subject at hand. Readers should not be surprised by where they end up. Test links regularly to make sure they still work. If it doesn't work, readers will be annoyed.

3. Only link once to the same site, not every time the subject is mentioned.

4. Keep writing about your subject. Don't switch to giving the reader instructions just because you have added a link:

Not: Go to reportsonline.com **for a transcript.**

Or: Click here **to access the transcript.**

But: The Federal Court posted the transcripts **online.**

5. Ensure that links are not to websites that are obscene, racist or otherwise offensive. In stories about such websites, it is not usually necessary to provide the address.

Source it

Avoid anonymity — the web is already anonymous enough. Be clear about where material comes from. Readers want to see a byline. On Canadian Press copy, our logo tells readers the material has our credibility behind it.

Copyright

News distributed on the Internet has no special status in terms of copyright law. A story published in an Internet edition of a newspaper is subject to the law just as it would be if it were in a newsprint edition. The same holds true for a Canadian Press story, or any material, available on a website that pays for or produces the content. Others must seek permission before reproducing or using those stories in substantially the same form.

Correcting mistakes

It is just as important to fix errors in online stories as it is in stories published in print. The Internet presents special challenges because once an incorrect story has been sent on the net, it is virtually impossible to ensure the corrected version replaces the incorrect version everywhere it appeared. Was the mistake in a fleeting headline appearing on a BlackBerry? Was it stored in a database that did not receive the corrected version?

There is also an added problem: Internet reading habits are not nearly as predictable as those of newspaper readers. Newspapers traditionally run a correction to a story in the same spot in the newspaper each day, which allows readers to easily find it. Alternatively, they run the correction in the same page or section of the paper where the original story ran, hoping to catch the readers who saw the earlier piece. But how do we catch an Internet reader? Say she plugs into a website every day at 6 a.m. to read the news. One day there is a mistake in a story, which is fixed after our reader logs off. She isn't going to go back and read that same story again the next time she logs in — unless we give her a heads up to do so.

If the mistake is a minor factual one, or a spelling or grammatical problem, it should be fixed as soon as it is noted. But for more serious errors and changes, The Canadian Press kills the problem story and replaces it with a corrected one as soon as it is known to be wrong. On the Writethru, a publishable note is added that can be put at the bottom of the story to alert readers that the story has changed.

➤ See **Corrections and Correctives**, page 466.

In addition, for the most serious errors, online clients are alerted by email that a story should be deleted from any archives. Seriously wrong stories are also removed from databases that are accessible by Canadian Press clients, and the corrected versions, complete with any Correctives that were moved, are filed in the database. Correctives also appear on The Canadian Press website.

Style specifics

1. If providing an actual web address (URL), follow upper and lowercase exactly: **thecanadianpress.com**. The http:// or **www** does not need to be included because almost all web software supplies it. Some addresses begin with other expressions (**ftp://**, for instance) and these should be included. Long web addresses should be allowed to wrap.

Note: Web addresses don't always belong in news stories. They have to work their way in as a piece of information the reader is likely to find helpful. For instance, a story on the Bank of Montreal does not need to include the bank's website, any more than it needs to include the address of its head office. Stories on interest groups or commercial products do not require routine mention of a website as it amounts to free advertising. But if the site provides relevant, reliable and current material about the subject at hand, then including the URL will help readers obtain further information. For instance, a story on cancer survivors supporting each other online could include the URL of the site. Apply the same standards of relevance, balance and reliability that are applied to any piece of information in a story.

2. If a company uses a variation of its Internet address as its corporate name, capitalize the first letter: **Amazon.com**. Also capitalize the first letter when the reference is not to the URL, but to the domain name:

"The search engines I use the most are Google.com and Yahoo.com," he said.

3. Email addresses must be written the way they appear, which is usually all lowercase. Do not put them in angle brackets or parentheses.

4. Use **disc** for CDs (compact discs), CD-ROMs (compact disc-read-only memory) and laserdiscs. Use **disk** for the square plastic disks often called floppy disks (even though they are no longer floppy) or diskettes, and hard disks (found on a hard drive).

5. Filenames, including extensions, are case sensitive and should be written the way they appear.

➤ See also **Capitalization**, page 268.

Pictures

Pictures sell stories.

A good picture can carry a story onto page 1; lack of a picture can take a good story off the front page — and right out of the paper. The Canadian Press aims to illustrate every worthwhile story with photos, maps or graphics.

Having that happen depends on awareness. All editors, writers and photographers need to be alert to illustrating the story, whether it is a rewrite or the germ of an idea for a staff-written series. The story without pictures and graphics won't get the play it deserves.

Good photo work involves developing an understanding of what makes a good illustration and the mechanics of getting it from the photographer or artist to the network of receiving newspapers, magazines, television networks and websites.

The Canadian Press Picture Service began in 1948 as an exchange of mailed photos. The first Wirephoto network based on an analogue or sound signal transmitted over telephone wires began in Ontario and Quebec in 1954 and 10 years later was coast-to-coast. Wirephoto became LaserPhoto in 1978, when new transmission equipment using a laser beam was introduced. The network name was changed to PhotoNet in 1991 after digital transmission by satellite began.

A young girl plays on the rocks in Pangnirtung, Nunavut, in 2007. The contrast in the colours of the rocks and the red of her traditional dress make the photo unusually dramatic.

THE CANADIAN PRESS/ Jeff McIntosh

PhotoNet delivers more than 1,000 photos a day to Canadian daily newspapers, websites and other media. About one-fifth of the photos originate in Canada, shot by Canadian Press staff photographers and freelances hired by the news agency. The Associated Press and its photographers around the world provide the international content.

Every newspaper subscribing to the photo network is obligated to provide its local photos from spot news events to the news agency. Each newspaper subscriber has the capacity to transmit pictures directly to The Canadian Press by FTP.

Graphics, in French and English, are also delivered on the same satellite system.

Good illustrations

Good photos have similarities to good stories. They:

1. Are new and in some way unusual.

2. Show action the instant it happens.

3. Portray people and appeal to the emotions.

4. Relate to some important person, event or place.

5. Wrap up a story or provide an overall view of it.

6. Tie in with a current story, the season, the weather, a fad.

A good illustration will be marked by attention to **quality, content, composition, lighting** and **timing**.

A polar bear mother and her two cubs cuddle on the shore of Hudson Bay near Churchill, Man., in 2007. The unusual lighting, with the shadows on the bears, adds drama to this photo.

THE CANADIAN PRESS/ Jonathan Hayward

Quality

1. The main subject has clear, sharp details.

2. There are bright, natural colours or a gradual range of grey tones between black and white.

3. Skin tones for light-skinned people are a natural colour or light grey against a white shirt. There must be definition in the facial shading of people with darker skins.

A poor-quality picture might be slightly out of focus — look at the eyes. It might have heavy blacks and brilliant whites, or have an overall grey cast with no blacks and whites. Colours may be washed out or too dark.

The sole exception to these demands for quality is a shot of such outstanding news value that it will get into print despite poor quality.

Follow these basic rules when scanning negatives or acquiring and enhancing digital camera images to ensure maximum quality:

1. Start with an acknowledgment that "less is more" when enhancing images.

2. Do as many enhancements as possible in the pre-scan or when acquiring a digital image.

3. Keep enhancements in PhotoShop to a minimum. Often an unsharp mask is added in the pre-press handling of the image, making excessive use at the scanning stage unnecessary.

When toning, use levels or curves to adjust colour and tone rather than colour balance or brightness/contrast.

Director David Cronenberg at the Toronto International Film Festival in 2007. The simple composition of this photo puts the emphasis on Cronenberg's dramatic features.

THE CANADIAN PRESS/Nathan Denette

Content

1. Does the photo tell a story?

2. Is its subject important?

3. Is it appealing, well-composed and striking?

4. Is there outstanding human interest or some other quality that overrides minor news value?

Any newsbreak that is visually important or interesting makes the good-quality photo worth distributing. A window cleaner suspended in mid-air by his braces makes a good shot; a minor auto wreck usually doesn't because all wrecks tend to look much the same. A 20-car pileup, multiple deaths or trapped passengers can give an accident photo the news value needed to get it on the network.

Picture judgment is partly personal and partly a matter of experience. A photo is almost certainly worthwhile if an editor experienced in handling news finds it eye-catching. A newspaper photo editor's recommendation is usually a valid reason for selecting a picture.

A Ugandan
security guard is
reflected in the
window of Prime
Minister Stephen
Harper's car in
Entebbe, Uganda,
in 2007. The
unusual
combination of
images creates a
memorable photo.

THE CANADIAN
PRESS/Tom
Hanson

Composition

1. Are the main subject and its surroundings arranged so as to be attractive and cohesive? The right camera angle often allows information such as signs, buildings and other people to line up with the main subject, making the photograph informative and interesting.

2. Does the entire frame contain relevant content? Large empty areas that add little useful information limit the impact of the photograph.

3. Is the picture cropped to make the subject stand out clearly?

Standup group shots are not wanted, although sometimes the personalities involved create exceptions. The Queen with Commonwealth prime ministers or a new cabinet is usually newsworthy. In the best such photos, the group's attention is not centred on the camera and a side angle is used "to stack up" the subjects.

Be careful that the "arranged" photo does not turn into a picture that is contrived or set up by the photographer. There is no objection to cleaning up a cluttered background or moving the company president from behind his desk to stand in front of his widget-stamping machine.

The photo becomes contrived when elements or interpretations are added or subtracted to make a point that would not normally have been there. Spot news pictures should not be arranged.

Robert Doornbos of the Netherlands celebrates his win at the Champ Car race in Mont Tremblant, Que., in 2007. Every news photographer's goal should be to catch compelling content and good composition at the moment the action peaks.

THE CANADIAN PRESS/Paul Chiasson

Lighting and timing

1. Lighting gives two-dimensional photographs depth and contributes to the mood and impact of the picture or subject. Avoid flat, full front lighting or direct flash; they do nothing to emphasize the shape of a person or subject. Soft window light that strikes a person on an angle provides excellent light for an environmental portrait. Strong backlight will separate a subject from a dark background and early morning or late afternoon light makes architectural or wide scenic pictures dramatic. Good lighting can make a plain, information-only photo special and move it from the inside pages to a section front or home page.

2. Photographs that are a blend of compelling content and good composition that are made at the precise moment when the action peaks should be every photographer's goal. Timing is more than just pressing the shutter button when the ball is about to be grasped by a football player. It is the instant when all the other information around or behind the player is arranged and captured at the same time as the peak action. It is often characterized as the "decisive moment."

Photo manipulation

The Canadian Press does not alter the content of photos. Pictures must always tell the truth — tell what the photographer saw happen. Nothing can damage our credibility more quickly than deliberate untruthfulness. The integrity of our photo report is our highest priority.

PhotoShop is a sophisticated editing tool that allows photographic images to be manipulated easily. It's technically possible to change their content and impact on the reader, whether by accident or design.

Use of this tool must follow the long-established chemical darkroom standards of photo printing. Simple *burning* (making light portions of a print darker), *dodging* (making dark portions lighter), *colour balancing, toning* and *cropping* are acceptable. Exaggerated use of these features to add, remove or give prominence to details in the photo is not acceptable.

Retouching is limited to removal of dust spots, film scratches or abnormal marks and patterns.

Colour adjustment is to be minimal. Adjustments can be made to ensure honest reproduction of the original when the scanning and transmission processes alter colours.

Consult the Picture Editor first on any question of photo manipulation.

PhotoNet

The Canadian Press can get a picture across Canada in time to illustrate any breaking story if photographers move fast.

The large number of Internet sites and web portals dependent on the news agency for news pictures adds even greater urgency. Pictures must be transmitted as soon after an event starts as possible. The decades-old wire service saying "there is a deadline every minute" has never been more true. For newspapers, pictures that don't move in the same cycle with the story they illustrate will likely not be used, unless the content is exceptional or they illustrate a continuing story.

When a story breaks, The Canadian Press immediately co-ordinates coverage plans with its staff photographers, its client newspapers and AP. The most important consideration while setting up coverage is that a photographer must be at an event when it happens. Coverage must be lined up quickly.

Every paper uses photos to accompany local stories that could have wider interest. To get these on the network in the same cycle for use by others, papers should send their best pictures to the agency's photo desk as soon as they are available.

But what pictures should be sent?

1. Ask yourself whether you would be interested in the photo if you lived in a community 100 kilometres away. If the answer is yes, transmit it.

2. Send it if there is a story to go with it.

3. Does it pique your interest in any way?

The most frequent request from clients is for more news photos that can be used on inside pages and online photo galleries. Pictorially interesting weather and feature photos can help fill this demand. Watch for them.

Sending photos

Pictures sent to the Toronto Picture Desk for transmission must be of the highest possible quality. Full captions and relevant International Press Technical Committee (IPTC) field information — used to find and sort archived pictures — must be written and saved with the JPEG file before being transmitted.

Preparing pictures for transmission:

Canadian Press photographers and newspapers use digital cameras to make pictures and at times scan older negatives to digitize file photos. In both cases the pictures are imported into PhotoShop software for conversion to JPEG files. These are transmitted on PhotoNet.

Images should be scanned/acquired at a minimum 200 dpi. More and more newspapers and magazines are asking for 300 dpi originals. With higher-quality cameras now in use, the dimension on the longest side of the photo should be a minimum 25 centimetres. Keep the photo in the RGB mode. Conversion to CMYK from RGB results in the loss of colour information that cannot be recovered. Images should only be converted to CMYK as a final step before going to press.

Pictures should be compressed in standard JPEG format, at a ratio that results in an average 1.5- to two-megabyte file. When the file dips below 700 kilobytes it is clear they have been compressed too much.

Images downloaded from The Canadian Press Images Archive must be checked for size before they are transmitted on the network. Many files, including historical material, are stored at a much higher resolution and low compression and must be resized if they exceed the above guidelines.

IPTC fields

Take care when filling out IPTC fields, especially the caption field, which is publishable. Canadian Press member newspapers are able to read all IPTC information fields by using their picture browsers or opening the image *File Info* viewable in PhotoShop.

Captions are written in the same style used by most newspapers under the published picture. They should not include information from other IPTC fields.

These are the descriptions of the IPTC fields, and the information that should be placed in them:

Object name: This lists the story slug associated with the photo. For photos without stories, or when a slug is not available, photographers and editors should use a slug that would be a logical search criterion for a story that moves later. Use either the subject's last name, the name of the event, or a word that generally describes the photo.

Original transmission reference: This field lists a call letter-number combination associated with the photo. It includes an originating point's call letters and a picture number; for example, **CPT105** would be used for the fifth picture originating in Toronto.

Caption field: A standard caption would look like this:

> Prime Minister Stephen Harper gestures during a speech to the Canadian Club in Toronto on Tuesday, Feb. 13, 2008. Harper said that child-care funding would be addressed in the next federal budget. THE CANADIAN PRESS/Tom Hanson.

Regular captions have no **overlines** — all-caps descriptions detailing the type of picture. But instructive overlines should be used on file photos and specials as in these examples:

> FILE – Roger Clemens of the Toronto Blue Jays clenches his fist in victory in this Aug. 15, 1998, file photo during a game against the New York Yankees. THE CANADIAN PRESS/Frank Gunn

> SPECIAL TO LE JOURNAL DE MONTREAL – Montreal native Bianca Lallito, 13, poses for a photograph on Tuesday, Feb. 7, 2006 in Toronto. Lallito has won a trip to Turino, Italy, for the 2006 Olympic Winter Games (THE CANADIAN PRESS/Andrew Vaughan)

The full date — day of the week, date and year — should appear in the body of all captions. If only the month and year are known, use that. In file photos use the date the photo was originally shot. If the date is not known, use the year. If there is no known date, state **date of photo unknown** in the body of the caption and in the *special instructions file* of the IPTC header.

The sign-off for a Canadian Press staffer or freelancer is in parentheses: **THE CANADIAN PRESS/Frank Gunn.** If the name of the photographer is not known or needs to be withheld, the sign-off is **THE CANADIAN PRESS.**

Include the name of the newspaper for a member photo sign-off: **THE CANADIAN PRESS/The Globe and Mail-Peter Power.**

For a handout, use **THE CANADIAN PRESS/General Motors.** If the photographer is known, add the name: **THE CANADIAN PRESS/General Motors-John Smith. Note:** Handout photos should also use the code **HO** in the *byline title field* of the IPTC header, but do not put it in the sign-off.

For a pool photo sign-off, use **THE CANADIAN PRESS/Chris Wattie-Pool**. Do not name the newspaper or agency that shot for the pool in the caption sign-off. **Note:** The word **POOL** should be included in the *source field* and the *byline title field* of the IPTC file information.

Graphics sign-off follow the same style as photos: **THE CANADIAN PRESS/Sean Vokey**.

A TV frame grab photo sign-off is **THE CANADIAN PRESS/ CBC News. Note:** Often a mandatory credit is required when using a frame grab. This instruction should be included in the *special instructions field* and directly after the sign-off: **MANDATORY CREDIT REQUIRED WITH THE USE OF THIS PHOTO**.

Date: Date the photo was taken.

Filename: Name originally given to the file when it was saved.

Caption writer: This lists the initials of all the people who wrote or edited the caption, header fields or image file. This includes any toning of the photo file.

Headline: Lists keywords to aid in a more detailed search for a photo. It typically lists who is in the photo.

Special instructions field: Lists any special notations that apply uniquely to a photo such as CP Picture Archive, correction, outs, or mandatory credits.

Byline: Lists the name of the person who made the photo.

Byline title: Lists the title of the person who made the photo. Pick one of these categories:

STF — CP photographs by staff photographers, including Associated Press photographers.

FRL — CP photographs by freelance photographers.

MBR — Photographs from member photographers.

SUB — Photographs picked up by foreign subscribers.

MAG — Photographs provided by magazines.

TEL — Frame grabs from television.

POOL — Photographs by pool photographers.

HO — Handout photographs.

Credit: The name of the service transmitting the photo; almost always CP or AP.

Source: Lists the copyright holder or the original provider of a photo, such as CP, AP, a CP member, pool photo provider, or handout provider.

Category: Lists codes that aid in a more detailed search. Categories are:

A — U.S. news or features

C — Canadian news and features

F — Financial

I — International

S — Sports

V — Advisories

Supplemental categories: Lists codes that aid in a more detailed search for a photo. For example: **HKN** will show all NHL hockey photos. A list of categories is in the AP guide.

City, province, country: Lists the city, province or state and country where the photo was made. For file photos, do not use the transmitting point's city, province or country.

Keywords: Used by Canadian Press Images archive staff to add additional search terms.

Writing captions

Captions are always written in the present tense. They tell the reader, briefly and clearly, the basic details of the picture and tie it to the story it illustrates. Remember that photos attract even the most casual reader, so captions are probably the most-read words in the paper or web page, after headlines. Like headlines, captions must be crisp. Like stories, they must be readable and informative, interesting and lively.

Some reminders to make caption-writing easier:

1. Does the caption say when and where?

2. Does it identify, fully and clearly?

3. Are the names in the right order? List people in a group shot from the left, and specify position (left or front row, second from right).

4. Use at least two short, snappy sentences. One long, involved sentence is boring.

5. Stick primarily to explaining the action in the picture, but don't speculate. The prime minister's "grin" may be teeth-gritting anger. The "dozing" legislator may be reading a paper on his desk. Be sure or leave it out.

6. Watch attribution and don't let libel creep in.

7. Read what you've written. Are all the questions answered? Count the people in the picture and the number of names. Are the left-to-right designations correct? Is the action mentioned in the caption really shown?

Credit the photographer in the body of the caption if the picture has exceptional merit or the circumstances in which it was shot were very unusual. Say so when abnormal techniques such as multiple exposures or time exposures were used.

Kills and corrections

All picture kills and corrections are handled by the Toronto Picture Desk, which knows the exact distribution of a picture.

If you see an error in a caption or a graphic, phone the Picture Desk immediately.

Kills and corrections are transmitted on the same photo networks that carried the original. The style differs slightly from the style on news circuits. Kills are also transmitted on the English and French text wires.

CORRECTION: A caption correction is moved when a simple and non-libellous error occurs in a caption. Examples would be a misspelled name, or wrong hometown, sports score or slug. The procedure The Canadian Press uses to file a caption correction form is to point out the information that is being corrected in the *instructions field* of the IPTC header and write a corrected caption in publishable form. The word CORRECTION and the original photo's number are added to the object name field of the IPTC header. The photo follows the form with a corrected publishable caption noting so in the *instructions field* of the IPTC header.

ADDITIONS: A caption addition is moved when the original caption is incomplete, but otherwise accurate. It may add the name of someone in the photo or other important background information. The procedure for a caption addition is the same as that for a correction.

ELIMINATIONS: A caption elimination is moved when an acceptable photo has a caption that misrepresents the photo or is in bad taste. When this occurs a caption elimination form is moved alerting clients. Then the photo is retransmitted using the same procedure as a correction.

KILLS: A photo KILL is moved on PhotoNet for a photo that is objectionable and presents the possibility of legal action, libel or copyright infringement. Photo kills move in consultation with the Toronto photo supervisor and senior management.

Pictures and the law

The **Legal** section of the stylebook applies equally to the Picture Service. Ensure that neither the caption nor the contents of a photo violate the law or individual rights.

When photographing people in Quebec, take extra care not to violate the Quebec Charter of Human Rights and Freedoms as it relates to a person's right to privacy. The Supreme Court of Canada ruled in April 1998 that an individual's right to privacy under the Quebec charter includes the ability to control use of his or her image.

Although the ruling dealt with Quebec alone, its effect has been to change the way photos are handled in several other provinces with privacy statutes: Newfoundland and Labrador, British Columbia, Manitoba and Saskatchewan. It means care must be taken with some photos that feature identifiable people in them. Consent must be obtained from the subjects of such photos unless one of the following applies:

a) The people are incidental to the photo.

b) The identifiable person is not the subject of the photo but is one of a group in a public place — a crowd scene, for example.

c) The photo is part of coverage of a legitimate news event that the subject has a role in — a trial, for example.

d) The subject is a public figure.

e) The subject's success in her profession depends upon public opinion.

Otherwise, consent for use of the picture should be obtained and the subject's name and age must be included in the caption transmitted with the photograph.

Privacy is not the only consideration that should be taken into account when handling images of people in the news. In all jurisdictions, a picture of a person accused of a crime could prejudice the outcome of the court hearing if there is a question of identity. And there usually is. If in doubt, consult the editor before transmitting a picture.

Withhold immediately any picture questioned after transmission by sending a news-circuit advisory and a note on all photo networks that received the original. Send a followup advisory and note killing or releasing the picture as soon as the question is resolved.

Copyright photos

The Canadian Press owns the copyright of photos made by its staff and freelance photographers working on direct assignment for the agency. A freelance photographer who shoots a picture before selling it to The Canadian Press retains the copyright. The agency can use it only for the purpose agreed to when it was bought — usually unlimited editorial use by Canadian Press and Associated Press member newspapers and magazines.

Any unusual restrictions that the freelance demands must be noted in the *special instructions field* to avoid inadvertent violation of a copyright picture. These restrictions could include:

1. **One-time use only.** The photo can be used once with the current news story.

2. **Magazines out.** The photographer hopes to sell the picture separately to that market.

3. **Copyright photo, credit mandatory.** The newspaper must credit the photographer.

Photos provided by public relations firms or businesses may not be legally available for transmission other than at the time they illustrated a specific story. Always check with the photographer or the source before reissuing a picture of this type.

The Canadian Press Picture Service contract requires newspaper subscribers to include the newswire in copyright release of photos by their staff and regular freelances. Be especially careful of occasional freelance photos picked up from newspapers or borrowed later from their libraries. The libraries file every picture used, no matter what the source. Rights may not have been obtained for wire use and must be checked. Do not use a photo if the source is not indicated or cannot be determined from the newspaper's own publication.

Picturing money

It is generally against the law to picture in print any Canadian banknote or a recognizable portion of one. Such photos cannot be carried on PhotoNet. It's prohibited by Section 457 of the Criminal Code.

This does not apply to the printed likeness of a banknote if the length or width is less than three-quarters or greater than 1.5 times the length or width of the real one. Neither does it apply if the likeness is in black and white only or features just one side of the banknote. This gives photographers a fair amount of leeway in illustrating stories about money without breaking the law.

Occasionally the Bank of Canada will provide a replica of a banknote and agree to waive prosecution, usually to promote a newly issued note. These replicas may be transmitted.

It is generally against the law to picture Canadian money in print. But photographers have some leeway. Showing only one side of the bill is permitted.

THE CANADIAN PRESS/Tom Hanson

Cartoons

The Canadian Press picks up cartoons for use with news stories in special circumstances — for example, when a cartoon becomes the subject of political controversy, or to illustrate a story about a cartoonist.

Cartoons may also make good illustrations for a situational or analysis if they offer fair comment. Where there is controversy, more than one cartoon may be needed to reflect opposing views.

Newspapers are not obligated to provide The Canadian Press with their cartoons, and most editorial cartoonists retain and syndicate the rights to their work. Permission for the use of each cartoon must be arranged in advance with the newspaper or the cartoonist.

The use of any cartoon must be approved in advance by the Director of News Photography. Requests for such approval should include the name of the newspaper editor or cartoonist authorizing use.

Conservative supporters take shelter from the rain under a tree in Toronto during the 2004 election. Good political reporters search out the ordinary and make it sparkle.

THE CANADIAN PRESS/Jonathan Hayward

Politics and elections

When most people think of political reporting, they picture raucous question periods on Parliament Hill or in provincial legislatures. Or they see scrums where cameras, lights and microphones converge en masse on a political figure to draw out the truth. Those are essential elements to political reporting but it shouldn't stop there.

Experienced reporters dig hard to root out the stories behind the facades. What are government departments really doing? What policies are being developed that will affect people in Antigonish, N.S., or Courtenay, B.C.?

Good political reporters search out the ordinary and make it sparkle. They explain government policy in gripping detail. Top political stories pass the test of any good news story: Will people be repeating it on the bus, at the grocery store or over supper?

Political stories should be about real things. They should matter to readers and listeners. Not many people care to know which Liberal said what to which Conservative during a routine exchange at a committee meeting. What they want to know is how tax reform will affect their bank balances, whether they'll be able to get medical procedures quickly, whether the tax on beer is going up, and how much extra it might cost them to dispose of their garbage.

Basic tenets apply whether a reporter is covering politics at the federal, provincial, municipal or school board level: stories must be balanced, accurate, fair and clear.

Political gobbledygook can be suffocating. Political jargon is among the worst. Politicians adore bafflegab. It helps protect them from accountability and can effectively obscure truth. Plus, many politicians can get used to the sound of their own voices and find puffery appealing. News releases can be among the worst offenders. Watch for big words and ditto for clichés. Write copy that is clean, direct and conversational.

Beware of the pack mentality. It's easy to join other reporters and wander around "catching spit" in scrums in the lobby of the legislature. Scoops are the result of independent thinking, energy, initiative and digging.

Modern tools — access-to-information legislation, databases, BlackBerrys — can be very handy. But a good reporter remembers to use every means at their disposal to ferret out information.

On or off the record?

Reporters can be powerful allies or enemies for politicians. Remember they will try to use you to their advantage. Understand what their motives might be in providing information to you.

Avoid off-the-record chats with politicians whenever possible. While confidential conversations with sources can be invaluable (and not many readers or listeners want to know the name of some official anyway), if a politician is trying to speak on the QT, it's probably a sign there's something he or she does not want made public. You won't always be able to avoid it — but try. When you simply must resort to off the record, try to get a second source to go on the record. And don't ever let an anonymous source use the occasion to spout baseless critcism.

The matter of ethics is a tricky business where rules tend to shift. Cosying up to politicians might result in some great inside information. But the closeness might make it hard to stay objective. Decline all offers of freebies, even ones that don't fit the traditional definition. And full-time politics reporters should not join any advocacy groups or political movements.

Prime Minister Pierre Trudeau makes a face at a Canadian Press photographer in 1972. This photo was taken aboard the campaign plane where such antics were considered off the record. The photo was not made public until after the death of the prime minister.

THE CANADIAN PRESS/Peter Bregg

Some pointers

1. Try to retain a sense of human dignity in scrums. Reporters and technical people have a tendency to turn into wild animals, shouting and literally stomping on shorter and weaker people. Everyone, including the media's image, benefits from a little civility.

2. With 24-hour coverage of events around the globe, privacy is almost a thing of the past. And politicians are public figures — to an extent. When you dig out personal facts, ask yourself whether

readers, listeners and viewers really need to know and whether the information has a direct bearing on how the politician must perform his or her job.

3. Don't be a victim of technology. It's far too easy to tap electronically into news conferences, committee meetings, legislature proceedings and the like. These sorts of feeds are easily accessible and ubiquitous in the media. But you can't ask them questions like you can in person. Get out and be seen. Make sure people know who you are. Talk to live bodies. Visibility is a key asset.

Elections

Public-opinion polls and clever election strategists have dramatically changed the election process in Canada. So have skeptical and savvy voters.

Fundraising has become an art, candidates' personalities are carefully polished, campaigns are stage-managed for maximum television exposure, news is manipulated. And yet the voters grow ever more wary of elections and intolerant of manipulative politics. Voter turnout is at historically low levels in many jurisdictions.

News coverage must adapt to the changes, looking for more effective ways of describing the process and involving the voters.

Liberal Leader John Turner and Conservative Leader Brian Mulroney during their 1988 debate, considered a classic moment by political observers.

THE CANADIAN PRESS/Fred Chartrand

Some of the criteria for an effective news report on an election:

1. **Let the voters, not the politicians, decide what the issues are.**

Campaign coverage that is focused heavily on candidates' travels and statements may be irrelevant to readers. For example, if all the major parties are concentrating on constitutional issues, where does that leave voters worried about their jobs or the air they breathe or the fact that their kids have trouble reading?

Political reporters need to recognize that getting the *tough* one-liner snapped off by a cabinet minister with an eye on the 6 o'clock TV news is often less important than spending 20 minutes talking to voters in the minister's riding.

If reporters listen to what's on voters' minds, and put those concerns to the candidates, readers may decide the media are worth paying attention to.

The alternative is to allow politicians to decide what's news.

A sound election file can be built by focusing on the party leaders and the apparent issues in the first week or two of the campaign. From then until the final days, the focus should shift to pinpointing what's bothering the voters, explaining the background to the big issues and clarifying the parties' stands on voter concerns.

2. Be prepared.

Surprise elections are rare. Supervisors and political reporters aware of an impending election will (a) set up a clear organization for covering the campaign; (b) establish their news priorities; (c) put profiles of the party leaders and other basic backgrounders *in the bank* for use when the election is called.

As the campaign unfolds, measure out special takeouts on the issues dear to the voters' hearts. Some regional issues become important enough to swing whole areas, so they need sensitive explanation. Some unlikely candidates will come on strong and need profiling. Issues like party funding, television ads, all-candidates debates, minor parties and historical trends are often worth looking at.

Election campaigns are also a test of The Canadian Press's relationship with newspapers and broadcasters. Getting their news supervisors on side ahead of time can mean timely reports on major developments and a consistent supply of spot and feature material from all over a bureau's region.

Being prepared also means recognizing that the general public has lots of other interests besides politics. Campaign coverage shouldn't deprive readers of other news that's important to them.

3. Don't forget libel laws.

Statements are sometimes made in the heat of an election campaign that in other circumstances would be pretty good grounds for a libel suit.

Some basic legal ground rules:

a) A fair and accurate report of public statements made at a meeting that's open to the general public isn't usually risky. But that may not apply if only some members of the public (say, one party's members) are allowed into the meeting. And if a person attacked at the meeting wants to respond, the response must be reported.

b) Potentially libellous statements made in other circumstances — even a radio broadcast — are not safe to publish. Get legal advice.

c) Some provincial and federal laws limit certain forms of campaigning and advertising just before voting day. Check election laws for pitfalls.

4. **Provide context, colour, detail.**

Reporting on campaign activities means making sense of the political statements. It also means bringing the campaign to life.

Context: What would the promise of a new housing policy mean for house prices? Construction jobs? Increased government debt and taxes? How does the new policy compare with past promises, the other parties' positions? What do outside experts think of it? Not all such questions will be worth answering, but few political statements of any importance should be left to stand alone.

Colour: Most politicians are scarcely known to the public. They often need to be described in action, gesturing and raising their voices to emphasize a point or laughing at the hecklers or making small talk on the street. The towns and cross-roads where they campaign should be sketched. The campaign audiences should be shown responding or watching skeptically.

In both context and colour, be specific.

Not: The premier promised to cut government spending.

Instead: For the farm crowd in Ruralia, the premier promised to cut loan guarantees for big business. At the Middleton Rotary Club, she said there would be fewer tax concessions for shopping malls. Back in the capital, she worried about the cost of irrigation projects and secondary roads.

5. **For election night, again be prepared.**

Smooth, comprehensive coverage of election results depends on thorough advance work. It's too late to look for background information when the voting results are flooding in.

Prepare: profile material on the leaders and any candidates important to the over-all coverage; background on the major issues and how the parties stood on them; the range of public-opinion poll results; the best of the campaign anecdotes to lighten up the stories.

Also: statistical histories of which parties have formed the government and when; figures on the size of majorities for past governments; information on minority governments, the defeat of governments and their leaders, the national situation for each major party.

(Many newspapers, broadcasters and websites depend on The Canadian Press for detailed results, gathered progressively at a single election centre. The results are delivered in ready-to-use formats from a computer programmed to make instantaneous adjustments in vote totals, winners and losers, party votes and other categories. The material is invaluable for those writing stories at The Canadian Press and other media and is also used to instantly update interactive election maps on websites.)

6. Down with hype.

The frenzy of election night can be the enemy of clear thinking.

It's common in Canadian elections for one party to win a substantial majority of seats with barely 40 per cent of the votes. That doesn't constitute a **landslide** of popular support. Stories about the result need precise wording.

And sweeping statements about the voters' feelings or intentions are risky. Each voter in a federal or provincial election makes a choice among local candidates, period. Each constituency result is probably influenced by broader issues and the popularity of the party leaders, but they aren't on the ballot.

It's stretching things to write baldly that voters **rejected a spending freeze** or **punished the government for failing to cut unemployment**. The effect of all those individual votes will be a government with some stated commitments. That's the surest way to describe the election result. Informed political observers can help keep the influence of national or provincial factors in perspective.

7. Don't break the law.

It is against the law to transmit vote results into an electoral district before all the polling stations there are closed. This means that The Canadian Press doesn't transmit any federal election results on the Internet until polls close in British Columbia. Results for radio and television services are also moved regionally only, east to west, as polls close.

8. The cleanup.

Election campaigns don't end on election night. The days immediately following an election bring some of the most significant stories.

Supervisors need to ensure that fresh staff is available for two or three days after an election to complete reporting on how the results will affect voters.

Working from notes left over by election-night supervisors, the next-day staff should clean up loose ends — late polls, possible recounts, missing ballot boxes.

They can also concentrate on reaching the experts who will help make better sense of the results. They can examine the detailed results more closely for victories and defeats that were overlooked. And Canadian Press staff can exploit newspaper material that was neglected in the rush of election night.

9. **Plan for the next one.**

The start of good coverage of the next election begins with a thoughtful file on this one. Before the ink is dry on coverage of any election, a file should be opened that includes:

• Careful notes from supervisors on everything that went well and everything that went wrong — and why.

• Notes from reporters and deskers on how to improve election coverage. Everyone who took part should have something to contribute.

• Examples of the best and the worst stories from the campaign, your own or others'.

• Copies of all the memos, circulars, letters and other paperwork that will be needed as reminders the next time.

Stephen Harper and his family celebrate the Conservative election win in Calgary in 2006. Like politicians, the news media should always be ready for an election call.

THE CANADIAN PRESS/Jeff McIntosh

Polls

Public-opinion polls are like snapshots: it's not always obvious what they're showing. Is that woman on the right smiling or grimacing? Is she the mother of the young girl in the centre with the same blond hair? There are opportunities for misinterpreting the scene — particularly if you try to speculate that the snapshot is typical.

There's another similarity between polls and snapshots: there are too many of them, but no one wants to be the first to give them up. The Canadian Press limits its coverage to reputable polls dealing with topical issues.

Consider whether the polling firm belongs to a self-regulatory association. In Canada, the Marketing Research and Intelligence Association is the voluntary self-regulatory association that governs practitioners in the public opinion research industry. Members are required to meet the association's code of conduct and good practice, including specific provisions related to the conduct and reporting of polls. Further information on what constitutes a reputable poll, how results should be reported and a directory of the association's members can be found at www.mria-arim.ca.

By canvassing the opinions of a relatively small group of people, called the sample, pollsters are able to calculate how a larger population feels about a topic. Reputable pollsters do not state that the smaller group's views exactly mirror the larger one, and they acknowledge a poll's results could be significantly inaccurate in exceptional circumstances.

That said, properly conducted national polls using telephone or online methodologies are professionally designed to capture the opinions of a carefully constructed sample of the Canadian population, such that those opinions are projectable and can be said to closely approximate the views of the general population.

Reporting on polls

1. Stories about polls should use verbs like indicate and suggest, rather than show or report.

> TORONTO — Liberal support appeared to be holding stable across Canada in March as measured by the Harris-Decima polling organization.
> The Harris-Decima poll suggested little change from February for any of the major national parties among voters with an opinion ...

2. In stories on polls where a random probability sample was used, usually random telephone surveys, the margin of sampling error should be spelled out and its significance explained. Where

changes in comparative figures are smaller than the margin of sampling error, public opinion cannot be said with any certainty to have moved up or down. Stories should make clear that the margin of sampling error is the number of percentage points added to, or subtracted from, each poll number. Thus, a margin of error of 2.5 percentage points really represents a spread of five percentage points.

> Harris-Decima said the poll was reliable to within plus or minus 2.5 percentage points, 19 times out of 20. That means, when applied to the population at large, Liberal support in March could have been as high as 40.5 per cent or as low as 35.5 while Tory strength could range between 29.5 and 34.5 per cent. In one case in 20, the figures could be substantially different.
>
> Changes from February figures that are smaller than the margin of error have no polling significance. The apparent drop in Liberal support, for instance, is meaningless.

When selecting the sample for a random probability poll, researchers make sure that any adult in the population has a chance of making it into the sample. This is the foundation of probability sampling: every person in the population has some chance of being selected to participate. This has traditionally been accomplished with randomly dialed telephone calls. The polling firm must also randomly select an adult to interview in each of the randomly selected households, perhaps based on the household member with the most recent birthday.

3. Online research is gradually supplanting telephone surveying as the dominant methodology in Canada. Online survey participants are self-selected, which means a margin of sampling error cannot be calculated. Using margin of sampling error to describe the accuracy of online polling is misleading and prohibited under the marketing association's code of conduct.

Online polls use other techniques, such as weighting, to adjust for potential biases in survey data and produce reliable results when participants come from a panel of respondents who've been profiled in detail and when the study has been carried out by a reputable research firm.

Weighting adjusts poll data in an attempt to ensure that the sample more accurately reflects the characteristics of the population from which it was drawn and to which an inference will be made. Census data is often used to bring the sample into line with the characteristics of the population. Weighting does not involve any changes to the actual answers to survey questions.

Corporate members of the Marketing Research and Intelligence Association have agreed to comply with best practices standards, including weighting, when conducting online polls.

➤ See **Statistics,** page 171.

4. A national census is the ultimate poll. An election is a close second: it registers the opinion of all who vote. Comparing a poll

on party popularity with the most recent election result is sound practice. When comparing one poll with earlier polls on the same topic, however, don't assume that similar results make the polls more accurate. They don't.

5. Polls, like snapshots, show a moment in time. By the day after the questions were asked, people have already begun to change their minds. So it's wrong to suggest that a poll result can predict how people will behave — for example, a June political poll that's used to forecast an October election result. And it's wrong to take polling figures from the past and write about them in the present tense as if they are still just as valid.

6. The Canadian Press normally will not report national polls based on a random probability sample in which the sample size is fewer than 1,000 respondents. Given the size of the Canadian populations, this yields a margin of sampling error of between two and four percentage points. Always report the sample size. And when national figures are broken down into subgroups, such as regions, the margin of sampling error is much greater. Often there is no statistical support for drawing conclusions about subgroups. At the very least, the higher margin of sampling error needs to be provided and explained.

> By regions, the poll indicated NDP support was at a peak of 38 per cent in Ontario and a low of 12 per cent in Prince Edward Island. However, since the poll's accuracy depends on the number of people surveyed, the Ontario figure might range anywhere from 32 to 44 per cent while the P.E.I. sample was too small to be considered reliable.

7. There's a big difference between per cent and percentage points. The poll is accurate within 2.5 percentage points, not per cent. A political party whose support has apparently gone from a level of 16 per cent to 24 per cent has registered an increase of eight percentage points but its support has increased 50 per cent.

8. Non-political surveys produced by Statistics Canada and other government organizations are routinely based on a random sample of the general population and may not accurately reflect what's happening in the population as a whole. Margin of sampling error needs to be specified and explained, just as in a political poll. And suggest, not show, is still the verb of choice.

➤ See **Statistics,** page 171.

9. Some published polls cover a wide range of issues. In reporting on them, it's better to sacrifice polling results on secondary questions than to skip over essential information about the basic poll and its accuracy. Take a narrower focus and do it right. Consider using a Quick-style box to summarize some of the secondary results.

Some other pitfalls

Public opinion researchers recognize a number of other elements in polling that can affect the accuracy of a poll's results.

1. The sponsor of a poll may influence the questions asked and other aspects. The story should say if the poll was paid for by a political party, a lobby group or someone else with a vested interest in the outcome. And results from two different polling organizations can't be compared unless they were asking the same questions: for example, about the popularity of the Tories rather than Stephen Harper's Conservatives.

2. The dates a poll was taken can affect the outcome. If there was a significant event before or after the poll that could have coloured the result, say so.

3. If the people polled aren't a random sample of the population of interest — that is, with every person having an equal chance of being picked to respond — the results may be skewed. If there were a disproportionate number of middle-class people sampled on the question of income-tax rates, the poll might not give a true picture of society's attitudes as a whole. This is something for journalists to watch for and question, but it's also important to recognize that this is where weighting, quota controls and other techniques used by polling firms to adjust for potential biases in survey data come into play. This is how online research polls using convenience samples have produced results that have proven to be reliable predictors, including of election results.

4. The question asked can influence the result. Polls suggest most Canadians don't support abortion on demand, but a majority believe a woman whose health is at risk should be able to get an abortion. Depending on the question, poll results can claim to support almost any position in the abortion debate.

5. In public opinion research it was assumed until recently that if, for example, 40 per cent of a random sample of people couldn't be contacted, refused to answer a particular question or didn't know the answer, the significance of the remaining responses was reduced because they may not represent society at large.

Several recent studies have questioned the presumed positive relationship between response rates and quality and there is currently no consensus on the connection. That said, reporters and editors should insist on seeing a response rate. Other indicators of the quality of the poll, such as insignificant levels of bias, low levels of missing data, and conformity with other research findings, should also be considered.

Partisan polls

Polls are often used by interest groups to support their causes. The partisan group that pays for the poll gets to frame questions in their language, and may present the issues in an unbalanced or inaccurate way. A poll, for instance, paid for by a group opposed to the seal hunt could imply that the hunt is illegal in the wording of the questions, when it is not. But such an inference could influence responses and makes the poll's results questionable.

These dubious "push" polls are typically calls disguised as research that are designed to persuade large numbers of people to a certain point of view, not to measure opinion.

Not all political polls done by an interest group fall into this category. Message testing, when campaigns test the effectiveness of possible messages about opponents and even themselves, is a legitimate form of survey research.

In message testing, the survey will contain more than a few questions; the organization carrying out the survey will be identified; and the survey will include questions about the respondent's demographic characteristics. Message testing is usually based on a random sample of the populace. The number of calls will fall typically between 400 and 1,500 interviews.

Push polls, in contrast, usually ask one or only a few questions about a single individual or a single issue; the questions hinge upon uniformly negative (or sometimes uniformly positive) descriptions of the individual or issue; the organization carrying out the survey is not identified, or a phoney name is used; and unusually large numbers of interviews are conducted, with no concern given to the sampling technique.

Also be on the alert for news releases on such polls that make conclusions that cannot be supported by the poll results.

Partisan polls cannot be treated casually, especially when they deal with important public issues. Always weigh whether the results of the poll add anything of value to the reader's knowledge of the subject.

Polls during elections

Polls must be handled with care throughout any election campaign. All such poll stories should be seen by Toronto Main Desk or another senior supervisor.

The Canada Elections Act calls for specific information to be included in election survey stories transmitted in the midst of a federal election campaign. It also restricts when a new poll can be distributed.

When a poll story is transmitted within 24 hours of the poll first being released to the public, it must include: the name of the sponsor of the poll; the name of the polling firm; the date the poll was conducted; the group surveyed (Quebecers, Albertans, women in Ontario, etc.); the sample size; the margin of sampling error (if it is a random telephone poll); and unless the poll story is being transmitted by broadcast, directions on how to obtain more detail on the survey, including the wording of the question that was asked. These conditions do not apply to stories on polls after the first 24 hours of release.

The Canadian Press carries polls under the terms of the act on all text and broadcast services with the exception of headline-only services, where it is impossible to meet those terms. Canadian Press stories should include a mailing address or website address for the polling firm or the poll's sponsor, who by law must make the specific details of the survey available to the public.

Not all stories that touch on new polls will have all the information the act calls for. Roundups, QuickFacts and Graphics may have just a glancing mention of a new poll. However, at least one story should be carried that is focused solely on the poll and includes the required information. Tip publishers by advisory that the more complete story is also available:

EDITORS: Members publishing FedElxn-Roundup on Wednesday may also wish to consider publishing FedElxn-Poll, which carries information required by the Elections Act that is not in the roundup.

The Elections Act also says that any story on an unscientific poll (sometimes called a hamburger poll) should make clear that it is not based on recognized statistical methods if it is being transmitted within 24 hours of first being released to the public.

The act prohibits publication of previously unreleased voter preference polls on election day. This means that stories on polls released the day before the election could present problems, especially for newspapers that would be unable to publish the surveys until voting day. Supervisors should be consulted before a story on such a poll is carried. On election day, publishing exit poll information in regions where polls have not closed is also prohibited.

CFL 2008 SEASON PREVIEW

B.C.
LIONS
Still the class of the West after last year's CFL-best 14-3-1 record. Jarious Jackson and Buck Pierce are a solid 1-2 punch at quarterback. Slotbacks Geroy Simon (CFL-best 1,265 yards) and Jason Clermont (86 catches, 1,156 yards) anchor the receiving corps while running back Joe Smith ran for a league-high 1,510 yards. Defensive end Cameron Wake was the league's top rookie and defensive player last year. Mike Benevides replaces defensive co-ordinator Dave Ritchie.

CALGARY
STAMPEDERS
John Hufnagel takes over as coach and GM after last year's 7-10-1 record. QB Henry Burris was second in CFL passing with 4,278 yards and this year will have former B.C. starter Dave Dickenson behind him. Nik Lewis and Jeromaine Copeland are both 1,000-yard receivers while running back Joffrey Reynolds ran for 1,231 yards last year. Former Montreal defensive co-ordinator Chris Jones will look to work his magic with a Calgary defence that was pitiful in '07.

EDMONTON
ESKIMOS
After missing the playoffs for the second year Edmonton acquired receiver Brock Ralph, offensive lineman John Comiskey, cornerback Jordan Younger, defensive ends Fred Perry and Dario Romero, punter-kicker Noel Prefontaine and starter Ricky Ray, who is coming off a season-ending shoulder injury. Linebacker A.J. Gass has retired but is an assistant coach with the team.

SASKATCHEWAN
ROUGHRIDERS
GM Eric Tillman raised eyebrows this off-season when he let head coach Kent Austin go to Ole Miss and dealt Kerry Joseph to Toronto after their Grey Cup-winning season. Offensive line coach Ken Miller takes over for Austin while veteran QB Marcus Crandell, who led Calgary to the '01 Grey Cup crown, is now the starter. Defensive co-ordinator Ritchie Hall is one of the league's best and cornerback Omarr Morgan returns.

A new season kicks off

The 2008 CFL season kicks off with two games on Thursday night. Here's a quick look at each team with some statistics from last year and things to look for in '08.

SOME LEADERS FROM LAST YEAR:

TOUCHDOWNS Total	
Smith, BC	19
Reynolds, Wpg	18
Joseph, Sask	13
Rambo, Cal	10
Copeland, Cal	10

RUSHING Yards	
Smith, BC	1,510
Roberts, Wpg	1,379
Reynolds, Cal	1,231
Cates, Sask	888
Payton, MB	852

PASS RECEIVING Yards	
Simon, BC	1,265
Edwards, Wpg	1,250
Clermont, BC	1,156
Armstrong, Wpg	1,142
Cahoon, MB	1,127

PASSING Yards	
Glenn, Wpg	5,114
Burris, Cal	4,379
Joseph, Sask	4,002
Ray, Edm	3,852
Calvillo, MB	3,600

FIELD GOALS Total	
Setta, Ham	45
McCallum, BC	35
Fleming, Edm	34
Duval, MB	32
Congi, Sask	31

PUNTING Average yards	
Duval, MB	47.0
Prefontaine, Tor	45.9
Dales, Cal	44.7
McCallum, BC	44.3
Setta, Ham	44.0

2007 TEAM OFFENCE
Yardage is rushing plus passing minus team losses

TEAM	YARDS
Calgary	7,237
Winnipeg	6,832
Sask.	6,666
Montreal	6,308
B.C.	6,242
Edmonton	6,098
Hamilton	5,606
Toronto	5,523

2007 TEAM DEFENCE
Yardage listed is fewest yards total

TEAM	YARDS
Toronto	5,499
Winnipeg	5,906
B.C.	6,120
Sask.	6,367
Montreal	6,370
Edmonton	6,462
Calgary	6,715
Hamilton	7,094

2008 At-a-glance
Kickoff: The Montreal Alouettes kick off the 2008 season against the Tiger-Cats in Hamilton, starting at 7 p.m. ET, followed by the B.C. Lions' visit to the Calgary Stampeders at 10 p.m. ET. Both games are on TSN, which will carry all 72 regular-season and playoff games under a new exclusive broadcast contract with the league.

New coaches: Four teams have new head coaches. Marc Trestman takes the helm in Montreal, while John Hufnagel is the new man in Calgary. Rich Stubler makes his debut with the Toronto Argonauts on Friday night against the Blue Bombers in Winnipeg, while Ken Miller debuts Saturday for the Saskatchewan Roughriders at home against the Edmonton Eskimos.

New-look Riders: Saskatchewan begins defence of its 2007 Grey Cup title without last season's coach of the year Kent Austin or outstanding player Kerry Joseph, the star quarterback who was traded to Toronto in the off-season.

WINNIPEG
BLUE BOMBERS
In addition to its heralded aerial attack, Winnipeg boasts one of the CFL's top running backs in Charles Roberts. He was second overall in rushing last year with 1,379 yards and averaged a solid 5.3 yards per carry. Linebacker Barrin Simpson was second in the CFL in tackles with 112 while rush end Tom Canada was tied for third in the CFL with 12 sacks.

TORONTO
ARGONAUTS
Made a big off-season splash by acquiring QB Kerry Joseph, who led Saskatchewan to a Grey Cup title and was the CFL MVP last year. Michael Bishop, 11-1 as a starter last season, should provide stability coming off the bench. Defensively, linebacker Mike O'Shea needs two tackles to move past Alondra Johnson into second all-time. Mike Vanderjagt, who helped Toronto win consecutive Grey Cups in '96 and '97, returns to handle the kicking and punting duties.

MONTREAL
ALOUETTES
Montreal's 8-10 mark last year was its first losing record since returning to the CFL in 1996. Rookie coach Marc Trestman replaces GM Jim Popp on the sidelines and has veteran quarterback Anthony Calvillo back. Calvillo left the team late last year when his wife was diagnosed with cancer. Shoring up the defence was an off-season priority with Montreal signing linebacker Reggie Hunt, defensive back Tay Cody and versatile Canadian lineman Jeff Keeping.

HAMILTON
TIGER-CATS
New GM Bob O'Billovich takes over a team that was 3-15 last year. But Hamilton has quarterback Casey Printers to begin the season. Printers arrived late last year and at times look like someone who hadn't played since '05. Running back Jesse Lumsden has quickly become one of the CFL's top runners while linebacker Zeke Moreno had a CFL-high 114 tackles and is the defence's anchor. Defensive lineman Nautyn McKay-Loescher had a team-high 11 sacks.

SEAN VOKEY, DAN RALPH - THE CANADIAN PRESS

Lt.-Gen. Walter
Natynczyk

A sketch of Canada's next chief of defence staff:

Birthplace: Winnipeg

Age: 50

Personal: Married with three children; bilingual.

Education: Attended Royal Roads Military College in Victoria, and College Military Royal in St. Jean, Que. Graduated in 1979 with degree in business administration.

Military career: Joined the Canadian Forces in August 1975; NATO duty in Germany with Royal Canadian Dragoons; squadron commander at Royal Military College in Kingston, Ont.; six months of UN peacekeeping in Cyprus; command of Canadian Task Force in Bosnia; commanded Dragoons in Ottawa area during 1998 ice storm cleanup; deputy commander of U.S. Army Corps in Fort Hood, Texas; 15-month deployment in Iraq as Deputy Commanding General of the Multi-National Corps.

Current position: Vice-chief of defence staff since June 28, 2006. Becomes chief of defence staff July 1, when he will be promoted to general.

Quote: "The tactics and techniques and procedures are exactly the same and the risks are identical." – Natynczyk speaking Friday on what lessons from his experience in Iraq could be applied to Afghanistan.

Quicks and fact boxes

The traditional sentence and paragraph is not always the most effective way to present data, especially to time-strapped readers.

Many publishers, including newspapers, websites and magazines, use summaries, capsules and other digests of information — often along with eye-catching graphics — that can be absorbed quickly. It is usually possible to present information in such ways without sacrificing the detail that readers look for.

There is virtually no limit on the different formats that can be employed to help present information in a cohesive and accessible way. Some of the more common instruments are Quicks, Bullets, Glances, Q-and-A's and Highlights. Each has a different look but offers the same thing: fast access to information that is important, helpful or just plain interesting. These techniques can be embedded as well into a traditional story format through the use of bullets.

This packaging of information makes an easy jump into a graphic that combines the barebones information with photos and other illustrations for print publications, and video as well for interactive graphics, which are featured on websites. Graphics offer a dynamic way of presenting factual and background material.

See **Graphics**, page 75.

Information contained in a Quick can be transferred into an attractive graphic that gives editors visual content for their news pages.

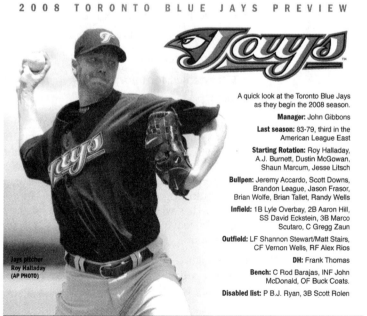

2008 TORONTO BLUE JAYS PREVIEW

A quick look at the Toronto Blue Jays as they begin the 2008 season.

Manager: John Gibbons

Last season: 83-79, third in the American League East

Starting Rotation: Roy Halladay, A.J. Burnett, Dustin McGowan, Shaun Marcum, Jesse Litsch

Bullpen: Jeremy Accardo, Scott Downs, Brandon League, Jason Frasor, Brian Wolfe, Brian Tallet, Randy Wells

Infield: 1B Lyle Overbay, 2B Aaron Hill, SS David Eckstein, 3B Marco Scutaro, C Gregg Zaun

Outfield: LF Shannon Stewart/Matt Stairs, CF Vernon Wells, RF Alex Rios

DH: Frank Thomas

Bench: C Rod Barajas, INF John McDonald, OF Buck Coats.

Disabled list: P B.J. Ryan, 3B Scott Rolen

Jays pitcher
Roy Halladay
(AP PHOTO)

THE CANADIAN PRESS

Quicks

Almost every good story presents an opportunity for a **QuickFacts, QuickList, QuickSketch** or **QuickQuotes**, whether hard news or feature.

Quickly defined, Quicks are short, sharp collections of information — facts, figures, trivia, biographical snapshots, memorable quotations.

These features are designed to accompany the main story. Newspapers can box the Quick to break up fields of grey type and offer interesting highlights, sidelights or insights into the news. Websites use Quicks to give readers some clickable options to explore.

There is no real limit on what can go into a Quick. For instance, they can:

• Provide a tight summary of main points from a high-profile meeting.

• Explain technical language from any kind of specialized get-together.

• Provide a calendar of main events at a multiple-day conference.

• Recite a selection of worthwhile jokes from a comedy festival or one-liners from an entertainer's news conference.

And especially, never neglect a Quick when it can give readers news they can use:

• What a new innovation means to you.

• How to tell if you've got the problem.

• What you can do about it.

• How the program works.

• Where to go for information.

• Pitfalls to watch for.

A Quick should never consist only of information already reported in the main news story. It may blend elements of the story with supplementary material from reference works or other sources. Or it may be a collection of related snippets not found anywhere else. It is also a good way to carry essential information that would bog down the main story. In a story, for instance, on the Canada's worst roads, the names of the roads can be listed in a Quick, leaving room in the story for quotes, comments and background.

Formats are highly adaptable. Informative, interesting and amusing are the main criteria. Question-and-answer formats are especially useful for complicated subjects.

Some guidelines:

• Quicks can be either placelined or undated. They carry the byline **The Canadian Press.**

• Quicks should be snappy and bare-bones, not in story form.

Not: Here are some tips to make a success of growing organic vegetables and herbs:

But: Tips on growing an organic vegetable garden:

Not: Early career: Born in 1920 to vaudeville entertainers, Rooney made his first stage appearance at 15 months. He made his film debut in silent-era short subjects at six and went on to star as perpetual juvenile Andy Hardy in a popular MGM series that ran from 1936 to 1946.

But: Early career: Born 1920 to vaudevillians. Stage debut at 15 months, on screen from age six. Top box-office draw in Andy Hardy series 1936-46.

• Quicks should be brief; 100 to 250 words is ideal. Anything longer should be packaged as something else.

• As in regular news copy, prefer the specific to the general. In some circumstances, Quicks can be used to provide detail that would clutter up the main story, such as province-by-province comparisons or statistical data.

Not: Showed interest in politics from early age.

But: At nine, insisted on joining father at Pierre Trudeau campaign rally.

Not: Woman threatens to complain to authorities about French use in pet store.

But: Woman warns owner of a Quebec pet store she might call language authorities because Peekaboo, a parrot for sale, didn't speak French.

• Try to include something offbeat in each Quick. A funny or shocking statement is a good lead-in to a collection of otherwise sober QuickQuotes or a good kicker to close a straightforward QuickSketch. An oddball statistic can enliven a businesslike QuickFacts (e.g. **stacked in a pile, copies of the committee's reports would reach higher than the 100-metre Parliament Building Peace Tower**). A memorable quote can enliven a QuickSketch.

• QuickQuotes can expand on statements that appear in the main story. They can offer more direct quotes on statements that are treated briefly, or actual words for paraphrased material, or new quotes that weren't essential to the story. Limit the selection to four or five, whether from a single person or several principals in an event.

• QuickTips can offer practical information for readers: five steps to healthier meals, seven ways to organize cupboards, etc.

• Don't use all-caps in headings.

Some examples

Bobsledder Pierre Lueders: an Olympic medal favourite
A quick look at bobsledder Pierre Lueders, one of Canada's Olympic medal hopefuls at the Vancouver Olympics:

Born: Sept. 26, 1970

Hometown: Edmonton

Event: Bobsled

Olympic competition: Feb. 20-21 (two-man) and Feb. 26-27 (four-man) at Whistler Sliding Centre

Past Olympic results: Gold medal at 1998 Nagano, silver medal at 2006 Turin.

Career highlights: 88 World Cup medals, eight world championship medals, six overall World Cup titles in the two-man, one overall World Cup title in the four-man, and four combined overall World Cup titles.

Did you know?: Lueders grew up idolizing the Edmonton Oilers and Wayne Gretzky and initially wanted to be a pro hockey player.

For the record: ``I realize if you don't win (at the Olympics), life goes on. I want to win, but I don't have to anymore." —Lueders on life after two Olympic medals.

Quebec's language watchdog no stranger to interventions over the years
The French-language office is investigating a complaint that a pub in downtown Montreal has English-only signs promoting Irish beers such as Harp and Caffrey. The language watchdog has responded to complaints from people seeking to protect the French language before:
1996: A woman warns a Quebec pet store she might get in touch with language authorities because Peekaboo, a parrot she wanted to buy, didn't speak French.
1999: The Old Navy clothing chain is asked to rename its stores La Vieille Riviere. It never happens.
2001: Some people express disappointment that race-car driver Jacques Villeneuve calls his restaurant Newtown.
2005: Language authorities say they will investigate complaints that Montreal Mayor Gerald Tremblay's party used the phrase Go Montreal in posters.
2007: Imperial Oil says it will keep its Quebec-only Marche Express name for its Esso gas stations after people protest a proposal to change the name to On the Run as they are known outside Quebec.

Bullets

Simple, yet effective formatting can be done within the body of a story with bullets. They can be either long or short, but should always follow a parallel structure.

Punctuation and capitalization in short bullets of a few words can be eliminated without hampering readability:

> The symptoms of a heart attack include:
> — dizziness
> — shortness of breath
> — confusion
> — chest pain
> — numbness in the left arm

But if the material is longer or would stand on its own as a sentence, uppercase the first letter of the first word in each bullet and use periods at the end of each one:

> The leaders of the Asia-Pacific Economic Co-operation forum outlined measures to combat bird flu at the end of their summit Saturday. The measures include:
> — Committing member countries to effective surveillance to prepare for and reduce the effects of a human pandemic.
> — Supporting the avian flu preparedness efforts of the World Health Organization.
> — Compiling lists of experts who could respond to the early stages of an outbreak.
> — Enhancing public awareness.

Glances

The **Glance** slug can also be used to explain a complicated story in a nutshell, to review the history of an event, to wrap up a sports tournament. It is also used when a major story is breaking here, there and everywhere.

But be sure to live up to the promise of the slug: it's a glance, not an encyclopedic look at a subject. Keep the language specific and easy to grasp quickly.

When the Glance is wrapping up events from all over the place, the format looks like this:

Terrorism-Glance ❶
Terrorism-at-a-Glance
                        By The Canadian Press ❷
 Major developments Thursday related to the war on terrorism:❸
   – ❹ Canadian military mission is to be operating by the weekend if everything goes according to plan in Afghanistan, commanding officer says.
                          — — — ❺
   – Canadian soldiers use beige paint, brushes and sand bags to adapt their forest-green camouflage for the desert environment of Kandahar.
                          — — —
   – President **George W. Bush**❻ says Geneva Convention applies to Taliban prisoners but not to captured al-Qaida terrorists; he refuses ❼ to classify either as prisoners of war.
                          — — —
   – 1,300 people give notice they may sue New York City for a total of $7.18 billion for alleged negligence during recovery and cleanup of World Trade Center site. ❽
                          — — —
   – Plane carrying 28 detainees lands at Guantanamo Bay❾ naval base in Cuba...❿

❶ **Keyword** slug is variation of the slug on the main story the Glance accompanies **(Terrorism)**.

❷ Not bylined except for the **agency credit**.

❸ Glances that accompany rapidly developing stories are frequently **updated** to keep pace with events.

❹ Each paragraph is indented and preceded by a boldface **dash** and a **space**. It ends with a period, not a semicolon.

❺ Each paragraph is separated by **three centred dashes**.

❻ **Names** are boldfaced.

❼ Entries are written in the **present tense** whenever possible to lend immediacy. Avoid headline writing that drops articles and auxiliary verbs. Each paragraph should be constructed in the same pattern for ease of reading.

❽ Paragraphs should not exceed **30 words**. Sentences are kept concise but not to the point where reader understanding or significant detail is sacrificed.

❾ **Location** is noted where the entry concerns a development away from the centre of the action.

❿ A Glance that wraps up different events related to the same story should be limited to eight or fewer entries.

Highlights

When complex elements of a story need summarizing, use Highlights.

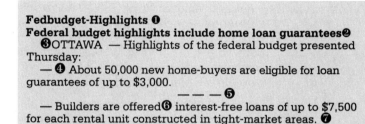

Fedbudget-Highlights ❶
Federal budget highlights include home loan guarantees❷
   ❸OTTAWA — Highlights of the federal budget presented Thursday:
   — ❹ About 50,000 new home-buyers are eligible for loan guarantees of up to $3,000.
                        — — — ❺
   — Builders are offered❻ interest-free loans of up to $7,500 for each rental unit constructed in tight-market areas. ❼
                 — — —
   — One-third of Canada's 16 million income-tax payers will be taxed less but few will save more than $100. ❽
                    — — —
   — Farmers facing bankruptcy ❾ . . .

❶ **Keyword** slug is a variation of the slug on the main story the Highlights accompany (**Bgt**).

❷ Carries **headline** but no **byline**.

❸ Usually **placelined** because it pulls together the key points of a major story focused in a single centre.

❹ Each paragraph is indented and preceded by a **dash** and a **space**. It ends with a **period**, not a semicolon.

❺ Each paragraph is separated by **three dashes**, boldface, centred.

❻ Entries are written in the **present tense** whenever possible to lend immediacy. Avoid headline writing that drops articles and auxiliary verbs. Each paragraph should be constructed in the same pattern for ease of reading.
— Sales tax rises to eight per cent Sept. 1.
— Single parents get child-care deduction up to $2,000.

❼ Paragraphs should not exceed 25 words. Sentences are kept concise but not to the point where reader understanding or significant detail is sacrificed.

❽ Highlights emphasize the key points of a story most closely affecting readers' lives, give specific examples and avoid jargon.

Not: Benefit eligibility for involuntary job-seekers reduced by one week.

But: Laid-off workers get unemployment pay after two weeks instead of three.

❾ Highlights include material that is dealt with at least briefly in the main story. Secondary items are not included. There should be no more than six entries.

Reading the news

Becoming a radio or TV news anchor, sportscaster or reporter requires a unique set of skills. Effective broadcasters are more than news readers — they're communicators. How does one become a good communicator? We know that some people are born with the gift of gab. But that doesn't make them good communicators. In fact, we tend to tune out or ignore individuals who run off at the mouth.

Good communication entails conveying thoughts and messages in an interesting and understandable manner. A natural voice with a pleasant, well-paced delivery and even, controlled breathing does the trick.

Several elements work together to produce good delivery. All of them are linked to the voice — our communication facilitator.

Breathing

Proper breathing is a basic function of good speech. In addition, it can help you control stress. This is where the diaphragm comes in.

The diaphragm is just above the stomach and is the muscle upon which the lungs rest. When you inhale, the diaphragm is stretched flat, forcing the stomach to protrude and the lungs to expand. When you exhale, the diaphragm returns to its normal dome-shaped position. Abdominal-diaphragmatic breathing is one of the best ways to maintain a healthy voice.

Put your hands on your sides, just above your hips. Push out your stomach and take a normal breath through your nose. Now exhale through your mouth. You'll find that it feels more comfortable and is much more effective than holding in your stomach and expanding your chest.

The everyday stresses of life, not to mention an intense newsroom environment, can affect your on-air performance — from your breathing to the speed and pitch of your voice. That's why it's important to look after your body with special emphasis on your vocal cords. Caffeine, coughing, shouting, clearing your throat, and dehydration all adversely affect the quality of your voice. Drink plenty of water because it keeps the vocal folds lubricated.

Resonance

In humans, the nasal, oral and pharyngeal cavities all contribute to vocal resonance. There are some things we can do to improve the quality of our vocal delivery.

The mouth is the most flexible and easily adjustable resonator we have. When the jaw is relaxed and fluid and the neck area is free of tension, we deliver optimum resonance. Opening the mouth more to provide a larger opening in the back of the oral cavity can provide a dramatically richer voice. But remember not to exaggerate lip movements.

Try to project from the diaphragm. This does not mean turn up the volume. Think of projection as an intense beam of light emanating from the lungs and directed to the rear of an auditorium.

Use warm-up exercises to hone the resonance of your voice.

Pitch

Just like any musical instrument, the human voice has the ability to alter its pitch. By changing tension in the throat, we produce sounds that assist in expression and effective communication. Use a natural pitch (your natural speaking voice) with a flexibility that is comfortable and doesn't tax the vocal folds.

Attempting to maintain a constant unnatural pitch (for example, lower pitch because you think your voice is too high) can cause physical problems and almost surely won't get you the job. But occasionally changing pitch for emphasis is a good technique and better than delivering in a monotone. If you don't sound interested in a story, how can you expect your audience to be? A good communicator is a talking storyteller, not a talking head.

Articulation

Proper articulation is a must. Our articulators are the lips, tongue, teeth, jaw, hard and soft palate, which work together for optimum performance. If any articulators aren't carrying their load, the result may be "marble mouth", or a sluggish delivery. The tongue must be flexible, the jaw fluid, and the vocal folds lubricated.

Clenching the teeth out of tension or stress limits the movement of the other articulators and adversely affects resonance. This can be alleviated through breathing exercises. A relaxed, open mouth is a must for proper articulation.

Lubrication is necessary, but tension or the consumption of certain foods and drinks often cause excess saliva and the need to swallow frequently. Foods that increase saliva include fried foods and those containing sugar or milk. Avoid them. Proper breathing will also help the problem.

Look up the pronunciation of unfamiliar words. Just as newspapers have an obligation to spell words correctly, broadcasters have the responsibility of pronouncing them correctly. Dictionaries and the daily pronunciation guide available on most wire services are great resources.

➤ See **Pronunciation Guide,** page 362.

Stress

Stress affects all the organs of the body, especially the heart and arteries. It isn't easy to control, but if you're a broadcast journalist, you've got to try.

The newsroom can be a very stressful place. A story can break at any time. There are deadlines to meet, interviews to conduct, reporters and field staff to deploy, budgets to meet, people to hire and train, etc. Shift work and personal responsibilities added to all that can make for many hectic and emotional days.

It is important to maintain good physical and mental health. Covering a big story, like a war, up close or even from afar, takes a toll on the body. You simply can't turn it off and forget about it when your shift is over.

Sleep: Try to get at least seven hours of sleep every day. It will pay off in the long run.

Exercise: Engage in cardiovascular exercise three or more times a week. Anything that sustains the heart rate at a targeted level for 20 minutes will improve your health and mindset.

Diet: Stress robs the body of vitamins and minerals. Try to eat five or six small meals a day, rather than three large feeds. Take a multi-vitamin every day. Avoid junk food, tobacco, and an excessive intake of caffeine and alcohol.

Express your feelings: Talk to someone close to you on a regular basis about your job, your boss, your performance. Getting it off your chest will lighten the load.

The bottom line is: Manage the stress before it manages you.

Delivery tips

The following tips will help you become a good communicator — and broadcaster.

1. Read aloud. There is no better training. Read all types of material aloud. It will help you to project your voice and get through a presentation without stumbling. It is also valuable — even essential — for proofing material prior to broadcast.

2. Be expressive. Use your voice naturally, as you would when telling a dramatic story to a friend. It is an instrument of thought and feeling.

3. Be natural. Don't strain your voice to produce a lower pitch to sound more authoritative. A deep voice used to be necessary to get a radio job, but no longer.

4. Be relaxed. Deep, abdominal-diaphragmatic breathing will help you cope with stressful moments. Regular, controlled breathing will allow you to glide through your presentation.

5. Pace yourself. Think of yourself as a smooth engine that runs at a steady speed. You will irritate your audience if you read one sentence rapid-fire and the next ploddingly.

6. Control the volume. Speak as you would during a friendly conversation. Shouting never increased the coverage area of any transmitter.

7. Sound conversational. Imagine you're having a conversation with a friend who is sitting across from you. This will help relax you and provide a smoother delivery.

8. Say what you mean and mean what you say. You are informing and, at times, entertaining the listening and viewing public — not just reading to it. You must understand what you are saying. If you don't, how can you expect your audience to?

Reporting

What image comes to mind when you think of a reporter? Is it the foreign correspondent, clad in a bulletproof vest, ducking for cover as he files from a war zone? Is it the TV reporter, microphone poised, firing tough questions as she races alongside a reluctant politician? Or a photographer chasing down a hurricane, recording the dramatic images?

As a journalist, you may get to cover such gasp-for-breath type of assignments. But you will also probably find yourself trying to build a story out of mind-numbing courtroom proceedings, desperately searching for the news hook in a repetitive political speech, and waiting in a hotel hallway until all hours of the night for the negotiators in a labour dispute to reach an agreement. You will also routinely battle fickle equipment and technical snafus, get rejected by newsmakers who will chat candidly and endlessly — until you pull your recording equipment out. And you will almost always be scrambling to meet deadlines. Much of your time will be spent hurrying to get to an assignment, only to end up waiting for something to happen.

News is information that affects people — their health, their families, their finances, and their communities. Journalists tell people what's going on in their world, often while it's happening.

Working as a reporter in the daily news industry means getting the facts, shaping them to make sense to people, and using words, sound and images to help bring the news to life.

Gathering news

People who read news in papers and online, listen to radio and watch TV often wonder where news comes from.

Some news is generated by reporters' observations or curiosity, by something they've heard or read, or by a tip. Stories can evolve out of anything, from a government decision to an unusual weather pattern.

Reporters routinely check to see if anything newsworthy is going on in the courts, on the police beat, or in government. They look to the worlds of business and entertainment, to social and labour activists. They make contacts among people who may tip them off to a potential story or verify rumours heard elsewhere.

Many stories stem from news releases or information received by their assignment editors. Reporters cover demonstrations, tragedies, entertainment, sports, and even the weather. And the one event reporters find themselves at time and time again is the news conference.

News conferences and scrums

News conferences are convenient places for journalists to get the information they need, along with some of the sound and pictures they require. The drawbacks are that interviews done at a news conference don't give the reporter an edge over her competitors and the audio and video she gathers at these staged events are rarely dramatic. For television, the news conference is often just the start of the assignment. The reporter and camera operator must gather further interviews and shots to adequately assemble their story.

A cardinal rule about covering a news conference is to get in and out as quickly as possible.

If the conference is being held to make a major, anticipated announcement (perhaps the resignation of a well-known politician), check to see whether a news release is being issued. Sometimes releases are handed out only minutes before the conference. If the information is not embargoed (cannot be broadcast until a specified time), call the newsroom and quickly file.

Get there early to make sure all your technical requirements are met. Some news conferences have sound equipment set up for you to plug into. Others don't, so you will have to set up your microphone on a table top. Be prepared to improvise and even get a little pushy. Some organizers welcome media to certain events (such as a speech), then don't provide proper access for recording equipment. Sometimes you have to be insistent to get the shots and/or audio required. In large scrums it can be a wrestling match just to get close enough to get your microphone in front of the newsmaker.

Once the news conference begins, it's imperative to listen carefully. You're not just listening for the news, but also for good quotes or clips that best sum up what the newsmaker is trying to say. Keep track of when those statements are made so you can quickly find them on your recording device.

Never wander too far from your equipment once the event is under way. Every now and then an interjection from the audience becomes more noteworthy than what's being said at the podium and you may have to record the unscripted action.

You have likely heard news conferences where reporters are all yelling questions at once. That can mean you don't get a chance to ask your question. Sometimes the newsmakers are available after the news conferences, so ask their handlers if something can be arranged. Unfortunately, the news subjects who spawn the most aggressive questioning aren't usually the ones who stick around.

Filing

The battle against the clock really begins once you've assembled your facts and are getting ready to file. The closer you are to deadline, the simpler you must make your story. For a major story, sometimes calling the newsroom to briefly report what happened will suffice until you have time to assemble a more complete story. Before you leave the conference or news event, you should have a clear idea what your story is going to be about, have crafted your lead, and know what quotes, soundbites or pictures you are going to use.

Understand the story before you attempt to write it. Some stories require further research or clarification. Don't make assumptions. It's better to ask a stupid or obvious question than to get the facts wrong. You can't be an expert in every field, and if you don't understand the material, you won't be able to make it clear for your audience.

Reporting from the desk

Today's journalists aren't always on the road. Some are back in the newsroom chasing stories from their desks. The telephone and the Internet are powerful, efficient tools for gathering news.

Just as much followup news work can be done over the phone (checking sources, pursuing story ideas), so can tracking down breaking news. If you're desk-bound and need to get details fast, you can find out a lot over the phone while your colleagues are travelling to the scene.

Think about who to call for information. Emergency officials (police, fire, ambulance, hospitals)? Transportation officials? Political sources? Then think about who else may be able to provide details or colour, preferably on tape for broadcast purposes.

Suppose there's an explosion and fire at a factory 80 kilometres away. It will take a while for a reporter and/or camera crew to get there. First, call all emergency services in that area to find out what is going on and how many people are affected. Use a phone book and a city or Internet directory to call people who live nearby, or the coffee shop across the street, to interview witnesses. Try to reach the mayor or another community leader. Many times all the details are a few phone calls away.

Remember to ask permission before broadcasting any interview. It's an ethical — and legal — requirement.

News releases and PR representatives

The job of most public relations people is to shape information for the media. They represent the views of the person, organization or company for whom they work. Sometimes the person who does this is the top official. Other times, he or she is lower down the corporate food chain or is hired on contract.

Though reporters dislike being "spun" by them, public relations people can quickly provide key interview subjects, sound and visuals, and information — of particular help in a chaotic situation. Occasionally, those in PR can come up with a decent story idea or even quietly pass on a tip. And the media relations department is often the place to find a warm body who will answer questions on tape or before a camera, particularly when a crisis erupts or after the 9-to-5ers have gone home.

Still, journalists must be aware that most public relations representatives will present only one side of the story — or at least one way of looking at the facts. Reporters must be sure that what they get is truly news and meets the standards of credible journalism. PR people are usually seeking publicity and positive exposure for their client. An endorsement, tacit or otherwise, in the news media is invaluable to them.

Courting the media usually begins with a news release. This missive often announces a news conference and provides little more than the subject, place, time and date. Often it can be ignored, but sometimes it provides solid information that may interest the public.

News releases seldom give all the details. If you decide to turn the information into a story, you will probably have to gather further information to provide balance.

To decide whether the information rates, ask yourself "is this new?" and "will it affect or interest anyone?" The first question is important. Those seeking publicity can repackage information several times to gain maximum exposure. For example, a public relations representative for a pharmaceutical company may send out a release when a new treatment has been invented, when the company has filed an application for approval with government, when the treatment has been approved, and again once it's on store shelves. How many times is this news?

Double check when using "firsts" and "only," popular claims with those who write news releases. It often turns out what was thought to be a "first" really wasn't.

Live news

The news on TV isn't the same as being there, but it gives journalists in the newsroom a window on developments, allowing them to keep their audiences up to date until their reporter on the scene files a more detailed story.

Events such as news conferences, parliamentary votes and debates, demonstrations, and speeches are often carried live on TV and radio.

If you're writing about a news conference that's being broadcast live, ask yourself the same questions the reporter on the scene would:

■ What is the news here, the main point?

■ Is there anything else to describe – the tone of voice, any obvious emotion?

Describe what you see on TV as if you were on the scene. Be careful, though, not to make assumptions about what cannot be seen beyond the narrow eye of the camera.

Big breaking news

The fast-breaking story goes to the very heart of The Canadian Press. The Canadian news industry — print, online, radio and TV — fixes its eyes on the wire when major news erupts. There is a potential deadline every minute. The story must be delivered at breakneck speed. But absolute accuracy and precise attribution rank ahead of speed in handling breaking news.

Getting organized

There is no textbook on handling the spot news break. Circumstances in any two breaks are never the same.

There may be official sources, such as police, to help. But there may not be — at least in the early stages.

Improvisation and resourcefulness are the standards. So are clear-cut organization, precise assignments, steady direction and cool heads.

Confusion at the scene of a plane crash, prison riot or tornado is the norm. Expect it but don't get caught up in it. Officialdom may be in a dither. The official version of what has happened may change in minutes. And then change again. Damage estimates and death tolls can swing wildly.

But disorder has no place in a newsroom when a big story is breaking.

Some basic guidelines:

1. Respond immediately to a tip of a major break. Assign someone to concentrate on getting it confirmed or denied. Notify supervisors so planning can begin immediately on staff assignments: on-site staff, main lead writer, other writers, chasers, editors; and on logistics like rental cars and chartered aircraft. Desks responsible for specific services, such as photos, must be alerted quickly. If a report of major news cannot be confirmed immediately, send an advisory on all services that The Canadian Press is checking an unconfirmed (repeat, unconfirmed) report or angle, and include the gist of what is involved. If the report is confirmed, send a publishable item first and work on the advisory next. The advisory should say as precisely as possible when copy is expected. Then deliver it on time. Or, in rare cases, send another note saying why it has been delayed. Never leave editors or news directors hanging.

➤ See **Advisories**, page 446.

2. Never move a story on a major break that isn't nailed directly to an identified source. That can be anyone from the prime minister announcing a declaration of war to a tow-truck driver at the scene of a multi-vehicle pileup. For most urgent breaking news, a **NewsAlert** is the first item that moves once the news is confirmed.

PENNFIELD, N.B. — Witnesses tell local radio station that a large plane has crashed in flames in southwestern New Brunswick.

Get the attribution in the NewsAlert. Every detail must be secure. Hold back if there is even the slightest doubt about a new development. But don't sit on a hot angle or wait for official sources to return calls. Nail down all sources. Ask them to spell their names. Ask for precise ranks or titles. This takes only seconds. Corrections take minutes, disfigure the report and are almost impossible to erase thoroughly once they have been transmitted to websites. Hold on to audio or original notes of who said what and when.

3. Then an urgent **QuickHit**, written to be used by all media platforms, takes over as the fastest way to provide details to broadcasters, websites and newspapers at once during the first hectic minutes.

> **PENNFIELD, N.B. — Eyewitnesses have told a local radio station that a plane has crashed in flames in southeastern New Brunswick.**
>
> **The plane, described by some as a four-engine aircraft, apparently went down in water near Pocologan in New Brunswick.**
>
> **RCMP have not confirmed the reports.**
>
> **Transport Canada says it has no reports of any missing civilian aircraft.**
>
> **Capt. John Pulchny, a military spokesman, told The Canadian Press that all military aircraft are accounted for.**
>
> **He said a Hercules cargo aircraft was in the area on a training mission but the control tower at its home base in Nova Scotia has been in contact.**

QuickHits are primarily written in a conversational style that serves the needs of broadcasters who may "rip and read" the copy on air, online clients who want a few details as quickly as possible, and newspapers that need information but not a publishable story.

QuickHits work best before 6 p.m. ET when the goal is to get the news out quickly for online and broadcast readers and listeners. After that time, the emphasis should be on newspaper-ready copy as deadlines approach.

Sometimes a series of QuickHits can serve a purpose, especially if it is early in the day, the story is continuing to change, and bureau or desk resources are limited. At other times, it makes more sense to hive separate reports off for each service to reflect their specific needs after the initial QuickHit. There are still other times when it is best to split a story into print and broadcast versions from the get-go. Consult with supervisors or Main Desk about what makes the most sense.

➤ See **QuickHits**, page 475.

4. After the initial details of the story are on the wire, move a coverage advisory as soon as plans are firm:

> **Ferry-Aground, Advisory**
>   **Editors:** Reporter Terri Theodore and photographer Jonathan Hayward are en route to West Vancouver, where a B.C. ferry has crashed into a marina near the Horseshoe Bay terminal. Information from the scene is expected by 2 p.m PT.
>   **THE CANADIAN PRESS Vancouver**

5. Quickly pin down the location, including the nearest town if the site is remote. Tip Graphics so a newsmap can get rolling. Keep the location high in all subsequent leads.

6. Don't wait for local authorities to get back from the scene. Chasers should not stop pressing while waiting for a promised call-back from an official source.

Scour phone listings — either through the Internet or the old-fashioned way with local phonebooks. Look for likely unofficial sources — a local service station or coffee shop. If there is nothing obvious, take a stab at random listed numbers. Chances are most people in the area will know something. Or know someone who does.

Caution: Don't say witnesses or sources when only one person is being quoted.

7. Aim to move a **1st Writethru** for print and online services within 20 minutes of moving a QuickHit. Alerts can and should interrupt the flow of Writethrus any time there is an official confirmation or significant story development. If newspaper deadlines are approaching yet the story is still being handled as an all-points QuickHit, a Writethru specifically intended for next-day publication should be moved as quickly as possible.

8. Don't bury the news when new — but less important — information becomes available. Survivors found staggering from the scene or casualties on the ground belong at the top. But don't leapfrog the real news with secondary information such as an RCMP announcement of a news conference on the plane crash. That sort of information is vital for the news media — but not the reader.

9. Try for fresh information for the top of Writethrus, but it must be pertinent to the main news. If necessary, stay with the original

lead and keep later secondary information lower.

Here is an example of a lead that keeps essentials at the top:

By Greg Bonnell
THE CANADIAN PRESS
   TORONTO – Air France said none of the 309 people aboard an Air France passenger jet perished Tuesday when it skidded off the runway, slammed into a stand of trees and burst into flames during a fierce thunderstorm at Pearson International Airport.
   Injured passengers and crew members aboard Air France Flight 358 from Paris, including one of the co-pilots, staggered a short distance from the wreckage to flag down commuters along Highway 401, Canada's busiest highway, in the moments after the crash, said Peel police Sgt. Glyn Griffiths.
   ``We located the co-pilot on Highway 401,'' Griffiths said.

Not all breaking news comes as a surprise and a writer can benefit from advance preparation:

By Greg Bonnell and Les Perreaux
THE CANADIAN PRESS
   STE-ANNE-DES-PLAINES, Que. – Karla Homolka was quietly spirited away from a Quebec prison Monday to face a daunting and uncertain future she fears will be fraught with peril after 12 years behind bars for her role in the sordid sex slayings of two Ontario schoolgirls.
   Homolka, the notorious ex-wife of convicted serial rapist and killer Paul Bernardo, was whisked out of the Ste-Anne-des-Plaines prison north of Montreal where she was transferred four weeks ago.
   Tim Danson, lawyer for the victims' families, said Homolka had been released but could not provide details.
   ``I just know that she's been released but I've still got one more family member to speak to,'' Danson said.
   Homolka's hopes of evading the glare of the national media spotlight appeared largely intact as she slipped past a gauntlet of reporters and photographers, apparently inside one of a pair of red minivans that drove away from the facility at the same time.

10. Give a wide berth to generalized and vaguely attributed statements, especially related to death tolls and damage estimates:

Not: Witnesses at the scene estimated about 20 people were killed and 40 or more injured.

But: "I counted 20 or 21 bodies and there must have been twice that many people who were showing some sign of life," said Jackie Lo, one of the first to reach the scene.

If figures prove badly out of line, it was Lo who was wrong — not those reporting her words:

> The official toll — 11 dead and 46 injured — was provided by RMCP Sgt. Laura Bridges and coroner Luis Alvarez. Earlier, one of the first volunteer rescuers to reach the area said she had counted 20 or 21 bodies.

11. Although initial QuickHits can be in the present tense because they are not intended to be published in newspapers, guard against slipping into the present tense in later Writethrus for newspapers, especially when picking up material from radio or TV. Writing in the past tense has two advantages: the story can be quickly led without having to change the tensing of the original; and the story stands up even if the situation changes after a paper has gone to press.

➤ For tips on writing breaking news for broadcast services, see **Writing for broadcast,** page 192.

Off-hours news breaks

Major news breaks at any hour of the day. A solo staffer who gets word on such a break should:

1. Brief the Main or National Desk, which can then alert other desks as necessary.

2. Move a NewsAlert or QuickHit, as appropriate.

3. Alert local supervisors who can call in reinforcements and start making plans for getting staff to the scene.

4. Send an advisory on coverage plans, even if it has to be tentative.

Organizing chaos

As noted, no two big news breaks are alike. But there are some tried and proven procedures to follow:

1. Get a strong lead writer in place immediately and let that person stick with the job. (Ask the National Desk for help if no one can be freed up locally.) The writer knows what information has been placed where in the story, where figures are first reported and where sources are first named and where new information can be smoothly blended in.

2. The lead writer should be assigned an editor who can work directly with the writer checking content and smoothing the flow. The editor keeps an eye on the clock to ensure updates are moving at reasonable intervals — she knows that last-minute detail or appealing touch of colour can go in the next Writethru rather than holding up the current one. The editor ensures the writer knows about any major changes being made in the story.

3. The writer and editor should not be involved in any other news while handling the big break. Their undivided attention is needed.

4. A bureau supervisor decides how much other copy is to be handled. Depending on available staff, or if the story is big enough, everything else may have to be put on hold. Often, though, the best course is to free one reporter-editor to handle all unrelated copy, likely in bare-bones form.

5. A supervisor, consulting with the writer and editor, decides what angles need chasing, who should go where and what information is needed for the next main lead or sidebars. If others are providing quotes or other details for the main story, remember this from the Old Lead Writer's Creed: Don't tell me — write it.

6. One supervisor or senior staff member should be the bureau funnel, dealing with supervisors at Head Office and monitoring other media to ensure the bureau or department is on top of the story. The lead writer and editor should not be answering phones and worrying about logistics and other details.

7. Don't be a bottleneck. Get others to help with chasing down a piece of background, checking a map for spelling or digging into electronic archives or library files. This staffer may also help Pictures and Graphics if a file photo needs to be transmitted or information is needed for a locator map or cutline.

Equipment

Proper equipment and fast action on logistics like transportation are critical when big stories break. Supervisors should ensure:

1. That electronic equipment (BlackBerrys, laptops, cameras and the like) are in top shape, fully charged and ready for action at all times. Company credit cards should be available for staff on short notice. There also should be some system in place for supplying cash in off-hours.

2. That each bureau has at hand the after-hours phone numbers for at least two charter plane companies. Phone immediately and get a quick estimate of cost and availability. Competition for charter aircraft can become intense when a big story breaks. It is often wise to make a tentative booking. Check other local media quickly about possible cost-sharing.

3. That reporters and photographers have current passports.

Sports

General

1. The standards of good general-news writing apply with equal force to the coverage of sports. People are the focus of reader interest. Bare results are the preserve of the agate page.

2. Remember that time is of the essence, especialy for major events. If there is a major trade in the NHL or a team has just won the Stanley Cup, a **NewsAlert** should lead the coverage, followed quickly by a **QuickHit** that wraps up the news development in four or so pithy paragraphs that can be used by broadcasters, online and print media.

3. The sensitive sports writer should know when a cliché has become threadbare. While athletes still profess to be *taking it one game at a time and giving it 110 per cent,* the days of reporting such mundane quotes are over.

4. When writing game copy, be concise. There's no need to describe every scoring play. Focus on the key play or performer and build the story around it. Pull together the remaining scoring plays into a paragraph or two. Sometimes, one sentence listing the remaining goal-scorers for each team in a hockey game, for example, will suffice. The reader who wants more can find it on the agate page.

5. Make sure the blinkers are off. Sports is more than what unfolds on the playing field. Capture the mood and size of the crowd and its impact on the game. Were the fans raucous, or sedate? Did they display banners or signs vilifying the visitors?

Watch for the interaction at the bench between players and coach, as well as between teammates. If the coach berates the star defenceman for giving the puck away on the decisive goal, let the reader in on it.

➤ See **More than a game**, page 154.

6. Make every quote in your story count. Each one should be there for a reason — it imparts colour or information that is not already in the story.

7. Finally, don't forget something so simple it's often neglected in stories: Was it a good game? Was it well-played? Was it entertaining?

Points to watch

1. The sport involved must be identified early in every story.

2. City names used as team names take singular verbs; team titles, even singular ones, usually require plural verbs: **Vancouver is**

last . . . but **The Canucks are last. Miami played its first game . . . but the Heat played their first game.**

3. Avoid unnecessary possessives. Write **The Canadiens centre stole the puck** not **The Canadiens' centre** . . . However, the possessive is required in the following: **The Canadiens' three straight losses are a season record.** When you are unsure whether the possessive is necessary, mentally substitute the city for the team nickname. By substituting **Montreal** in the examples given, it's quickly apparent which requires the possessive.

4. Avoid nicknames unless they are long-standing. If a person is known to readers by a given name and nickname, put the nickname in parentheses on first reference: **former CFL star Michael (Pinball) Clemons.** Usually, however, when a person is commonly known by a nickname, it is unnecessary to provide the given name as well: **star golfer Tiger Woods,** not **Eldrick (Tiger) Woods.**

5. Long-established and well-known leagues such as the National Hockey League, the Canadian Football League, the National Football League and the National Basketball Association may be referred to in first reference as **the NHL, the CFL, the NFL** and **the NBA.**

Initials are permissible on second reference for well-known minor leagues such as the American Hockey League **(AHL),** the International Hockey League **(IHL)** and Canada's three major junior hockey leagues. Otherwise, avoid initials even on second reference.

All leagues named in newspapers and other stories that might end up on non-sports pages should be spelled out in full.

6. Capitalize major events and trophies such as **the Olympic Games, the Olympics, the Pan Am Games, the Commonwealth Games, the Canada Games, the World Series, the Canadian Open, the Grey Cup, the Super Bowl, the Queen's Plate** and **the Vezina Trophy.** On second reference, refer to them simply as **the Games, the Open,** etc.

National and world championships are not capitalized. Write **the Canadian wrestling championships** and **the world hockey championship.**

7. The word *final,* meaning the last round of a competition, is singular in most cases. Write **Pittsburgh reached the Stanley Cup final** not **finals.** Exceptions: **Five swimming finals were scheduled Tuesday; the Boston Celtics are headed to the NBA finals** (official name of the event).

8. Don't expect the reader to have a medical dictionary next to the newspaper. What's an *anterior cruciate ligament* and why is it preventing Sidney Crosby from playing hockey? Make sure any medical jargon is explained and the extent of the disability is clear.

Sports ... More than a game

1. A sports writer who reports only what happens on the field or rink and ignores what takes place off it is being negligent.

2. On many sports pages today, the daily game is often summarized in a few paragraphs or worked into a roundup. Line stories tend to be analyses, backgrounders and profiles, or else they focus on trades, drafts, salaries, racism, substance abuse and legal problems.

3. Certain stories invite a blind eye: substance abuse, racial tension, disciplinary problems. These are not merely personal questions for publicly acclaimed athletes. Writing about these issues may require legal advice, but it should be part of the sports beat.

This photograph of Wayne Gretzky, wiping a tear as he announced his trade from the Edmonton Oilers to the Los Angeles Kings in 1988, dramatically showed how the business of sports takes a human toll.

THE CANADIAN PRESS/Ray Giguere

4. Sports pages must reflect the evolution of the multibillion-dollar sports entertainment industry. Every sports writer takes time to interview a team's general manager about a new prospect or a hot trade rumour. But a good sports writer will also get to know a team's business manager to write about attendance, television revenue and taxes.

5. Don't leave the business end of sports out of so-called amateur events. Members of Canada's national teams are no longer amateurs. Appearance money is now the main criterion for most track meets, so don't ignore it in the story.

6. As well, Canada's amateur sports federations are part of a substantial bureaucracy and should come under the same journalistic scrutiny as any government department.

7. The only true amateurs left in sports are people like weekend softball players and neighbourhood joggers. While recreational athletes aren't usually newsworthy, the sports they play are. Keep a close eye on trends in recreational sports. Why are people willing to spend hundreds of dollars on running shoes? How many weekend warriors are seriously injuring themselves on the softball diamond?

Women in sports

1. Sports pages tend to be filled with stories about male athletes. Despite that, a survey by the National Hockey League found more than 40 per cent of its fans are women. The crowd at any major sports event can show a similar ratio.

2. Sexist language, stereotypes and references have no more place in sports pages than in any other part of the newspaper.

3. A few anachronisms survive in sports: **the Ladies Professional Golf Association**. But generally, female athletes are no more *ladies* than males are *gentlemen*.

Beware of sports stereotypes. This picture is proof that hockey – and wrestling – aren't just for men. Gillian Apps of Team Canada is upended by a Team Russia player during the 2006 Winter Olympics in Turin, Italy.

THE CANADIAN PRESS/Ryan Remiorz

4. There's no justification for always leading with the men's competition in events, such as marathons, where both sexes compete. If separate stories aren't warranted, the most competitive, exciting race deserves the lead — and that's not always the men's event.

5. Be on the lookout for sexism in sports. Female athletes, particularly in golf and tennis, get a disproportionately smaller share of prize money compared with men. If an amateur program seems to be devoting more resources to male athletes, find out why.

6. Physical descriptions of athletes — male and female — are sometimes appropriate, and their personalities and gestures will enliven quotes. But avoid gratuitous descriptions that have sexist undertones. The simple test: Would this type of thing be written about a male athlete?

7. Any sports writer who refers to a female gymnast as a **pixie** or a basketball player as an **amazon** is not relying on a cliche, but is being sexist. Don't patronize. Be thoughtful and tasteful in your use of language.

8. In sports such as women's hockey, sex-specific terms such as **defenceman** and **two-man advantage** are usually preferred over **defencewoman** and **two-woman advantage**, as those in the sport use the traditional terms. But follow personal preference if it is different. Another option is to use a neutral term, such as **defender**.

➤ See **Sexism**, page 21.

Thinking visuals

1. When developing a story, think immediately about illustrations. Discuss the story with a staff photographer or photo editor and the video desk. Rely on their talents to make your story more complete.

The Masters: Players to watch

A look at some of the players in the spotlight and a few flying below the radar ahead of the 70th Masters tournament, which runs from Thursday to Sunday:

THE CANADIAN PRESS PICK
The no haircutting bet with Adam Scott and Tim Clark is over and so is Sergio's inability to get it done in golf's biggest events. The combination of some hot putting – and a little grooming – will make for a picture-perfect moment Sunday, when Garcia puts on a green jacket for the first time.

THE FAVOURITES

Tiger WOODS
Tiger's stellar Masters record (four green jackets before the age of 30) and a lengthened Augusta National course have made him the consensus favourite to repeat as champion this week. Has already won three times around the world in 2006, but it's unclear how father's deteriorating health may or may not affect his game.

Phil MICKELSON
Lefty has created a stir by carrying two drivers and winning last week's BellSouth Classic by 13 strokes. After several near-misses in the majors, Mickelson won the 2004 Masters and followed it up with last year's PGA Championship. Phil knows he can win golf's biggest events now and may just do it again here this week.

Retief GOOSEN
The forgotten man in golf's Fab Five, Goosen has the length and patience to win at Augusta National. If conditions at the course stay firm and fast, expect him to grind his way to the top of the leaderboard while much of the field falters – the same way he did in winning U.S. Opens in 2001 and 2004.

THE CONTENDERS

Sergio GARCIA
Golf has been waiting for one of the young players to break through and win a major title. Sergio's the top of the under-30 class and could find himself at the top of the leaderboard if his putter gets hot. He hits the ball a mile and strikes his irons beautifully, which should give him as many putts for birdie as anybody this week.

Luke DONALD
Britain's most promising player arrives in Georgia with loads of confidence after his second PGA Tour win at the Honda Classic a few weeks back. It's been 10 years since Nick Faldo won Britain's last green jacket, but Donald could parlay his sound swing into Masters glory. Finished tied for fifth in his tournament debut last year.

David TOMS
Could this be the week for major title No. 2? Toms has been one of the steadiest players on tour this year, having won the Sony Open and finished second, third and ninth in three other events. Doesn't drive the ball as far as the big boys, but is a solid iron player and putter, which serves him well on any golf course.

THE LONGSHOTS

Colin MONTGOMERIE
Oh Monty. He's 0-for-56 in major championships, but remains a sentimental favourite after so many near misses. The past year has seen Monty rediscover his game and finish second to Tiger Woods at the British Open. A lengthened Augusta National will be a challenge, but his accuracy and a little luck might make him an unlikely champion.

Arron OBERHOLSER
Last seen outplaying Canada's Mike Weir to win at Pebble Beach, Oberholser is making his Masters debut. While experience certainly counts at Augusta National, Oberholser is a player who finds a way to get it done – and sports one of the lowest scoring averages on the PGA Tour.

Thomas LEVET
You should be able to find his picture beside the entry for longshot in your dictionary. The Frenchman's best result in eight PGA Tour events this year is a tie for 33rd, but he played well at Augusta National a year ago and has contended in majors before.

CHRIS JOHNSTON / SEAN VOKEY - CP

2. The same holds for graphics. Many sporting events leave writers with more statistics than should be used in a story. The unused stats can make a timely graphic. Sports lends itself to graphics and a good one can sell a story to editors and readers.

3. As well, QuickSketches, QuickFacts and QuickQuotes are welcome complements to sports stories. They can spell out essential background material, leaving more room for colour and personality in the story.

Sponsorship in sport

Sponsorship has crept into every corner of sports, making it difficult to separate the commercial sponsor from the event title.

Avoid unwieldy titles, at least on first reference, but be fair about how sponsorship is handled. It is not fair to write about the **Buick Open** but call it the **Canadian Juniors** for curling when the full title is the **M&M Meat Shops Canadian Juniors**.

Sports are inevitably an advertising vehicle, but the sponsorship should have a legitimate connection to the event in order to rate being mentioned. References to the sponsorship should not be unduly emphasized.

Skip Sylvie Robichaud of New Brunswick faces Team Canada at the Scotties Tournament of Hearts curling championship in Regina in 2008. Sponsorship is an inevitable part of sporting events.

THE CANADIAN PRESS/Paul Chiasson

Metric, measurement and numbers

1. The Canadian Press generally uses metric to measure distances and calculate speeds. However, some sports — baseball, golf, football, horse racing and certain classes of auto racing, for example — are reported in imperial. Use the measurement the

sport uses. For further information, see sections dealing with individual sports.

Remember, however, that virtually two generations of Canadians have been brought up on metric and may be confused by imperial references. Unless precise imperial field demarcations are involved, as in football, or race distances, such as the Indianapolis 500, use metric wherever it's a sensible option.

Note: Many figures, imperial or metric, are rough estimates. When translating imperial to metric, don't use exact conversions unless precision is essential, such as in field events at an athletics meet. Round figures off.

2. Although some sports use metric for weight classes and the like, personal measurements continue to be imperial. When referring to heights, write **The centre stood six foot three**; as an adjective, it's **the six-foot-three centre**. If it's clear from the context, it's permissible to say **Jones, 6-3, 220 pounds, came to the Blue Bombers** . . .

Don't mix imperial and metric in one sentence: **The six-foot-three runner is the Olympic 200-metre champion**. Rephrase it or use separate sentences.

3. When measurements consist of two or more elements, do not use commas. Write **She stood five foot three** and **She was timed in two hours 15 minutes 35 seconds**.

4. In times, a colon is used between hours, minutes and seconds; a period before decimal fractions of a second. Write **0:27** (27 seconds), **0:27.7** (27.7 seconds), **2:00.1** (two minutes one-tenth of a second), **3:47:39.67** (three hours 47 minutes 39.67 seconds). Note that times involving only seconds include a zero before the colon.

5. When not expressing fractions in decimal terms, write **8-100ths of a second** and **3½ minutes**, but **two-thirds of an inning**.

6. Odds are listed as **20-1**, not **20 to 1** or **20-to-1**.

➤ See **Numbers**, page 335.

Records

When records are established, put them into perspective:

• Compare a national standard with the world mark.

• Try to explain why the previous record had been one of long standing or why it has been broken three times in the last year.

Statistics and formats

Agate

Agate, or scoreboard, pages allow newspapers to present the essential aspects of a game or competition concisely. In many instances, they provide the option of not carrying a story on the event. These pages also satisfy the appetite among sports readers for more background statistics and comparison tables.

Reporters and editors should think constantly of ways to supplement stories with agate tables, fact boxes and graphics.

Consult desk books for details on tabulating material and slugs.

Results formats

Most results are presented in one of three formats: **bare score, basic summary** or **head-to-head result**.

Canadian results in international competitions are boldfaced. Hometowns for Canadians are provided; others are listed by country.

Bare score

The winning team is listed first, with the exception of European soccer results where the home team is listed first, regardless of the outcome.

Wednesday's list
THE CANADIAN PRESS
NHL
    Toronto 3 Montreal 3

Later scores go as follows:

Add Wednesday's list
Add NHL
    Calgary 6 Vancouver 4

Basic summary

Sports that use a basic summary include bobsled/skeleton/luge, canoe/kayak, equestrian, diving, figure skating, gymnastics, judo, rowing, sailing, shooting, skiing, speedskating, swimming, track and field and weightlifting.

EDMONTON — Results Sunday from a World Cup track meet (distances in metres):

WOMEN
100 Hurdles
Semifinals

Heat 1: 1. Perdita Felicien, Pickering, Ont.,, 12.75 seconds; 2. Joanna Hayes, U.S., 12.75; 3. Nichole Denby, England, 12.79.

MEN
High Jump
Qualifyiing
(q-advanced to next round)

Group A: 1. q-Mark Boswell, Brampton, Ont., 2.29 metres; 2. q-Yaroslav Rybakov, Russia, 2.25; 3. q-Mickael Hanany, France; 2.20; 4. (tie), Jacques Freitag, South Africa, and Kyle Lancaster, U.S., 2.15.

Note: Where the field is particularly large, such as in a marathon, results are broken into paragraphs, approximately of equal length. For example, a 20-member field would be broken into two paragraphs of 10 competitors each. Paragraphs end with periods.

Head-to-head result

A head-to-head format is used for boxing, fencing, squash, tennis, volleyball and wrestling.

LONDON — Results Wednesday from the Wimbledon tennis championships (seedings in parentheses):

MEN
Singles
Final

Goran Ivanisevic, Croatia, def. Pat Rafter (3), Australia, 7-6, 3-6, 6-3, 2-6, 9-7.

Field summary

Sports that use a field summary include auto racing and cycling.

MONTREAL — Results and grid positions after qualifying Saturday for the Canadian Grand Prix at the 4.42-kilometre Gilles-Villeneuve Circuit (with name, country, team and time):

1. Michael Schumacher (Germany), Ferrari, one minute 15.782 seconds (average speed 210.018 km/h); 2. **Jacques Villeneuve, Iberville, Que., BAR-Honda, 1:17.035**; 3. Eddie Irvine (Britain), Jaguar, 1:18.033 . . .

Athletics   ➤   See **Track and field.**

Auto racing

1.   Report Formula One racing in kilometres, but NASCAR, Indy Racing League and other North American circuits in miles.

Baseball

The first linescore of the day follows this style:

Thursday's major league linescores
THE CANADIAN PRESS

AMERICAN LEAGUE
ChiSox   000 100 210— 4   8   1
Toronto   020 020 01x— 5   14   0

   Buehrie (L,1-4), Dotel (5), Wassermann (8) and Pierzynski; Halladay (W,21-5), Tallet (7), Ryan (S,33) (9) and Zaun, Barajas (8). **HRs:** ChiW — Thorne (9); Tor — V.Wells (17), Stairs 2(20), Hill (6).

Canoe/kayak

1. Categories are listed as *C-1* (canoe singles), *K-2* (kayak pairs), etc.

Cricket

1. International cricket competition generally consists of *Test matches* and one-day *international matches*. Test matches last five days and involve teams given Test status by the International Cricket Council. The current Test-playing countries are Australia, Bangladesh, England, India, New Zealand, Pakistan, South Africa, Sri Lanka, West Indies and Zimbabwe.

Test matches take daily breaks at lunch and tea before the end of day's play (sometimes called *at stumps*). In moving copy, take care to ensure the story covers the day's play and not just a portion.

2. An explanation of some common cricket terminology:

Innings — An innings (singular) is completed when: (1) 10 of a team's batsmen have been dismissed; (2) the batting captain "declares" (voluntarily ends the innings); or (3) a specified number of overs have been bowled.

Overs — consisting of six balls delivered from alternate wickets.

Wickets — three stumps topped by crosspieces (called *bails*) situated at either end of the pitch (field) and from which the ball is bowled.

Curling

1. Rinks are named in this order: *lead, second, third* (or *vice-skip*), *skip*.

2. Do not write *curling bonspiel*.

3. Abbreviations when necessary in linescores are: **Alta, B.C., Man, N.B., N.L., N.Ont, N.S., Ont, P.E.I., Que, Sask** and **Terr** (Territories).

4. Linescores follow this style:

> **MOOSE JAW, Sask.** — Linescores Tuesday at the Canadian women's curling championship:
> | | **Round 10** |
> |---|---|
> | P.E.I. | 001 010 201 1 — 6 |
> | Manitoba | 200 101 010 0 — 5 |

5. Standings follow this style:

> **VERNON, B.C.** — Final round-robin standings and Sunday's playoff result at the Ford World Women's Curling Championshp at the Greater Vernon Multiplex:
>
> | Country (Skip) | W | L |
> |---|---|---|
> | x-China (Wang) | 7 | 0 |
> | x-Canada (Jones) | 7 | 1 |
> | x-Switzerland (Ott) | 7 | 1 |
> | t-Japan (Meguro) | 6 | 2 |
> | Denmark (A.Jensen) | 5 | 3 |
> | Sweden (Victorsson) | 6 | 5 |
>
> x–clinched playoff berth
> t–played tiebreaker
>
> **Sunday Result**
> **Gold medal game**
> Canada (Jones) 7 China (Wang) 4
>
> —
>
> **Saturday Results**
> **Semifinal**
> Canada (Jones) 9 Japan (Meguro) 8
> etc.

Figure skating

1. The four disciplines of competitive figure skating are *men's singles, women's singles, pairs* (man-woman) and *ice dancing* (man-woman). *Singles* begins with a short program in which skaters must attempt predetermined jumps or movements in not more than two minutes 40 seconds. The majority of the marks are then available in the free-skating program in which competitors choreograph their own combinations of jumps, spins and steps within three to 4 1/2 minutes depending on whether it's a men's or women's competition and on the age group. Skaters select their own music for both the short and long programs. Judges assign points for every element in a performance based on a grading system that takes into account the level of difficulty in each move. Points also are awarded for the artistry conveyed to the audience.

Pairs skating consists of a short program with required jumps, spins and lifts and a free-skating portion which contains moves similar to singles skating but executed simultaneously by both competitors. Free-skating programs last four minutes at the senior level and, like singles, judges award marks taking into account the level of difficulty of each move and the artistic impression conveyed. Again, the majority of the marks are available for the longer-free-skating program.

Ice dancing is easily distinguished from pairs skating in that jumping is not allowed. The couple seldom separate. Competitions include three phases — compulsory dances such as the waltz, tango and foxtrot in which couples skate three repetitive sequences of steps to their own choreography, and free dance in which competitors select their own moves and music.

2. Some of the more common jumps (named after their inventors and, therefore, capitalized):

Axel: Skater, facing forward, takes off on the outside edge of either foot, rotates up to 3 1/2 times and lands on the outside edge of the other foot, facing backward.

Lutz: Skater starts with a lengthy glide backwards down the ice, then takes off on the outside edge of either foot and, after up to three rotations, lands on the outside edge of the other foot, facing backward.

Salchow: Skater, facing backward, takes off from the inside edge of either foot and, after up to three rotations, lands on the outside edge of the other foot, facing backward.

Football

1. Style for game summary:

TORONTO — CFL Wednesday night:

SUMMARY
First Quarter
    Tor — Safety Dales concedes 5:15
    Cal — FG Maver 21 11:08
    Tor — Safety Dales concedes 14:04
Second Quarter
    Tor — FG Shaw 46 2:25
    Tor — FG Shaw 12 8:11
    Cal — TD Lewis 39 pass from Burris (Maver convert) 11:50
    Tor — FG Shaw 40 13:18
Third Quarter
    Cal — TD Browner 23 fumble return (Maver convert) 6:30
    Cal — TD Lysack 77 interception return (Maver convert) 10:26
    Tor — Safety Dales concedes 15:00
Fourth Quarter
    Tor — Single Shaw 49 1:58
    Tor — FG Shaw 48 3:54
    Tor — TD Johnson 1 run (Lemon to Owens for two-point convert) 13:02
    Cal — FG Maver 51 15:00
First Overtime
    Cal — FG Maver 35
    Tor — FG Shaw 22
Second Overtime
    Cal — TD Lewis 17 pass from Burris (Two-point convert unsuccessful)
    Tor — TD Boyd 22 run (Lemon to Johnson for two-point convert)
Calgary 3 7 14 3 3 6_36
Toronto 4 9 2 12 3 8_38
    Attendance — 20,242.

2. Style for game statistics:

VANCOUVER - Statistics from the Saskatchewan-B.C. CFL game Saturday night:

	Sask	B.C.
First downs	26	16
Yards rushing	188	89
Yards passing	252	317
Total offence	440	406
Team losses	20	41
Net offence	420	365
Passes made-tried	18-29	19-29
Return yards	165	157
Intercepts-yards by	0-0	0-0
Fumbles-lost	2-1	2-1
Sacks by	4	2
Punts-average	5-41.4	8-43.4
Penalties-yards	8-100	16-116
Time of possession	34:51	25:09

Net offence is yards passing, plus yards rushing, minus team losses such as yards lost on broken plays.

Individual

Rushing: Sask — Cates 16-93, Charles 4-47, Durant 4-33, Dressler 3-15; B.C. — Robertson 10-54, Joran 1-13, McCallum 1-9, Printers 1-8, Lulay 2-5.

Receiving: Sask — Rodriguez 5-58, Getzlaf 2-55, Fantuz 4-55, Dressler 3-53, Charles 1-17, Cates 3-14; B.C. — Simon 6-169, Armstrong 6-76, Arceneaux 3-39, Wilson 2-22, P.Jackson 1-7, Robertson 1-4.

Passing: Sask — Durant 18-29, 252 yards, 1 TD, 0 ints; B.C. — Printers 10-14-12 0-1-0; Lulay 9-15-19 7-1-0.

Golf

1.   Write **par 4, par-4 hole, five-iron** or **No. 5 iron, three-wood** or **No. 3 wood, 1 over par for the round, shot a 1-over-par 73, parred, birdie, birdied, bogey, double-bogey, triple-bogey 7, bogey-free** (not **bogey-less**), **bogeyed.**

2.   There are two basic types of play: *match* and *stroke*.

In *match* play, the individual or team wins a hole by taking fewer strokes than the opponent. The entry winning the most holes wins the match. Stroke totals are not kept.

In *stroke* play, the individual or team keeps a running total of strokes taken at each hole. The one taking the fewest strokes overall is the winner.

3.   Match-play tournaments follow this style in head-to-head results:

   Bill Richardson, Creston, B.C., def. Ian MacDonnell, Antigonish, N.S., 3 and 2.

(Richardson had an insurmountable lead of three after 16 holes. As a result the final two holes were not played.)

   Bill Richardson, Creston, B.C., def. Ian MacDonnell, Antigonish, N.S., 1-up.

(Richardson led by one after 18 holes or after extra play. If two players are tied after 18 holes, play continues until a hole is won.)

Hockey

1. Style for game summaries:

> VANCOUVER — NHL Saturday night:
> **First Period**
> 1. Montreal, A.Kostitsyn 21, 0:54
> 2. Montreal, Latendresse 12 (Smolinski, Sperra) 8:19 (pp)
> 3. Montreal, Kovalev 33, 12:49 (penalty shot)
> **Penalties** — Isbister Vcr (tripping) 2:04, Kostopoulos Mtl (obstruction-hooking), Cowan Vcr (diving) 5:45, Brown Vcr (goaltender interference) 7:32, Price Mtl (delay of game; served by Fisher) 17:59.
> **Second Period**
> 4. Vancouver, Pyatt 8 (H.Sedin, Ohlund) 2:52 (sh)
> 5. Vancouver, Cowan 5 (Brown, Ohlund) 6:22 (pp)
> 6. Montreal, Kovalev (Smolinski, Dandenault) 6:35
> 7. Vancouver, Pyatt 26 (D.Sedin, McIver) 8:00
> **Missed penalty shot** — Bieksa Vcr, 16:45.
> **Penalties** — Ritchie Vcr (holding) 2:11, Latendresse Mtl, (double roughing), Pettinger Vcr (roughing) 5:04, Vancouver bench (too many men; served by Rypien) 14:06, Ryder Mtl (slashing) 19:42.
> **Third Period**
> 8. Montreal, A.Kostitsyn 12 (Eaves) 8:11
> 9. Vancouver, Piekanec 9, 12:29
> 10. Vancouver, D.Sedin 13 (H.Sedin, Ohlund) 19:15
> **Penalties** — McIver Vcr (holding stick) 2:31, Begin Mtl (fighting), Lapierre Mtl (roughing, hitting from behind major, game misconduct), Koivu Mtl, Fitzgerald Mtl, Shannon Vcr, Cowan Vcr (roughing, fighting, misconduct), Luongo Vcr (leaving the crease; served by Rypien), Pettinger Vcr (roughing, fighting), Jaffray Vcr (instigating, fighting, game misconduct) 16:45.
>
> **Overtime**
> No scoring.
> **Penalty** — Latendresse Mtl (cross-checking) 3:21.
> **Shootout**
> Vancouver wins 2-1
> Montreal (1) — Kovalev, miss; A.Kostitsyn, miss; Latendresse, goal; Ryder, miss; Smolinski, miss.
> Vancouver (2) — Pyatt, goal; Isbister, miss; H.Sedin, miss, Brown, miss; D.Sedin, goal.
> **Shots on goal by**
> Montreal 12 6 9 3—30
> Vancouver 7 14 9 1—31
> **Goal (shots-saves)** — Montreal: Price (L,23-15-2); Vancouver: Luongo (W,21-16-4)(start, 6:35 second)(22-17), Sanford(12:49 first)(8-8).
> **Power plays (goals-chances)** — Montreal: 2-7; Vancouver: 0-4.
> **Referees** — Paul Devorski, Mick McGeough. **Linesmen** — Mark Pare, Dan Schachte.
> **Attendance** — 17,242 (17,439).

Note 1: The number after a scorer's name is his season goal total. The (pp), (sh) and (en) notations designate power-play, short-handed and empty-net goals.

Note 2: The time of each goal is computed from the start of the period.

Note 3: The winning goaltender is the one in net when the winning goal is scored. The NHL defines the winning goal as the goal which is one more than the opposition's final total. For example, if the final score is 8-4, the fifth goal scored by the victorious team is the winner.

Horse racing

1.   Terms to watch include *colt* (an uncastrated male aged four or less), *horse* (an uncastrated male aged five or more), *stallion* (an uncastrated male, especially one used for breeding), *gelding* (a castrated male of any age), *filly* (a female aged four or less), *mare* (a female aged five or more), *quarter-horse* (a horse bred to run a quarter-mile), *standardbred* (bred chiefly for harness racing; a pacer or trotter), *thoroughbred* (of pure or pedigree stock; chiefly for flat racing and steeplechase).

Lacrosse

1.   *Field lacrosse* is played on an open field roughly the size of a soccer pitch. Each team can have 10 players at a time on the field. *Box lacrosse* is played in arenas with each team allowed to dress about 18 players and have a goaltender and five runners on the floor at any one time.

2.   Both are full-contact sports in which players catch and throw a solid rubber ball using sticks comprised of a plastic head around leather or string webbging attached to a metal or wood shaft. the object is to put the ball in the oppoisition's net.

3.   Games in the professional National Lacrosse League consist of four 15-minute quarters, while most amateur leagues use a format with three 20-minute periods. Sudden-death overtime settles ties.

Mixed martial arts (MMA)

1. Mixed martial arts is a growing combat sport combining boxing, wrestling, jiu-jitsu and other martial arts. The sport is not sanctioned in every jurisdiction. In most places where the sport is permitted, it is regulated by the same bodies that govern boxing.

2. The dominant organization in the sport is the Ultimate Fighting Championship although there are rival promoters.

3. Fights are held in rings or cages, with the UFC's Octagon the most famous example.

4. In the UFC, fights last three five-minute rounds, unless there is a stoppage by knockout, technical knockout or submission. UFC championship bouts last five rounds. Three judges score the fights, as in boxing, if the bout goes the distance.

Rowing

1. A *regatta* is a knockout competition ending with a race or races between two or more finalists. A *repechage* is a second chance to qualify, used only in the preliminaries. The boats used in sculling and rowing are *shells*, not sculls.

In sculling (*singles, doubles* or *four-member crews*), each competitor rows with two oars called *sculls*. In rowing (*pairs, fours, eights*), each competitor uses one oar.

Fours and eights are *crews*, never teams. The competitors are *scullers* or *oarsmen* or *oarswomen*, never rowers. The terms *rowing* and *oars(wo)men* may be used in a general sense referring to regattas and the scullers who take part.

2. Identify events as *single sculls, double sculls, pairs, pairs with coxswain, fours, fours with coxwain* and *eights*.

Rugby

1. There two versions of the game: *rugby union* and *rugby league*.

Rugby union is the 15-man game that is played around the world and contested at the Rugby World Cup, held very four years. *Rugby league* is a 13-man game played primarily in England, Australia and New Zealand (countries where rugby union is also played). As the most widely played version, rugby union can be referred to simply as rugby to differentiate itself from rugby league.

2. Rugby positions include *prop, hooker, second-row* or *lock forward, flanker, No. 8, scrum half, fly half, centre, winger* and *fullback*. Top-level international rugby fixtures are known as *Test matches*.

3. Both codes play 40-minutes halves. Rugby scoring has a *try* worth five points, *conversion* two and *drop* or *penalty goal* worth three. In rugby league, a try is worth four points, a conversion two, a penalty goal two and drop goal one.

Sailing

1. In Olympic sailing (formerly yachting), races fall into two categories: *fleet racing* and *match racing*. In fleet racing, all competing boats race against each other at the same time. In match racing, two boats compete one on one. All events are fleet races except the *Soling* event, which starts with a series of six fleet races to determine the top 12 competitors, who then advance to a match racing elimination series.

Boats are categorized into classes based on the weights and measurements of the boats. This changes frequently as the popularity of various boats waxes and wanes. In general, the trend is toward smaller boats with fewer crew members. There are men's, women's and mixed events.

2. The America's Cup is a *formula* class event. For a yacht to qualify for this challenge series, its size must not exceed a given limit. That limit, which approximates the length of the boat, is arrived at using a complicated mathematical formula that factors in such things as length, draft and sail area. In 1992 a 24-metre limit was set.

3. Where names of yacht classes include an imperial measure (e.g. *Whatsis 30:* a 30-footer), a sentence of explanation may be necessary if there's a risk of confusion.

4. Some races are still measured in nautical miles. Convert these to kilometres but retain an initial nautical-mile equivalent in parentheses. A nautical mile is equivalent to 1.852 kilometres.

Skiing

1. Skiing is divided into four categories: *alpine, nordic, biathlon* and *freestyle*. Alpine includes downhill, slalom, giant slalom, super giant slalom and a combined event. Nordic includes cross-country, ski jumping and a combined event. Biathlon combines cross-country skiing with rifle shooting. Freestyle includes moguls, aerials, skier cross, halfpipe and table top (big air).

Soccer

1. For British and European leagues, the home team is listed first in scores; in standings, the order for *T(ies)* and *L(osses)* is reversed from standard North American tables.

Speedskating

1. Speedskating consists of long-track and short-track events. Race distances include 500, 1,000, 1,500, 3,000 (women only), 5,000 and 10,000 metres (men only).

2. Scoring is in minutes, seconds and tenths of a second. Extend to hundredths if available.

Tennis

1. Use head-to-head results format. Grouped results should be graded in order of seedings. See example page 160.

2. Tiebreakers are used to avoid marathon sets. The first player to win six games wins the set, unless the opponent has won five games. In that case, the player with six games may take the set by winning the next game. If that player loses it, (a) play can continue until either player wins two straight games, or (b) a tiebreaker may be played in which the winner is the first player to score seven points with at least a two-point lead. If the score

reaches 6-6 in the tiebreaker, play continues until one player leads by two points. In some events, doubles matches include a "super tiebreaker" instead of a third set. In this case, the first team to 10 points with at least a two-point margin wins the match.

Track and field (Athletics)

1. Olympic and other international events are measured in metric, although some imperial distances are still raced in the United States. Distances and heights in such field events as the high jump, long jump, pole vault, shot put, discus, hammer and javelin should be reported in metres. But the 100-yard dash, for example, is not converted to the 91.44-metre dash.

2. Use the metric distance for marathons — 42.195 kilometres (not 26 miles 385 yards).

Wrestling

1. Identify events as *Greco-Roman* or *freestyle* for men. Women compete only in *freestyle*. In the Greco-Roman style, a wrestler is not allowed to attack an opponent's legs or use his legs to execute other moves. In freestyle, the wrestler can use his arms and legs to execute holds and defend against his opponent.

Statistics

Statistics can be pillars of the day's news. They are also the devil's playground, luring reporters into errors of interpretation, assumption and fact.

Some of the problems with statistics would diminish if the news media would regularly treat them with the care — and the skepticism — they need. The quote credited to Benjamin Disraeli is deservedly famous: **"There are . . . lies, damned lies and statistics."**

The value of statistics, intelligently used, can hardly be overstated. They help to give substance to stories on hundreds of topics. But there are pitfalls:

1. Some statistical reports rely on actual counts: the number of new cars sold in Vancouver in March, based on sales reports from all dealerships. Some are estimates: the number of unemployed in Canada in August, based on extensive samplings of households. These poll-based statistics are subject to error and reporting on them needs some of the same care applied to writing about public-opinion polls.

➤ See **Polls**, page 124.

2. Some statistical reports are issued on a preliminary basis, subject to adjustments later. The federal government's figures on international trade are one example. Some of the later adjustments can be substantial. That means the figures must always be described as preliminary, and early in the story the importance of the adjustment process needs to be spelled out each time. When the final figures are available, they should be reported and comparisons made with the preliminary figures. Since the preliminary figures are tentative, it doesn't make sense to attribute great significance to the precise numbers. If that makes a story less interesting and less authoritative, so be it.

3. Statistics are usually relevant only for the time period concerned. There can be substantial changes from one year to the next in all sorts of statistics. An obvious example: a poll on the number of homes with high-speed Internet access in 2005 says very little about how many families had jumped on the Net by 2010.

4. Comparisons of statistical studies on the same topic can be useful in detecting trends, such as employment in the manufacturing sector over a few months or even years. However, comparisons between one time period and an earlier one should take account of how the population and other crucial factors have changed in the interim. A 25 per cent increase in auto thefts from 1995 to 2005 might actually represent a decline in the rate of thefts, if population and car ownership figures are taken into account. (Rates are more telling when they're available: the number of murders per 100,000 population.) Similarly,

comparisons of value over time must take into account the decline in purchasing power of the dollar.

5. The bases of comparison shouldn't be decided routinely. Comparing January retail sales figures with December's can be meaningless because of the Christmas rush; comparing them with the previous January's is usually best. But when the economy is reaching a peak or a trough, a year-over-year comparison may not be as revealing as month-over-month or some other comparison thoughtfully chosen.

6. The significance of statistics can't be safely stretched. If Canada's overall cost-of-living index goes up mainly because of higher taxes in Ontario, many Canadians will not be affected and a story should make that clear from the start. If a provincial study reports that the number of homeless people in the province has declined eight per cent from a year earlier, that alone can't be taken to suggest declines in other provinces.

7. Similarly, it's risky to assume that American statistical studies are equally valid in Canada. Some academics find it hard to resist using the floods of American studies to buttress arguments about conditions in Canada, adding casually that "there's no reason to think the same figures don't apply in this country." Don't believe it. Check some authorities; there are numerous differences between the two societies.

8. Phrases like **seasonally adjusted, gross domestic product** and the like may be understood by specialists, but the ordinary reader can use help. The methods of calculating changes in such basic measurements as the consumer price index or the unemployment index should also be explained from time to time. When available, sample size — 700 of the 2,000 sporting goods stores, for example — should be mentioned. People want to know how reliable these indicators are.

Some terms

Average refers to the result obtained by dividing a sum by the number of quantities added together. The average of 10, 20, 30 and 40 is 100 divided by four, or 25.

Mean usually designates a number in the middle of two extremes.

Median is the middle number of a series arranged in order of size. The median in the group 55, 62, 70, 81 and 95 is 70. The average would be 72.8.

Norm implies a standard of average performance. **The snowfall is below the norm for January in Alberta.**

Travel writing

Travel stories share many of the requirements of other features: effective use of quotes and people, a lively writing style, a good lead that grabs the reader's interest.

But more than most other features, travel stories must usually convey a sense of place. The writer draws a picture for the reader by selecting vivid detail and using description effectively.

1. Travel writers need to make their stories interesting — a mere listing of information from travel brochures and government tourist boards won't do.

The airily upbeat style more common in promotional travel literature doesn't work either.

2. The proper approach is somewhat sharper and reflects the writer's personal observation.

What is it about a particular place that is distinctive, that catches the writer's senses?

What do the city streets look like? What do the people wear? What is striking about the markets, the countryside?

The writer should try to get real people into the story — a street vendor, a passerby, a museum guide. Anyone but the overused taxi driver or hotel desk clerk.

3. The best travel stories will capture the genuinely interesting aspects of a destination without glossing over harsh reality: poverty, inefficient transportation, anti-tourist sentiment. Experienced travellers expect some discomfort but they also want practical information on what to be prepared for.

At times, the need for plain-speaking will be paramount. When travel is likely to be affected by political developments, earthquakes or floods, terrorist threats or other newspage developments, a travel-page report can hardly ignore it.

4. Good travel topics include an offbeat site, a new attraction, any interesting destination.

Trends that affect tourists are also worth considering: the popularity of adventure travel or eco-friendly trips.

A narrow focus often provides the best opportunity for colourful writing — for example, a market street in Lima, a festival in Barcelona, a museum on prairie dogs in Alberta. But a large-topic story — travel in eastern Europe, London in summertime, cruising the Caribbean — is also worthwhile.

If the reporter can add some perspective — a sense of familiarity with the country and the people — all the better.

5. Unlike some magazine material, travel stories for newspapers and websites must be punchy and concise. Interesting historical background can be woven in judiciously.

6. An **If you go** fact box — with websites, details on accommodations, directions, prices and other similar information is often desirable.

7. The use of the first person is occasionally acceptable when giving a personal account of an unusual adventure, but it should not be overdone.

8. Photos are essential for travel stories.

9. Travel stories do not need exotic placelines. Many people want ideas on cheaper or shorter holidays within Canada.

10. When a freelance writer's trip is subsidized, a line is added at the end of the story: **John Smith is a Toronto-based freelance writer. His trip to France was sponsored by the French tourist office.** (Canadian Press staff are not allowed to accept subsidized travel.)

Video

General

Today's video stories can come from a television crew, a reporter with an inexpensive digital camera or a member of the public wielding a cellphone. With the likes of YouTube and other video-sharing websites, video stories have a wide reach and considerable shelf life online.

Visuals are at the heart of the video story and at times the pictures essentially stand on their own: security video of a gunman firing shots into an apartment building entrance or protesters harassing the Governor General. Other times, video needs additional footage to tell the story: so-called B-roll that breaks up footage of talking heads or illustrates something mentioned in the report.

In telling the video story, reporters have to think about the building blocks needed. While some shots may spontaneously happen, others require some advance planning. In the case of a junior hockey team playing its last game, for example, footage of the clock counting down the final period tells the story and you only get one crack at it.

In deciding how to assemble a video, reporters and editors have to choose the most effective form. Is a voiceover needed or do the visuals tell the tale? Are there audio clips or still photos that bolster the storytelling? Should the reporter place himself or herself on camera?

In most cases, online video is short. The average Canadian Press video report runs two minutes. While consumers have wide-ranging appetites for video, they tend to snack when they consume content online. Video can come from many sources and reporters need to be on the lookout for third-party footage. Universities, foundations, even police forces can furnish video that can be used to enhance a story. Reporters and editors have to evaluate the pluses and minuses of such video and its source.

Remember that video, a warts-and-all medium, can be intrusive. While reporters should not shy away from news, they need to show the same sensitivity in reporting it with a video camera that they do in other media.

What to shoot

1. Some types of stories just don't lend themselves to video. Focus on the ones that have potential, such as spot stories with compelling images (natural disasters), lots of motion (performances, sport events) or an emotional element in a bigger story (one survivor's version of a tragic event). Slice-of-life or humorous stories, first-person accounts and how-to or how-things-work stories are also prime candidates for feature videos.

2. A-roll is the core of the video — footage of the newsmakers or event itself. Short segments of quality material work better because they can be stitched together. For instance, shoot a couple of interview questions per person only. If you've shot more than that, send only the best to the video editing desk. Unless the visuals are extraordinary, shooting footage for longer than 10 minutes is excessive.

3. B-roll is illustrative footage that is spliced into the primary video to fill out the story. It also gives video editors pictures to run with voiceovers providing key information. A good selection of B-roll is needed. Footage of signs is always useful. Think variety — don't just shoot the TV monitors, but also people looking at the TV monitors. Get people entering and leaving the frame. If police are holding a press conference, shoot the police logo on the wall, the participants coming into or leaving the room and any "props," such as evidence on display. About 15 seconds of each will fill out a report.

4. Try to imagine what a "storyboard" for the piece would look like, then make sure you shoot the building blocks. Just as sentences need pronouns as well as adjectives and nouns to complete a thought, video requires different visual elements to present a story. What would be a compelling opening shot? Is it a close-up of the face of the survivor of a fire? Or a wide shot of the fire itself? Do you have footage of both? Then think through the story to ensure you have enough shots to tell the story. For a story on the flooding of a community, for instance, wide shots that establish the overall scene are needed, as well as closer-up video of a flooded area, perhaps, and then a close-up of particular damage. For an interview with a resident, it is easier to tell the story visually if you get shots of him standing or walking around his flooded basement, as well as close-ups of his face as he talks about the damage.

How to shoot

1. The rule of thirds, popular with artists, is a good one to follow. Imagine lines drawn horizontally and vertically that divide the screen into a tick-tack-toe board, producing a grid of nine boxes. Place the important elements of your shot where these lines intersect rather than smack in the middle of a box. This helps produce pictures that are nicely balanced to the human eye.

2. When shooting someone speaking, get close, although give them space in front of their face. Videos viewed online are relatively tiny and it can be hard to see people who are far away. Keep the camera at eye level — the positioning of the camera may accidentally add bias. The speaker's shoulders and face should fill the frame and the eye line should be in the top third of the frame. If it is lower, the name tags that go on the bottom of the frame will chop off the person's mouth.

3. Shoot with light facing your subject, not coming from behind her back. The light should illuminate her face. Ask the subject to move if necessary.

4. Keep the camera steady. One way to do this is to keep your elbows tucked in to your sides, or lean against something.

5. For B-roll, move around to get different points of view, which creates much more interesting video. Shoot a variety of angles — high, low, wide, tight. Hold the camera above your head at a wide angle setting. Stand on a chair or table to get a high shot of a group of people. Put the camera close to the ground to get dramatic shots of people's feet or traffic passing by.

6. If using a basic point-and-shoot camera, do not zoom while recording. Get physically closer to what you want to shoot and resume shooting. Or stop recording, zoom, and restart recording.

7. Avoid panning as well — it is tough to watch and tough to edit. Don't move the camera to catch action — let it happen within the frame.

Sound

Most built-in style microphones on cameras do not record audio at an acceptable quality. Ambient noise, from traffic, music or other background sounds, can ruin audio on a clip. Whenever possible, use a separate recording device to get matching audio. The best solution is a camera with an external microphone jack that a mike can be plugged into. If relying on the camera for audio, get as close as possible to the subject who is speaking.

2. If you are shooting one person who is talking into the camera, try plugging a microphone (with a Canadian Press flash) into the audio recording device and ask the interview subject to hold and talk into it. It looks better than having the recording device in the picture.

3. Remember to ask questions that will produce sentences, not one-word (yes, no) answers. Try "command" questions: Tell me why you're here; tell me about your book; tell me what happened. Rephrase the question if you don't get an answer that works. And resist the urge to encourage the speaker with verbal injections like "really" or "yeah." Nod silently instead.

Editing video

Video editing is a language. It can convey meaning or emotion just as the written and spoken word can.

Voiceover scripts

1. If using a voiceover, the script should be focused on context and background, not repeat what the viewer can see in the video. And write to the video — don't make the script longer than the video material.

2. Videos can persist online for more than 24 hours so avoid putting time references in scripts. Use the day of the week instead of today, tomorrow and yesterday.

3. Place names and peoples' names can be put in a tag instead of the script to save time.

4. Break it up — listening to someone talk for a minute or more without pause in a voiceover can quickly become too much. Interrupt long passages of voiceover with interview clips or the natural sound on the video.

5. In the script, mark where there should be breaks so the person recording the voiceover knows where to pause. It also helps the editor figure out which clip goes where.

File or stock footage

1. Identify as file footage any generic or stock material. If the material being re-used illustrates a specific event, include the date, month or day it took place.

2. Video, such as a movie trailer, taken from other sources must be credited.

For movies and TV, the credit should be to the original production company, broadcaster or Canadian distributor. For music videos, credit should be to the artist's record label.

3. Efforts should be made to get material from high-quality sources such as production company or broadcaster websites. YouTube should be a last resort.

4. If video from YouTube is used, credit YouTube and the screen name of the person who posted it. If the name is offensive, credit YouTube only.

The YouTube component should be an element in the video, not the entire video. In most cases, YouTube clips should be used only when they are timely and relate directly to a developing news story. The YouTube clip should not be used in followup videos.

Copyright rules apply to video in the same way as they do to print. See **Sources**, page 25, and **Online news**, page 95.

Visual effects

1. Use **cuts** (from one clip to another) if a series of shots are all happening at the same time at the same place.

2. **Dissolves** (where one image fades smoothly into another one) are an excellent tool, but should not be overused. Too many dissolves can slow down the pace and reduce the energy of a sequence. Dissolves are best saved for significant jumps in time or place or if two back-to-back shots look jumpy as a cut and there is no additional shot to put in between. They are also a good bridge when moving from a still photograph to a live action sequence; otherwise, the move can be jarring. The standard duration for dissolves is 12 frames.

3. **White flash** transitions, which are a rapid dissolve to and from a white frame, work well when jumping from place to place in a news roundup from across the country or around the world, or when making huge leaps in time or showing something radically out of sequence. Don't use them to get in and out of interview clips.

4. **Fade-through-black**, where the screen slowly turns black, conveys a sombre, slow-paced mood, the opposite of a white flash. Use sparingly when the subject matter is appropriate, such as a funeral.

Video manipulation, music, special effects

1. The Canadian Press does not manipulate video footage or audio in a way that might mislead viewers. Beyond routine adjustments for brightness or contrast, video images should not normally be altered.

2. Audio and video should always relate to one another. For example, file audio should not be used with fresh footage to make up for the fact that new sound is not available.

3. Music is not usually appropriate in a news video unless it is part of the story. Sometimes music can be used in a lighter or playful feature piece. Special effects, such as highlighting certain parts of the screen with colour, can be used in some non-news videos. Check with a supervisor before adding music or special effects.

Captions, headlines, snapshots

Videos are filed with three other elements: **headlines, captions** and **snapshots**. The headline (no more than eight words) and caption (around 40 words) entice website readers to click on the video. They should reflect the actual content of the clip. The snapshot is a screen grab from the video showing a representative scene or person. It will be displayed in a small size so the image must be clear — the simpler the better. Try to use someone's face or a scene with one familiar object, not one with many elements.

Raw audio

The tearful plea of a mother begging abductors to return her daughter.

Police officers shooting a confused man with Tasers as he asks for help.

The solemn ramp ceremony as the latest soldier killed in Afghanistan is returned to Canada.

These are all compelling images in themselves that need no voiceover or fancy editing techniques. It doesn't matter if the camera is moving or not always in focus or if the sound is muffled. Such powerful content offsets technical inadequacies. Always be on the lookout for raw video clips that tell a story.

Work and the workplace

General

Most people spend more of their waking hours at work than at anything else, including time for friends, family or leisure. They can have strong opinions about work.

That's one of the factors that make reporting on work and the workplace so demanding. There are many other complications that increase the need for care in maintaining accuracy and fairness.

For instance, relations between employee and employer, between labour and management, tend to be complex and sensitive.

Workers go through periods of great ambition and satisfaction and swings of unproductiveness and discontent. They are often part of a business or profession that can boom one year and go bust the next.

And they are an increasingly transient and adapting force. Where a generation ago someone had a lifelong career, today workers can expect to have two or more different careers, sometimes at the same time.

That means workers, and people seeking work, must be thoughtfully portrayed.

The workforce

1. Although contract disputes provide the most drama, coverage of work needs to go far beyond the union-shop floor. A majority of the workforce is not unionized.

2. Technology has increasingly meant that many employees cannot or do not end their work day at a specific time. BlackBerrys, wireless networking and a host of other communications technology also allow many workers to create a virtual workplace far from the physical location of their employer. Increasingly, work has moved offshore or far from head office. Do not assume that a company's workforce is located in one building.

3. There has been steady growth in the number of term contract employees — people hired for a specific function for a specific period of time. They are often paid a lump sum in lieu of benefits or pensions.

4. Whether it's the effects of contract work or the legacy of the "downsizing" phenomenon of the past few decades, today's employees are less likely to stay with the same employers for their entire careers.

The workplace

1. If the nature of labour is changing, so is the nature of management. Experts say more duties are being delegated, more decisions are being made by workers and more ideas are working their way up to the boardroom from the office or factory floor.

2. Consultation between workers and managers is becoming more common. The *us-against-them* approach is slowly breaking down, and partnerships among business, labour and governments in industrial and professional risk-taking have begun to appear. *Interest-based bargaining*, where employers and unions focus on developing mutually beneficial agreements based on their interests, is replacing *positional bargaining*, where each side starts with opposing viewpoints and one side must compromise to reach an agreement.

3. These changes in turn produce other changes in traditional practice. Workers make concessions on salaries in exchange for bonuses tied to performance. Managers make concessions on professional leaves even if that creates short-term expertise problems.

Coverage of news about work and the workplace has to reflect such changes.

But even when covering more traditional union-management situations, the goal should be perspectives that are tied to human beings: how someone is making ends meet during a strike; how a local merchant is coping with a lockout; the effect of multinational ownership on labour relations in a Canadian town.

Conditions of work

The basic document governing conditions for employees and workers in un-ion-ized plants and offices is the contract. Non-unionized workers generally live under more casual arrangements. Complicated economic times bring complex work arrangements that require careful, clear explanations.

Some general guides:

1. **Wages:** In contracts, always compare the previous basic or average wage with the new rate, using a recognizable job (a bricklayer in the construction industry, a production line employee in an auto plant, a senior reporter at a newspaper). When wage changes vary according to the job category, the range should be specified.

When using percentage changes in wage stories, always use actual examples of change. And compare like elements: report a $50 weekly increase in a $700 weekly salary, not a 50-cent hourly increase in an $800 weekly salary. Beware of baldly totalling percentage increases. An increase of 10 per cent now and 10 per cent next year is not a 20 per cent increase; compounded, it is 21 per cent. Don't make readers do math.

2. **Dates:** In contract stories, spell out the starting date to indicate how much retroactivity is involved in a contract settlement. Spell out the dates of further changes in the contract during its identified full term. Don't say a new contract gives workers $4 an hour more, when in fact it gives $2 now and $2 in two years' time.

3. **Inflation protection:** Mention when wage arrangements provide for additional increases if inflation is a specified rate, commonly called **indexation** or a **cola (cost-of-living-allowance) clause**, terms to be avoided except in quotes and to be explained no matter what.

4. **Job protection:** Summarize measures that shield workers from unemployment, including advance notice of layoffs or plant closings, guaranteed payments for those laid off, retraining programs, pension protection and offers of corporate trans-fers to other communities.

5. **Worker concessions:** In contract stories, summarize changes that might limit strikes or other activities to protest work conditions, or agreements to limit salary increases in order to protect jobs or increase the workforce.

6. **Non-monetary issues:** Contracts are often fought over conditions of work, including the flexibility of work hours, the ability of workers to curtail their work hours or to share jobs, the amount of continual worker training a company will provide, or health and safety issues.

These should be highlighted as interesting elements for readers with similar or contracted jobs. When estimates of the value of these benefits are carried, the source of the estimate must be given: **The company says the new child-care provisions are worth $100 a week per employee.**

When neither workers nor companies mention these aspects of a contract, try to get the information independently.

Labour organizations and affiliations

Unions are grouped in national and regional groups but have a large measure of autonomy within them.

The largest federation in Canada is the **Canadian Labour Congress,** with more than three million members. A majority of the national and international unions in the country belong to the congress. Affiliated secondary bodies include all provincial and territorial federations and more than 100 district labour councils. CLC headquarters is in Ottawa.

People are members of the CLC only through their affiliated unions. In most provinces, such unions are grouped in provincial federations — the Saskatchewan Federation of Labour, for example. CLC unions also maintain district labour councils in most urban areas.

Large unions in Canada, especially those spread over a wide area, are usually broken down into locals. The biggest unions include the *Canadian Union of Public Employees, the National Union of Public and General Employees, the National Automobile, Aerospace, Transportation and General Workers Union of Canada* (formal name for *Canadian Auto Workers*), the *United Food and Commercial Workers International Union* and the *United Steelworkers of America.*

Note: When writing about a union that has a French name only, avoid using the French name unless the story requires it. Paraphrase the nature of the membership — a **Quebec civil servants union** — rather than invent a capitalized English name.

Union membership

Specific terms describe the various forms of union membership.

Closed shop: an employer may only hire people who are members of the union.

Union shop: an employer may select employees but all are obliged to join the union within a specified time.

Maintenance of membership: employees must retain membership for the duration of the contract.

Open shop: employees are free to join or not join a union. Workers who don't join are commonly called **free riders**, a term to avoid.

Rand formula: named after Justice Ivan Rand, who arbitrated a 1945 Ford strike. It requires all members of a bargaining unit to pay union dues but makes membership in the unit voluntary.

Checkoff: The employer acts as a collecting agent for a union by deducting dues from the employee's pay.

Laws and courts

Labour relations in Canada are divided into federal and provincial jurisdictions, each governed by a labour code.

The Canada Labour Code covers employees of federally chartered companies like banks, Crown corporations and those in such regulated businesses as transportation and communications that have interprovincial dealings. Provincial codes cover all others.

The federal code is enforced by the Canada Industrial Relations Board, a quasi-judicial body that investigates and rules on union accreditations and violations of the code, such as illegal strikes and lockouts, unfair labour practices and inter-union membership raids.

Similar bodies exist in the provinces. Such functions in Quebec are filled by a labour court.

Federal civil servants are governed by the Public Service Staff Relations Board and disputes are regulated by a special act.

Conciliation

When the federal government intervenes in a dispute, there are several stages:

Stage 1: A **conciliator** is appointed who tries to get the sides talking.

Stage 2: A **conciliation commission**, often the original conciliator, is next appointed. The commission studies the issues and, unless it is felt the sides are too far apart for agreement, writes suggestions for a settlement.

Stage 3: A **mediator** goes back and forth to the parties and tries to craft a report for a vote by management and union membership.

Stage 4: An **arbitrator** can be brought in to devise a binding settlement. Arbitrators are also used in grievance procedures and, on occasion, for contract negotiations.

Provincial governments intervene in different ways, and a reporter covering a dispute under provincial jurisdiction should be aware of specific procedures that apply.

Strikes and lockouts

Strikes are the cessation of work to press the workers' position. **Lockouts** are the closure of all or part of an establishment to counter a work slowdown, to gain concessions from workers or to resist their position. Always distinguish between the two.

Stories should make clear the reasons for the dispute, how long the strike or lockout has been in effect and the number of employees involved.

Reporters should seek out the human elements when strikes or lockouts occur. There are economic consequences from a prolonged dispute for both the workers and their industry, and occasionally there are moments of violence and high drama. Less well explored are the psychological impacts for healthy workers to be away from their jobs and for managers to be in open conflict with employees.

Vocabulary

Labour-management reporting is loaded with euphemisms and pejoratives, so tread warily.

1.   People are not **terminated** and workforces are not **downsized** or **consolidated**. People are **laid off** or **fired** and

workforces are **cut**. (Avoid the term **cutbacks**. It's simply **cuts**.) Always say whether layoffs are temporary or permanent.

2.   Employees are not **engaged in study sessions** or job actions. They have **stopped work** or **slowed work**.

3. **Scab**, a term used since 1777 for a worker who refuses to join a strike or who takes over the work of strikers, is permissible only in direct quotes; even so, use with discretion. **Strikebreaker** is a vague, rarely accurate term — a strike is seldom broken by the hiring of people to replace striking workers. A more accurate term — even though it doesn't reflect the hostility of strikers that can accompany such hiring — is **replacement worker**. In Quebec, companies are forbidden to hire outside workers to do the jobs of strikers.

4. Avoid **company offer** and **union demand**. **Proposal** and **counter-proposal** are neutral terms.

5.   A **picket**, borrowed from the military term for a small body of soldiers on guard duty, is a force of workers stationed outside an establishment to dissuade customers or workers from going in. A **sympathy picket** involves people outside the bargaining unit joining in. A **demonstration picket** is a temporary form of protest by workers about employment conditions or bargaining talks. An **electronic picket** involves a striking union tying up all incoming lines to an establishment relying on telephones for business.

Avoid the term **honour a picket line**. It implies some legal obligation which may not exist. Report that someone or some group **refused** or **declined to cross a picket line**. Similarly, do not write that pickets **barred access** to a struck establishment unless someone was actually prevented from entering.

6.   Avoid the term **union bosses**. Union leaders in some cases may not legally order members to walk off the job. Strike decisions and executive appointments in unions depend by law on a majority vote of union members or of members present and voting at a union meeting.

7. A **wildcat strike** is a strike for which union leaders disclaim responsibility. It is not an **illegal strike**, which comes when workers leave their jobs when under contract, strike when they are legally prevented from doing so, or continue a strike when they have been ordered back to work by a court.

8. A number of specialist terms deal with workforce reduction. **Attrition** involves reduction through normal retirement, leaves of absence and resignation. A **buyout** involves a company offer to pay special compensation — improved pension, generous severance or the like — to employees who will retire early or quit. In some cases, if attrition or a buyout doesn't achieve the desired workforce reduction, **layoffs** would be the next step. But a buyout is not a layoff.

World news

Canadians play an active role in world affairs: as soldiers in trouble spots, diplomats advancing Canada's objectives abroad, business people getting a share of the global market. The Canadian Press gives the Canadian angle due attention in the flow of international news.

A Canadian soldier pats a boy on the head during a visit to a refugee camp in Kabul, Afghanistan, in 2003. News photographers and reporters travelling abroad can bring home stories that are of particular interest to Canadians.

(THE CANADIAN PRESS/Tom Hanson)

The Canadian Press has an exclusive relationship with The Associated Press to cover much of the world. AP, the world's largest news agency, offers a comprehensive report but its stories are not written with a Canadian readership in mind. Canadian reporters abroad and their editors back in Canada are more likely to notice parallels of interest to Canadian readers. They can make foreign developments understandable in Canadian terms.

So when there is a Canadian angle to hit, The Canadian Press prefers to send its own reporters or chase the Canadian elements from its own desks and laptops. There is also a Canadian Press correspondent in Washington and a bureau in Kandahar, Afghanistan, where Canadian fighting troops are stationed. These efforts add a Canadian dimension

At the same time, it is important to ensure that Canada's influence on the international stage is seen in the proper context. For example, the activities of the Canadian delegation at a major international conference are certainly worth reporting in detail, but a balanced story should contain the most important overall developments spearheaded by other countries at the conference. A complete world report includes stories on how other nations try to solve issues that Canadians also face. A report on how problems such as health care, pollution and taxation are handled abroad can provide Canadians with fresh alternatives to ponder. And in the same way that Canada isn't just Mounties and snow, other countries are more than the stereotypes for which they are known.

Foreign reporting

Before you go

Depending on your assignment, and the conditions in the country you are travelling to, there can be lots of work before you ever leave Canada. Some issues you will need to consider:

Medical: A travel clinic can ensure you have the appropriate vaccinations. A medical exam — note your blood type — is also recommended if the assignment is going to be fairly long.

Documents: Ensure your passport is current; check visa requirements. Get extra passport photos for visa and other uses. If your assignment involves working or living with the Canadian Armed Forces, ensure all necessary documents they require are completed.

Gear: Ensure all equipment and other gear is in full working order. Make sure you understand how everything works. Practise everything well before your departure date — not the night before! If you are not sure how to dress or what to take, ask others who have been on similar assignments.

Background: Do some research about the country or countries you are going to. If it is a war zone, educate yourself on such issues as military organization, ranks and the like and how to protect yourself in a hostile environment.

Money: In many countries, you can visit a bank machine or use your credit card if you run low on cash. In some countries, you will have to bring all the cash you need with you. If this is the case, make a plan for transporting it. Money belts are available at travel stores. Don't pack it in your checked baggage. Familiarize yourself with how to receive money via Western Union or another such agency.

Packing: Do not overpack. You don't want to be tied down with luggage when news breaks. For most assignments, you should be able to easily carry all your own gear. And luggage gets lost. Don't pack vital medications, work gear or money in your checked baggage.

Reporting from a war zone

Every assignment is different. However, there are certain common themes if you find yourself reporting from a war zone. The following tips are provided by Canadian Press reporters who have worked in Afghanistan covering the Canadian military.

1. Always travel with a couple of telephones and basic reporting gear. As technology gets more and more complex, you can still accomplish a lot with a telephone, paper and pen.

2. Military personnel will encourage you to cover aspects of their mission that are particularly good public relations. Evaluate each trip based on the risk you will take versus the potential story value.

3. Covering the army outside camp can be as simple as a day patrol in an armoured vehicle to hand out aid or as intense as a two-week hike in the mountains. Often trips will take you to forward operating bases or FOBs — basic camps with outhouse toilets, sometimes cots and a few extra supplies. It's not luxury. It's wise to bring your own toilet paper and hand sanitizer. For filing, forward bases sometimes have electrical generators but your most frequent source of electricity is the standard electrical plug-ins found in the back of Light Armoured Vehicles, or LAVs. Bring a small extension cord or power bar. And keep your batteries charged — you never know when that plug-in will be the last you see for awhile.

4. On any overnight trip, bring your computer and transmitting gear. A two-day trip can easily turn into a week when you are with the military.

5. Time "outside the wire" follows the old cliché of 99 per cent boredom, one per cent sheer terror. When the one per cent kicks in, you may react with paralysis or the overwhelming desire to run. Be on your toes and stay calm. Follow the soldiers and do what they say. Their training should get you through.

The female perspective

Female correspondents face an added challenge reporting from a country where customs prevent women from appearing in public with uncovered heads and western-style dress. Many men in these countries may never have seen the hair or uncovered face of a woman to whom they're not related. You will be stared at constantly.

It is a good idea to adopt local clothing styles, up to and including a burka. They are hot and obstruct your vision, but can give you freedom to roam that you wouldn't have otherwise. Less restricting and usually acceptable in a Muslim country is a shalwar kameez, including headscarf, which will cover your arms and upper body.

Fixers

Working with a fixer — a local citizen who speaks the language, understands the customs and can drive you around — can be frustrating at times, but he is also a reporter's lifeline to the civilian population. Writing stories that reflect the reality of ordinary people living in a war zone is probably the most difficult part of the assignment. Fixers can make it happen.

Back to reality

Every person who goes on assignment to a war zone has a different experience. Some reporters end up in combat. Others rarely get a chance to leave the base. Many have both experiences on the same tour. The time is stressful, whether they are directly touched by violence or not.

Some people feel an extraordinary energy boost from being in a combat zone. Be aware that coming down from that high can make the adjustment to ordinary life very difficult. Your friends, family and colleagues may not understand. A few days of decompression on neutral ground can help you find an even keel.

Professional counselling can be helpful. You don't need to be waking up with night sweats or diving under tables at every loud noise to benefit from this help. It may be as simple as discussing a strategy to readjust to covering B-grade politicians in your town.

Chasing world news from a desk

The phone is also a prime tool in tracking down news involving Canadians abroad. Some tips:

1. Make calls early in a breaking story. Interview subjects are usually talkative within the first few hours of major news. After that window of opportunity, many clam up on their own or officials put up roadblocks. And you avoid the problem of media fatigue by the subject.

2. Operators can be a tremendous source of help. When calling overseas, identify yourself and explain the urgency of your call. If the operator is not very helpful or not willing to stay on the line, ask for a supervisor.

3. If you know the name of the contact, always make a person-to-person call. With the meter running, person-to-person may end up saving money — and ensures the operator stays with you.

4. Remember when calling abroad that almost anyone you reach is likely to know more about the country and its information sources than you do. Ask them who they would call if they were trying to get the information you need. And always ask the person you've managed to contact for the names and numbers of anyone else who might also be able to help.

5. Sometimes, it helps to be a human being first — and a journalist second. When you are the first person to reach the horrified Canadian teenager who has just been caught in a gang shootout in Mexico, offer to call her parents and let them know she's OK. That can also be a good way to get to the folks at home for some comments.

6. If your subject is reluctant to talk, explain why the information is important or try to empathize, ask how they're coping and make a joke if appropriate. A laugh can be a great equalizer. This is particularly important when talking to newsmakers who are thousands of kilometres away. You may not get another chance to interview them.

7. When calling an embassy after hours, make sure the security guard (who usually answers) understands that it's an urgent news media call and the ambassador or other senior staff should be alerted. If there's a delay, leave a number you can be reached at, collect.

8. Once you've established a reliable and helpful contact during an ongoing story, let them know you'll be checking in often. Leave them numbers so they can get in touch with you about new developments.

9. The Internet and email are invaluable tools to communicate with newsmakers and correspondents abroad and overcome time-zone barriers. Keep such messages clear and concise to avoid misunderstandings arising from unintended distortions in the meaning of the written word.

Editing world news

1. Keep in mind the changing complexion of Canada's population. Most newcomers now come from countries outside the traditional European sources of immigrants. Slang once commonly understood among people from Britain, for example, may be indecipherable to new immigrants from another part of the world.

2. Stories from abroad can refer to local currency figures if it serves a purpose, such as to add colour or a regional flavour to copy. The U.S. dollar is widely used in international transactions and most Canadians know roughly how much it is worth. There is no need to uniformly convert all U.S. dollar references into their Canadian equivalent — do the conversion only when it is needed to enhance understanding of the story.

➤ See **Foreign currencies,** page 52.

3. Keeping the news report free of legal problems presents special challenges for editors. U.S. libel laws, for example, permit the reporting of statements that would be dangerous in Canada. Check with a supervisor or legal counsel before releasing doubtful material. Kill any story found to be dangerous. Withhold any story that has given rise to legal questions.

➤ See **Legal,** page 215.

Writing for broadcast

Good broadcast writing shares many of the same traits as writing for print. The differences all relate to the fact it will be heard, rather than read.

Paint a picture

The demonstration turned ugly after the first rock was thrown. People in balaclavas knocked over a fence and set fire to some garbage cans. Then police jumped on a young protester, pinned him down and dragged him away screaming. Now, officers in riot gear are advancing on the protesters, pounding their shields with batons in an intimidating beat. Tear gas fills the air. Other protesters are dropping their signs and fleeing. Some trip and fall.

Good broadcast writers paint pictures with words, in concise, everyday language, putting the viewer or listener at the scene.

There's nothing magic about broadcast writing. It's a craft, and like every other craft, the more you work at it, the better you get. Think of the suggestions and examples in this chapter as guidelines, not rules. Strict adherence to rules can result in stale, formulaic writing.

Leads

The first line of a story should catch the ear of the listener or viewer and make her want to find out more.

Residents of Buffalo, New York, who wanted a white Christmas got their wish, and a whole lot more.

The listener, intrigued, learns more about the extraordinary snowstorm in the next line.

The city has been whacked by a storm that has dumped 40 centimetres of snow.

Leads in broadcast journalism should be short and punchy. Don't try to cram in all the facts. To determine the lead, ask yourself "What about this story grabs my attention?" And then "How does this story affect people?"

The soulful voices of a choir and notes from a mighty pipe organ fill the cavernous Notre Dame Basilica as a nation honours the late Pierre Trudeau.

Make sure, though, that for the sake of cleverness, you don't bend the facts.

It's a budget that's big on security. The federal government will spend 7.7 (b) billion dollars over five years on new security programs.

Long identifications bog down a lead. The following one looks better on paper than it sounds. Read it aloud.

U-S Environmental Protection Agency on-scene co-ordinator Richard Rupert says poisonous gas pumped into the Hart Senate office building appears to have killed any remaining anthrax spores.

Break up the information into two or more sentences and shorten the lengthy title.

It appears all the anthrax has been removed from a U-S government building. Richard Rupert of the Environmental Protection Agency says preliminary tests suggest the fumigation of the Hart Senate building was successful.

If you want to use an attribution in the lead, use the person's occupation, then state his title in the next sentence.

A U-S environment official says it appears all the anthrax has been removed from a government building. Richard Rupert, the Environmental Protection Agency's on-scene co-ordinator, says preliminary tests suggest the fumigation of the Hart Senate building was successful.

Incomplete sentences work in broadcasting, especially as leads. But don't overdo it.

A terrible tragedy on the roads of eastern Quebec. Provincial police say several people have been killed in a crash on Highway 185 near Degelis (DAY - zhay - lee).

To tie two or more stories together, try "umbrella" leads. But make sure there are comparisons to be made and it isn't a stretch to tie them together.

There have been political upsets on both coasts tonight.

or

Weather is causing chaos in different parts of the country.

Don't mix metaphors.

Another war of words is brewing.

And avoid cliches **(war of words)**. Strive to find more original ways of expression. Avoid general leads **(The finance minister has presented his budget)** and unimaginative ones (It's back to the bargaining table for the two sides in the civic workers' labour dispute).

Avoid quotes as leads because the listener can't tell whether you're making the statement or quoting someone else. An exception can be made for famous quotes — **"We shall never surrender"** or **"...one small step for man, one giant leap for mankind"**, which are immediately recognized by most listeners.

In some cases, attributions must be made in the lead, even if it takes away a bit of the punch. The listener may be left with the impression that the lead is a statement of fact rather than someone else's conclusion:

The movie industry is doing a good job, but retailers and the recording industry need to do better. That, according to a followup report by the U-S Federal Trade Commission following last year's critical assessment of the entertainment industry's marketing practices.

Do not assume listeners are as up to date as you on names in the news. Some people are indisputably well known. Most are not. (Describing someone as well known or famous often means they aren't.)

Question leads often work with lighter stories, but can become tiresome if overused.

Remember the 12-hundred pound man who got wedged in the doorframe of his house last fall? Well, he's been on a diet.

In this age of swift communications, reaction to a major story often comes quickly, before many have heard the big news. While a reaction may seem like a strong fresh lead after you've written the main story for the past four newscasts, think it over carefully. Some stories are so big you have to let the basic facts remain on top for several hours. The night Diana, Princess of Wales, died in 1997, reporters were gathering reaction the moment the story broke. However, the death itself remained the lead for many hours because of its impact and also because it happened late at night on a summer weekend and many people didn't hear the news until the following morning.

Make each word count

News broadcasting is a constant battle against the stopwatch. Every word must count. You quickly learn it's a lot harder to tell a story in few words than in many.

The essential elements of all news stories can usually be summed up in one sentence. The rest is detail, context and colour.

The key to paring down your story is to get to the heart of the matter. The best way to do this is to pretend you're telling someone you know what has happened. When you do this, you are doing two things — boiling down the story to its key elements **and** telling it in your own words in plain, conversational English. All broadcast writing should be conversational because you're writing for the ear. Unlike newspaper readers, listeners can't check what you just said.

It's critical to understand the story before you write it. All stories must answer the five Ws (who, what, when, where and why) and how. If you have questions, the listener likely will too. If you're rewriting copy, write from the original, not from a rewrite, to avoid misinterpretation.

Try to restrict each sentence to a single thought. Cram too much information in the sentence and you lose the listener. As well, long sentences are difficult to read aloud.

A good way to keep sentences short is to eliminate wordy phrases. Say **charged** instead of **charged in connection with**, **because** instead of **due to the fact that**, **violated** rather than **in violation of**.

Trim titles as much as possible. It's **finance minister** instead of **minister of finance**, and **A-B-C Company official John Smith** instead of **A-B-C Company vice-president of exports and imports John Smith**.

Bringing life to your copy

News stories are about people. Listeners and viewers want to know how events affect them and others. A newswriter's job is to make information interesting. A well-written story will always make it to air before a factually correct, but poorly written, one does.

Use colourful, descriptive language. Be specific about what you see. Dramatize — but don't embroider.

Panicked demonstrators. Air clogged with tear gas. Screams of rage.

Its immediacy gives broadcast journalism the edge over other media. Therefore, it's imperative to use the latest information. Check with your sources on an unfolding story before heading to air. Has the legislation passed as expected? Has the plane landed? Has the death toll changed? Be sure your audience gets the latest details.

Avoid dating a story by putting **yesterday** in the lead. If you're writing about an event that happened yesterday, freshen the story with reactions or an idea of what's expected to happen next.

Always write in the active voice. It gives the story a sense of immediacy. We speak in the active voice, so it's a natural for broadcast writing.

Not: The signs are being dropped by the fleeing protesters.

But: The protesters are dropping their signs and fleeing.

Write in the present tense, but don't sacrifice accuracy to make a story sound current. It's **The Queen will visit Ottawa this morning** until her plane lands. Then, it's **the Queen has arrived in Ottawa** or **The Queen is in Ottawa**.

Write the way you speak. Say **Jane Doe has been dropped from cabinet** rather than **dropped from cabinet is Jane Doe**.

Be careful of word order.

Not: The Queen had several children for breakfast.

But: The Queen had breakfast with several children.

Don't be afraid of repeating the word "says" in broadcast copy, because that's the way we speak. There are some acceptable alternatives — **states, maintains, notes, points out, adds, asserts, claims** — but be cautious. If you say someone claims something, that casts doubt on his statement. If someone notes something, that makes her statement true. If someone admits something, it implies a confession. On the other hand, if someone is speculating on or predicting something, spell it out.

Candidate Jane Doe predicts she'll defeat the incumbent in the election.

Be consistent in sentence structure.

Not: The farmers say the best policy is to impose tariffs on imports and encouraging consumers to buy Canadian.

But: The farmers say the best policy is to impose tariffs on imports and to encourage consumers to buy Canadian.

Beware of descending into bad taste. Reporting on deaths or serious injury is not the time to be using cute turns of phrase. Never trivialize death. Also, eliminate unnecessary references to race, sex or religion. And think twice before including gory details or vulgarity.

Don't raise questions that you don't answer. For example, if you're writing that something is second on a list, make sure you mention what's first.

Always back up your facts unless whatever is being stated is obviously true. **The suspect was carrying weapons and heroin when he was arrested** needs a source. **The stock market sank 200 points today** does not. Also, unlike newspaper style, make sure your attribution is at the beginning of a sentence, not at the end.

Do not assume what a newsmaker is feeling.

Not: The community activist is furious about the tax cuts.

But: Pounding the podium, the community activist shouted that the tax cuts hurt the poor.

Avoid using an entire sentence for attribution.

Not: Jim Robinson is the manager of the liquid waste plant. He says if it weren't safe, he wouldn't work there.

Better: Manager Jim Robinson says if the liquid waste plant weren't safe, he wouldn't work there.

Don't generalize. If one person on the street in Halifax laments the lack of snow at Christmas, that doesn't become **People in Halifax are unhappy about their green Christmas.** Refrain from jumping to conclusions. A reduction in the number of drunk driving charges over the Christmas holiday doesn't necessarily mean fewer people are driving while impaired. It could mean fewer drivers were stopped and checked by police.

Numbers, dates, time elements

Numbers can be confusing in a broadcast story.

Not: Last year, U-S police reported 5.5 homicides for every 100,000 population, triple the Canadian rate of 1.8.

Better: Last year the homicide rate was three times higher in the United States than in Canada.

Express large numbers in ways listeners can relate to.

Two-million people live in an area about the size of Vancouver Island.

Be general about dates. It's easier to understand **John Doe will appear in court next Thursday** than **John Doe will appear in court January 16th.** Instead of saying **the strike began November 3rd** say **the strike began three weeks ago.**

Time elements usually come after the verb.

The commission announced last Tuesday it's starting cross-country hearings.

"Midnight" needs clarification. If you say taxes are due to be mailed no later than midnight on Wednesday, that's technically first thing Wednesday morning. But many listeners would think that's Wednesday night. It's best to spell it out.

Taxes must be mailed before midnight Tuesday night.

Or

Taxes must be mailed by 11:59 p-m Tuesday.

Direct quotes

Avoid direct quotes unless they add something to the story that would be lost if the statement were paraphrased.

The prime minister admits the issue has caused a rift among some Liberal leadership candidates. But in his words, "It's democracy, you don't want to vote for a pussycat."

Quotes with "I" in them rarely work because they sound like the newscaster is talking about himself.

Words to watch

None is a word that often causes confusion. Does it take a singular or plural verb? The rule of thumb is to use a plural verb when **none** stands for **not any**, but a singular verb if what you mean is **not one**.

None of the people on board were Canadian.

Ten climbers have tried but none has succeeded.

Anybody, anyone, another, anything, each, either, every, everybody, everyone, many a, neither, no one, nobody, somebody and someone take a singular verb.

Be consistent. If something is singular — for example the jury — don't later refer to the jury as they. If you need to use the word they to get your sentence to make sense, start out by calling those on the jury the jury members.

Keep the article (a, an, or the) when writing about a series of things.

The area has been devastated by an earthquake, a hurricane and a tsunami.

Compared to and compared with are tricky. When comparing two like things, use compared to. Use compared with when showing similarities or differences.

He compares the two countries to brothers who sometimes argue.

The company's profits are down four per cent compared with last year.

Excessive alliteration can get you in trouble.

Sea Shepherd Conservation Society spokesman Sandy Smith says the "Sea Shepherd Two" will set out today.

This is hard on the ear — and hard on the newscaster who has to say it.

Avoid the word respectively as it can be confusing in broadcast copy.

Not: Jones and Smith won three-million and two-million dollars respectively.

But: Jones won three-million dollars and Smith won two-million.

Eliminating that can improve the flow of a sentence. Compare:

He says the winters are growing steadily warmer and He says that the winters are growing steadily warmer. The first sentence has a better flow when spoken.

But that has its place. Throw it in if leaving it out could cause confusion. The Opposition warned the Commons faces chaos unless the bill is changed. Did the Opposition warn the Commons? Or does the Commons face chaos? A simple that would clear it up. The Opposition warned that the Commons faces chaos unless the bill is changed. The most effective way to determine whether that is needed is to read the sentence aloud.

If you end a sentence with a person's name, don't start the next sentence with the same name. It's hard on the ear.

A choir sang as the award was presented to an emotional Fred Smith. Smith wiped tears from his eyes before making his acceptance speech.

Spelling counts

A rookie may think, "Spelling doesn't matter. No one is reading this but me." That's wrong. For one thing, reporters are in the accuracy business and spelling is part of it. Also, the correct spellings of names may be needed for television graphics. And you can no longer assume only you will read your copy. The story you wrote may be used for a web page or as part of news headlines for an electronic billboard.

Editorializing

We all have opinions and biases. Being in the media and absorbing so much information often adds fuel to those fires. But a newscast is not the place to express such feelings and you must be on guard to keep those biases out of copy. If you don't, your credibility will suffer and you will hear from your listeners and viewers, especially those who disagree with you!

The easiest way to keep the copy neutral is to stick to the facts. Report what you see and hear. Let the events speak for themselves.

Remember that words are loaded. The expression "the pen is mightier than the sword" is still relevant today. So choose your words carefully. One person's **nagging** is another's **reminding her of her responsibilities.**

It's **left without taking questions from reporters,** not **sneaked out the back door.**

Be careful when reporting the words of others. Don't report their opinions as fact. If a cabinet minister says: "I'll introduce this desperately needed legislation in the spring session," don't write **The cabinet minister says he'll introduce the desperately needed legislation this spring.** Write **The cabinet minister says he'll introduce what he calls the "desperately needed legislation" this spring.**

Avoid jargon — such as **collateral damage** to describe people killed in war — and officialese — such as **rightsizing** to describe a company's layoffs. These words and phrases take away from your report's objectivity.

➤ See also **Common faults,** page 292; See also **Writing for print,** page 203; See also **Editing for print,** page 54.

Newscasts

Creating a newscast is really all about using your words and your voice to get someone to stop what she's doing and listen to you. Otherwise, you're nothing but background noise.

Rule No. 1 is to use attention-grabbers — words that are active, words that engage. Imaginative, creative words.

Since radio is a highly intimate medium, write and deliver your newscast to just one person — someone you visualize sitting there, listening to you.

You have the power to take that person around the world in a matter of minutes; to make them imagine the sights, scents, and sounds of each and every place.

Where to start

It's your job to determine what's important, what's timely, what's interesting, what's relevant to your audience, what's new. So much to say — so little time.

Be concise in your writing — and clear. Your listener can't go back to figure out what you just said. Put the news event in context, but don't try to squeeze in every fact. Don't use a lot of numbers. What little on-air time you have goes by quickly.

Each hour or half-hour, survey the material at your disposal — local, regional, national and international news.

Each potential item needs to be put through your own subjective filter. It could be a need-to-know story, a good-to-know story or a water-cooler story (one you know will get talked about, not necessarily for its hard-news value, but because it's interesting and fun.)

You may pick 20 or 30 stories, but end up with only eight or 10 in your newscast.

Follow this rule: if the stories you've chosen don't hold your interest, chances are they won't hold your listeners' interest either.

Picking a lead

"What should I lead with this hour?"

That's a question many a newscaster has asked many a time.

The key phrase here is "this hour," because in 60 minutes, there'll be a "next hour" and the news may change dramatically in that time.

What constitutes a lead story? One school of thought says the lead must always be a hard-news story. Perhaps so, if such a story presents itself, and can be told in many ways as it unfolds and develops. But perhaps not . . .

Try this: strive to make your lead the most recent, interesting, informative, compelling, serious, or humorous story you have on hand. Think of it also in terms of sound, so you can transport your listeners to where the news is happening and stimulate their senses with the sights, sounds, and experiences of the people who are actually there.

Lining it up

So, you have your lead. Now you have to think about the rest of the newcast.

Think of your second story as your sub-lead. It could be related to the lead, or have the next best piece of audio. If you can find some way to connect the stories, you will create a good flow. The flow of the cast is just as important as the lead if you want to keep the listener interested.

Using sound

Take stock of what kind of sound is at your disposal. In many instances, sound may determine your lead. Ideally, you would have a blend of sound, combining the words of the reporter, the voice of the newsmaker, and raw sound of the event itself.

If voice reports (voicers) are available, ask yourself: is the story important enough to use a 35-second voicer? If not, you may want to use only part of it. But using audio of the newsmaker is generally preferable because that's whom the story is about. This is especially true in stories where emotions are running high.

Natural sound from an event helps bring the listener to the scene. You can capture the sorrow of a memorial service through music or take your listener to a crowded street where protesters are shouting and choking on tear gas. Radio, remember, is a medium of the imagination.

On major breaking news stories, consider incorporating live broadcasts from your audio service into your newscast, or going live to one of your own reporters.

Kicker versus closer

When it comes to kickers, it's usually feast or famine. Some days there are a million stories — people and animals doing silly, even stupid, things that make us smile or roll our eyes.

Other days, zaniness seems to have taken a holiday. On these occasions, a thought-provoking science or medical story can be just as effective as a kicker in closing your newscast.

Entertainment stories can be used, too. So can weather stories.

Remember, you don't necessarily have to leave 'em laughin'.

Writing to your audience

Variety is the spice of life — and also the essence of putting together a newscast.

Strive to find a newscast that will keep your audience rapt from start to finish. Remember, you've got to be both informative and entertaining. It's not easy.

First of all, you've got to strike the right blend of politics, business, health, lifestyle and entertainment. You've got to juggle local and regional news with national and international stories. And to accomplish this, you've got to keep your copy fresh and choose stories that have relevance.

Understanding your station's demographics will help you determine the relevance of your stories and write them so their relevance is immediately apparent to the listener.

Timing out

Eventually, you will get a feel for how much copy and audio you need to fill your newscast. Some newscasters can tell just by looking at their copy. Others use the word count on their computers.

If your station is automated during some parts of the day, you may find yourself having to time out to the second to catch the start of a satellite program. In that case, it's a good rule to time out your kicker so you know when to start reading it. As you reach the last 30 seconds or so of your newscast, you can still do a couple of one- or two-line stories and be confident you'll get your kicker in.

Writing for print

The first page of an early Canadian Press stylebook had this to say about writing news:

"Every story worth printing can be written for The Canadian Press."

That remains the case, although much about writing news has changed.

No longer is the role of the news writer merely to inform. Readers (call them news consumers, if you like) are bombarded with information.

But what many modern-day messengers fail to provide, whether they are delivering the news over the Internet or on a traditional newsprint page, are context, background, balance and the sights, smells and sounds of the news. Such details tell readers why the news is important and what it means, in terms that strike home.

Newspapers are fighting to attract new readers and hold the ones they have. Readability has always been an issue in the newspaper business, but never more than in today's reality: Fewer people are reading traditional printed newspapers. Those who are reading papers spend less time at it.

Many people do pick up on news via the Internet or a wireless device. But news organizations must compete with the many distractions that lure the reader to other online destinations. To help, reporters and editors must present news stories that are uniformly appealing.

Readability is often tied to sentence length. Sure signs of trouble: too many ideas, too many subordinate clauses.

It's possible to write brightly and clearly in sentences that run to 30 words and more. Possible — but not probable.

Be human

Stories must be human, specific, clear, concise, imaginative and factual.

1. Write about people. Personal words like **father, pilot, nurse, welder** put life into news stories:

> An ice fisherman trudging along the edge of an isolated lake found the wreckage.

> A power failure crippled most of Quebec's electricity network Tuesday afternoon. It left about six million people without heat and light in freezing temperatures.

A five-year-old girl lies with her teddy bear as she is airlifted to a hospital from Walkerton, Ont. She was one of the victims of the tainted water tragedy in the town in 2000. The photo brings a huge news story down to a human scale.

THE CANADIAN PRESS/Kevin Frayer

Look for the human angle in every story: the sheet-metal worker replaced by a robot, the single parent whose rent has doubled, the teller robbed by a gunman with a shaking hand. A roundup on unemployment could open this way:

> Like anyone buying insurance, Donald Good hoped he wouldn't need it. He insured himself last March against being laid off. As it turned out, he did need it.

Put things in real-people terms:

Not: An Alberta provincial court judge has thrown out charges against two men, ruling that the six days they spent in a Camrose jail constituted cruel and unusual punishment.

But: Two young Alberta farmhands were freed from jail after telling a judge their cell had a broken window and was so cold the water pipes to the sink and toilet froze for days on end.

2. Relate the news to the reader's life whenever possible, which is often:

> Airfare negotiations between Canada and the United States broke down Wednesday, dashing the hopes of thousands of travellers for bargain flights over the Labour Day weekend.

> Scientists believe they have detected the deadly chemical dioxin in the lake, but they say the levels appear too low to harm cottagers who drink its water or swim in it.

> The ruling means the plant workers will be eligible to apply for unemployment benefits within a week.

3. Quotes are a vital element that give the story dimension and character. Take pains to choose them carefully, paraphrasing those that merely deliver information and keeping the ones that set the scene, capture the flavour of the news or provide insight:

> Cho, said Violand, began "methodically and calmly shooting people down."
> "It sounded rhythmic, like he took his time in between each shot and kept up the pace, moving from person to person.
> "After every shot I thought: 'OK, the next one is me.'"

> "I've dealt with the Raineys ever since I've been a cop," said Ephraim H. Branton, the affable deputy sheriff of the Lake County police and a 24-year veteran.
> "A lot of 'em came from ol' river rats. I've dealt with 'em on everything from runnin' moonshine to huntin' gators illegal."

4. Perk up stories that are devoid of anything human, except perhaps some unnamed spokesman or official. Season them with examples that bear directly on the lives of readers:

> Just when you thought you had finally caught up with the Joneses, along came Statistics Canada on Tuesday announcing that 1.2 million households have more than one high-definition television.

Be specific

1. Give the reader specific details. Ask yourself: How does this look? Sound? Feel?

> ASTOR, Fla. — Inland from the shimmering beaches and swaying palm trees featured on garish postcards is where many locals say you will find the real Florida.
> Swampy bogs and inky rivers are stealthily patrolled by alligators. Snakes slither across the sun-baked asphalt greased by constant humidity. And every kind of criminal has come here to either ply their trade or escape from the law.

2. Get interesting human nuggets into the lead:

A prison guard killed in the Archambault Penitentiary last July "was looking at pictures of his family and crying like a baby" when convicts burst in on him, a murder trial was told Tuesday.

Carolyn Kay shakes her gnarled, 91-year-old fingers, still bloody from the caribou she's been butchering, as she emphasizes the message she wants taken to hearings on a northern gas pipeline.

This morning they were young offenders, breathing the stale air of jail.
This afternoon they are hunters, zooming over the snowy tundra in snowmobiles and sleds.

3. Paint word pictures:

Not: The accused were overjoyed.

But: The accused kissed and hugged each other.

Not: Candidates often encounter strange things while campaigning for the election.

But: In at least one riding, voter nudity overshadows ferocious dogs, slippery walks or long-winded residents as the greatest test of a candidate's composure.

Not: The MPs showed disgust at a rape scene in one of the censored films.

But: The MPs winced as the Confederate soldiers grabbed and raped a black slave in one of the censored films.

Be clear

1. Always organize the story in your mind before you start writing.

Decide what the news is and put that in your lead. Stories with leads like these stand a good chance of flowing smoothly:

Canada's outgoing Governor General laughed at the notion of a career in politics Thursday while the party that appointed Michaelle Jean five years ago refused to say if it might try to convince her to make a run.

Those on the hunt for student "bookleggers"' trafficking in stolen texts at Canada's universities know the fraudsters come in all shapes and with all kinds of scams.

2. But there are other ways to a reader's heart as well:

> The old Tory tune played in Alberta again on Thursday, but a lot fewer people got up to dance.

> For 40 minutes at least, Joannie Rochette found solace in the soft crunch of her leather boots and the crackle of the ice breaking beneath her blades.
> The Canadian figure skater wiped away tears, took a deep breath and then stepped on the Pacific Coliseum ice, seven hours after receiving the devastating news that her mother and No. 1 fan, Therese Rochette, had died overnight in Vancouver.

> The diapers hold nine cups of fluid, are made of six layers of cotton and micro-fibre, dry in an hour, are reusable and come stylishly in white or burgundy with Velcro closures. A company is advertising them on the Internet, saying they are a perfect fit for "gamblers at all-night casinos."

3. Use plain words, but always the right words. Make it **wicked**, not **nefarious**; **remaining**, not **residual**; **tone down**, not **modulate**.

4. Use specific words when details are useful. Write **hamburger and french fries**, not **food**; **shouting and laughing**, not **making a noise**; **a man of 87**, not **an elderly man**.

Be direct

1. Don't write **a number of cars** if you can say **five cars**; **a six-figure income** if you can say **an income of $415,000**; **a long dry spell** if you can say **37 days without rain**.

2. Don't use lazy terms for unknown quantities that either fail to inform or force the reader to backtrack for more details: **fairly, really, pretty, few, quite, very, this**.

Not: It's been fairly hot in Kandahar lately, but farmers recently received quite a bit of ran.

But: Temperatures in Kandahar topped 42 C last week before the region received more than two centimetres of rain.

Not: Magna's board of directors hasn't recommended how shareholders should vote, as is usually the case in transactions like this.

But: Magna's board of directors hasn't recommended how shareholders should vote, as is usually the case in transactions that involve executive compensation.

3. Translate pompous phrases.

Not: A poor public response.

But: Only a quarter of the tickets were sold.

Not: There is a doctor availability problem in the health delivery system.

But: There are not enough doctors in hospitals and private practice.

4. Avoid putting more than one thought in a sentence. In general, the contents and structure rather than length itself make sentences hard to understand.

Not: Union leader John Dickerson declared, "I have no regrets and would do the same again" as he entered prison Thursday to begin serving a three-month sentence imposed last week for defying the legislature and refusing to call off a strike of civil servants angered by wage rollbacks.

But: Union leader John Dickerson said he had "no regrets and would do the same again" as he entered prison Thursday to begin serving a three-month term.

Dickerson was sentenced last week for defying the legislature and refusing to call off a strike of civil servants angered by wage rollbacks.

5. Beware of too many dependent clauses, especially in mid-sentence where they break the flow. Each clause adds more ideas to the sentence, making it harder and harder to grasp.

Not: The U.S. vice-president flew into Berlin from Bonn, along with the German chancellor, with whom he held talks Monday on disarmament strategy on the first stop of a seven-country tour.

But: The U.S. vice-president flew into Berlin from Bonn on the second stop during his seven-country tour. With him was the German chancellor, with whom he held talks Monday on disarmament.

6. Keep introductory phrases and clauses short and simple.

Not: Noting spirited and repeated suggestions from the floor that the group should press Ottawa for a higher salmon quota for British Columbia fishermen who have complained bitterly about competition from foreign fishing fleets, especially the Japanese and American, but to some extent the Russians, association vice-president Hedley Evansson said ...

But: As for higher salmon quotas, Evansson said ...

7. Sentence length can grow comfortably when the sentence is simply a list of closely linked ideas referring to the same subject:

In the dead stillness of the summer afternoon, when heat waves shimmer, purple clouds gather and echoing thunder heralds the deluge to come, Jamie Holtom is pulled back to the awful day 10 years ago when a tornado wrenched his two-year-old son from his arms and took his boy's life.

Be concise

Keep your story tight in content as well as phrasing. Stick with the truly significant angles. A *full* report can often mean a dull report.

Be aware that a 1,000-word story in standard newspaper print would cover the back of a corn flakes box. Ask if the story would really hold a reader through an entire bowl of cereal.

If a story threatens to run long, consider whether some of the material could be broken out as highlights, a chronology or a point summary.

Clutter chokes meaning. Simplify:

1. Ditch the long word that says no more than the short: **attempt** (try), **approximately** (about), **preponderance** (most), **consequently** (so), **substantiate** (prove), **initiative** (plan).

2. Ditch the laborious phrase: **despite the fact that** (although), **at this point in time** (now), **in the event that** (if), **ahead of schedule** (early), **in the majority of cases** (usually).

3. Ditch ponderous euphemisms and gobbledygook: **correctional facility** (prison), **job action** (strike, slowdown), **depressed socio-economic area** (slum), **in a classroom setting** (in a classroom), **resource centre** (library or lab), **lower rates of infant mortality** (fewer baby deaths).

4. Ditch words that aren't doing any work: **He said** (that) **the cut**(back)**s in** (the) **health care** (field) **have put hospitals in a crisis** (situation).

Next-day stories

Newspapers usually prefer an analytical approach on stories, especially staged news events, as a way to attract readers who are likely to have already heard the facts from last night's TV newscast, a 24-hour news channel or a website headline. Copy for papers must keep alive a story that may have already been reported for more than 24 hours. Take advantage whenever a story's subject matter lends itself to a present-tense or forward-looking approach: **Canada can no longer export goods to Spain**, rather than, **The government imposed export restrictions Tuesday**.

Don't place undue emphasis on minor developments to freshen a story. But do look for a different perspective. For example, on a provincial budget: Were human-interest angles neglected? How will the budget influence the next election? On an important government announcement: can a behind-the-scenes account on how the decision came about be constructed?

The essential details of the news must be covered so it is understandable to readers who may be hearing about it for the first time. If these details are lengthy or complex, they can sometimes be handled in a Quick so they don't burden down a lead that is taking a new approach.

A writing checklist

1. Is the lead right? Does it capture only the most significant angles? Is there secondary information getting in the way of the main points? Is there an appealing human touch or quotation deep in the story that would fit in the first paragraph? Is the time element placed where it falls naturally in speech?

2. Does the writing appeal to a reader's senses? Are there gobs of *officialese*, jargon or abstractions? If so, can they be translated into direct language? The language people use when they're discussing events of the day over dinner?

3. Would a point summary help the reader? With the main news angle covered in the lead, should readers be given a capsule taste of other interesting angles awaiting them lower in the story?

4. Does the story give the reader any sense of where the news happened and how it happened, how people in the immediate area reacted? Did some of the audience start to leave before the speech was over? Did the speaker seem to notice?

5. Is there another side to the story? Is one side buried, throwing the story off balance? If someone whose viewpoint is obviously part of the story was unavailable, does the story say so? When pertinent, does it spell out what efforts were made to reach the unavailable source?

6. Have legally questionable elements in the story been cleared by a lawyer?

7. Is there overattribution? Are all those *he said*s necessary? Does every direct quote need attribution tacked on?

8. How about sentences? Is each sentence limited to one thought or a closely connected range of thoughts? Can a subordinate clause be changed into a sentence to give the reader a clearer path? Are the sentences active? Are inactive verbs adding fat to sentences? Is there an idea that needs explaining? If so, find a way to explain it better. Or could the problem sentence be cut without loss?

9. How about quotes? Could the story be brightened with stronger human voices? In cutting quotes, have the strongest been saved and the weaker sacrificed? Can some quotes be cut because they aren't controversial and don't give any character to the speaker? Is the story sprinkled with fragmented quotes? Is it necessary to say, **He said he was "out of touch"**?

10. Have words been wasted? Can single words replace phrases: **placed under arrest** (arrested), **in the vicinity of** (near), **charged in connection with** (charged), **in the shooting incident** (shooting)?

11. Can shorter or more familiar words be used: **They attempted** (tried) **to expedite** (speed up) **what they perceived** (saw) **as a viable** (workable) **plan?**

12. Has bafflegab been translated? Have **accommodation units** been turned into **houses and apartments;** methods of intercity transportation into **planes, trains, buses and cars;** disadvantaged into **poor; upwardly mobile** into **ambitious?**

13. Does the writing read like normal English? Is any of it unlike anything you would ever say: **the six-foot-eight 290-pound University of Manitoba product;** Paramount vice-president of corporate communications Deborah Rosen?

14. Are there stale expressions? Is the story dulled by clichés: **court was told; 14-hour marathon session; grim-faced delegates?**

15. Do the transitions lead the reader smoothly from one idea to the next? Could a bump between two sentences be removed with an **and, but, meanwhile** or some other transition? Would it help to repeat a key word or phrase from the preceding sentence or paragraph? **This new strategy . . . ?**

16. Is the tone right? Is the writing too formal, slangy or trendy? Has sexist, racist or other tasteless language slipped in?

Legal

Legal

Although this section provides general information on journalism and the law, it is written for Canadian Press editors and reporters and reflects the news agency's needs. The guidelines and policies in this section do not represent an agreed professional standard; nor do they represent the practices of all newspapers. Its main focus is to alert news agency staff to situations that may require advice from legal counsel. It is not a substitute for such advice and should not be used in that way.

Engraved in the memory of every reporter and editor should be:

1. Carelessness and bad judgment on legal questions can ruin people's lives. Every journalist must weigh this responsibility when working.

2. It is dangerous to publish statements that damage a person's reputation or livelihood unless the statements are provably true or unless the law clearly provides a special exemption.

3. It is particularly dangerous to suggest criminal conduct unless it has been proved in the courts.

4. Every person charged and before the courts is entitled to be presumed innocent and to receive a fair trial. It is forbidden to publish anything that passes judgment on an accused or that could hinder a fair trial unless it has been admitted in court as evidence. (Of course, the court's judgment is publishable.)

5. Juveniles involved with the law — accused, witnesses or victims — must not be identified, even indirectly, without legal advice.

6. In cases where legal action is a possibility, or could involve a dispute over what was said, reporters should keep notes, audio tapes and related documents for three months. It's expected that notification of any legal action would be given by that time. Reporters should also note that during examination for discovery they may be required to make available to the court all material related to the story in question — including such things as emails to sources or other versions of the story.

Follow these rules:

1. Check legal authority before writing anything legally doubtful.

2. Cut out anything that looks legally questionable until it can be cleared for use.

3. If legal doubts arise after a story has been distributed, order the story killed or withheld immediately until the doubts can be resolved.

Crime

Reporting on crime

No area of reporting requires greater care than crime.

People's reputations and livelihoods are at stake. Concepts of fairness that are at the core of Canadian democracy come regularly into play.

On the other hand, a justice system that deals effectively with criminals is a legitimate goal of every democracy. And one of the bases of an effective justice system is public scrutiny: the public must see justice being done, if not in person then through the media.

Courtrooms are natural theatres of human drama and good court reporting takes the reader to the heart of the drama — but always with fairness and objectivity in the recording of testimony and the description of witnesses.

Reporters and editors should make themselves familiar with the entire legal section of this stylebook in a general fashion. The subsections are set out in such a way that those working on a specific step in the legal process can refer to the portion dealing with that step. The worst pitfalls are highlighted at the start of each subsection.

However, the law is complex. A stylebook is no substitute for legal counsel on doubtful issues.

Criminal cases

Some general rules:

1. Court reporting must be fair and accurate to be legally protected. Otherwise, the protection is lost. That means straightforward coverage of testimony, even-handed descriptions of accused or witnesses, balance between Crown and defence cases, no plain or implied taking of sides.

2. Coverage must also be contemporaneous. It is risky to report well after the fact on a criminal proceeding, particularly if the accused was acquitted. It can seem like an attempt to blacken the accused's name needlessly. Consult counsel before reporting on an old proceeding.

3. Give the exact charge in a criminal case, not a generality. If the charge is sexual assault, don't write **attack**.

4. Don't refer casually to a defendant's religion, race, political party, profession or other qualification unless it's directly relevant. Beware of categorizing an accused in a way that could reflect on an entire group of people.

5. Identifying alleged victims or other witnesses in sexual assault cases and some other sensitive areas may be banned by the court. Even if not banned, it is usually wrong to identify alleged victims of sexual assault without their active consent. Always consult a supervisor if an exception is being considered.

6. In important cases, provide the possible penalty, but also mention that the maximum penalty is rarely imposed and prison terms are rarely served in full.

7. When substantial prison terms have been imposed, specify promptly how much time must be served before parole can be considered.

8. Don't total concurrent sentences (**sentenced to a total of 120 years**). Report the individual sentences on various charges and the actual maximum prison term.

9. Don't attempt to pull together two or more court cases into one story unless they were linked in court. Such natural linkages are rare anyway, but on days when a number of parallel cases are going on in different courts — say, concerted disturbances by activists — publishing a roundup can risk influencing a sitting jury or potential jurors.

Some general background:

1. Criminal offences are generally of two types, **summary conviction** (less serious) and **indictable** (more serious). Some offences such as theft under $1,000 may be prosecuted either summarily or by indictment, at the discretion of the Crown.

2. Summary conviction offences are dealt with in a streamlined procedure under which the accused goes directly to trial without a preliminary hearing. Examples include causing a disturbance, indecent exhibition in a public place or being found in what are called **common gaming-houses** or **bawdy-houses**.

3. Summary conviction offences are tried by a justice of the peace or by the lowest of a province's courts. There are no jury trials at this level.

4. Indictable offences generally involve a choice of courts, at the discretion of the Crown, and sometimes a choice of trial with or without jury, at the discretion of the accused.

5. For many indictable offences — including armed robbery, breaking and entering, forgery and arson — the options are:

a) Trial by provincially appointed judge (lower courts) without jury and without first undergoing a preliminary inquiry.

b) Trial by federally appointed judge in a provincial superior court without jury but with a preliminary inquiry.

c) Trial by a federally appointed judge with jury in a provincial superior court. Such courts have a variety of names in different provinces: Court of Queen's Bench, Supreme Court, Superior Court.

6. For the most serious indictable offences, such as murder or treason, there is no option. They must be tried in a superior court. And they must be heard by a jury unless the accused and the provincial attorney general both agree otherwise.

7. Appeals of convictions for indictable offences are heard by provincial courts of appeal. Appeals for summary conviction offences are heard by a variety of courts depending on the province.

8. The Supreme Court of Canada hears criminal appeals only if a point of law is involved and if leave to appeal is granted by a panel of three justices or by a provincial appeal court. Leave to appeal is not necessary if a provincial appeal court has reversed an acquittal won in the trial court; if at least one justice has dissented in the appeal court's decision; or if a co-accused, having been tried jointly, has had an acquittal sustained on appeal.

Before charges are laid

Dangers:
1. Naming a person before formally charged.
2. Providing past criminal record.
3. Linking a suspect to a crime.

Police take an interest in many people. Often nothing comes of it. But to write that someone **is under investigation** for a criminal offence can cast a cloud over the person's life. The courts consider a false allegation of criminal conduct among the worst forms of libel.

Therefore, special care must be taken with any story identifying a person being investigated but who has not been charged or has not appeared in court to answer a charge.

The Canadian Press does not normally name individuals until they face formal charges. There may be exceptions depending on particular legal circumstances and news value, but the exceptions are rare.

Always check supervisors or seek legal advice before using doubtful information. With that caution, following are some general comments and examples:

1. Contempt of court — appearing to influence a court proceeding — becomes more of a risk as a trial nears. The most sensitive time is when a jury is about to be chosen.

2. Even if not contemptuous, a report that police are **investigating** a specific person, or **considering charges** against a specific person, can be libellous in some cases.

3. Depending on the circumstances, it may be permissible to report that **an investigation is under way** or **searches have been carried out.**

4. It is proper to publish the fact that a warrant has been issued for the arrest of a named person, or that he or she has in fact been arrested, or has received a summons to appear in court, or has signed a promise to appear.

5. The exact nature of the charge can be stated if the person has appeared before a judge, or if the charge is outlined in a warrant, summons or other document. It is probably dangerous to go into further detail without documentary evidence or testimony in open court.

6. Relevant references to the criminal record of an accused are routinely included in stories at the time of arrest. But care should be taken to ensure the information is legally sound. The reference to a past record should be relevant and in the public interest, and the information must be presented concisely and fairly. Toronto Main Desk should vet stories that delve into past records.

7. Guard against using information on past criminal records as an accused's trial approaches. Stories that move just before the trial should not draw from early stories on the accused's record. This information could be possibly be held in contempt by a court if it is published just as a jury is being chosen.

8. The contempt risk from possibly prejudicial information on past record increases as the legal process goes forward and the time for possible jury selection nears. There is not a clear guideline that applies to all situations for when such information should be dropped. Consult Main Desk and counsel.

9. Even when it's permissible to mention the background, a story must never imply that the suspect's record means he or she is guilty of the new offence.

10. Occasionally, a criminal comes before the courts who's so notorious that virtually anything may safely be written about the person's past and character until trial is imminent. Resist the temptation to abuse this liberty. If the criminal is truly notorious, the public doesn't need constant reminders of the reasons. And such stories can send the wrong signal about the media's concern for fair play.

11. On rare occasions — a hostage-taker who surrenders, a bank robber wounded in the act — the suspect's identity may be obvious even before being charged. In such cases, write only that a named person has been arrested or is in custody, without going into detail.

12. A suspect must be kept separate from the crime. For example, it may be all right to say: **A robbery was committed. John Doe is being held.** It is never all right to say: **John Doe committed a robbery.** Similarly, it is not acceptable to write: **A drug ring was broken today with the announcement of charges against three people.**

13. Witnesses can be interviewed when a crime is committed, but their statements should not be used to link a specific suspect to actions that could be disputed later in court. Witnesses must not be interviewed once a suspect has come before the courts.

14. Reporting police statements carries no immunity from the risk of libel or contempt. Such statements have to be weighed as carefully as any other information and checked for accuracy when possible. Whether a particular police force can be depended upon for fairness and accuracy is a matter of past experience. It is no defence against a libel or contempt charge to say the police were thought to be trustworthy.

Inquests

Dangers:

1. Publication bans.
2. Later use of incriminating evidence.

1. Coroner's inquests — sometimes called **fatality inquiries** — are held to investigate the cause of a violent death and make recommendations designed to avoid future deaths. They are presided over by a judge or coroner, depending on provincial law.

2. Inquests are usually open to media and public. The general rule holds that public hearings may be reported fairly and accurately.

3. However, the person presiding may order the inquiry closed, temporarily or permanently, because of possible prejudice to a potential accused, national security, public safety or intimate testimony, depending on provincial law. In such cases, whether evidence from the inquiry becomes public later is a matter for the presiding officer and/or provincial law.

4. An inquest may hear evidence that would be inadmissible at a later court proceeding, such as a confession. It may be reported at the time, unless the presiding officer directs otherwise, but it should not be repeated without legal advice once the case is before the courts.

5. Inquest juries are usually forbidden to make any finding of civil or legal responsibility. However, their investigations can sometimes lead to questions of who might have committed a crime, in a way not normally open to the courts, and that could lead to criminal charges. It's unwise to speculate about such possibilities without legal advice, however.

6. Inquest juries, like those at criminal trials, are forbidden by law from disclosing any information about their deliberations.

7. In Quebec, among things the law forbids:

a) Publishing a photograph of the dead body without consent.

b) Publishing any identifying information about a witness under 18 years of age implicated in the events.

c) Publishing autopsy reports.

Arraignment and bail hearing

Dangers:
1. Violating publication ban.
2. Reporting confession or criminal record.

1. Arraignment is normally the first step in a criminal court proceeding. It usually involves just an appearance by the accused before a judge, reading of the charge, making a plea and selecting a trial option. It's not essential that the accused enter a plea; the court may record a plea of **not guilty** if no plea is entered.

2. The court may hear evidence from a psychiatrist or other qualified person and order a psychiatric examination to test the accused's fitness to stand trial. The judge usually orders a ban on publication of such evidence; if not, it may be reported. There are normally no other restrictions on reporting arraignments.

3. A decision on bail may be made at arraignment, or at a separate bail (or **interim release**) hearing. If the accused requests a ban on publicity, the judge must grant it. It is then forbidden to publish testimony or the judge's reasons for granting or denying bail. The fact of whether bail was granted, and any conditions for release, may be reported.

4. Even without a publication ban, no confession offered in evidence by police or other witnesses may be reported at this stage without legal advice. There should be no mention of a criminal record without approval from a supervisor or counsel.

Change of venue

Danger:
1. Reporting court decision.

1. When a criminal case becomes so notorious in a community that it would be almost impossible to find jury members who could be impartial, a change of location (**venue**) can be ordered by the court to ensure a fair jury trial for the defendant. The change is usually to a community well removed from the scene of the crime.

2. Since the point of changing location is to find untainted jury members, the court may order severe limitations on what can be published about the case.

3. On occasion, the court may ban publication of anything about the change of location — including the fact that a change of venue has been requested or granted.

4. When the trial begins in the new location, the court can order a ban on reporting that a change of venue has taken place. The ban remains in effect until a verdict has been handed down or the trial otherwise ends.

Preliminary inquiry

Dangers:

1. Violating a publication ban.
2. Reporting a confession.

1. A preliminary inquiry is held to determine if there's enough evidence to warrant a trial. The accused usually asks for a ban on publicity. The judge is required to grant it on request, and no evidence may then be reported.

2. What may be reported:

a) Whether the accused is sent to trial.

b) The exact charge on which the accused was brought to preliminary hearing and, if appropriate, on which he or she was sent to trial.

c) The number of witnesses heard.

d) Any comment by the lawyers, or the accused, or any part of the judge's decision not referring to the evidence heard.

3. Even without a publication ban, the Criminal Code prohibits reporting any confession — by the accused at the hearing (rare) or mentioned in evidence by police or other third parties at this stage — at risk of a fine, time in jail, or both.

4. A confession in this context can mean a literal admission of guilt or any statement or action implying guilt. For example, if police testify that the accused led them to the body in a murder case, it should be avoided as an implied admission of guilt.

5. Any publication ban remains in effect until the conclusion of any subsequent trial, defined as the point at which a verdict is reached, regardless of intention to appeal. At that point, testimony at the preliminary hearing becomes publishable.

6. If the accused is discharged at the end of a preliminary hearing for lack of sufficient evidence, the banned testimony becomes

publishable. An exception is a confession offered as evidence by police but not admitted by the judge; in such cases, consult a supervisor or counsel.

Trial

Dangers:

1. Reporting what the jury hasn't heard.
2. Evidence of criminal record.

---

1. The general rule is that any evidence admitted by the judge at a public trial can be reported. This includes confessions and other evidence that may have been excluded at previous stages, if the evidence is presented again in open court.

2. It is dangerous to resurrect any other previous submissions made at a preliminary inquiry until the trial ends.

3. Evidence or arguments presented with the jury absent should not be reported, except in the rare cases where the jury has been sequestered. For example, no reference should be made to evidence at a hearing (**voir dire**) held to determine whether certain evidence, such as confessions or wiretaps, may be legally presented to the jury.

4. If such evidence is admitted by the judge, it can be reported when presented to the jury. If not admitted, it may not be reported until the jury is sequestered and retires to reach a verdict.

5. Statements ordered struck from the record by the judge may still be reported. The judge's ruling has the effect of erasing the statements only from the trial record.

6. Any reporter who starts to cover a trial part way through must confirm that there is no voir dire or other restriction on what may be reported.

7. Evidence of previous convictions is usually not admitted at trial. If an accused presents evidence intended to show good character, he or she may then be asked about any prior criminal record.

8. On rare occasions, the public is excluded from all or part of a trial:

a) Trials of young people under the federal act dealing with youth crime.

b) Trials in which there is risk of disclosing information affecting national security or defence, international relations or the public interest.

c) Cases where the judge orders a trial closed in the interests of maintaining order or the proper administration of justice. No testimony may then be reported, but the verdict can be.

9. If the public is excluded to maintain order but the media are allowed to remain, the proceedings may be reported unless the judge directs otherwise.

10. Immediately after a verdict in a criminal trial has been rendered — and even if one of the parties plans to appeal — it is permissible to report fair and accurate comments by editorial writers, columnists and legal experts on the facts of the case, the parties, their lawyers, the judge's conduct and the administration of justice.

11. There is increasing leeway now to criticize the administration of justice, including the conduct of judges and the validity of their judgments. But to suggest unworthy motives by a judge is courting a contempt citation.

Undercover police in court

Danger:

1. Identifying and endangering undercover police officer.

1. When an undercover police officer testifies at a trial, courts often order bans on publication of any information, including images, that could serve to identify the officer or other undercover officers mentioned in testimony.

2. Such a ban is very broad and reporters should assume that it includes any reference made in court to a first name used by the officer. This may seem unusual since a first name may not normally amount to identifying an individual. However, it is not unusual for an undercover officer to be identified on the street by first name only. Such officers regularly use their real first names and could be in serious danger if they are discovered to be undercover officers.

3. Reporters should never use the first name or any identifying information of the undercover officer when reporting on the matter without specifically checking with the Crown attorney for bans. Even if there are no bans, reporters should strive to ensure that their report does not imperil the safety of undercover officers.

Appeals

Danger:
1. Suggesting bias.

1. Normally, anything and everything said at an open appeal court hearing can be reported.

2. Appeal court judges are generally considered to be above being prejudiced by the publication of comment or opinion about a case being heard on appeal.

3. Nonetheless, to suggest bias or prejudgment on the part of a judge — appeal court or otherwise — is tempting fate.

4. And of course the normal rules of court reporting — fair and balanced coverage — apply to appeal court hearings.

Retrials

Dangers:
1. Recalling previous verdict.
2. Recalling previous evidence.

1. When a trial ends in a hung jury, or when a conviction or acquittal has been overturned on appeal, a new trial may be ordered. That means that for the accused, the slate has in effect been wiped clean. It is as if the first trial did not take place.

2. The appeal court's decision may be reported at the time with full background. But well before a new trial begins there must be the same restraint in reporting on evidence or testimony as would have applied before the first trial, especially if a jury trial is possible.

3. Unless specifically banned, it is permissible to report that a previous trial ended in a hung jury, or that the verdict of the previous trial was overturned on appeal. When retrial is imminent, it is not normally permitted to report what the previous verdict was, or that there was a hung jury, since that could influence the new jury.

Young persons

The Youth Criminal Justice Act, which covers people from their 12th to their 18th birthdays, replaced the Young Offenders Act in April 2003. It is significantly different from its predecessor.

1. All trials of people aged 12 to 18 take place in youth courts. No one is transferred to adult court.

2. The act bans publishing the name or other identifying characteristics of the accused through at least until sentencing.

3. The only youths who can be identified after sentencing are those sentenced as adults, and then only if a court has not issued a publication ban.

4. Once persons turn 18, they can consent to be identified as having been prosecuted under the act, as long as they are not still incarcerated for the crime.

5. The act bans publishing the names and other identifying characteristics of juvenile victims of youth crimes, including deceased victims. It also bans identifying young people as persons who have appeared as witnesses at youth court hearings. Exceptions to both restrictions involve permission from the court, parents, and — in the case of witnesses or victims who have turned 18 — the young people themselves. When dealing with possible exceptions to the ban, make sure there are no court orders affecting identification; and ensure identifying the witness or victim will not also identify another young person whose identity is protected.

6. An unusual aspect of the Youth Criminal Justice Act is that media cannot immediately identify a deceased juvenile who is believed to be the victim of a crime in which an accused is being dealt with under the act. Media must first get the consent of both parents. If one media outlet obtains proper consent, then the publication ban is lifted for all media. Discuss with Main Desk before identifying the dead person.

7. If police ask, the court can allow the identification of young people they are trying to arrest. Such a court order can last five days.

8. The prohibitions against identification of some young people include carrying information that could identify them, such as where they live, where they go to school, sports teams they belong to, the names of members of their families, and the institution where they are held.

9. When a young person is suspected in a crime involving family members, no story may include both the victim's name and her or his relationship to the suspect, since this could identify the young person. When the first news of such a crime becomes available:

a) Do not name the victims or describe their relationship with the suspect until it is clear where the chief news interest will lie: in the relationship or in the stature of the family.

b) Try to develop a consensus with other media on what to publicize — the names or the relationship.

c) Once a decision is made on which element to publicize, do not switch tracks without consulting counsel. Anyone putting together the names from one story and the relationship from the other can identify the suspect.

Child protection laws

1. A big red flag should go up whenever a court and-or an agency is involved in the custody or care of a child. It may be in violation of provincial child protection laws to provide information that would tend to identify the child or the child's parents or guardians. These publication bans may even be triggered in some provinces before there is any court involvement in a case. The matter should be referred to Main Desk, which can consult counsel.

2. There are also instances in which government agencies are involved in the custody or care of a child with the co-operation of the parents and without court involvement, and in which a publication ban does not apply. Counsel's guidance will be needed in recognizing these instances.

3. When it comes to media, child welfare laws are simple: protect the child from publicity that could be harmful to the child's future. But recognizing the signals that indicate when those laws might come into play is less straightforward. Some wording that might appear in stories that would indicate there could be a ban on identification of the child and the child's parents or guardians, include references to actions by the Children's Aid Society, or government social workers or a court hearing to determine whether a family member can get a child back from government care.

4. The child protection laws differ province to province and go by different names. Alberta's law is very broad, and some argue that its ban on identifying a child under the care of the government continues even after the child is dead. The welfare of a child is often a sad element in a story of domestic violence or other such tragedy. It is natural in such instances for media to want to report what becomes of the child. However, if that involves revealing an intervention by the government to take the child to a place of safety, then media may not be able to tell that part of the story. It can be reported that the child is safe, unhurt and being cared for but the involvement of child protection authorities may not be reported.

5. As an example, Ontario's Child and Family Services Act prohibits the identification of a child as a person involved in a proceeding or hearing under the act. The act also prohibits identifying the child's parents, foster parents or other family members. It is OK to identify John and Jane Doe and write that they are in court on drug trafficking charges. But it contravenes the act to include that the daughter of the two named accused was taken into protective custody by the Children's Aid Society.

It is permissible, to report the traffickers have a daughter unless the court has made an order banning publication on information that would identify the daughter. And it is not uncommon that a publication ban is sought and granted in a criminal matter where the child has been abused or has been living in an undesirable environment. A proceeding under the Child and Family Services Act begins as soon as a child protection worker intervenes to take a child to a place of safety.

Sensitive cases

1. In cases involving sexual offences, extortion or usury, a judge must ban publication of the identity of victims or a juvenile witness if asked to do so by either the victim, the witness or the Crown.

2. In such cases, it is forbidden not only to name the victim or witness but also to provide any information that could disclose their identity.

3. Among information that could reveal their identity would be a family relationship, address, place of employment or other characteristic that could allow some members of the community to make an identification.

4. Even where no ban is in effect, it is usually wrong to identify alleged victims of sexual assault without their active consent. CP does not name minors who are victims of sexual assault, even with the consent of their parents.

5. In rare cases, a victim's name somehow becomes widely known in the community and publication of the name is not banned. Nevertheless, editors should still weigh whether using the name will send a signal to readers that the media are indifferent to the problems of sexual assault victims in general. Any story that does contain the name of an alleged sex assault victim should include a reference explaining why the person is being identified.

6. Reporting on divorce and annulment proceedings is subject by law to restraints. Generally, only a bare identification of those involved, the main issues and the judgment can safely be reported.

7. Generally, provincial legislation that requires the reporting of communicable diseases also provides for strict confidentiality. It is therefore risky to breach the anonymity of those with a sexually transmitted disease, AIDS or other reportable infection without their consent.

8. Certain offences are regarded by the law as relatively minor, subject to small fines at most. But publicly naming those accused of communicating with a prostitute, indecent exposure or similar offences can have ruinous consequences. It should be done rarely.

9. The law, not just ethics, can determine what gruesome or indecent details to publish in court cases. The law forbids reporting on indecent matters or indecent medical details that could injure public morals — phrases that are vague enough to require legal advice when in doubt.

Amber Alerts

When a child is reported missing, police can issue an Amber Alert — a warning to the public to be on the lookout for a child. The warning gets to the public via broadcasters and digital highway signs and other media.

The declaration of the alert confers no special rights on media and it doesn't trump statutory publishing bans such as child welfare laws. However, if the police are giving information to the media that is truly pertinent to the recovery of a child, it is almost certainly going to be legally defensible. There are strong defences for carrying information as it becomes available from police on where the child was taken from, who is believed to have taken the child and the nature of any threat from the suspect — information important to the recovery of a child. There may be reasons to consult legal counsel on some facts that come to light related to the Amber Alert, but the core information released by police to help in recovery of the child should make its way to wire quickly.

However, if the child has been found alive, consult with counsel for guidance on whether it is wise to continue to publish these facts, given that the reason it was OK to do so earlier — to help find the child — is no longer applicable.

Civil cases

While criminal cases involve society's attempt to control wrongdoing or protect the public good, civil cases involve disputes between private individuals or corporations. Society provides the court structure and a set of laws designed to make the settlement of grievances an orderly process.

Civil cases require the same care and dispassion of reporters as criminal cases do.

Vocabulary:

1. In civil cases, there is no **prosecutor**. Nobody is said to be **charged**. At the end of a court hearing, no one is **convicted** or **acquitted**, nor found **guilty** or **not guilty**.

2. The person initiating a civil case is the **plaintiff** or **petitioner**. The process involves **bringing suit** or **taking action** or **seeking damages**. The other party is the **defendant** or **respondent**.

Claims

1. Small claims are heard in a variety of lower courts depending on the province. The upper limit for the amount claimed in such cases also varies with the province.

2. Small claims are usually heard directly by a judge, without lawyers acting for the contesting parties.

3. Intermediate claims are heard at lower or intermediate court levels, with lawyers representing the parties. Jury trials are rare.

4. The largest civil claims are heard in provincial superior courts, by judge alone or with jury.

5. Jury trials are no longer provided for in Quebec for civil suits.

Class action lawsuits

1. Class-action lawsuits are often announced by press release. Publicity is important to many of these suits because it allows other prospective members of the class represented in the suit to learn of it.

2. Such press releases do not have the protection that court documents or court proceedings do. A story repeating defamatory claims from a press release *cannot* be defended by saying the story accurately conveyed the contents of the press release. If possible, use court documents, such as a statement of claim, rather than a release as the basis for a story. Reporters should also seek a statement of defence, both immediately and in subsequent days. The rule: Make sure any story based on a press release that refers to a lawsuit poses no legal risk even if a lawsuit is not actually filed or if the lawsuit filed doesn't represent some of the language in the press release.

Other civil cases

1. Surrogate or probate courts exist in some provinces to deal with wills and estates. In other provinces, such cases are heard by the courts that handle other civil actions.

2. The Federal Court of Canada has jurisdiction over citizenship, taxation, immigration, copyright, trademark and patent cases, judicial review of federal administrative tribunals, and claims brought against the government of Canada.

Appeals

1. Appeals in civil cases are heard by the appeal division of a provincial superior court or court of appeal. Leave to appeal must almost always be sought from the higher court.

2. The appeal division of Federal Court hears appeals from decisions of that court.

3. The Supreme Court of Canada hears appeals on civil cases if there is a matter of public importance or an important point of law at issue.

Examination for discovery

1. Before trial of a civil suit, a process called examination for discovery is normally held. It allows the parties to examine each other's case and to clarify the issues to be resolved at trial.

2. Although the testimony is recorded and those testifying are under oath, the evidence at examination for discovery is not subject to all the normal safeguards of a courtroom.

3. Such examinations are not considered public hearings. The transcripts are not public documents and are not normally accessible to the media. However, one of the parties to a case may place them on the public record, and as such they may be subject to reporting. However, publication of such evidence should not be considered without legal advice.

Damage suits

Dangers:
1. Quoting from one-sided documents.
2. Referring to amount claimed.

1. When one party files suit for damages against another, a writ or statement of claim is issued. A fair and accurate account of what is in the writ normally may be carried, but the story should strive for balance by:

a) including comment from principals named in the writ;

b) making clear the writ consists of allegations that are still to be tested in court.

A report on a statement of claim could present a libel risk if the above conditions are not met. In cases where a writ contains extremely defamatory information, it is prudent to seek counsel's advice before filing a story.

2. When a jury is hearing a civil suit for damages, it is not supposed to be informed about the amount of damages sought, for fear it will be misled. There is no real limit to the damages a person can claim and the amount may be ridiculous. As a working (but not infallible) rule, don't report the amount of damages sought during a jury trial or for a month before such a trial. Once a case has been decided, there is no such restriction.

3. The restriction does not apply to cases heard by a judge alone, nor to civil cases in Quebec where there are no longer jury trials in civil suits.

Contempt of court

Every journalist must be on guard against contempt of court in reporting on crimes, investigations and court cases.

Contempt of court doesn't mean despising a judge or the justice system. It's an old usage of the word **contempt**, meaning to **interfere** with the administration of justice or **disobey** the courts.

Controlling contempt is intended to protect a person's right to a fair trial, a cornerstone of democracy.

General guidelines

Dangers:

1. Defendant's confession.
2. Previous convictions.
3. Speculation.
4. Ignoring publication bans.

---

1. When a story is known to be in contempt, kill it at once. If contempt is suspected, withhold the story from publication, check it with counsel and keep editors advised.

➤ See **Libel**, page 235.

2. It is a basic rule that nothing must be published that interferes with the proper course of justice. That particularly includes anything that impairs an accused person's right to a fair trial.

3. Even if a statement is true and not libellous, it may be in contempt of court if it hurts a person's right to a fair trial.

4. A statement made in a legislature, court or other place of privilege is not protected from contempt. If an MP makes a statement in the Commons that could be prejudicial, it should not be published without consulting counsel.

5. There is a particular risk of prejudice in reporting on a defendant's confession unless it has been accepted as evidence in open court.

6. Check counsel before referring to previous convictions unless they are mentioned in open court. Such information is not necessarily admissible at trial.

7. The publication or repetition of a statement in contempt of court is itself contempt. The source of the statement or its accuracy doesn't matter.

8. Guilt or innocence should not be imputed to any party in a court case. It is also dangerous to speculate on possible motive for a crime, the credibility of witnesses or the likely outcome in a jury trial.

9. Do not report testimony or other material from previous stages of a criminal proceeding — preliminary hearing, death inquiry or the like — unless it is introduced again in open court.

10. At a jury trial, it is a crime to report evidence heard by a judge at a *voir dire,* a hearing held to determine whether certain evidence will be presented to the jury. Such hearings are always held with the jury excluded. However, publication of voir dire evidence may be allowed when it involves a case being tried by judge alone or in those rare cases where a jury is being sequestered. If in doubt, check counsel.

11. Any restriction imposed by a court on publication remains in effect until the court sets it aside.

12. It is a crime in Canada for jurors to disclose any information on their deliberations. While there's no law forbidding reporters to interview jurors, the reporter could be charged with inducing a juror to break the law by encouraging the juror to reveal protected information.

13. Once a case has ended, it is usually permissible to report criticism of the administration of justice or the conduct of a judge. It is risky to suggest the judge had improper motives. In some provinces, a statement may also be in contempt if it vilifies a court or judge. Check counsel when in doubt.

Foreign cases

1. Exercise care on any story from abroad that includes out-of-court statements by police or others about Canadian individuals or businesses if a subsequent trial is likely to take place in Canada.

2. In particular, beware of assuming that U.S. laws and legal procedures apply in this country. Statements about an accused person from police and other authorities of a kind that are routine in the United States can be considered contempt in Canada.

Libel

Remember:

1. Statements damaging to reputation must never be published unless there is a clear legal basis for doing so.

2. Anyone who repeats a libel is fully responsible for the libel, no matter what its source.

3. A libel can cause great damage to a person's life.

4. Individual reporters and editors can be sued along with their employers for libels they permit to be published.

---

1. Libel is the publication of a false and damaging statement. It is part of the broader legal category known as **defamation**, covering **slander** (ordinary conversation) and **libel** (published or broadcast).

2. Defamation is a statement that tends to lower a person in the opinion of others, or exposes the person to hatred, contempt or ridicule. Defamation is also a statement that injures another's reputation in a way that affects that person's livelihood — work, trade or profession — or financial credit.

3. When a story is known to be libellous, **kill** it at once.

> **EDITORS: Kill Toronto Accusations for LEGAL reasons. Story contains wrong name. Will be sub.**
>
> **THE CANADIAN PRESS Halifax**

A Writethru Correction should also move at once, removing the troublesome content. When even a slight doubt exists, move a Writethru deleting the material so the information is immediately dropped from online services. If a check determines that the material can be used, another Writethru, reinstating the information, can be moved.

➤ See **Corrections and Correctives**, page 466.

4. The Canadian Press newswires provide instant publication of every word filed. As soon as stories are sent to wire, they immediately reach a lot of people. Aside from quickly being posted on websites or read by TV and radio news presenters, many stories, as well as advisories, are automatically routed to clients who subscribe to databases of Canadian Press content. This means all words — slugs, headlines, update notes — have the same potential to be legal risks. If a story about alleged transgressions of a public figure were cavalierly slugged **Nailed-the-Stinker**, for instance, this could be used in court to suggest

the subject of the story was not given fair treatment.

5. Emails between reporters and editors about the way a story is being handling must always reflect the professional, unbiased approach to news by The Canadian Press. Avoid casual chatter in emails that might leave the impression the news agency has a bias regarding the subject matter of the story. Once notice of a legal action is given, the emails can be brought before a court; any move to dispose of emails or other documents related to the story would be looked on unkindly and could complicate the agency's legal position. The moment there is a suggestion of a legal action, consult counsel.

General information

Key points:

1. Truth difficult to prove.

2. Public interest must be weighed.

1. Libel has serious potential to harm not only the news agency and its employees, but any newspaper or broadcaster using the material. A plaintiff can sue everyone, or pick and choose arbitrarily — even to the point of aiming at the weakest links, those with the smallest resources who are most likely to pay to settle a libel suit without contest.

2. Libel involves an untrue report. Truth is a **complete defence** against a libel suit. A true statement of fact is not vulnerable even if it is damaging. But the one who publishes a damaging statement is responsible for proving the truth of the statement, and that is often extremely difficult. In some cases it may be impossible. It's not up to the plaintiff to prove the statement is false.

3. In Quebec, in addition to truth, the Civil Code requires that publication be in the **public interest** and **without malice**.

4. **Public interest** and **lack of malice** are not specified by law elsewhere in Canada. However, professional ethics dictate that before publishing a truthful but damaging statement, the press will weigh carefully whether the public interest is served by publication. And absence of malice must be a foregone conclusion in the publication of any news report.

5. The Canadian Press and other media whose reports reach an audience within Quebec must take into account Quebec's legal requirements when considering publication of potentially libellous material from elsewhere in Canada, particularly if the report concerns a Quebec resident.

6. Consent can be used as a defence in a libel suit, but it requires proof that:

a) the person defamed has been informed defamatory information will be published, and

b) the person knows what he or she is consenting to, and

c) the person consents to publication.

If consent is to be used as a defence, the proof of it will have to meet certain standards that stand up in court. A signed formal statement or an audio tape of an interview may be called for. Consult with counsel beforehand to work out details.

7. Except in Quebec, it is virtually impossible to libel the dead. And a libel suit launched by someone who subsequently dies is normally dropped. However, it could be dangerous to defame a dead person in a way that affects the living: for example, suggesting a man sexually abused his children before he died.

Privilege

Key points:
1. Fair, accurate, no malice.
2. Right to rebuttal.

---

1. Privilege means **protection from legal action**, even when defamatory material has been published. Privilege is based on two traditional assumptions:

a) It would be in the public interest for every citizen to attend certain events or read certain reports. Failing that, all citizens should have access to fair and accurate reports of such events.

b) In some cases, the public good is better served through unrestrained debate and the free communication of information than it is through a normal concern about accuracy or defamation.

2. Privilege is never absolute. At its most fundamental, it still requires that any report be **fair**, **accurate** and **without malice**:

a) **Fairness** means lack of bias, not taking statements out of context.

b) **Accuracy** means reporting the facts correctly. A report need not be textual or complete; it can be a fair synopsis.

c) **Lack of malice** means there is no dishonest or hidden motive nor reckless disregard for the truth.

3. The protection of privilege is also lost as a defence in a libel action if there has been a refusal to publish a reasonable statement of explanation or contradiction despite a request from the person defamed to do so.

4. Privilege does not extend to matters of contempt. Statements that could interfere with a person's right to a fair trial risk contempt even if made by an elected representative during an open session of a legislature. A fair and accurate account of a court case could be in contempt as well if it prejudices another case.

5. A statement of claim filed in court as part of a libel action is a privileged document and often provides the legal basis needed for reporting the alleged libel. Any story on the libel action should be fair, accurate, without malice and contemporaneous to the action in order to preserve the privilege. This means including views from both sides in the case. Source the material to the statement of claim, and consult Main Desk before moving the story on the wire.

What's protected

Key points:

1. Legislative bodies, courts.
2. Quasi-judicial bodies.
3. Meetings, reports.
4. Public proceedings.
5. Notices to the public.

1. The common law — that is, traditional rights recognized by the courts — and the Civil Code in Quebec provide general principles for the protection known as privilege.

2. In addition, all provinces have specific statutes dealing with libel and privilege. The statutes vary; in tricky cases, get legal advice. However, the following may be considered privileged:

a) Debates and committee meetings of the House of Commons, the Senate and provincial legislatures, as well as public reports and documents issued by these bodies.

Note: The privilege doesn't extend to statements made outside of a chamber or committee hearing, such as in a scrum.

b) Proceedings heard in public before any court exercising judicial authority, and reports issued by courts. The privilege doesn't extend to hearings from which public and press are excluded, nor to any matter on which the court has banned publication. If a report is not contemporaneous, consult counsel.

c) Death inquiries or coroner's inquests, royal commissions and other commissions of inquiry are not strictly courts but their proceedings and reports or documents are generally privileged.

d) Hearings of federal and provincial regulatory agencies and administrative tribunals, such as labour relations boards and human rights tribunals, and their reports or documents.

e) Meetings and reports of local government bodies and their agencies, such as municipal councils, municipal planning boards, school boards, boards of health.

f) Public meetings. This broad category can be tricky. It is usually defined as a meeting open to the general public, lawfully convened, to discuss a matter of public interest. It probably doesn't cover a news conference, nor a political meeting to which only supporters of one party have been invited. When in doubt, check counsel.

g) Any bulletin, report, notice or other document issued for the information of the public from a public authority, such as a government office or department, police service, medical officer of health or local board of health. This would include, for example, a warning that a particular product is dangerous to health.

h) Any notice or report issued by any government or municipal official, commissioner of police or chief constable for the information of the public, and published at that person's request. The most common example is a police appeal for public help in locating a fugitive or missing person.

Provincial statutes

Key points:
1. Professional, business, sports bodies.
2. Right of rebuttal.
3. Retraction, apology.

1. Each province in Canada has some form of libel legislation, dealing with issues of defamation and protection from legal action under certain conditions.

2. In addition to the categories of privilege listed previously, most provincial laws extend privilege to the findings and proceedings of professional, business and sports organizations that are formed in Canada. Included would be the disciplinary proceedings of law societies, medical associations, trade and business associations and sports leagues.

3. However, provincial law states that refusal to carry a reasonable statement of explanation or contradiction from the complainant, if asked to do so, will wipe out the privilege.

4. The law also specifies that a full and fair retraction for a defamatory story, if published with equal prominence to the original story and within *three days* of receiving legal notice, will

reduce damages. The provision doesn't apply to a story that suggests a criminal offence was committed.

5. Damages may also be reduced if a full apology is published either before legal action was started or promptly afterwards.

6. The Quebec Press Act, in addition to most of the above, also extends privilege to the reports of the provincial ombudsman when tabled in the legislature, and to reports by the government or an authorized person about the financial solvency of companies or the value of certain stock and bond issues.

7. The Quebec law provides for reduced damages by apology, but that doesn't apply when a criminal offence is suggested. Nor does it apply when the defamation involves a candidate for Parliament, the national assembly or municipal office and when it is published in the period extending from three days before nomination day until election day.

Special concerns

1. People in certain areas of society make outrageous statements as a matter of course. Politics and sports are prime examples.

2. Public statements from people in these fields are routinely harsh, overstated and malicious. If such statements were made by others under different circumstances, the courts would be much busier.

3. The fact that political or sports comments rarely result in libel claims does not mean there is no need for caution in reporting them. Libel is libel. Check counsel before taking chances.

4. A separate concern involves non-Canadians who have business or other interests in Canada. Such people can sue for libel in this country if news from abroad is published in Canada which affects their reputation or livelihood in Canada. Thus, for example, a report from somewhere in the United States that alleges drug-taking by a football player now in the Canadian Football League — or even with CFL prospects — would be dangerous. So would a report from abroad that damages the reputation of a Hong Kong businessman with Canadian business interests.

Good faith

1. If a statement is false, it is no defence to claim that it was thought to be true at time of publication.

2. However, the damages awarded in a libel suit may be reduced because of absence of malice and evidence of good faith:

a) if there were reasonable grounds for believing the defamatory statement was true, and

b) if an apology was published when the statement was discovered to be false.

Fair comment

Key points:

1. Honest opinion.
2. Based on provable fact.
3. Public interest.

1. Commentary involves questions of opinion and interpretation. A different test is applied to commentary than to factual reporting. Comment or opinion (**the government's program is ruining the economy**) need not be proved true in the sense that an objective fact (**the government has increased the sales tax**) is true.

2. The defence of fair comment has often been applied to editorials and to artistic criticism such as book, film or theatre reviews. But it isn't limited to such material. It can be used to defend any story that mixes factual material with interpretation and analysis.

3. To be defensible, comment must meet these criteria:

a) It must express an opinion honestly held. It can't be presented maliciously or out of a hidden motive.

b) Most important, it must be based on facts *presented in the story* that can be proved to be true. An honest opinion based on false information cannot be defended.

c) It must relate to a matter of public interest, not a purely private matter.

4. Public interest is roughly parallel to news value. But publication in one province on the grounds of public interest could be libellous in another province.

5. The basic rule holds: When in doubt, get legal advice.

Responsible communication

Key points:

1. Public interest
2. Responsible reporting.

1. In 2009 the Supreme Court of Canada established a new defamation defence called responsible communication. It permits the publication of defamatory statements in a story about a matter of public importance even if the publisher cannot prove the truth of such statements, as long as responsible steps were taken to

verify the information. A court would consider the following criteria when determining if adequate steps were taken to verify information:

a) the seriousness of the allegation:

b) the public importance of the matter.

c) the urgency of the matter.

d) the status and reliability of the source.

e) whether the plaintiff's side of the story was sought and accurately reported.

f) whether the inclusion of the defamatory statement was justifiable.

g) whether the public interest in reporting the defamatory statement lay in the fact that it was made rather than its truth.

h) any other relevant circumstances.

Copyright

Dangers:

1. Substantial quotes without OK.
2. Permission not in writing.

1. Copyright is what gives the creator of an original work the exclusive right to benefit from it.

2. Copyright covers such creations as books, films, songs, articles and essays, letters, diaries, pictures or anything else that's original and in some permanent form. It can even extend to distinctive titles.

3. The copyright owner controls the right to reproduce the work, in whole or in substantial part.

4. For the press, this means there can be no substantial quotations from copyrighted material without written permission of the copyright owner. Giving a mere credit to the copyright owner isn't sufficient.

5. *Substantial* has different meanings for different works. A complete stanza from a short pop song could be substantial. Generally, copying the heart of a work would be against copyright law. Check counsel when in doubt.

6. An exception is made for quotations used in a review or critique, but it must be a bona fide review and the quotes should be no more than needed to make a critical point.

7. Generally, government documents, speeches and most other material used in daily journalism are not copyright.

8. Over time, copyright protection is lost and the work falls into the public domain. In Canada, literary and artistic copyright expires 50 years after the author's death. Copyright on photographs expires 50 years after the negative has been processed.

9. Information cannot be copyrighted, only the form in which it is presented. Although newspapers frequently identify a story as being copyright, the actual news in the story cannot be protected. Someone else using an original method of expression may reproduce the information. Making a few changes in expression is not sufficient; the presentation must be substantially original.

10. The Canadian Press has first right to use staff-written local news from newspapers that are part of the co-operative news agency, whether or not the newspaper declares it to be copyright.

11. However, worked-up exclusives or news from beyond the newspaper's normal coverage area cannot legally be distributed in their original form by the news agency without permission from the managing editor or other senior officer at the paper. Giving credit to the paper is not a substitute for getting permission if there are to be substantial quotes or reproductions from the original. Permission can be assumed if the paper has transmitted the story to The Canadian Press electronically

12. Like anyone else, in the absence of permission, the news agency may distribute a report based on the information in the copyright story. It must use substantially different words and it should be brief — no longer than needed to report the substance of the story. Direct quotes of more than a sentence or two are not allowed.

13. The Canadian Press may also not normally use a published feature created by a freelancer, even if it involves local news. Freelance work is usually identified by a different credit line (e.g., **Special to the Mirror**) than staff work. Ignoring the copyright owned by a freelance can be costly.

14. The copyright in a Letter to the Editor is held by the letter writer, who automatically gives a right of publication to the newspaper that receives the letter. To reproduce all or part of the letter elsewhere would require written permission from the copyright holder, in strict legal terms. But in practical terms, verbal permission from the newspaper will do. (Few letter writers are likely to sue because their views have been given a wider audience, and if they won a suit the damages would likely be minimal.)

15. Freelance photographers hired by The Canadian Press negotiate in advance the ownership and resale rights for their film. The work of newspapers' regular freelance photographers is available to the agency. In most instances of spontaneous photography — the bystander's shots of a hot news event — the freelance is told by the paper to negotiate directly with The Canadian Press.

➤ See **Pictures**, page 101.

16. News distributed on the Internet has no special status in terms of copyright law. A story published in an Internet edition of a newspaper or any other website is subject to the law just as it would be if it were in a print edition. Permission must be given by the copyright holder before it is reproduced in substantially the same form.

➤ See **Internet and social media sources,** page 29.

Privacy, wiretaps

Dangers:
1. Disclosing others' communications.
2. Broadcasting private conversations.

1. Anyone may record their own conversations, without the permission of the other party, whether in person or on the telephone or other circumstance.

2. However, it's illegal to intercept or record conversations or private communications of other people without the consent of one of the other parties.

3. It's also illegal to broadcast on radio (but, oddly, not on TV) any part of one's own conversation with someone else without the consent of the other person. An exception is when the other person has phoned in to participate in the broadcast.

4. And it's illegal to use or disclose anything about others' private communications without the consent of one of the parties.

Media and police

Police in Canada sometimes turn to the print and broadcast media for information and evidence. They have been known to demand the use of photographs and film to document charges against possible rioters and others involved in public disturbances, and have made other demands on news people to support police work.

The media have generally resisted. If people come to view the media as an arm of the justice system, they will lose confidence in the media as an intermediary between ordinary citizens and authorities.

Following are normal guidelines for dealings with police:

Public notices

1. The media normally co-operate when police ask for publicity about the hunt for suspects or lost persons. Accuracy in identification is essential. Racial description and other characteristics — not usually part of a news report — are a normal part of such published identification material.

2. Do not casually refer to a person as dangerous. The description would be prejudicial if referring to someone whose jury trial is imminent. It should be based on a *written* release from police intended for the public.

Co-operation with police

1. There is normally no objection to providing police with copies of stories or photographs that have already been published, or other routine material of a non-confidential nature, as a matter of courtesy.

2. However, reporters' notes, unpublished film, background files, email and other material dealing with ongoing stories or anything of a private or confidential nature should not be provided to police unless they produce a search warrant.

3. Material gathered by reporters and other employees in the course of their work is the property of the employer. No employee has the right to turn over such material to police without permission from a senior supervisor.

Newsroom searches

1. Police will sometimes provide advance notice that they intend to present a search warrant. In any case, police arriving in a newsroom with a search warrant — with or without notice — must not be delayed, obstructed or resisted. They are not obliged to wait until legal counsel is on the scene.

2. However, police should be referred immediately to a senior supervisor, and legal counsel should be informed immediately by phone.

3. The arrival of police with a warrant in a newsroom during a busy time could hamper efforts to get the news out. It is permissible to ask police to arrange a more convenient time. The Supreme Court of Canada said in a 1991 ruling that an "unreasonably conducted" search could make the search invalid and that a newsroom search should be conducted in a way that does not interfere unreasonably with the news operation.

4. The warrant should be inspected closely to ensure that

a) all factual references (address, name of company or person, date) are accurate;

b) a suspected offence is specified;

c) it is properly signed by a justice of the peace.

4. If there are errors, the police should be asked to leave. If there aren't, the supervisor can watch any search being conducted. Others on staff can observe and, if necessary later, serve as witnesses about the way the search was conducted, but only the supervisor should talk to police.

5. While not obliged to assist searchers, the supervisor may decide it is best to direct them to a specific desk or area and otherwise help them if the alternative is a wide sweep that could uncover unrelated confidential material elsewhere in the newsroom.

6. The supervisor should ask permission to photocopy any material that is to be seized. If the request is refused, legal counsel should be consulted immediately.

7. If the searchers intend to take confidential material relating to sources, or unpublished material, the supervisor should insist that it be placed in a sealed envelope until the question of privilege can be decided in court.

8. Legal counsel should be consulted promptly about any question that arises as a result of being served with a search warrant.

Legal vocabulary

The language of courts and lawyers is extremely precise, but it can be distant from plain speech. Latin terms and jargon abound. Legal language may find its way into a story legitimately for effect or precision, but in most cases a plain substitute or clear explanation is best.

Some standard legal terms:

affidavit: sworn written statement to be used as evidence.

arraign: charge before the courts.

bawdy-house: archaic term still used in Criminal Code for brothel.

common law: unwritten law based on ancient custom and judicial precedent.

    common-law marriage: relationship based on living together without legal recognition. **Note:** It is not usually necessary to specify if a relationship is common-law.

concurrent: at the same time; of a number of jail sentences, to be served simultaneously (as opposed to consecutively).

contempt (of court): not disdain for the judge, but interference with justice or disobedience of court order.

copyright: protection of exclusive use of original work.

ex parte (Latin for *from one party*): one-sided; submission by one party in legal dispute without contest from other side.

habeas corpus (Latin for *You have the body*): writ requiring person be brought before court, usually to test whether person's detention is legal.

house arrest: detention in one's own home instead of prison.

in camera (Latin for *in a room*): private(ly); hearing with public excluded.

indeterminate sentence: of no fixed term, dependent on prisoner's conduct.

indict, indictment: formally accuse of crime; formal accusation or charge.

    indictable offence: more serious level of criminal charge (less serious is called summary offence).

interim release: term increasingly used instead of **release on bail**.

leave: permission, as in **leave to appeal**.

open custody: assignment of offender to group home or other lightly supervised environment, usually for juveniles.

plaintiff: person who brings complaint to court in civil case.

plead no contest: in the United States, the name of a plea in a criminal action that has the same effect as a guilty plea.

pré-enquête (*pre-inquiry*): rare form of private hearing by judge or justice of peace to decide whether charge should be laid.

privilege: immunity granted under certain conditions to speak without fear, or to report such speech.

remand (from Latin for *commit*): return to custody or the order doing so.

stayed charges: a direction of the court that charges not be acted on at least until some other step is taken.

sub judice (Latin for *under a judge*): before the courts; for the court alone to decide.

subpoena (Latin for *under penalty*): writ commanding presence in court.

surety (from Latin for *security*): person who takes responsibility for another's performance, such as appearing in court; also the money given as a guarantee.

suspended sentence: unenforced sentence that is subject to good behaviour.

venue (change of): location; move trial to another community to avoid prejudice against accused.

voir dire (Old French for *say the truth*): hearing within a trial, with jury excluded, to test admissibility of confession or other evidence.

writ: court order requiring specified act or giving authority to someone to have act done.

writ of certiorari (from Latin for *inform*): demand from higher court for records from lower court.

writ of mandamus (Latin for *We command*): command to inferior court, or to person to perform legal duty.

young person: in law, male or female between 12th and 18th birthdays.

child: person under 12.

Canadian courts

Each province has different names for its courts. Here is a list, including federal courts, with upper courts listed first . Capitalization is in Canadian Press style, which is lowercase for lower courts in keeping with general capitalization rules. This is not the style used by the courts:

Federal:
Supreme Court
Federal Court of Appeal
Federal Court
Tax Court

Alberta, New Brunswick, Manitoba:
Court of Appeal
Court of Queen's Bench
provincial court

British Columbia:
Court of Appeal
Supreme Court
provincial court

Newfoundland:
Supreme Court (Court of
  Appeal and trial division)
unified family court
provincial court

Northwest Territories, Yukon:
Court of Appeal
Supreme Court
territorial court

Nova Scotia:
Court of Appeal
Supreme Court
provincial court
family court

Nunavut:
Court of Justice

Ontario:
Court of Appeal
Superior Court of Justice
Ontario court of justice

Prince Edward Island:
Supreme Court (appeal
  division and trial division)
provincial court

Quebec:
Court of Appeal
Superior Court
Quebec court (provincial)

Saskatchewan:
Court of Appeal
Court of Queen's Bench
unified family court
provincial court

Tools and technical guides

Abbreviations and acronyms

General

1. Text studded with abbreviations is hard to read and unsightly. Avoid when an option exists.

2. Use only abbreviations and acronyms (abbreviations pronounced as words) that are familiar to ordinary readers.

CN, CTV, MP; Stelco, NATO, radar

3. An abbreviation is sometimes acceptable to avoid an unwieldy lead: **a PLO rocket attack**. But in general, provide the full name later: **Palestine Liberation Organization**.

4. Abbreviations that have become household terms are acceptable in all references. That is, they need not be spelled out, though the full word or phrase may make for more graceful reading.

CBC, MP, NATO, NDP, PoW, RCMP

Note: As to familiarity, it is impossible to set lasting rules. The once-familiar **RAF** (Royal Air Force), for instance, no longer commands widespread recognition, whereas **BBC** does. When in doubt, spell out.

5. When abbreviations follow indefinite articles, the way the abbreviation is pronounced determines whether a or an is used.

a WHO spokesman, an EKG

Acronyms are read as words and rarely require an article.

the bookstore sells CD-ROMs, VANOC ran the Olympics

6. In general, do not put a bracketed abbreviation after the name of an organization: Transportation Safety Board (**TSB**), World Health Organization (**WHO**).

Abbreviations that need this device to be clear should rarely be used.

7. For ease of reading or variety, a general term is often preferable to an abbreviation.

the industrial relations board, mad cow disease, the union, the autoworkers, the company, the association instead of **CIRB, BSE, CAW** and the like.

8. Do not spell out common abbreviations if the full term is not in general use or is hard to pronounce: **TNT** (for trinitrotoluene), DNA (deoxyribonucleic acid), LED (light-emitting diode).

Where necessary, include a brief description to help the reader: **DNA, the carrier of genetic information; LED lights, which don't burn out or get hot.**

9. Abbreviations suitable in one context may be unsuitable in another. **MLA**, for instance, might puzzle readers in Newfoundland and Labrador, Quebec and Ontario, and should be spelled out for general service: **member of the legislative assembly,** or **member of the legislature.** IPO (for **initial public offering)** might work in a business story but not in a general story.

Similarly: **MHA — member of the** (Newfoundland and Labrador) **house of assembly; MNA — member of the** (Quebec) **national assembly; MPP — member of the** (Ontario) **provincial parliament.**

10. Non-English abbreviations that may be unfamiliar to English-speaking readers should be explained at some point.

the terrorist group ETA, the acronym for the Basque name meaning Basque Land and Liberty; the French union federation CGT, short for Confédération générale du travail; the Quebec steel company Sidbec; Soquip, which stands for a French name meaning Quebec Petroleum Development Corp.

➤ See **Plurals of nouns,** page 356.

Style for abbreviations

1. Omit periods in all-capital abbreviations unless the abbreviation is geographical or refers to a person.

AD, CST, IPO, UBC, UFO, VIP, URL; B.C., P.E.I., N.W.T., U.S., T.O., L.A.; J. R. Ewing, J.R., E.T., good ol' J.B.

Note 1: Some public figures become known by initials without periods.

FDR (Franklin Delano Roosevelt), **JFK** (John Fitzgerald Kennedy), **PET** (Pierre Elliott Trudeau), **GBS** (George Bernard Shaw)

Note 2: Compound abbreviations are written without spaces.

M.Sc., P.Eng.

Note 4: Omit periods from currency abbreviations.

US$500, C$800

2. Most lowercase and mixed abbreviations take periods.

f.o.b., Jr., lb., No., m.p.h., B.Comm.

Note: Metric symbols are not abbreviations and take periods only at the end of a sentence.

m, l, km/h

3. Mixed abbreviations that begin and end with a capital letter do not take periods.

PhD, PoW, MiG, U of T

4. Single-letter abbreviations are followed by a period.

36 King St. E. (for **East**)

But **brand X, the letter E**

Style for acronyms

1. Acronyms formed from only the first letter of each word are all capitals.

NATO (North Atlantic Treaty Organization), **AIDS** (acquired immune deficiency syndrome), **CD-ROM** (compact disc read-only memory)

2. Acronyms formed from initial and other letters should usually be written in caps and lowercase.

Dofasco (Dominion Foundries and Steel Corp.), **Nabisco** (National Biscuit Company)

However, sometimes general usage leads to all-caps forms: **BMO** (Bank of Montreal); **VANOC** (Vancouver Organizing Committee for the 2010 Olympic and Paralympic Winter Games). In these cases, keep in mind readability; in some cases it is preferrable to use a descriptive instead: **the Vancouver Olympics organizing committee.**

3. Acronyms that have become common words are not capitalized.

radar (radio detection and ranging), **scuba** (self-contained underwater breathing apparatus), **snafu** (situation normal, all fouled up), **laser** (light amplification by stimulated emission of radiation), **zip** (zoning improvement plan)

Academic degrees and honours

1. In general, avoid the abbreviation and use a phrase instead: **John Woo, who has a doctorate in chemistry.**

2. If it would be cumbersome to follow No. 1, or if the degree is well-known, the abbreviation can be used.

The teen actor earned his BA while working on his first movie. Pauline Regan, MA, and Ann Bullock, B.Sc., spoke to the homeless about educational programs.

3. Follow usual style for abbreviations, as spelled out on page 255: **B.Sc., BA, LLB, M.Sc., MA, B.Comm., PhD, OBE, VC, P. Eng.**

Dates and times

1. For months used with a specific date, abbreviate only **Jan., Feb., Aug., Sept., Oct., Nov.** and **Dec.** Spell out standing alone or with a year alone.

Oct. 1, 1999, was a Friday. January 2006 was wet.

Note: Do not abbreviate a month spelled out in the name of an organization: **the November 17 terrorist group.**

2. In tabular matter, use these forms without periods:

Jan, Feb, Mar, Apr, May, Jun, Jul, Aug, Sep, Oct, Nov, Dec

3. Days of the week are abbreviated only in tabular matter and without periods.

Sun, Mon, Tue, Wed, Thu, Fri, Sat

4. **AD** is acceptable in all references for **anno Domini** (Latin for *in the year of the Lord*) and **BC** for **before Christ**. AD precedes the year; BC follows it.

AD 410, 55 BC

But write **12th century AD.**

5. Write **10 a.m., 3:30 p.m., EDT, AST**

➤ See **Time**, page 407.

Measurements

1. In general, spell out such terms as **kilogram, metre** and **minute.**

A five-kilogram packet costs $2.

2. A few common terms — **km/h, mm, m.p.h., c.c.** — are acceptable on second reference when used with figures.

70 km/h, 105-mm cannon, the old 30-m.p.h. limit, 2,000-c.c. engine

3. Terms may be abbreviated in tabular matter and if used repeatedly.

kg, l, cwt., min.

4. Use this style for imperial abbreviations, both singular and plural, in tabulations:

in., ft., yd., mi.; oz., lb., cwt.; sq. ft.

Similarly: **sec., min., hr.**

5. Use this style for metric symbols, both singular and plural, in tabulations:

mm, cm, m, KB, km, kg, g, t, ml, l, ha, kPa

➤ See **Metric**, page 315; **Numbers**, page 335.

Organizations

1. Use **Bros., Co., Corp., Inc.** and **Ltd.** with corporate names and without commas.

Texaco Inc. has announced a new oilfields development.

Note: Spell out **company**, etc., in the names of entertainment groups unless the group name includes an abbreviation.

Canadian Opera Company, Blues Brothers

2. Do not abbreviate other terms — **association, department, division, organization** and so on — in corporate and government names.

Reader's Digest Association, Justice Department

3. An ampersand is acceptable in corporate names if the organization uses it: **AT&T, A&P, S&P.**

4. Spell out **United Nations** as a noun, but the abbreviation **UN** may be used as an adjective with well-known organizations.

The United Nations will meet. The UN Security Council voted no.

Places

1. For Canadian provinces and territories, use these abbreviations after the name of a community:

Alta.	N.B.	N.S.	Que.
B.C.	N.L.	Ont.	Sask.
Man.	N.W.T.	P.E.I.	

Note 1: After the name of a community or when standing alone, use **Yukon.**

Note 2: An abbreviation has not yet been established for **Nunavut,** so it should be written out in all references.

2. For American states, use these abbreviations after the name of a community.

Ala.	Kan.	Nev.	S.C.
Ariz.	Ky.	N.H.	S.D.
Ark.	La.	N.J.	Tenn.
Calif.	Md.	N.M.	Vt.
Colo.	Mass.	N.Y.	Va.
Conn.	Mich.	N.C.	Wash.
Del.	Minn.	N.D.	W.Va.
Fla.	Miss.	Okla.	Wis.
Ga.	Mo.	Ore.	Wyo.
Ill.	Mont.	Pa.	
Ind.	Neb.	R.I.	

Note: Do not abbreviate **Alaska, Hawaii, Idaho, Iowa, Maine, Ohio, Texas, Utah;** or **Puerto Rico, Virgin Islands.**

➤ See **Placelines,** page 347; **Place names,** page 353; and **People, places,** page 340.

3. Generally do not abbreviate the names of countries, provinces or states when standing alone or used adjectivally.

The United States (not U.S.) declared war. The Nova Scotia (not N.S.) cabinet met. The United Kingdom (not U.K.) consists of Britain and Northern Ireland.

Note: The abbreviations **U.K., U.S., B.C.** and **P.E.I.** may be used adjectivally to reflect spoken usage.

the B.C. legislature, a U.K. bank holiday, rival U.S. teams

4. In numbered addresses, write **Ave., Blvd., Cir., Cres., Dr., Hwy., Pky., Rd., Rte., Sq., St., Ter.**

36 King St. E., 111 Sutherland Dr., 9 Binkley Ter.

Note 1: Spell out general locations.

on King Street, down Portage Avenue, the Yonge Street subway

Note 2: Spell out these official residences:

24 Sussex Drive, 10 Downing Street.

5. In general, abbreviate Saint and Sainte in place names.

St. John's, N.L., Sault Ste. Marie

But Saint John, N.B.

Note: Use a hyphen instead of a period after **St** and **Ste** in Quebec place names.

Ste-Agathe, St-Eustache

➤ See **French**, page 304.

6. Do not abbreviate **county, fort, mount, point** and **port** as part of a proper name.

Fort McMurray, Mount Everest, Port Stanley, Ont.

Titles

1. Abbreviate **Gov. Gen.** and **Lt.-Gov.** before names on first reference.

Gov. Gen. Pamela King, Lt.-Govs. Joan Pappas and Alan Bucyk.

Note: Lowercase former governor general (not former Gov. Gen.), former governors general Georges Vanier and Adrienne Clarkson, the late lieutenant-governor Pat Filippo, the then-president John Redway (but prefer a more graceful construction: John Redway, who was president at the time).

2. Do not abbreviate **attorney general, auditor general, district attorney, postmaster general, secretary, secretary general** or **treasurer.**

3. Abbreviate **Dr., Msgr., Prof., Rep., Rev., Sen., Sgt.** and the like before full a on first reference.

Dr. Pamela Gucci, Msgr. Brian Doyle, Profs. Eva Oberast and John Green, Rev. Freda Cernetig, Sen. Kevin Ward.

Miscellaneous usages

1. When necessary, use this style for bracketed political affiliations in parliamentary and legislature copy:

Tom Arlee (NDP-Edmonton East), Sen. Mary Atkins (Con-Man.), Myron Martin (Lib-Snowy River), Rep. John Whyte (R-Pa.), Sen. Obie Black (Ind-Va.), state Sen. Darleen Healey (D-Queens)

Note: In general, prefer a descriptive phrase to the bracketed style.

➤ See **Government**, page 310.

2. Abbreviate ship and plane designations.

HMCS Restigouche, USS Johnson, SST (but spell out on first reference: supersonic transport)

Note: The is not required before HMCS or HMS, since HM stands for Her Majesty.

➤ See **Ships,** page 262.

3. Do not abbreviate books of the Bible.

Genesis, Leviticus

4. In general, spell out serial terms, but **article (Art.), number (No.), page (p.), section (Sec.)** and **volume (Vol.)** may be abbreviated before a number.

Block 1, Chapter 2, page 3, p. 3, Vol. 9

➤ See **Numbers**, page 335.

5. Do not use periods with clipped forms that have become accepted as complete words.

ad, disco, exam, gym, hi-tech, lab, math, polio, porn

6. Do not use periods with shortened forms of first names if they are pronounced as spelled.

Al, Alex, Barb, Ben, Ed, Fred, Marj, Pat, Sam, Will

But **Danl., Geo., Thos.** when such terms appear in textual matter.

7. Do not use periods when letters designate persons or things.

the spy chief Z, exhibit A, the mysterious Madame X

But use a period if the letter is an abbreviation.

Mrs. G., (shortened from **Gamp**)

8. In general, do not use such shortenings as **Penetang** (for **Penetanguishene**), **Peterboro** (for **Peterborough**), **Soo** (for **Sault Ste. Marie**) and **Xmas** (for **Christmas**).

Note: Write **Soo Greyhounds**, the official name of the Ontario Hockey League team.

Aboriginal Peoples

First Nations, Métis, Inuit

Canada's Aboriginal Peoples comprise three distinct groups: First Nations (sometimes called Indians), Inuit and Métis. Their numbers are estimated at more than one million. In the 2006 census they made up four per cent of the Canadian population. This group is younger than the general Canadian population and is growing at a much higher rate.

It is a common misconception that most Aboriginal Peoples live on reserves. In fact, Inuit and Métis generally do not, and a large proportion of those who identify themselves in the census as North American Indians live off reserves, many of them in large urban centres.

Three subgroups apply to First Nations in Canada. **Status Indians** qualify as Indians under the Indian Act and can take advantage of certain rights reserved for them. **Non-status Indians** are those who have never registered or are not eligible to register under the terms of the act. **Treaty Indians** are those who are registered with a treaty band and are descended from Indians who signed treaties with the Crown.

By agreeing to treaties most Canadian Indians exchanged some interests in their ancestral lands in return for various payments and promises from Crown officials.

There are about 600 First Nation bands in Canada. A **band** is a First Nation community for whom lands have been set apart and for whom money is held in trust by the Crown.

Writing about Aboriginal Peoples

1. Canada's Aboriginal Peoples are not a homogeneous group with a standard set of interests and grievances. An effort should be made to reflect their diversity in stories specifically dealing with aboriginal groups.

Saying someone is **an Alberta native** is unhelpful. Try to identify the tribal affiliation or the reserve.

Milton Born With a Tooth, an Alberta Peigan; Barbara Harris of the Six Nations of the Grand River Territory; Neil Sterritt, hereditary chief of the Gitxsan-Wet'suwet'en Nation in British Columbia; Angie Wahienhawi Barnes, grand chief of the Mohawk council at Akwesasne Territory near Cornwall, Ont.

2. If a language other than English or French is spoken, include it in the body of the story: **John Mark, who addressed the forum in Cree.**

3. Use the style and spelling preferred by aboriginals for the names of their communities: **Nickel Palm Reserve, Grassy Narrows First Nation**. A good resource is the Indian and Northern Affairs Department's website, which lists the names of most aboriginal communities.

Identities

1. The term **First Nation** or **Nations** is widely used by status and non-status Indians. It does not have a legal definition. Others still prefer to be called **Indian**. When known, use the preference of the group or individual.

First Nation, rather than **reserve**, is also used by many bands in the name of their community: **Gameti First Nation**.

2. Originally, the word **Métis** was applied to descendants of French traders and trappers and Indian women in the Canadian northwest. Now it is usually taken to mean anyone of mixed Indian and European ancestry. Many Canadians have this mixed ancestry but not all describe themselves as Métis. Even Métis organizations have different definitions of who is Métis.

3. There are about 56,000 **Inuit** (never Eskimo) in Canada. They live in about 50 small settlements above the treeline from Labrador to Alaska. The Inuit population is growing rapidly. Inuit make up 85 per cent of the population of the territory of Nunavut.

The singular of Inuit is **Inuk**. Their language is **Inuktitut**.

The Inuit of the western Arctic call themselves **Inuvialuit**.

Note: Do not confuse the **Inuit** and the **Innu**, a First Nations people who live in Labrador and northeastern Quebec.

Languages

There are many different aboriginal languages spoken in Canada. **Cree** is the most common, followed by **Inuktitut** and **Ojibwa**. Many of the other languages are spoken by only a couple of thousand people.

Iroquois languages are spoken by such groups as the Six Nations, including the Mohawk and Oneidas.

Northern aboriginal people speak **Athapaskan** languages, while those in British Columbia speak languages from several families, the most common being **Salishan**.

Aircraft, ships, guns

Style for names

1. For the names of aircraft, guns, tanks, rockets and the like, use a hyphen when a figure follows a letter.

a DC-10 jetliner, a CF-18 fighter, an M-16 rifle, an M-60 tank, a Russian SSN-8 rocket

Note: Satellite names do not take a hyphen: **Anik F1, Anik F2.**

2. Do not use a hyphen when a letter follows a figure.

an FA-18A fighter, a 727-100C cargo plane, the JT-15D fan-jet engine

3. Do not put a hyphen between a spelled-out name and a number.

a Dash 8-300, an F-4 Phantom 2 fighter, a Leopard 2 tank, a Polaris A-3 rocket

4. Form plurals by adding *s* without an apostrophe.

two Dash 7s, a shipment of AK-47s, 15 M-60s

Aircraft

1. Refer to an aircraft with or without the name of the maker or designer.

Lockheed L-1011 TriStar, Lockheed L-1011, L-1011, TriStar

2. North American military aircraft carry a prefixed letter to indicate the basic function: *A* for *attack, B* for *bomber, C* for *cargo* or transport, *F* for *fighter, H* for *helicopter, S* for *anti-submarine, T* for *trainer.*

Note: Do not confuse the prefix *C* for *Canadian* (**a CF-18 fighter**) with the *C* for *cargo* (**a CC-130 Hercules**).

3. A jumbo jet is any very large jet aircraft, such as a *DC-10, Boeing 747, L-1011* or *Airbus.*

Ships

1. The terms **ship** and **boat** are less than precise. A good general rule is to use **boat** for smaller inshore or lake craft, **ship** for larger ocean-going craft. **Vessel** is a handy catch-all for anything bigger than a rowboat. Deepsea freighters, tankers, bulk carriers, container ships, ocean-going passenger liners and most naval ships should never be called boats. (Naval exceptions: motor torpedo boats and submarines.)

2. Words to describe boats and ships vary from region to region. **Laker** is a common term for Great Lakes vessels but may be unfamiliar to readers in some areas of the country. **Fish boat** is an everyday term on the West Coast but unheard of on the East Coast, where such craft are called **fishing boats**.

3. Avoid *nauticalese* that is indecipherable to the average reader — or be prepared to translate it: **fo'c's'le** (forward part of a ship where crew live); **bottom** (a freighter or tanker); **hawser** (cable or heavy rope used to secure a ship to a wharf); **dead-reckoning** (fixing a ship's position by instruments when observation of stars is not possible); **"It's going down by the head."** (A ship is sinking bow-first.)

4. For numbers in ships' names, use the vessel's own style: **Queen Elizabeth 2, Bluenose II**.

5. The Canadian navy has a variety of ships. The most powerful are its **command and control destroyers**, with a complement of nearly 250-300 sailors, but the backbone of the navy is its 12 **patrol frigates**, which have between 225-250 sailors. The navy also employs **submarines** with a crew of 55-60; **replenishment ships** — often called tankers — with a crew of 300; and smaller **coastal defence vessels** with a crew of 37-41, most of whom are naval reservists. Canada does not have cruisers, battleships or aircraft carriers. With the exception of the replenishment ships, each navy vessel can properly be referred to as a warship and its crew **the ship's company**.

6. The familiar abbreviations **HMCS, USS** or **HMS** may be used before the name of a military ship: **HMCS Terra Nova, USS Coral Sea**, etc.

Note: Do not put *the* in front of HMCS or HMS for reasons that are obvious when the abbreviation is written out: *(the)* **Her Majesty's Canadian Ship Halifax**, etc. Naval tradition also drops *the* on second reference to military ships: **The damaged tanker was escorted by Terra Nova into port at Vancouver**. But use the article *the* before names of non-military ships: **The Titanic sank off Cape Race, N.L.**

Graphics can be particularly useful in presenting technical details to the reader.

7. Avoid or spell out less familiar, cumbersome or archaic abbreviations: **MV** (for motor vessel) **Lollipop**; **CCGS** (for Canadian Coast Guard Ship) **Louis S. St. Laurent**; **RMS** (for Royal Mail Ship) **Titanic**, etc.

8. Avoid terms like **seamen** and **fishermen** unless the sex is important and known to be male. **Crew members** and **crew** are always serviceable.

Graphics can be particularly useful in presenting technical details to the reader.

A look at HMCS Halifax

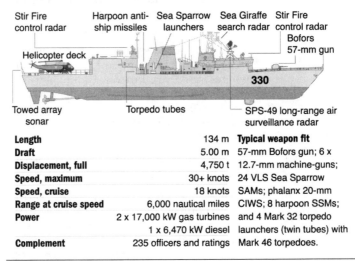

Stir Fire control radar

Harpoon anti-ship missiles

Sea Sparrow launchers

Sea Giraffe search radar

Stir Fire control radar

Bofors 57-mm gun

Helicopter deck

330

Towed array sonar

Torpedo tubes

SPS-49 long-range air surveillance radar

		Typical weapon fit
Length	134 m	57-mm Bofors gun; 6 x
Draft	5.00 m	12.7-mm machine-guns;
Displacement, full	4,750 t	24 VLS Sea Sparrow
Speed, maximum	30+ knots	SAMs; phalanx 20-mm
Speed, cruise	18 knots	CIWS; 8 harpoon SSMs;
Range at cruise speed	6,000 nautical miles	and 4 Mark 32 torpedo
Power	2 x 17,000 kW gas turbines	launchers (twin tubes) with
	1 x 6,470 kW diesel	Mark 46 torpedoes.
Complement	235 officers and ratings	

Source: Saint John Shipbuilding   THE CANADIAN PRESS

9. Ships have been referred to in the feminine form — **she** and **her** — for generations. But some readers find it objectionable, especially if the statement being made is sexist (**she's temperamental**). Use **it**, except in direct quotes.

10. Ships' tonnage is measured and expressed in several ways, all of them complex. In general, the tonnage of warships reflects their weight, while the tonnage of other ships reflects their capacity. Never write that a ship **weighs** such-and-such. If appropriate, try to express dimensions in everyday terms to provide a sense of size: **The tanker is about as long as 40 transit buses parked bumper to bumper.**

11. A ship's country and port of registration may have nothing to do with the vessel's ownership or the nationality of its crew. Many ships sail under what is known as a **flag of convenience**, meaning they are registered in countries with lower registry charges and wage rates than the owners would pay in their home countries. Hence, a ship identified as **Panamanian-registered** may in fact be owned in a country halfway around the world from Panama. Shipping agents may be able to help with such details as the nationality of the crew, the nature of the cargo, last port of call, etc.

12. Some marine measures:

nautical mile 1.853 kilometres (6,080 feet)
knot one nautical mile an hour
fathom six feet (slightly under two metres)

Guns

1. A **rifle** has a grooved bore and fires bullets from cartridges. A **shotgun** has a smooth bore, may be double-barrelled and fires shot from shells. A **pistol** may be a revolver, which holds cartridges in a revolving cylinder, or an automatic, which holds cartridges in a magazine. A **cartridge** is a case consisting of an explosive charge and a bullet or shot. Shotgun **shells** are filled with powder and shot made of lead or steel.

2. When reporting crime stories, avoid the casual use of the term **hunting rifle**, which wildlife and hunting organizations argue is accurate only when used in context with a hunter legally pursuing game. Try to get a precise description of weapons from police and other authorities.

3. Precision is also welcome in military stories. Aside from the fact a military audience is quick to correct mistakes, even for the lay reader there is a difference between an **assault rifle** and a **.50-calibre machine-gun**. Similarly there is a huge difference between a **mortar bomb** and an **artillery shell**.

4. Rifles, pistols, revolvers and other small arms are usually described in **calibre**, which is a measurement of the diameter of the inside of the barrel and is expressed in decimal fractions of an inch or in metric. The word calibre is not used in metric measurements. Write **a .22-calibre rifle, a 9-mm pistol**.

5. More precise description of calibre is expressed by an added set of figures (after a hyphen) to designate load, speed of bullet or year of adoption: **.30-30, .250-3000, .30-06**. Often such precision is necessary to differentiate among .30-calibre guns.

6. Shotguns are measured in **gauge**. Gauge refers to the number of balls, with a diameter the size of the inside of the barrel, that can be made from a pound of lead. For a shotgun with a barrel 0.729 inches in diameter, for instance, a pound of lead yields 12 balls, so the gun is called a **12 gauge**. The .410 is a calibre but is commonly called a gauge. Other gauges have no decimal point.

7. **Gun** is an acceptable term for any firearm; it may also be used to describe larger weapons, such as artillery pieces.

8. Large naval and artillery guns fire **shells**; mortars fire **bombs**. A **round** is one shot, whether from a handgun, a rifle or a cannon.

9. The **magazine** of a firearm simply refers to the reservoir or device holding extra rounds of ammunition to be fed into the chamber through spring, bolt or some other action. The magazine can take various forms, such as the **rotary** (as found on the Thompson machine-gun or **tommy-gun**), **tubular** (in some bolt action, semi-automatic, lever and pump-action rifles), **belt** (which feeds ammunition into rapid-fire automatic weapons) or **box** (either a fixed or detachable compartment).

The term **clip** describes a detachable magazine used with bolt-action, semi-automatic and automatic rifles, as well as some shotguns and handguns (usually semi-automatic or fully automatic) holding a varying number of cartridges, from two up. Note that a magazine is not always a clip.

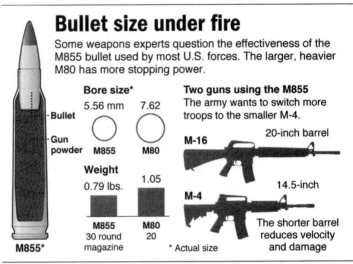

Bullet size under fire

Some weapons experts question the effectiveness of the M855 bullet used by most U.S. forces. The larger, heavier M80 has more stopping power.

Bore size*

5.56 mm   7.62

M855   M80

Weight

0.79 lbs.   1.05

M855   M80
30 round   20
magazine

M855*

Two guns using the M855
The army wants to switch more troops to the smaller M-4.

M-16   20-inch barrel

M-4   14.5-inch

The shorter barrel reduces velocity and damage

* Actual size

SOURCE: Defense Department   AP

10. A **semi-automatic** reloads itself after each shot and fires once each time the trigger is depressed. An **automatic** weapon fires continuously as long as the trigger is depressed and there are rounds in the magazine.

11. The production and use of anti-personnel **landmines** are banned by an international treaty, although a number of countries, notably the United States, are not signatories. The treaty bans only anti-personnel mines. Anti-tank mines and weapons such as Claymore mines are legal. The former only go off under the weight of a heavy vehicle. The latter are command-detonated, that is they must be manually triggered.

➤ See **Military**, page 322.

Types of landmines

The four basic types of anti-personnel landmines:

▶ **BLAST MINES:** Laid on ground or buried just beneath surface. Usually detonated by pressure of footstep on top of mine. Upward explosive blast maims or kills victim.

◀ **FRAGMENTATION MINES:** Usually laid above ground, often camouflaged and fixed to stakes, detonated when person walks into tripwire. Typically projects damaging fragments over 20-metre-radius circle.

POMZ-2

Valsella VS-50

▶ **BOUNDING MINES:** Usually buried. Pressure to tripwire or fuse atop mine causes small explosion that projects mine body upward to height of one metre or more, where main body explodes and scatters fragments.

Valmara 69

◀ **DIRECTIONAL FRAGMENTATION MINES:** Mounted above ground, packed with steel balls or metal fragments in front of explosive charge. Detonated by trip wire or remote control. Scatters fragments frontward. Typical version, U.S. Claymore, propels balls 50 yards in a 60-degree arc.

M18A1 Claymore

Sources: AP reports, The Arms Project of Human Rights Watch / Physicians for Human Rights, Red Cross, United Nations

THE CANADIAN PRESS / AP

Capitalization

General

The Canadian Press follows a modified down style. That is, where a reasonable choice exists, we use lowercase. This is the basic rule:

Capitalize all proper names, trade names, government departments and agencies of government, names of associations, companies, clubs, religions, languages, nations, races, places, addresses. Otherwise lowercase is favoured where a reasonable option exists.

Here are some guidelines:

2. Capitalize common nouns — base, drive, ocean, church, department — when they are part of a formal name: **Canadian Forces Base Trenton, Sussex Drive, Atlantic Ocean, Catholic Church, Fisheries Department.** Generally, lowercase them when standing alone in subsequent references: **the Canadian Forces base, the drive, the ocean, the church, the department.**

Note: In sports references the words **Games** (as in **Olympic** or **Commonwealth Games**), **Plate** (as in **Queen's Plate**), **Series** (as in **World Series**) and so on are capitalized when standing alone in subsequent references. This is to avoid confusion with the generic use of the words (as in **a series of rained-out games**). Also, it is three **Cups,** in second references for such awards as Stanley Cups.

3. Lowercase the common-noun elements of names in plural uses: **the Atlantic and Pacific oceans, John and Leslie streets, prime ministers Marie Leclair and James Dunn.** But retain capitalization for the plurals of abbreviations: **Lt.-Govs. Michael O'Hara and Robert Bernard, Drs. (Revs., Profs., Sgts.) Fraser Douglas and Berthe Lucas.**

4. Capitalize formal titles directly preceding a name: **Energy Minister Marcie Edmond.** Lowercase them when standing alone or set off from the name with commas: **the energy minister; the energy minister, Marcie Edmond; Marcie Edmond, the minister of energy.**

5. As a rule of thumb, formal titles are those that could be used with the surname alone: **Bishop Vardy.** These embrace government titles (**Prime Minister Brown, Ald. Chester**), professional titles (**Dr. Masse, Prof. Seguin**), military and paramilitary titles (**Pte. Kirkup, Insp. Low**) and religious titles (**Rabbi Dubuc, Brother Agnew**).

6. Lowercase occupational titles and job descriptions: **GM president Andre Lefort, general manager Sally James, news editor Agathe Simard, author Susan Sontag, nurse Tom Atfield.**

➤ See **Titles**, page 410.

7. The instruction *capitalize* refers only to the first letter of a word. If other letters are to be capitalized, *all-caps* or other specific instructions are given.

8. In sections dealing with the capitalization of book, film, music and other such titles, the term *principal words* means nouns, pronouns, adjectives, adverbs, verbs, the first and last word of the title, as well as prepositions and conjunctions of four letters or more.

9. Many organizations, including The Canadian Press, capitalize staff titles (even when standing alone), department names and the like in internal documents. If this policy is used, be consistent.

the President; Editor-in-Chief, Head Office; Personnel

Alliances

1. Capitalize alliances and similar groupings.

Confederation, the European Union, Commonwealth, NATO allies, Warsaw Pact, East and West (ideological groupings), **Allies** (in world wars), **Group of Eight** (industrial countries)

2. Write **western allies, imperial ambitions, the coalition against Iraq.**

Animals and birds

1. Generally lowercase the names of animals, birds, fish and so on.

collie, dachshund, pit bull, grizzly bear, palomino, pinto, quarter-horse, shorthorn, blue jay, herring gull, mallard, phoebe, robin, snowy owl, eastern cottontail rabbit, brown trout, snapping turtle, western rattlesnake, red admiral, hawk moth, dragonfly

2. Capitalize names derived from proper nouns except where usage has established the lowercase.

angora (cat, goat, rabbit), **Angus cattle, Baltimore oriole, Canada goose, Clydesdale horse, Dalmatian, German shepherd, Great Dane, Guernsey cow, Holstein-Friesian, Irish terrier, Kodiak bear, mandarin duck, Newfoundland dog, Percheron, Rottweiler, St. Bernard, Shetland pony, Siamese cat, spaniel**

Note: Unless the sex has been established, refer to an animal as *it.*

The dog wolfed its dinner. Toby, who was famished, wolfed his dinner. A bull gored his tormentor. The doe licked her leg.

3. In scientific names, capitalize only the first word.

Orcinus orca (killer whale), **Ovis canadensis** (Rocky Mountain bighorn sheep), **Ursus arctos horribilis** (grizzly bear), **Branta canadensis** (Canada goose), **Cyanocitta cristata** (blue jay), **Grus americana** (whooping crane)

Awards

1. Capitalize awards, honours and decorations.

Order of Canada, Order of Merit, Governor General's Awards, National Newspaper Awards, Nobel Peace Prize, Nobel Prize for chemistry, a Nobel Prize winner, Pulitzer Prize for international reporting, a Pulitzer Prize-winning writer, Victoria Cross, Bronze Star.

Note: French awards follow French style: **Croix de guerre.**

2. Lowercase common-noun references standing alone.

the order, the awards, the prize, the cross

Buildings

1. Capitalize the proper names of well-known buildings, bridges, canals, parks, roads, rooms and other manufactured features.

Parliament Buildings, East Block, White House, Oval Office, Buckingham Palace, U.S. Capitol, Archambault Penitentiary, Calgary City Hall, Lions Gate Bridge, St. Lawrence Seaway, Welland Canal, Laurentian Autoroute, Vancouver International Airport, Union Station, War Memorial, CN Tower, Montreal Neurological Institute, Toronto Hospital, Square of Heavenly Peace, Hall of Mirrors, Sistine Chapel, Fundy National Park, French Embassy

2. Lowercase general terms standing alone, in plurals or in descriptive uses.

the palace, the international airport, the capitol, the city hall, the hospital, the Panama and Suez canals, a St. Lawrence bridge, Banff and Jasper national parks

The Canadian Press, Associated Press, AFP

1. Capitalize **The Canadian Press** and **The Associated Press** when the full names are used. On second reference, it is The Canadian Press but **the AP** (lowercase *the*).

Note: Where the use is possessive, *The* is capitalized: **The Canadian Press's membership, The Associated Press's reporter.** But where the use is adjectival rather than possessive, the article is lowercased and the apostrophe omitted: **the Canadian Press membership, the Associated Press reporter.**

2. The name of The Canadian Press's French-language operation is **La Presse Canadienne**.

3. **Agence France-Presse** is so spelled. **AFP** is acceptable in second reference.

➤ See **Newspapers and magazines** below.

Compositions

1. Capitalize the principal words in the titles of books, broadcast programs, films, plays, poems, songs, speeches, works of art and other compositions. For a definition of principal words, see page 271, No. 8.

The Watch That Ends the Night, CBC's World at Six, Gone With the Wind, The Taming of the Shrew, In Flanders Fields, Gettysburg Address, The Da Vinci Code, the Mona Lisa

Note: Composition titles, except for the Bible, can be written in italics to differentiate them in regular copy, when technically possible, or enclosed in quotation marks when italics are not an option. If they are already set off as a list or differentiated in some other way such as font style, as above, there is usually no need for quotation marks or italics.

2. Do not capitalize *the* at the start of names of almanacs, the Bible, dictionaries, directories, encyclopedias, gazetteers, handbooks and the like.

the Canadian Almanac, the Canadian Oxford Dictionary, the Encyclopaedia Britannica, the Canadian Press Stylebook

3. **Volume, chapter, section, act, scene**, etc., are capitalized when they precede a number. But **page, paragraph, verse** and **line** are lowercase in keeping with widespread practice: **page 20, line 7**.

See Numbers below.

4. Use this style for references:

Act 1, Scene 2; 1 Kings 15:5-7 (i.e. First Book of Kings, Chapter 15, verses 5-7); Henry IV, Part 2 or 2 Henry IV

5. Lowercase art styles, schools and movements unless the word is derived from a proper noun or can be confused with a common word:

art deco, art nouveau, baroque, cubism, **impressionism, neoclassical**

But Dada, Gothic, Renaissance, Romanesque, the Bloomsbury Group

➤ See **Music** below.

Courts

1. Capitalize superior, including appeal, courts.

Privy Council, Supreme Court, Federal Court, Court of Queen's Bench, Superior Court (Quebec, Ontario), Appeal Court, International Court of Justice (the World Court), European Court of Justice, High Court of Justice (the High Court), U.S. Tax Court, U.S. Court of Military Appeals, U.S. Court of Appeals

Lowercase divisions.

the appeal division (or trial division) of the Supreme Court

2. Lowercase lower courts.

family court, youth court, U.S. customs court, U.S. district court

➤ For a full list of Canadian courts see page 250.

3. Capitalize **Crown** when referring to the supreme governing power.

The Crown dropped the charge. The matter was in the hands of the Crown attorney.

Derivatives

1. Lowercase proper names that have acquired independent meaning.

arabic numerals, bohemian, brussels sprouts, cardigan, chinese red, draconian, duffel coat, dutch oven, french fries, mackintosh, manhattan, manila paper, morocco leather, oxford cloth, plaster of paris, portland cement, roman type, sandwich, scotch whisky, spartan, venetian blind, watt

2. Medical terms tend to retain the capital longer than commoner words.

Achilles tendon, Fallopian tube, Pap smear, Freudian slip

But **caesarean section**

Note: When in doubt, capitalize.

Food and drink

1. Brand names of foods and drinks are capitalized.

Alphabits	Skor bar
Timbits	Pepsi-Cola

2. In food names, there is no consistency in the capitalization of proper nouns. Some are capped: **oysters Rockefeller, McIntosh apple, Bing cherries.** Others are not: **baked alaska, cheddar cheese, caesar salad.** Follow the *Canadian Oxford Dictionary* unless *Caps and Spelling* shows otherwise.

3. The names of drinks are generally lowercased: **brandy, manhattan, champagne, scotch.** But wines named after grape varieties are likely to be capitalized: **Zinfandel, Pinot Noir, Sauterne.** Follow Oxford unless *Caps and Spelling* shows otherwise.

4. At the start of a recipe list, capitalize the name of the dish being made:

Apple Oatmeal Squares
250 ml (1 cup) all-purpose flour
250 ml (1 cup) quick-cooking rolled oats, etc.

➤ See **Metric**, page 321, for more on recipes.

Foreign personal names

Such particles as **de, des, di, du, le, la, lo, van** and **von** are usually lowercase except when they begin a sentence.

Charles de Gaulle. De Gaulle said no. Manfred von Richthofen was nicknamed the Red Baron. Von Richthofen was a flying ace.

Note 1: Observe personal preferences.

Pierre De Bane, S. S. Van Dine, Martin Van Buren, Jean de La Fontaine

Note 2: Particles are sometimes dropped on second reference.

Ludwig van Beethoven, Beethoven; Guy de Maupassant, Maupassant; Jean de La Fontaine, La Fontaine; Joachim von Ribbentrop, Ribbentrop; Lorenzo de Medici, the Medici

Geography

1. Capitalize geographic and widely recognized descriptive regions.

the North (Canada), **Far North, Northern Canada, High Arctic, Western Canada, Central Canada, East Coast** (region, not shoreline), **Maritime provinces, Prairies, Barrens, the Front, Niagara Peninsula, Nile Delta, Alaska Panhandle, Downtown Eastside** (Vancouver), **Lower Manhattan** (New York City), **West End** (London), **Upstate New York, Far East, Orient, North Atlantic, Central Africa, Central Asia, Western Hemisphere, North Pole, the Pole, Tropic of Cancer**

Note 1: Write **eastern Quebec, southern Ontario, northern Ontario, southern California.**

Note 2: The **Atlantic provinces are New Brunswick, Newfoundland, Nova Scotia and Prince Edward Island. The Maritimes consist of New Brunswick, Nova Scotia and Prince Edward Island.**

Note 3: Write **English Canada** and **French Canada** but English-Canadian and French-Canadian.

➤ See **Political divisions** below.

2. Capitalize specific natural features.

Canadian Shield, Gulf Stream, Rocky Mountains, Mackenzie River, Yellowhead Pass, Niagara Escarpment, Lake Winnipeg, Great Lakes

3. Capitalize fanciful or imaginative terms.

Rust Belt, Deep South, Down Under, Bible Belt, Ho Chi Minh Trail, Promised Land, Eternal City, Silicon Valley

4. Lowercase points of the compass, mere direction and location, and descriptive regions not widely recognized as such.

north, to the west of Newfoundland, rain sweeping south, east coast (shoreline, not region), southern Saskatchewan, northwestern Ontario, eastern Newfoundland, downtown Calgary, north-end Toronto

5. Lowercase **northern, southern, eastern** and **western** in terms derived from regions.

a northern custom, southern hospitality, an easterner, eastern provinces, a western Canadian, a westerner, western armies, far eastern peoples

Note: In Western Canada, Ontario people are referred to as **easterners**. In Ontario, Maritimers are referred to as **easterners**. Don't use **Eastern Canada** unless the meaning is clear.

6. Lowercase **parallel** and the like.

48th parallel, international date line, equator

7. Lowercase generic terms standing alone except when they are conventionally used as a short form of the proper noun.

Lake Erie, the lake; Rocky Mountains, the mountains; Grand Canyon, the canyon

But the Interior (for instance, British Columbia), **the Island** (for instance, Prince Edward Island), **the States** (the United States), **the Continent** (Europe), **the Channel** (English Channel), **the Lakes** (Great Lakes)

8. Lowercase the common-noun element in plurals.

lakes Superior and Erie, Red and Assiniboine rivers, the Northern and Southern hemispheres, King and Front streets

9. Lowercase **province** and **state** used in a geographic sense.

Quebec province, New York state

But capitalize as part of the corporate name.

Province of Quebec bonds, New York State vs. Smith

➤ See **Political divisions** below.

Government departments

1. Capitalize specific international, national, provincial and state government departments, ministries, agencies, boards, etc., including short forms of the proper name.

World Health Organization, United Nations Children's Fund, Department of Agriculture, Agriculture Department, Canada Post Corp., Canada Post, St. Lawrence Seaway Authority, National Parole Service, Library of Parliament, Canada Industrial Relations Board, Pensions Appeal Board, Census Bureau (U.S.), Vietnam Health Ministry, Ukrainian Embassy, Italian Consulate, Secret Service, Office of the Commissioner of Official Languages, Ontario Ministry of Labour, Ontario Labour Ministry, B.C. Highways Ministry, Georgia Department of Human Resources

Otherwise, lowercase branches and sections within government ministries.

communications branch of the Ministry of Labour, regulations section of the Natural Resources Ministry

2. Capitalize cabinet portfolios only as part of a title directly preceding a name: **Finance Minister June Atkins.** But **June Atkins, minister of finance.**

3. Capitalize proper-name elements of a department or ministry when they stand alone and are being used as a noun to represent the ministry. Otherwise, lowercase.

The cuts will affect Justice and Communications. In those 25 years, she worked in Housing and Natural Resources.

But not Ellen Howe, a former Justice minister

4. Lowercase common-noun elements standing alone and in plurals.

the department, a ministry spokeswoman, board figures, the authority, the service's record, departments of Justice and Defence

5. Lowercase local government councils, departments, boards, etc.

Peel regional council, Edmonton city council, Saskatoon board of education, Moncton development department

Historical terms

Capitalize the names of historic periods and events.

Stone Age, Dark Ages, Middle Ages, Crusades, Norman Conquest, Reformation, Industrial Revolution, the Depression or the Great Depression, Dirty '30s, Cultural Revolution, Creation, Exodus, the Flood, Civil War (American), Battle of the Plains of Abraham, War of 1812,

Reign of Terror, Riel Rebellion, First World War, Prohibition, Holocaust, Battle of Britain, Vietnam War, Quiet Revolution, October Crisis, Winnipeg General Strike, Montreal Massacre

But **medieval**, a **reformation**, a **renaissance** in painting, **19th century**, **ice age** (no single period)

Note: Capitalize **Confederation** in references to Canada: **Fathers of Confederation.**

Holidays

Capitalize holidays, religious feasts and all special times.

New Year's Eve (but in the new year), **Ash Wednesday**, **April Fool's Day**, **Mother's Day**, **Canada Day**, **St-Jean-Baptiste Day**, **July Fourth**, **Fourth of July**, **Halloween**, **Christmas Day**, **Hanukkah**, **Yom Kippur**, **Passover**, **Ramadan**, **D-Day**, **Education Week**

Note: Write **election day, census day.**

Internet terms

1. Capitalize specific proper names.

World Wide Web, Internet, Adobe Acrobat, Windows Explorer

2. Lowercase descriptive or generic terms.

chat room, cyberspace, domain name, email, home page, intranet, web, web browser, webcam, webcast, webmaster, website

3. Use all-caps for such abbreviations and acronyms as:

HTML (Hypertext Markup Language); **CD-ROM** (compact disc read-only memory); **RAM** (random access memory); **URL** (universal resource locator)

➤ See **Online news,** page 95.

Laws and documents

1. Capitalize proclaimed laws, treaties, important legal codes and historic documents.

British North America Act, Constitution (Canada), **Charter of Rights, Colombo Plan, UN Charter, Criminal Code, Declaration of Independence, Magna Carta, Kyoto Protocol**

Note: Constitution is capitalized in all references when the Canadian Constitution is meant. Otherwise it is capitalized only when preceded by a name: **the U.S. Constitution, the constitution.** Also lowercase **constitutional: the constitutional crisis.**

2. Lowercase proposed and defeated legislation, amendments,

general references and plurals.

the proposed charter of rights, the Privacy Act amendment, the Charlottetown accord, a disarmament treaty, the code, the BNA and human rights acts

3. Lowercase speech from the throne, royal assent, third reading, the president's state of the union message, white paper, green paper.

Legislative bodies

1. Capitalize international and national legislative bodies and their equivalents, including some short forms.

UN Security Council (Security Council), UN General Assembly (General Assembly), Parliament (national), House of Commons, the House, the Commons, the Senate, House of Lords (the Lords), House of Representatives (the House), Chamber of Deputies (the Chamber), Bundestag, Cortes, Diet, Knesset, National Assembly (French)

Note: Generic uses of parliament are lowercase: **the Knesset, Israel's parliament; the Sejm (Polish parliament).**

2. Lowercase general terms, informal terms (except short forms listed above), plurals and derivatives.

the administration, the council, an assembly motion, government, cabinet, lower house, the Canadian and British parliaments, parliamentary, senatorial

But the Commons motion

3. Lowercase provincial, state and regional legislatures and local councils.

Quebec national assembly, Ontario legislature, Ontario provincial parliament (but avoid), Newfoundland and Labrador house of assembly, New South Wales parliament, the Virginia senate, the Northwest Territories council, Peel regional council, Victoria city council

4. Lowercase committees and subcommittees.

the committee on communications and culture

5. Capitalize the full name of royal commissions. But lowercase more informal references to commissions of inquiry.

the Royal Commission on Corporate Concentration, the Royal Commission on Bilingualism and Biculturalism, the Gomery inquiry

But the royal commission, the bilingualism commission

➤ See **Laws and documents** above.

Military

1. Capitalize **Canadian Forces, the Forces** (Canada only).

2. Capitalize **Canadian Army, (Royal) Canadian Navy** and **(Royal) Canadian Air Force** in references to pre-unification forces (before 1968).

3. The general terms **army, navy** and **air force**, written lowercase, may be used of the appropriate branches of the unified Canadian Forces: **a Canadian navy boat.**

4. For foreign forces, lowercase **army, navy** and **air force** when they are preceded by the name of a country.

Lebanese army, U.S. air force, Russian navy

Note: This style is intended for consistency. Many countries do not use **army, navy** or **air force** as the proper name.

5. Otherwise capitalize full, specific names of formations, both military and paramilitary.

Royal Navy, U.S. 8th Air Force, the 27th Army, French Foreign Legion, Royal Marines, Canadian Coast Guard, U.S. National Guard

But the army, the navy, the air force, the legion, the marines, a marine, the coast guard, a coast guard plane, the national guard, a national guardsman

6. Capitalize specific bases, commands, schools and ships.

Canadian Forces Headquarters, Canadian Forces Base Comox, the Citadel (Quebec City), **Joint Chiefs of Staff, French General Staff, 6th Fleet, Royal Military College, HMCS Restigouche, HMS Antelope, USS Iowa**

But a Canadian Forces base

➤ See **Aircraft, ships, guns**, page 262.

7. Capitalize official names of units.

Royal 22e Regiment, 3rd Battalion, B Company, 3rd Infantry Division, 126 Squadron

8. Capitalize nicknames of units.

Van Doo, Desert Rats, Green Berets

9. Capitalize major armed conflicts and rebellions.

Battle of Marathon, Wars of the Roses, French Revolution, U.S. Civil War, Boxer Rebellion, Bolshevik Revolution, Battle of Britain, Battle of the Bulge, Six-Day War, Cultural Revolution

10. Capitalize fronts and important positions.

Western Front, Maginot Line

➤ See **Abbreviations**, page 253; **Military**, page 322.

Music

1. In general, capitalize the principal words in the English titles of musical compositions.

Tchaikovsky's *Symphony No. 4 in F minor*, **Tchaikovsky's** *Fourth Symphony*, *Light My Fire* **by the Doors, Avril Lavigne's** *Complicated*

Note: The words **major, minor, sharp** and **flat** are written lowercase in keeping with widespread practice.

2. When the opus number is given, set it off with a comma.

Handel's Concerti Grossi Nos. 4-6, op. 6; Mozart's Exultate, Jubilate, K. 165; Bach's St. Matthew Passion, BWV 244

3. Translate a foreign title into English unless the work is commonly known by its foreign name.

La Bohème, L'Après-midi d'un faune, Eine kleine Nachtmusik

4. For non-English titles the style varies.

In French titles, capitalize the first word, and the second word too when the first word is an article, and proper nouns: **Mon rêve, Le Rêve passé.**

In Italian, capitalize the first word and proper nouns: **La donna e mobile, La clemenza di Tito.**

In German, capitalize the first word and every noun: **Du bist mein ganzes Sehnen.**

In Latin, capitalize each word: *Te Deum.*

Names

1. Except in the cases of all-lowercase or all-uppercase names, follow the capitalization used by the organization or person unless it hampers readability.

eBay, iPod, WestJet, PepsiCo, MuchMusic

Note: Capitalize lowercase names at the beginning of a sentence: **EBay.**

2. If a corporate or promotional name is all lowercase, cap the first letter for clarity.

Adidas (not **adidas**); **Citytv** (not **citytv**)

For names of people, follow their preference.

k.d. lang

2. If the name is all uppercase, cap only the first letter.

Band-Aid (not **BAND-AID**), **Scrabble** (not **SCRABBLE**), **Via Rail** (not **VIA Rail**)

Note: Initials are capitalized: **IBM, CTV, EMI.**

Nationalities and race

1. Capitalize the proper names of nationalities, peoples, races, tribes and the like.

Aboriginal Peoples, Arab, Arabic, African, African-American, Asian, Caucasian, Chipewyan, Chinese, English-Canadian, Gypsy, Hispanic, Indian, Inuk, Inuit, Jew, Jewish, Latin, Negro, Nordic, Pygmy

2. Write aboriginal (but Aborigine for the Australian race), black, brown, white.

Newspapers and magazines

1. Lowercase the in names of newspapers.

the Toronto Star, the Star; the New York Times, the Times

2. For French-language papers, write Montreal La Presse rather than the Montreal La Presse in first reference. In subsequent references avoid sentence constructions that juxtapose the and le or la: the La Presse editorial. Alternatives include La Presse's editorial, an editorial in La Presse, La Presse said in an editorial.

3. The Canadian Press includes qualifiers like daily, evening and Sunday if the paper prefers them: New York Daily News.

4. Capitalize magazine only when it is part of the title.

Maclean's magazine, Harper's Magazine

Nicknames

Capitalize fanciful names and nicknames.

Iron Curtain, Third World, Boat People, Red Power, Little Italy, Golden Horse-shoe, Old Guard, Big Three, Grits, Grand Old Party (GOP, but avoid), Tiger Williams, Herman (Babe) Ruth, Mack the Knife, Ethelred the Unready, Coeur de Lion, the Sun King, Mother Nature

➤ See also **Names, nicknames, initials**, page 332.

Note: Father, Mother, Mom, Uncle and the like are capitalized when used as a name: The doctor told Father that Aunt Jane is worse. After a personal pronoun, they are lowercased: The doctor told my father that my aunt Jane is worse.

Numbers

1. In general, capitalize a noun followed by a number denoting place in a numbered series.

Act 1, Article 29, Book 3, Channel 2, Chapter 10, Cloud 9, Cosmos 150, Figure 13, Grade 3, Part 2, Pershing 2, Phase 1, Room 125, Square 1, Volume 12, Ward 7

Note: Avoid roman numerals except in personal sequences and in proper names where specified. **Henry Ford III, Bluenose II, Rocky IV**

2. Lowercase such words in plural use.

acts 3 and 5, chapters 1-3, grades 9 through 11

3. Lowercase **page, paragraph, sentence, size, verse, line.**

page 36, paragraph 2, line 3

Organizations

1. Capitalize the full names of organizations and institutions, but lowercase general references, with the exceptions noted below.

American Airlines, the B'nai Brith, the National Organization for Women, Queen's University, the airline, the autoworkers, the organization, the university

Note 1: Company, Limited, Incorporated, Brothers and similar words are abbreviated as part of a name, **General Motors of Canada Ltd.**, except in cultural references: **Canadian Opera Company, Jonas Brothers.**

Note 2: For consistency, lowercase **the** in the names of organizations, except for those noted in *Caps and Spelling*.

➤ See **The** below.

2. Capitalize the names of major subdivisions of an organization.

the General Council of the United Church of Canada, the Chevrolet Division of General Motors

3. Lowercase ordinary internal elements of an organization.

the United Church's division of mission, the board of directors of General Motors, the mortgage department at Bank of Montreal

4. Retain capitalization when the short form of a name is a household word. But use lowercase when referring to members of an organization.

Scouts Canada, the Scouts but **two boy scouts; International Brotherhood of Teamsters, Chauffeurs, Warehousemen and Helpers of America, Teamsters union, the Teamsters; Ku Klux Klan, the Klan, a klansman; Odd Fellows** and **an Odd Fellow** (capped to avoid ambiguity); **Knights of Columbus, the Knights.**

5. Retain capitalization when popular usage has reversed a name and eliminated **of, of the** and the like.

Department of Justice, Justice Department; Ministry of the Interior, Interior Ministry

➤ See **Abbreviations and acronyms**, page 253.

Plants

1. In plant names, capitalize proper nouns and adjectives derived from proper nouns.

Scotch pine, Kentucky blue grass, Douglas fir, white Dutch clover

2. In botanical names, capitalize the first word, lowercase others.

Primula japonica (Japanese primrose), **Taraxacum officinale** (dandelion), **Acer rubrum** (red maple), **Cornus florida** (dogwood)

3. Capitalize the names of fruit and vegetable varieties.

McIntosh, Delicious (apples); **Yukon Gold** (potatoes)

4. Capitalize wheat varieties generally except where usage has established the lowercase.

Selkirk, durum

➤ See **Technical terms**, page 403.

Political divisions

1. Capitalize specific political and administrative divisions.

British Empire, Dominion (Canada), **United Kingdom, French Republic, Greater Vancouver Regional District, Montreal Urban Community, Ward 2, 11th Congressional District, Precinct 2, Muskoka District, McGillivray Township, Niagara Region.**

But **Niagara region, Muskoka district** when referring to the geographical area.

2. Lowercase such words as **city, county, province** and **state** except when they are part of the incorporated name.

in the **city** of Halifax, the **City of Halifax's** credit rating; in Quebec **province**, the **Province of Quebec** vs. Smithers; the California **state** capital, the **State of California's** damage suit; **Quebec City, New York City, Kansas City, Greenwich Village**

Politics

1. Capitalize the full names of political parties and movements, but lowercase **party** in short forms.

Liberal Party of Canada, Liberal party, Conservative Party of Canada, Conservative party, Green Party of Canada, Green party or Greens, Christian Heritage party, Communist party, Young Liberals, National Liberation Front

But **New Democratic Party, Saskatchewan Party, Bloc Québécois, Parti Québécois**

2. Capitalize **Communist, Conservative, Democrat, Fascist, Liberal, Nazi, New Democrat, Socialist** and the like when they refer to a specific party or its members.

3. Lowercase these words when they refer to a political philosophy, except when they are derived from a proper name.

communism, democracy, fascism, socialism, separatism, democratic rights, conservative principles, independent nations, republican system, the left, right-wing group, liberals, communists, social democrats

But **Marxism, Marxists, Nazism, Nazis**

4. Capitalize fanciful names and nicknames.

Grits, Tories, Grand Old Party (GOP, but avoid), Old Guard, Young Turks, Black Power, Greens

5. Capitalize **Leader, Chairman** or **Secretary** when used with the name of a party and directly preceding a name, but lowercase as the title for others.

New Democrat Leader Jack Layton (but **party leader Jack Layton; Communist party General Secretary Do Muoi** (but prefer **Do Muoi, the Communist party general secretary**)

But **Libyan leader Moammar Gadhafi, NDP chairman Roy Brown, party secretary Ann Rogers**

6. Capitalize **Politburo** and **Central Committee**, but lowercase other principal political bodies as well as political conventions.

the government, the administration, the cabinet, Liberal leadership convention, Republican platform committee

➤ See **Legislative bodies** above.

Quotations

1. Capitalize the first word of a complete quotation.

Pickets yelling "Scab!" deterred 200 men from entering.

McCabe replied to the lawyer's "Ah, Mr. McCabe" with an "Oh, hello, Mr. Trout."

Poirier asked, "Did you expect to hear shouts of 'Well done' and 'Good luck'?"

2. Do not capitalize a word or phrase that is quoted merely for discussion or because it is controversial or used ironically or oddly.

What does "gating" mean?

One of the words used was "scab."

The "gift" cost $10.

➤ See **Punctuation**, page 378.

Religion

1. Capitalize sacred names.

Adonai	Lord of Lords
Allah	the Madonna
the Almighty	the Messiah
the Angel Gabriel	Mother Mary
the Apostle Paul,	the Omnipotent
Paul the Apostle	the One Great Spirit
the Baptist	our Lady
Blessed Virgin	Prince of Peace
Buddha	the Prophet (Muhammad)
the Child Jesus	the Saviour
Divine Providence	Siva
Father	the Son
God	the Son of Man
the Godhead	the Twelve Apostles
the Guru	the Virgin
the Holy Family	Vishnu
the Holy Spirit	the Word
Jehovah	Yahweh
King of Kings	

Note: Lowercase **fatherhood, providence** (in a general sense), **messianic, a saviour** (in a non-religious sense), **the angel, an apostle, holy father** (for the Pope).

2. Capitalize personal pronouns referring to God: **He, Him, His, Me, My, Mine, Thou, Thee, Thine** and so on. Lowercase relative pronouns: **who, whom, whose.**

3. Capitalize the proper names and nicknames of the devil.

Satan, Lucifer, Father of Lies, Old Nick, the Antichrist

Note: Lowercase **satanic,** capitalize **Satanism.**

4. Lowercase **god** and **goddess** in references to pagan gods but capitalize their proper names.

the sun god, the gods of Olympus, the goddess Venus, the god Thor

5. Capitalize the names of religions, faiths, their current heads and their adherents.

the Baha'i faith	Islam	Parsee
Buddhist	Jain	the Pope
Christianity	Jew	Shintoist
the Dalai Lama	Muslim	the Sikh religion
Hinduism	Neo-Confucianism	Zen-Buddhism

Note: Lowercase **pagan, atheist, agnostic** (in a general sense), **gentile, spiritualist, theosophist.**

6. Capitalize the names of religious denominations, movements, orders and their adherents.

an Anglican
Baptist
Catholicism
Christian Science,
  a Scientist
Church of Jesus Christ
  of Latter-day Saints,
  a Mormon, Mormonism
Eastern Orthodoxy
Franciscans
Grey Nuns
High, Low Church
Jehovah's Witness,
  a Witness

New Age
Oxford Movement
Papists
Pharisees
Protestantism
Reform Jews
Salvation Army,
  the Army
Sephardism
Seventh-day Adventist,
  an Adventist
Sons of Freedom,
  a Freedomite

7. Capitalize sacred writings and their parts.

the Bible
Book of Genesis
the Epistles
Laws of Manu

Lord's Prayer
New, Old Testament
the Qur'an
Romans

Scripture
Shariah
the Talmud
the Vedas

Note: Lowercase **fisherman's bible, biblical, the gospel truth, a parable, an epistle, apocryphal, talmudic, vedic.**

8. Capitalize such familar references as the following.

Garden of Eden
the Chosen People
Tower of Babel
Noah's Ark
Ten Commandments
City of David
Day of Atonement
the Second Coming
the Last Day

Holy Week
Good Friday
the Crucifixion
the Resurrection
the Prodigal Son
Three Wise Men
Good Samaritan
Yom Kippur

the Shroud of Turin
Diet of Worms
the Hegira
  (Muhammad's)
Ramadan
Festival of Sacrifice
Sabbath
Council of Trent

Note: Lowercase **heaven, hell, paradise, purgatory, nirvana.**

9. Lowercase sacraments, rituals, meetings and the like.

aqiqa
baptism
bar mitzvah
christening
confession
  eucharist

evensong
high mass
holy communion
kaddish
mass
seder

shiva
stations of the
  cross
synod
way of the cross

10. Capitalize **church** as part of the name of a building, a congregation or a denomination.

St. Paul's United Church, the Anglican Church

Note: Write **an Anglican church, the Roman Catholic and Anglican churches, church and state.**

11. Capitalize major subdivisions or sections within a church, but lowercase ordinary internal elements.

the General Council of the United Church, the Anglican Communion, the church's division of mission, the church's revitalization committee.

➤ See **Capitalization**, page 284 and **Titles**, page 411.

Schools

1. Capitalize universities and colleges but not their departments.

Simon Fraser University, Macdonald College, McGill medical school, department of dentistry, English department, faculty of education

2. Uppercase the proper name of schools. Otherwise, lowercase.

York Collegiate Institute, Banff High School, St. John's Catholic School, London School of Economics, Harvard Graduate School of Business, University of Toronto Schools (proper names); **York high school, Rolph Road elementary school, St. John's separate school** (not proper names).

3. Lowercase the names of courses and programs.

political studies program, world history course

Slogans, headlines, greetings

1. Capitalize the principal words of written slogans and newspaper headlines when quoted in the body of a story, but do not use quotation marks.

On one placard was written Restraint — Practise What You Preach. Another sign read Help the Economy.

The editorial appeared under the heading Show Some Leadership.

➤ See **No. 8**, page 278, for a definition of principal words.

➤ For rules on **Headlines**, see page 80.

2. Capitalize common specific greetings such as **Merry Christmas, Happy New Year** and **Happy Birthday.** Lowercase **season's greetings.**

Space

1. Capitalize the proper names of asteroids, comets, constellations, planets, satellites, stars and other unique celestial objects, and nouns and adjectives derived from proper names.

Ceres, Andromeda, Great Bear, Ursa Major, Charles's Wain, Big Dipper, Milky Way, Anik E1, Martian, Jovian, Venusian

2. In general, lowercase the common-noun element of the names of celestial objects.

Ceres asteroids, the constellation of Andromeda, Halley's comet, Crab nebula, Barnard's star

But the North Star (Polaris)

3. Lowercase **earth** except when referred to as a planet. Lowercase **sun** and **moon** in all instances.

down to earth, move heaven and earth, returned to Earth from Mars, Earth's atmosphere, the new moon

4. Lowercase the names of meteorological phenomena.

northern lights, aurora borealis

Sports

1. Capitalize major sports events and trophies.

Olympic Games, Winter Olympics, World Series, World Cup, Canadian Open, Canada Cup, Grey Cup, Queen's Plate, Stanley Cup playoffs, Super Bowl, Vezina Trophy

2. In second references, capitalize **Games, Series, Cup, Open, Plate, Stakes** and the like: **the Series' leading batter, the Plate also-rans.** This is an exception to the rule that common nouns standing alone are lowercased.

➤ See **Sports**, page 152.

The

1. The word **the** (or its non-English equivalent) is capitalized at the start of titles of books, magazines, movies, TV programs, songs, paintings and other compositions, as well as specialty TV channels when **the** is part of the name.

The Last Spike, The New Yorker, L'Amour masqué, The Journal, The Holly and the Ivy, The Artist and His Model, The Sports Network

2. **The** is not capitalized at the start of the names of such works as almanacs, the Bible, directories, encyclopedias, gazetteers and handbooks.

the Canadian Almanac, the Reader's Encyclopedia, the Concise Oxford Dictionary, the Canadian Press Stylebook

3. When **the** is capitalized in a geographical name, retain the capitalization.

The Pas, The Hague, El Salvador

But the Netherlands, the Congo, the City (London financial district), **the Front** (sealing ground off Labrador), **the Barrens**

4. In rare instances, **the** can be capitalized when it is used to give a singular meaning to an ordinary word.

The Change (menopause), **The Show** (baseball's major leagues)

5. For consistency, lowercase **the** in all other names: companies, associations, institutions, newspapers, documents, laws, awards, ships, trains, nicknames, rock groups and so on.

the Bay, the Royal Canadian Legion, the House of Commons, the Foreign Affairs Department, the Anglican Church, the Gazette, the Constitution, the Juno Awards, the Transcontinental, the Royal York Hotel, the Boss (Bruce Springsteen), **the Beatles, the Doors, the Prince of Wales**

Note: Capitalize the definite article in the names of French-language newspapers in accordance with French style: **Le Droit.**

➤ See **Newspapers and magazines** above.

Times and seasons

Lowercase the seasons and spelled-out references to time.

**spring, winter
mountain standard time, eastern daylight time,
Atlantic daylight time**

But MST, EDT, ADT

Titles

1. Capitalize formal titles — those that are almost an integral part of a person's identity — when they directly precede the name.

Pope Benedict, Queen Elizabeth, Prime Minister Gordon Brown, Dr. Hans Selye, Prof. Harold Smith, Sgt. Ann Rutherford, Brother Marcus, Mayor David Miller

Note: With few exceptions, a title more than two words long should be set off from the name with commas: **Arnold Schaur, trade and commerce minister,** . . .

2. A title set off from a name by commas is lowercased. **The prime minister, Gordon Brown, will represent Britain at the talks.**

3. Lowercase occupational titles and descriptions. Titles of officials of companies, unions, political organizations and the like are also lowercased.

Widget president Barbara Sansom, CAW secretary Margaret Wilson, defenceman Patrick Keenan, general manager Art Simpson, commissioner Bert Nobby, coach Guy Lebrun, contralto Maureen Forrester, astronaut John Young, school principal Paul Chambers

Note 1: Avoid the inelegant practice of invariably affixing the description to a person's name as a false title: **rock star Bill Glass, bus driver Mary Owens, Niagara Falls businessman Mario Gucci.** Offer occasional relief by using a **the** phrase: **the contralto Maureen Forrester, the English historian Arnold Toynbee.** Or use a comma construction: Violet Haynes, a Liberal member, disagreed. The spokesman, Tom Jameson, refused to comment. Ford's president, Alain Batty; a truck driver, Mary Owens.

Note 2: Avoid such pileups as **public relations director John O'Connor's department; best-selling Canadian mystery writer Eric Wright.**

4. Capitalize all references to the current Pope, Canada's reigning monarch and the current Canadian Governor General. But lowercase most formal titles standing alone.

the Pope's visit, the Queen's family, wrote to the Governor General

But the king of Denmark, the prime minister, the president, the Communist party chairman

Note: Lowercase **pontiff.**

5. Capitalize **Royal Family** when referring to the British Royal Family. Also **Queen Mother, Her** or **His Majesty** and **Her** or **His Royal Highness,** whether standing alone or with names. For former and future British monarchs, capitalize the title: **the former King.** With foreign royalty, capitalize all current titles used with a proper name and lowercase others: **Queen Astrid, former king Farouk.**

6. Royal — as in **royal visit, royal assent** — is lowercase.

7. **Crown** is capitalized when it refers to the state.

the Crown corporation, the Crown alleged, the Crown jewels; but **the Queen's crown**

8. Capitalize titles of nobility, religion and such that are commonly used instead of the personal name. Lowercase on subsequent references.

the Prince of Wales, the prince; the Duchess of Cornwall, the duchess, the Archbishop of Canterbury, the archbishop

9. Capitalize terms of honour, nobility and respect.

His Excellency, His Honour, Your Honour, Hon. John Jones, Her Worship, His Grace, My Lord

Note: Use such terms only when they appear in direct quotations.

10. To avoid ambiguity, all references to legislative **Speakers** are capped.

11. Lowercase titles preceded by **former, acting** and so on.

prime minister-designate Mary Brown, acting prime minister John Burgess, president-elect Tony Leech, the onetime president Gerald Ford, former mayor Joanne Lesniak

But Deputy Prime Minister Oskar Arendt

Note 1: Abbreviated titles are capped: **the late Dr. Jean Savard.**

Note 2: In references to past events, titles are capped when words like **former** and **the late** are dropped:

The official opening of the St. Lawrence Seaway — on June 26, 1959 — was attended by Prime Minister John Diefenbaker and U.S. President Dwight Eisenhower.

12. Lowercase plural uses of titles.

premiers Jean Martineau and Gertrude Germain, popes John Paul II and John XXIII

Note: Capitalize the plural use of abbreviations: **Profs. Giuseppe Gucci and Helen Bruno.**

13. Lowercase derivatives.

presidential, papal, ministerial, senatorial, mayoral

14. Variations on the titles of cabinet ministers are not capitalized.

junior finance minister Robert Jack; acting health minister Kim Shen

Note: Titles of government officials below cabinet rank are lowercased: **deputy minister Eva Swartz, House leader Ian Loy** (federal), **house leader Ian Loy** (provincial).

15. Following titles are in Canadian Press style:

Prime Minister Stephen Harper
Deputy Prime Minister Tony Soprano
the prime minister, Stephen Harper
former prime minister John Turner
junior finance minister Jean Fortin
deputy trade minister Aldo Conti
Liberal Leader Maxine Hyde
the Speaker
the Governor General
Gov. Gen. Michaelle Jean
lieutenant-governor
Lt.-Gov. Norman Kwong
Senator Donald Oliver

➤ See **Government**, page 310; **Titles**, page 410. Also, **Government departments**, **Military** and **Religion** above. For composition titles, see **Compositions** and **Music** above.

Trade names

1. Capitalize all trade names but use them only when they give point, colour or impact to a story.

The doctor refused to prescribe Tamiflu.
She blew the inheritance on a Mercedes.
He lived for a year on Big Macs and Timbits.

2. A generic term can often be used instead.

headache pill (Aspirin); **adhesive bandage** (Band-Aid); **cola** (Coca-Cola); **fibreglass or glass fibre** (Fiberglas); **tissues** (Kleenex); **heat-resistant glass** (Pyrex); **cotton swabs** (Q-Tips); **plastic foam** (Styrofoam); **petroleum jelly** (Vaseline); **photocopier** (Xerox), **stun gun** (Taser)

Note: Trade names subject to protection in Canada are normally listed in the *Canadian Trade Index*. Do not follow the capitalization in the *Canadian Oxford Dictionary*.

➤ See **Trade names**, page 415.

Common faults

The most common faults in writing are lack of imagination, muted curiosity, and a deaf ear and closed eye for the reader's interests.

These faults lead straight to stories that are predictable, unfocused and boring.

By turn or together, they may confuse readers with conflicting information, leave them gasping for missing facts or infuriated at what they know is misinformation.

Such stories can puzzle readers with fog and bafflegab, and have them wondering what the news means to them and their everyday lives.

Bluntly put, they turn readers off.

Active vs. passive

Think of active verbs as power words — words that drive your sentences, keep the reader's attention and move her briskly along.

Not The economy experienced a quick revival.

But: The economy revived quickly.

Not: At first light there was no sign of the ship.

But: The ship vanished in the night.

Use the passive when a switch in emphasis is helpful, for instance, to put the news ahead of the source:

Not: A grievance board has ordered the reinstatement of a counsellor fired for kicking a patient.

But: A counsellor fired for kicking a patient has been ordered reinstated by a grievance board.

And the passive may lighten a sentence by removing secondary information that can wait: **A banker wanted for questioning in the disappearance of $1 million is believed to have flown to Mexico, police said today.** (But be sure a later paragraph gives reasons for the belief.)

Arithmetic

Writers should mind their math when dealing with statistical percentages and other figures. Never make the reader do the arithmetic.

Reporting that the number of flagpole-sitters in Canada has increased 100 per cent in the last year is meaningless without the base figure. An increase from five flagpole-sitters to 10 is 100 per cent but the percentage figure alone suggests a population explosion.

Take care as well in phrasing changes in percentage statistics. A poll that suggests a drop in government support to 25 from 50 per cent does not mean a 25 per cent drop. It's a change of 25 percentage points.

Clichés

Tired expressions are indeed tiresome. No one needs to read about a program being unveiled or the lucky lottery winner for whom Christmas came early.

But use a cliché if it expresses your meaning exactly and if it will spare the reader some cumbersome second choice. It would be hard to improve on such gems as **sour grapes, cry wolf** or **tip of the iceberg** which sum up complex ideas in a few words.

Avoid the automatic or lazy cliché:

Grind to a halt, a parent's worst nightmare, in the wake of, in happier times, seriously consider, shock waves, lucky to be alive

And the fad term:

Downsize, peer group, quantify, wannabe, yuppie, couch potato

And the fossil that no longer raises the faintest image:

Moot point, short shrift, at loggerheads, by the same token

Dig for treasure

Search a story for hidden angles that would snatch a reader's attention if even a hint of the buried treasure were woven into the lead.

Not: A local man faces three counts of attempted murder and four counts of assault with a weapon causing bodily harm after a hotel brawl at a wedding reception sent seven men to hospital, six with knife wounds, early Saturday morning.

But: A brawl at a wedding reception between friends of the bride and friends of the groom left seven men hurt and a country lodge with a heap of shattered furniture, antiques and chandeliers early Saturday.

Everyday words

Treat the reader to words and phrases that are short and familiar.

About, not **approximately**

Met, not **held a meeting**

Approve, not **authorize**

Improve, never **ameliorate**

Plan or **program,** not **initiative** or **strategy**

Front-end loading

Avoid it like the plague.

Not: United States envoy Herman Cohen said in London after meeting government and rebel representatives at peace talks that the two sides had agreed to a ceasefire.

But: The two sides have agreed to a ceasefire, United States envoy Herman Cohen said after ...

Not: In an email to Prime Minister Stephen Harper urging that the offices Canada Post plans to eliminate be retained, the union said it was appalled by the proposed measures.

But: The union said it was "appalled" by Canada Post's plans to close the offices. It urged in an email to Prime Minister Stephen Harper that all the post offices be retained.

Not: An official of the Nova Scotia Environment Department, who was at the scene on the Annapolis River near the small community of Paradise about 170 kilometres west of Halifax, said both tractor-trailer units were spilling chemicals into the river.

But: Both tractor-trailer units were spilling chemicals into the Annapolis River near the small community of Paradise, a Nova Scotia Environment Department official said from the scene, about 170 kilometres west of Halifax.

Not: British Columbia and Yukon Birders Association executive director Anne-Marie Sheehey will be the featured speaker.

But: Executive director Anne-Marie Sheehey of the British Columbia and Yukon Birders Association will be the featured speaker.

Formula leads

Avoid the formula approach, where every story sounds the same.

Not: BARRIE, Ont. — Three men suffered minor injuries when their light plane crashed into a field Friday.

But: BARRIE, Ont. — A light plane hit power lines while taking off in a rainstorm Friday, flipped and crashed upside down in a farmer's potato field. The three men aboard escaped with minor injuries.

Headline language

Keep headline language out of the story.

Not: Joseph inked a six-year contract.

But: Joseph signed a six-year contract.

Not: The commission will launch a three-pronged probe into the fire.

But: The commission will investigate the fire in three ways.

Short general-purpose words may fit in a headline, but not in a story.

Avoid words like **cop, ink, ire, laud, lash, rap, shun, vow**

The headline-writer's practice of dropping **a, the, of** and the like to save space leads to lumpy sentences in the body of a story.

Not: He was intrigued by Canadian Imperial Bank of Commerce chairman Sarah Stanley's defence of Big Oil Co.'s rescue.

But: He was intrigued by the defence of Big Oil Co.'s rescue offered by Sarah Stanley, chairman of the Canadian Imperial Bank of Commerce.

Lazy words

Cast an inquisitive eye on words like **colourful, controversial** and **zany**. An editor who asks why Mayor Horsefall is **colourful** may learn Horsefall once ate his hat on the town hall steps when he lost a hockey bet with the mayor of a rival town. Tell the reader.

Mind-reading

Reporters and editors should not consider themselves mind-readers who can somehow measure others' true feelings.

Not: Genereux believes the government is corrupt.

But: Genereux said he believes the government is corrupt.

Not: Iroshima is furious about the layoffs.

But: "We're not taking this lying down," Iroshima said, shaking with anger and smashing his clenched fist into the factory fence.

More than words

Tell the reader what has happened, certainly. But also help the reader understand why and how it has happened in terms that strike home:

Not: The hurricane caused widespread damage to buildings, farm equipment, trees and hydro lines.

But: The hurricane's winds lifted roofs off houses and barns and flipped over cars, tractors and even lumbering dump trucks used to carry grain. Almost every fruit and shade tree in the region was knocked over, and linemen said about 3,000 hydro poles had been snapped off.

Overloads

The overloaded lead is sure to turn the reader off:

Not: The family and friends of William John Fortune have raised enough money to rescue the stranded Canadian tourist and, with the help of volunteers from the Barbados police department, will send an airplane on Tuesday to lift him and his two daughters, Louise and Samantha, from a tiny sandspit north of the Caribbean island, longtime friend Lorne Pulsifer said Tuesday.

But: An airplane will head for a tiny Caribbean sandspit north of Barbados on Tuesday to rescue a stranded Canadian tourist and his two daughters, a family friend said Tuesday.

The overblown statement is another turnoff:

Not: Once the wind was at his back, the hometown quarterback wreaked as much havoc on the defence as hurricane Katrina did in New Orleans.

But: The hometown quarterback, with the wind now at his back, threw touch-down passes on three consecutive drives.

Overwriting weakens stories and repels readers:

Not: The legislation was greeted with howls of protest.

But: One opposition member after another criticized the legislation, calling it ill-conceived and dangerous.

The facts are best presented in plain conversational style with deft phrasing, touches of human interest, significant details and strong quotes.

Avoid overcharged words: **blast, charged, chastise, flail, flay, lambaste, enraged, lash** and **slam**.

Simply report in an even tone what was said:

Not: Labour leader Ken Lewenza launched a bitter attack on the company's offer.

But: "It is the most preposterous company offer I've seen in the last 15 years," said labour leader Ken Lewenza.

Say and variants

Early Canadian Press stylebooks described **say** and **said** as honest and inconspicuous. They are also not to be toyed with.

Say and **said** should be attached to words and ideas that exactly mirror the speaker's, not an interpretation or extension. Words like **indicate** or **suggest** may be appropriate where **said** is not and are mandatory in stories on opinion polls.

Not: The poll shows fewer than 10 per cent of Canadians believe . . .

But: The poll suggests fewer than 10 per cent . . .

Many substitutes for **say** and **said** are risky or, at best, vague:

Admit implies confession, **affirm** states a fact, **assert** declares strongly, **claim** and **maintain** hint of doubt, **confide** implies a confidence, **declare** states explicitly, **disclose** and **reveal** presume earlier concealment.

Be especially wary of **explain, point out, claim** and **note.** They all imply that what is being said is fact. **According to** and **said she believes** may question the speaker's credibility.

Words like **recalled** and **predicted** can be tricky. Make sure they fit the circumstances.

Sentences and paragraphs

Readability has never been more important. People are busier and have less time than ever to read news. They will quickly bail out from a story that is heavy and dull.

One key factor in readability is sentence length.

A sentence is more likely to be clear if it is short and conveys one idea:

People with near-death experiences agree about details to a remarkable extent.

A longer sentence which closely connects several ideas also works:

Many of them say they float out of their bodies, encounter God or a spirit figure, meet deceased relatives, review their past lives, feel great peacefulness and finally return to their bodies.

That sentence runs to 32 words, but its meaning never falters because everything relates to the same subject and the language is simple.

Try to begin sentences with words that have punch and power. Avoid starting with phrases, longer clauses or attribution.

Keep paragraphs short and active. Paragraphs of two or three tight sentences are inviting. Long, grey blobs of print are not.

Splits and prepositions

The normal position for an adverb that modifies a compound verb (**is missing, was reached**) is between the parts of the verb: **The plane is still missing. Agreement was soon reached.**

Split an infinitive (**to satisfy, to keep**) rather than create a confusing or unnatural sentence: **The discovery is expected to more than satisfy investors. Godfrey told him to kindly keep his opinion to himself.** But don't split infinitives unnecessarily: **The parents asked the babysitter to quietly leave by the back door.**

If a preposition falls naturally at the end of the sentence, leave it there: **Reuben wants to know which team he'll be on.**

That

Dropping **that** often makes for smoother reading, especially in shorter sentences.

She said (that) **she wanted to be alone.**

But retain it to avoid misleading the reader even momentarily.

Carr said that on May 1 he was in Halifax; Finance Minister Jim Flaherty warned that the government would step in.

That should also be retained and repeated with two or more clauses.

He promised that the singer would appear and that the evening would be a success.

That-which

When it comes to introducing a clause in the middle of a sentence, there's sometimes confusion about whether **that** or **which** is correct. **Which** sounds grammatical somehow, so it ends up being used too often.

That is generally used when the clause is essential to the noun it defines or narrows the topic: **The movie** that **opened at the Roxy last week.** (It's not just any movie, it's the one that opened last week at a specific theatre.)

Which clauses give a reason or add a new element: **The movie, which cost $4 million to make, has done landslide business.** (The assumption here is that the reader already knows which movie is being discussed, and its cost is an added bit of information.)

A helpful distinction: **which** clauses generally need commas, **that** clauses don't. Read the clause over in your mind. If it makes sense using **that** instead of **which**, chances are **that** is the right word to use.

Time element

Put the time element where it falls naturally in speech, usually right after the verb or at the end of the sentence.

Not: Veterans Affairs Minister Jean-Pierre Blackburn Thursday said the new policy . . .

But: Veterans Affairs Minister Jean-Pierre Blackburn said Thursday the new policy . . .

Try to put the time element at the end if putting it directly between the verb and its object is awkward:

Not: Finance Minister Jim Flaherty announced Wednesday a $2-billion job program.

But: Finance Minister Jim Flaherty announced a $2-billion job program Wednesday.

There are situations where the time element is at home either in the middle or at the end.

Dawn Coe-Jones came out of the pack Saturday to score a five-shot victory in the Canadian women's golf championship (Saturday).

Trippers

Be alert for words, phrasing and sentences that will cause a reader to stumble:

Not: Manness said he met with trucking industry officials earlier this year who said they were concerned about taxes.

But: Manness said he met earlier this year with trucking industry officials who said they were concerned about taxes.

Not: After dining on hundreds of pet cats and dogs, the provincial Environment Ministry has decided to round up coyotes and ship them to remote parts of the province.

But: Coyotes have killed dozens of pet cats and dogs, so the provincial Environment Ministry has decided to round up the predators and ship them to remote parts of the province.

Not: The bears were destroyed when they would not leave a tree in which they were munching leaves.

But: The bears were shot when they could not be coaxed out of a playground tree where they were munching leaves.

Unanswered questions

Never leave basic questions unanswered.

Not: The price of gasoline has gone up by 20 cents in New Brunswick today.

But: The price of gasoline in New Brunswick has gone up today by 20 cents to $1.40 a litre. It is the second such increase in three days.

Not: She was sentenced to life in prison.

But: She was sentenced to life in prison with no chance of parole for 17 years.

Not: A police officer was shot Friday as two men sped away from the scene of a bank holdup in downtown Brandon.

But: A police officer was shot in the chest and seriously wounded as two men sped away ...

Not: Canadian shoe manufacturers say a federal government plan to lift import quotas on leather footwear will deliver a severe blow to the industry.

But: Canadian shoe manufacturers say a federal government plan to lift import quotas on leather footwear will ultimately lead to higher shoe prices for Canadians, especially women. It will also mean hundreds of Canadians will lose their jobs in shoe factories, they said.

Verbs ending in -ize

Verbs ending in *-ize* strike many readers as ungainly, although some have gained acceptance.

Accessorize, capsulize, decimalize, definitize, hospitalize, therapize

Accept them when there is no satisfactory alternative.

Who and whom

Correct usage of these two eluders can be determined by dividing a sentence in two. Use **who** when it stands for **he, she** or **they**. Use **whom** when it stands for **him, her** or **them**.

The police issued a public alert for a man who they said was armed and dangerous. (They said **he** was armed and dangerous so **who** is correct.)

She took refuge with her next-door neighbour whom she had trusted in the past. (She trusted **her** so **whom** is correct.)

Word order

Words out of order can create chaos.

Not: After falling from the ceiling for years, the Hamilton-Wentworth school board will remove tiles containing asbestos this summer from an area high school.

But: After falling from the ceiling for years, tiles containing asbestos will finally be removed from a Hamilton-Wentworth high school this summer.

Not: She has a six-figure income as a model, a horse and a Jaguar.

But: Modelling has given her a six-figure income, a horse and a Jaguar.

Compound words

General

General

1. In the absence of widely agreed rules, writers and editors sometimes have to decide whether a compound word should be written open (**knuckle ball**), hyphenated (**knuckle-ball**) or solid (**knuckleball**).

2. In practice, a new compound is normally written at first as two or more words (**on line**), becomes increasingly hyphenated (**on-line**) and is then combined into a single word (**online**).

3. In North America, the tendency is to drop the hyphen as soon as a new compound becomes familiar.

4. For compound nouns, follow the *Canadian Oxford Dictionary* unless *Caps and Spelling* differs. If neither offers help, write it as separate words.

Note: Compound nouns are not necessarily created from nouns but may be combinations of verbs, adverbs and so on.

teeter-totter, know-how, the down-at-heel, letdown

Guidelines

1. Hyphens are used to unravel meaning.

an old-book collector, an old book-collector; a white-slave racket, a white slave-racket; a light-blue coat; a dry-ice machine

2. Compound adjectives are often hyphenated before the noun they modify.

a world-class athlete, up-to-the-minute fashion, a 12-year-old child, a cease-trade order

3. When the words forming a compound adjective stand alone in a sentence, they are usually not hyphenated.

an athlete of world class, fashion that's up to the minute, the child is 12 years old, an order to cease trades

Note: In the sentence The 12-year-old is from Vancouver, 12-year-old is properly hyphenated as a noun. Similarly: a race for three-year-olds.

5. Compound verbs are usually either hyphenated or written as one word.

hand-picked, babysit, whitewash, deep-six, pop-up

6. Compound verbs ending in an adverb or a preposition are not hyphenated.

break away, hold up, shoot out, run in, lean to, clip on

Note: The same two words used as nouns or adjectives are written solid. But if the solid form would be hard to grasp, use a hyphen.

breakaway, holdup, shootout

But run-in (not runin), lean-to (not leanto), a clip-on lid (not clipon)

➤ See **Punctuation**, page 387.

French

The Canadian Press delivers its news report in English for an audience that is not necessarily bilingual. Stories peppered with French break the flow and make reading difficult. At the same time, it is not always possible to avoid the use of French in the names of organizations or movie and book titles. In that case, a translation that remains as faithful as possible to the French should be provided. If a precise translation is impossible, an explanation or description can be used.

The aim is always ease of understanding without sacrificing the meaning of the French text.

Names of organizations

1. In most cases, use the English form for the names of organizations.

Quebec Liquor Corp. (not Société des alcools du Québec); Montreal Transit Corp. (not Société de transport de la communauté urbaine de Montréal); Quebec Federation of Labour (not Fédération des travailleurs du Québec); Quebec provincial police (not Sûreté du Québec); Museum of Fine Arts (not Musée des beaux-arts); Great Whale hydro project (not the Grande baleine project)

2. The names of some organizations cannot readily be translated. Others become familiar in their French version, or have no official English version. In such cases, the French name should be accompanied by an explanation.

Conseil du patronat, the largest employers group in Quebec; Centrale des syndicats du Québec, the teachers federation; Société pour vaincre la pollution, an environmental group; Union des producteurs agricoles, the farmers union; Ecole polytechnique, the engineering school affiliated with the Université de Montréal

Note: Be careful with the following agencies set up in conjunction with Quebec's French-language law (Law 101).

Office de la langue française, the agency that administers the provisions of the provincial language law; Conseil de la langue française, a research and advisory body on language issues.

3. For some organizations, known even to English speakers in Quebec by their initials, use a substitute rather than the full name or initials.

CEGEP (Collège d'enseignement général et professionel): junior college; CLSC (Centre local de services communautaires): community health centre

4. Some Quebec titles have equivalents in other provinces. Use a similar form for the Quebec version even if that means the translation is not identical to the French.

Corporation professionnelle des médecins du Québec: Quebec College of Physicians rather than the Professional Corporation of Quebec Doctors; Directeur général des élections: chief electoral officer

5. A few organizations, titles and the like are commonly known by their French names and need not be followed by a translation.

Le Droit, Société St-Jean-Baptiste, Notre Dame, Université de Montréal

Books, movies, etc.

1. Prefer the English form for the titles of books, movies and the like if the English name is widely known.

Remembrance of Things Past (not *A la recherche du temps perdu*); *Jesus of Montreal* (not *Jésus de Montréal*); *The Decline of the American Empire* (not *Le Declin de l'empire américain*)

2. When a French name or title is used in a quotation, a list of awards or a review, it should be followed by the official translation, if available, in parentheses.

Le Malade imaginaire (The Imaginary Invalid); Le Matou (The Alley Cat); Dans l'oeil de l'aigle (In the Eye of the Eagle); Dans le ventre du dragon (In the Belly of the Dragon)

3. When there is no official translation — for example, if the movie or book has not been issued in English — provide a translation in parentheses that accurately conveys the meaning of the French title.

Au revoir, les enfants (Goodbye Children); Les Belles-soeurs (The Sisters-in-Law)

4. When there is no official or simple English title of a novel, TV program, movie or the like, or when the English translation conveys a different meaning from the French, an explanation is in order.

Bonheur d'occasion **by Gabrielle Roy, which translates as Second-Hand Happiness but was issued in English as** *The Tin Flute*

Un Train d'enfer, **a movie whose title translates as A Train From Hell, but which also carries the meaning of breakneck speed**

René Lévesque's *Memoirs,* **whose original title,** *Attendez que je me rappelle*, **had a typically offhand suggestion of Hang On, It'll Come to Me — with a hint of Quebec's official motto**

Accents

1. When technically possible, use accents on French proper names, including place names, and on the rare instances when French common words are not translated into English.

Jean Chrétien, L'Actualité, Trois Rivières, Fête nationale, raison d'être

Note: Accents are not used on **Quebec** and **Montreal**, which have long-established English versions, unless they are part of a proper name: **Le Journal de Montréal**

2. Follow Oxford for English words.

cliché, resumé, café, debut

Capitalization

1. For most names in French, capitalize the first word, the second word too when the first is an article, and proper nouns.

This applies to:

a) Titles of books, songs, movies and the like.

De la terre à la lune, Sur le pont d'Avignon, Les Liaisons dangereuses

b) Names of newspapers and magazines.

Le Journal de Montréal, L'Actualité, Le Courrier du peuple, L'Acadie nouvelle, La Voix de l'Est (l'Est, meaning **the East**, is capitalized as the name of a region)

Note: When referring to a French newspaper, avoid repetition of the article. **La Presse reported today** (not **the La Presse report said today**).

c) A variety of other kinds of names.

Fête nationale (a holiday), **L'Auberge bonne nuit** (a hotel), **La Petite marmite** (a restaurant), **L'Académie canadienne-française** (an association), **Place d'armes** (a city square), **Conseil du patronat** (employers' organization), **Office de la langue française** (government agency)

2. For names of corporate organizations, The Canadian Press uses the English article preceding the name. Otherwise, capitalize the first word and proper nouns, lowercase other words.

the Service de perception, Emballages St-Laurent ltée, the Caisse de dépôt et placement

3. The main exception to the basic rule is for place names, which follow normal CP capitalization.

La Tuque, Pointe-aux-Trembles, St-Basile-le-Grand

4. Franco-Albertan and Anglo-Quebecer take capital letters; francophone and anglophone do not. Generally, prefer French-speaking and English-speaking. The word allophone is also entering the vocabulary to describe someone who is neither French- nor English-speaking, but it should be avoided.

5. Fleur-de-lis is capitalized when it refers to Quebec's flag.

Hyphens in place names

1. Most multiple-word place names in Quebec and other French-speaking areas of the world are hyphenated.

Iles-de-la-Madeleine, Trois-Rivières, St-Georges-de-Beauce, Stanstead-Est, Que.; Petit-Rocher, N.B.; Iles-de-la-Madeleine, Que.; Val-d'Isère, France

Note: In names preceded by the definite article, do not put a hyphen after the article.

La Malbaie, La Pocatière

2. Hyphens are omitted from purely English place names.

Stanstead Plain, East Broughton, Otterburn Park

3. Hyphens are omitted in the names of natural features such as lakes and mountains.

Lac Barrière, Baie des Chaleurs, Rivière des Prairies

Note: A natural feature can be part of the name of some municipalities. They are hyphenated: Baie-Comeau, Lac-Beauport, Mont-Laurier.

4. Street names take hyphens.

Ste-Catherine Street, 136 René-Lévesque Blvd.

Saint

1. Family and place names that include *saint* or a variant are tricky, needing the same care in checking as *Mac* and *Mc* names.

2. In Quebec place names, *saint* and *sainte* are abbreviated to *St* and *Ste* (no periods) and joined to the next word by a hyphen. Elsewhere in Canada, practice varies.

St-Jean-Port-Joli, Que; Ste-Anne-des-Monts, Que.

But St. Boniface, Man.; Sault Ste. Marie, Ont.; Saint John, N.B.; St. John's, N.L.; St. Brieux, Sask.; Saint-Antoine, N.B.; St. Jacques, N.L.

Note: It is not always obvious that a name is feminine or masculine (e.g. St-Hyacinthe); check if in doubt.

3. Quebec family names may be written either with **saint** and **sainte** spelled out (**Louise Saint-Pierre, Marcel Sainte-Marie**)

or in abbreviated form (**Chantal St-Amour** or **Pierre Ste-Croix**). Check with the person for a preferred spelling; if that is not possible, prefer the long form.

4. For the names of saints, follow normal English practice and use St. for female as well as male saints and do not hyphenate.

St. Jean de Brébeuf, St. Marguerite Bourgeoys

5. For institutions, follow their preference.

Saint Mary's University, Auberge Saint-Antoine

Translation

1. The Canadian Press avoids double translation. The risk of error is compounded when a quotation moves from one language into another and then back again. Paraphrasing a quotation reduces the risk.

2. When translating from an interview or from a French text, avoid awkward literal translations. Translate to convey the meaning of the quote or French text while remaining as true as possible to the original. If that requires too many contortions, paraphrase.

"Il a réussi à sauver les meubles": not **"He managed to save the furniture"** but **"He was able to salvage the essentials."**

3. Be alert to words that look alike in French and English but have different meanings.

amateur (in sports, **fan**); **bulletin d'information** (**news report**); **circulation** (**traffic**); **commission parlementaire** (**legislature committee**); **déception** (**disappointment**), **déçu** (**disappointed**); **éditeur** (**publisher**), **rédacteur-en-chef** (**editor**); **exploiter** (**operate**); **formation** (**training, education**); **ignorer** (**be unaware of, not know**); **impliquer** (**involve**); **militant** (**member** of a political party); **nomination** (**appointment**); **populaire** (**popular,** but more often **of** or **for the people**); **sécurité** (**safety**); **sensibiliser** (**educate**), **sensible** (**sensitive to**)

4. **Business terminology:** The business world uses some terms that present translation problems.

actif (**assets**); **action** (**share**); **administrateur** (**director**); **bénéfice net** (**profit**); **chef de l'exploitation** (**chief operating officer**); **chiffres d'affaires** (**income**); **membre de la direction** (**officer**); **obligation** (**bond, debenture**); **passif** (**liabilities**); **président-directeur-général** — **pdg** (**president and chief executive officer** — **ceo**); **président du conseil** (**chairman of the board**); **société** (**company** or **corporation**); **société fermée** (**private company**); **société ouverte** (**public company**)

5. **Legal terminology:**

effraction (break and enter); homicide involontaire (manslaughter); mandat de perquisition (search warrant); outrage au tribunal (contempt of court); voies de fait (assault)

Note: In Quebec, the Civil Code based on the French Napoleonic Code is used in civil litigation. The Canadian Criminal Code applies in criminal cases.

As a result, many procedures differ from elsewhere in Canada.

➤ See **Legal** section, page 215.

Government

Capitalization

➤ For questions of capitalization on government, parliaments, laws, royalty, etc., see the chapter **Capitalization**, starting page 268.

National and provincial legislatures

1. Ministers with more than one portfolio should be referred to by the title most appropriate to the story. **Intergovernmental Affairs Minister Kathleen Keenan** becomes **Sport Minister Kathleen Keenan** in stories about the Olympics.

2. The **official Opposition** is the opposition party with most seats: **the Opposition Liberals, the two opposition parties.**

3. **MP** is always acceptable for member of Parliament. Don't use an abbreviation for members of provincial legislatures, since the title varies from province to province.

4. Write **Senate, Sen. Nate Nurgitz, a senator, former senator Robert de Cotret.**

5. Make it **Parliament Hill, the Hill, Parliament Buildings, East Block, Peace Tower, lower chamber, upper chamber, lower house, upper house.**

6. The official residence of the Canadian prime minister is **24 Sussex Drive**; that of the Opposition leader is **Stornoway.**

7. Write **prime minister-designate** Stephen Harper, not **prime minister-elect** Stephen Harper, because the Canadian electorate does not vote for a prime minister or premier as such. But **president-elect** Barack Obama is correct in U.S. contexts.

8. Federally, it is the **Conservative Party of Canada,** formed by the merger of the Canadian Alliance and the federal Progressive Conservative party. **Conservative** is also acceptable, as is Tory. The form **Progressive Conservative** is still in use for provincial parties.

Political affiliations and designations

1. The political affiliation of elected members and the names of their constituencies are specified when they are relevant. For members of Parliament and provincial legislatures, give the party and constituency; for senators, party and province.

2. Streamlined abbreviations for party designations are fine in routine parliamentary and legislature copy, or in stories where many members are named. They are also used in election results. They are avoided otherwise, except for **NDP** and **PQ.**

Abbreviations for some of the better-known parties are: **ADQ** (L'Action démocratique), **BQ** (Bloc Québécois), **CHP** (Christian Heritage party), **Con** (Conservative), **EP** (Equality Party), **GRN** (Green Party), **Ind** (Independent), **Lib** (Liberal), **NDP** (New Democratic Party), **PC** (Progressive Conservative), **PQ** (Parti Québécois), **SP** (Saskatchewan Party), **SC** (Social Credit).

Style is **(Lib-Winnipeg North Centre)**. The abbreviation is separated from the constituency by a hyphen with no spaces on either side.

Usually, a descriptive phrase reads better than a streamlined style: **David McGuinty, the Liberal for Ottawa South, a riding held for many years by his father.** Sometimes a fuller description is desirable. For example, in a debate about federal transfer payments to Ontario: **David McGuinty, Liberal member for Ottawa South, is the brother of Ontario Premier Dalton McGuinty.**

3. In the bracketed style, the names of federal constituencies not easily identified are followed by the name of the province: **(Lib-Egmont, P.E.I.)**.

4. The names of cities are given when they have more than one seat: **Toronto Danforth** (city first).

First minister

Where the choice is between **prime minister** and **premier**, use **prime minister** for the heads of national governments in general but **premier** for the heads of government in France and its former colonies, Canadian provinces and Australian states. Some West Indies governments also have premiers; follow individual preferences.

Monarchy

The Queen and members of the Royal Family deserve normal respect for their constitutional role in Canada, but coverage of their visits to this country and other activities is governed by basic news standards.

In particular, that means stories should not gush (**looking radiant**). Nor should they pretend the visitor's casual asides are profound or witty, nor quote meaningless exclamations from bystanders (**"It's the most thrilling day of my life," said 11-year-old Melanie Simpson**), nor be littered with royal this's and that's (the **royal breakfast**, the **royal limousine**, etc.).

The best stories tend to focus on one or two events in the visitor's day, stressing human elements that are genuinely newsworthy and describing them fully and frankly. The organization is also worth a story at times: in Halifax, they once used green paint on a bald stretch of the common as part of their spruce-up.

1. The Queen is Canada's **head of state**; the prime minister is **head of government**.

2. The **Governor General** represents the Queen in Canada on a daily basis and as such is Canada's de facto head of state. Canada's governors general are appointed by the Queen on the advice of the prime minister. The Governor General is also the commander-in-chief of Canada, which includes such responsibilities as appointing the chief of the defence staff (on the advice of the prime minister), approving military insignia and awarding military honours.

2. Unless there are problems with identification — for instance, in a story dealing with a number of monarchs — the preferred term is **the Queen**, rather than **Queen Elizabeth**. Use **Queen of Canada**, never **Queen of England**. Prince Charles is not **heir to the British throne**; he is **heir to the throne**.

3. Camilla, wife of Prince Charles, uses the title **the Duchess of Cornwall**.

3. Don't refer to the late Princess of Wales as **Princess Diana**, since she wasn't a princess by birth.

➤ See **Titles**, page 410.

Succession

Order of succession to the throne:

1. Prince Charles, Prince of Wales (Queen's eldest son)
2. Prince William (elder son of Charles)
3. Prince Henry (second son of Charles)
4. Prince Andrew (second son of the Queen)
5. Princess Beatrice (elder daughter of Andrew)
6. Princess Eugenie (second daughter of Andrew)
7. Prince Edward (third son of the Queen)
8. James, Viscount Severn (son of Edward)
9. Lady Louise Windsor (daughter of Edward)
10. Princess Anne (only daughter of the Queen)

Ceremonies

1. The Queen and other members of the Royal Family receive a **royal salute** — the playing of *God Save the Queen* by a royal guard.

2. The Governor General and lieutenant-governors are accorded a **vice-regal salute** — part *God Save the Queen*, part *O Canada*.

3. The prime minister, visiting heads of state and political leaders, etc., are greeted with a **general salute** — a few bars of music other than *God Save the Queen* or *O Canada*.

➤ See **Military**, page 328.

First lady

The Americanism **first lady** refers to the wife of a U.S. president. Avoid. Never apply the term to the Queen or to the wives of Canadian governors general, lieutenant-governors or prime ministers.

Nationhood

Nation means the people of a country; **country** is the territory of a nation. Hence avoid **nationwide** when used in a geographical sense, **the nation's capital** (for Ottawa), etc.

Canada

1. The national flag is the Maple Leaf.

2. The national anthem is *O Canada;* the royal anthem, *God Save the Queen.* The patriotic song *The Maple Leaf Forever* enjoys semi-anthem status outside Quebec.

3. The national emblem is the maple leaf. The beaver is a semi-official emblem.

4. Canada's coat of arms bears the inscription *A Mari Usque Ad Mare* (From Sea Even Unto Sea).

5. Canada's patron saint is St. Joseph (March 19).

Government jargon

1. Avoid using the jargon that often flows so freely from government news releases or officials' mouths. Jargon fails to convey information to those unfamiliar with the term and can even mislead.

2. Steer clear of pompous or awkward phrasing. Not **government initiative**. Initiative means **personal drive**. Use **government program** or **plan**. Not **referenced** (use **refer to**), not **impact on** (use **affect**), not **negatively impact on** (use **hurt**).

3. Government budgets are rife with specialized terms. Keep it simple. **A negative growth in revenues** means government took in less money. **A surplus on the ordinary account** should not find its way into copy. Explain it instead: **The government showed a modest $10-million surplus on day-to-day operations, but once money spent on capital projects was taken into account — such as road repairs and a new court building — it ran a deficit of $500 million for the year.**

4. Provinces are often described by politicians and the media as being "have" or "have not." Have-not provinces receive **equalization payments** from the federal government, which is constitutionally obligated to ensure similar services are available

to all citizens. Beware leaving the impression that there is a fund that some provinces pay into and others take from. In fact, Ottawa calculates the fiscal capacity of each province based on revenues from various taxes. It averages these to provide a standard and provinces below the standard receive money, funded through Ottawa's general revenues.

Many institutional stories, such as annual budget coverage, can be illustrated with graphics that help a reader navigate through numbers and other material that is easier to understand in a visual format.

FEDERAL BUDGET 2008

Budget winners | **Budget losers**

SENIORS Tax rules changed to allow seniors to shelter more of their Gauaranteed Income Supplement from taxes even if they earn extra income. Extension of program to help older workers stay in the workforce.

SAVERS Introduction of flexible tax-free savings vehicle to help plan for purchase of house, car, trip, retirement or other.

MANUFACTURERS $1 billion in relief for three extra years of accelerated capital cost allowance for new machinery and equipment. Another $250 million over five years for an Automotive Innovation Fund.

ABORIGINALS Relatively modest $270 million over two years to clean up drinking water and improve education and health on reserves.

HOMELESS No new funding for affordable housing.

CHILD CARE No measures to create new spaces or enhance tax benefits.

WORKING POOR No change in minimum wage in federal sector, which activists say needs to be at least $10 an hour.

Source: Department of Finance

THE CANADIAN PRESS

FEDERAL BUDGET 2008

Revenues and expenses

Budgetary revenues are expected to total $241.9 billion in 2008-09 while total expenses are expected to be $239.6 billion resulting in a surplus of $2.3 billion.

*Numbers may not add due to rounding

Revenues	$ billions	Expenses	$ billions
Income tax		**Major transfers to persons**	
Personal income tax	118.6	Elderly benefits	33.3
Corporate income tax	36.8	Employment insurance	15.3
Other income tax	5.9	Children's benefits	11.9
Excise taxes/duties		**Major transfers to other levels of government**	
Goods and services tax	27.6	Federal transfer support for health and other programs	33.1
Customs import duties	4.2	Fiscal arrangements	15.3
Other excise taxes/duties	10.1	Alternative payments for standing programs	-3.3
Employment insurance premium revenues	16.5	Cities and communities	1.0
		Direct program spending	101.5
Other revenues	22.3	Public debt charges	31.5
	Total **$241.9 billion**		Total **$239.6 billion**

Source: Department of Finance

THE CANADIAN PRESS

FEDERAL BUDGET 2008

Budget balance

The government expects a budgetary surplus of $2.3 billion for 2008-09.

$ billions

2.3

'06-'07 '07-'08 '08-'09 '09-'10 '10-'11 '11-'12 '12-'13

Projected

Source: Department of Finance

THE CANADIAN PRESS

Metric

General

The Canadian Press uses metric for most measurements. As with any measurement, the most important instruction is: **Be clear.** Specific descriptions are often needed, but comparative examples from everyday life can be even more helpful: **big as a truck, small as a thimble, knee-deep snow** and the like.

When metric?

1. Among the lingering exceptions to metric are cases where some other measurement remains conventional — personal weights and heights, precious metals in troy ounces, two-by-fours, quarter-inch screws and the like.

2. Metric measurements are not put into the mouths of those who speak in the inch-pound system, either in direct quotes or in indirect speech. Rephrasing can be used to limit such occasions.

3. In most other cases when imperial must be used, it should be accompanied by a metric equivalent. For example, Canada's 200-nautical-mile (**370-kilometre**) fishing limit, or the number of litres in a 35-gallon barrel of oil (**about 159**).

4. But when repeated use of bracketed equivalents may slow down or annoy the reader, consider a separate line or paragraph giving the metric equivalent. Thereafter let the specialists speak in their own tongue.

5. Speed and distances are expressed in metric, including very great distances such as the number of kilometres between planets in the solar system. Certain astronomical distances, such as those between stars or galaxies, are often measured in light-years — the distance light travels in one year moving at almost 300,000 kilometres a second, or about 9.46 trillion kilometres.

6. The altitude of airplanes and the height of mountains are expressed in metres, not feet, and distances at sea are expressed in kilometres, not miles or nautical miles. Measure speeds in kilometres an hour, not knots.

7. The size of animals is expressed in kilograms and metres (centimetres and the like for extremely small animals). Meat on the store shelf is in kilograms.

Let logic be your guide

1. In handling material from U.S. sources, it is usually possible to make a straight conversion from imperial. **The plane crashed about 90 metres from a home for the elderly.** (The source material reads **100 yards.**)

2. But tend to use round figures. Most of the world uses metric and material routed through the United States from abroad has possibly gone through one conversion already.

3. In converting to metric, do not use figures that imply greater accuracy than justified by the original data. For instance, using 2.54 centimetres to the inch, convert 35 inches to 89 or even 90 centimetres, not 88.9.

4. Don't needlessly mix imperial and metric in comparisons in the same sentence. Make it **the 60-pound boy was attacked by a dog almost twice his weight.** Save the exact weight of the dog (50 kilograms in this case) for another sentence.

5. People often talk in imperial. Again, try to avoid juxtaposing a quote containing imperial with metric.

6. And, of course, it's axiomatic that a writer doesn't meddle with the idiomatic: **The crowd inched forward.**

Sports

1. Most Olympic and many non-Olympic sports are contested and reported in metric. But others, including baseball, basketball, golf, horse racing, soccer and North American football, continue to use imperial. Boxing uses both: professional weight classes are imperial while amateur divisions are metric.

2. Different types of motor racing use different measures. Grand Prix and motorcycle racing are in metric, but NASCAR and IndyCar racing are in imperial.

➤ For details, see **Sports**, page 152.

Odds and ends

1. The names of metric units are usually spelled out: **a 20-kilogram sack**, not **a 20-kg sack**; **covering 50 hectares**, not **covering 50 ha**; **ran 10 kilometres**, not **ran 10 km.**

2. There are no abbreviations in metric, only symbols. These symbols take periods only at the end of a sentence, never take *s* in the plural and are separated from a number by a space. In adjectival uses, the space is replaced by a hyphen.

3. **C** (for Celsius) can be used on first reference. Other common symbols such as **km/h, mm** and **KB** should be written out in first reference but may be used on second reference when preceded by a number: **at 70 km/h, a 105-mm cannon, a 112-KB file.**

4. A number less than one has a zero before the decimal: **0.25 ha**, not **.25 ha**; but prefer **a quarter hectare** and the like when common fractions are involved.

5. Treat the names of metric units as singular when the number preceding them is less than one: **0.25 litre** but **2.5 litres.**

6. For temperatures less than 0 C, use a minus sign as in **-5 C**. The minus sign is a hyphen preceding a number with no space between.

7. The clipped form **kilo** is not acceptable for **kilogram** or **kilometre** since kilo simply means a thousand and is not a specific unit.

8. Superior numbers are not available on many keyboards for the preferred symbols for square metres (**m2**), cubic centimetres (**cm3**) and such. Instead write **sq. m, cu. cm**, etc. The symbol for degree (¬∞) is unavailable; for **15˚C** write **15 C**, or **15 degrees C**.

9. Symbols may be used in tabular matter and certain sports and financial routine.

10. Metric units named after people have capitalized symbols (**A** for Andrew Marie Ampere, **C** for Anders Celsius, **Pa** for Blaise **Pa**scal and **W** for James Watt); but when the name of a unit is written in full, only Celsius is capitalized. Otherwise write ampere, pascal, watt, etc.

11. A few symbols for metric prefixes are capped, including **M** for **mega** (one million) and **G** for **giga** (one billion); for example, **MPa** (megapascal), **GJ** (gigajoule). But avoid prefixes denoting extremely large multiples and such small fractions as **pico** (one-trillionth), **nano** (one-billionth), **micro** (one-millionth).

➤ See **Abbreviations and acronyms,** page 253.

Different strokes

1. In much of the world, spaces are used to separate long numbers into blocks of three digits (**25 353 425**) and a comma is used as a decimal mark (**245,3**). Canadian Press style is to separate figures with commas rather than spaces (**25,353,425**) and to use a period rather than a comma in decimals (**245.3**).

2. In Quebec, French-language media have adopted the international style: a space instead of a comma in long numbers, a comma instead of a decimal point and a currency symbol after an amount instead of before. Thus **12,24$** is used for **$12.24**.

Metric conversion table

Into metric

If you know	multiply by	to get
Length		
inches	25.4	millimetres
inches	2.54	centimetres
inches	0.0254	metres
feet	0.3	metres
yards	0.91	metres
miles	1.61	kilometres
Area		
sq. inches	6.45	sq. centimetres
sq. feet	0.09	sq. metres
sq. yards	0.84	sq. metres
sq. miles	2.59	sq. kilometres
acres	0.4	hectares
Mass (weight)		
ounces	28.35	grams
pounds	0.45	kilograms
tons (short)	0.907	tonnes/metric tons
Volume		
Imp. — not U.S.		
fluid ounces	28.41	millilitres (cu. cm)
pints	0.57	litres
quarts	1.13	litres
gallons	4.54	litres
cubic inches	16.39	cubic centimetres
cubic feet	0.03	cubic metres
cubic yards	0.76	cubic metres
Temperature		
Fahrenheit	Subtract 32, then multiply by 5/9ths	Celsius
Temperature variations		
Fahrenheit	.555	Celsius

Out of metric

If you know	multiply by	to get

Length

millimetres	0.04	inches
centimetres	0.39	inches
metres	3.28	feet
metres	1.09	yards
kilometres	0.62	miles

Area

sq. centimetres	0.15	sq. inches
sq. metres	10.76	sq. feet
sq. metres	1.19	sq. yards
sq. kilometres	0.4	sq. miles
hectares	2.47	acres

Mass (weight)

grams	0.035	ounces
kilograms	2.2	pounds
tonnes/metric tons	1.1	tons (short)

Volume

		Imp. — not U.S.
millilitres (cu. cm)	0.03	fluid ounces
litres	1.76	pints
litres	0.88	quarts
litres	0.22	gallons
cubic centimetres	0.06	cubic inches
cubic metres	35.31	cubic feet
cubic metres	1.31	cubic yards

Temperature

Celsius	Multiply by 9/5ths, then add 32	Fahrenheit

Temperature variations

Celsius	1.8	Fahrenheit

Common metric units

	CP style for symbol		CP style for symbol
Length			
millimetre	mm	metre	m
centimetre	cm	kilometre	km
Area			
square millimetre	sq. mm	hectare (10,000 sq. m)	ha
square centimetre	sq. cm	square kilometre	sq. km
square metre	sq. m		

Note: To convert hectares to square kilometres, divide by 100.

Volume			
millilitre	ml	cubic centimetre	cu. cm
litre	l	cubic metre	cu. m
Mass (weight)			
milligram	mg	kilogram	kg
gram	g	tonne/metric ton (1,000 kg)	t
Electricity			
volt	V	ohm	ohm
ampere	A	hertz	Hz

Energy		**Power**	
joule	J	watt	W
kilojoule	kJ	kilowatt	kW
megajoule	MJ	megawatt	MW
kilowatt hour	kW-h		
Pressure		**Temperature**	
pascal	Pa	Celsius	C
kilopascal	kPa		
megapascal	MPa		
Speed		**Memory**	
metres a second	m/s	kilobyte	KB
kilometres an hour	km/h		

Converting

1. Fuel consumption of automobiles is given in number of litres per hundred kilometres, written **l per 100 km**. The lower the figure, the lower the rate of consumption. To convert miles per U.S. gallon into litres per 100 kilometres, divide 234.2146 by the number of miles. To convert miles per Canadian gallon into litres per 100 kilometres, divide 282.48 by the number of miles.

2. To change Fahrenheit to Celsius, subtract 32, then multiply by five and divide by nine. To convert Celsius to Fahrenheit, multiply by nine, divide by five, then add 32.

3. Convert large numbers of hectares into square kilometres. To do so, divide the number of hectares by 100.

4. In Canada the results of cholesterol tests are given in millimoles per litre (mmol/l). In the United States, the results are in milligrams per decilitre (mg/dl). To determine the Canadian equivalent of an American cholesterol reading, multiply by .0259. For example, 140 mg/dl is about 3.6 mmol/l.

Recipes

Follow this style for recipes, where imperial continues to be in wide use:

Apple Oatmeal Squares
250 ml (1 cup) all-purpose flour
250 ml (1 cup) quick-cooking rolled oats
125 ml (1/2 cup) firmly packed brown sugar
5 ml (1 tsp) nutmeg
2 ml (1/2 tsp) salt
175 ml (3/4 cup) butter
6 medium cooking apples
50 ml (1/4 cup) sunflower seeds

In a bowl, combine flour, oats, sugar, nutmeg and salt. Cut in butter until mixture is crumbly. Measure out 125 ml (1/2 cup) and set aside for topping. Press remaining mixture evenly in bottom of greased 23-cm (9-inch) square pan.

Peel and core apples, cut in halves lengthwise. Place cut side down on oatmeal base. Add sunflower seeds to reserved crumb mixture and sprinkle over top. Bake at 190 C (375 F) for 40 to 45 minutes. Cut into squares and serve warm or cooled.

Makes 12 squares.

Note: To save space, punctuation in abbreviations (tsp, tbsp) can be eliminated and numbers below 10 don't need to be written out.

Military

General

1. All Canadian servicemen and servicewomen are members of the **Canadian Forces**, often shortened to the **Forces**.

Note: Uppercase **Forces** applies only to Canadian forces; all others are down.

2. The Canadian Forces are headed by the **chief of the defence staff**, who is responsible to the minister of defence and oversees all aspects of military policy. The chief is in charge of all three branches of the Forces and is therefore properly described as **Canada's top military commander**, not top soldier. The **vice chief of defence staff** is primarily responsible for operational matters.

3. There are eight commands: **Navy, Air Force, Army, Military Personnel, Canada Command, Canadian Special Forces Operational Command, Canadian Operational Support Command** and **Canadian Expeditionary Force Command**. Each branch command is headed by a lieutenant-general, with the exception of the navy, which is headed by a vice-admiral. The general in charge of the army can properly be described as **Canada's top soldier**.

4. The Department of National Defence is divided into two separate and distinct sections. The **military branch** is overseen by the chief of defence staff, who is equivalent to a deputy minister in the federal civil service. Then there is the **civilian side**, which is responsible for defence procurement, contracting, maintenance and administration. The civilian side is overseen by a deputy minister, who also reports separately to the minister of national defence.

5. The army, air force and navy have formed joint commands in each of the six geographic regions of the country: **Atlantic, East, Central, West, Pacific** and **North**. Each of these is properly referred to by its location. For example, there is **Joint Task Force Atlantic**. The joint task force commander, who reports to Canada Command at National Defence headquarters in Ottawa, decides on what resources — ships, aircraft, troops — are deployed for specific missions.

6. Units making up land, sea and air formations go by a variety of names. The main field units are **division, brigade, regiment, battalion, squadron, company, troop** and **platoon**; naval units are **fleet, squadron** and **ship**; air units are **division, group, wing, squadron** and **flight**.

7. The terms **army, navy** and **air force** are acceptable, and personnel may be referred to as **soldiers, sailors** and **airmen** or **airwomen**.

8. One rank structure, based on army grades, is used for army and air force personnel, another for navy personnel.

➤ See **Ranks**, below.

Bases

1. National Defence Headquarters in Ottawa is the headquarters of the Canadian Forces and the Defence Department.

2. Major service establishments include **Canadian Forces bases: Canadian Forces Base Comox, B.C.,** or **CFB Comox** in second reference. There are smaller establishments called **Canadian Forces stations** and specialist installations such as **Canadian Forces ammunition depots**.

3. Canada's three **rescue co-ordination centres** — at Halifax, Trenton, Ont., and Victoria — are jointly staffed by the Canadian Forces and the Canadian Coast Guard. The Forces co-ordinate air searches and the Coast Guard co-ordinates marine searches. The Forces contribute most of the aircraft used in searches while the Coast Guard contributes most of the marine vessels.

4. Avoid the abbreviations **CFS, CFAD** and **RCC** as being unfamiliar to readers.

5. When conducting operations in the field, the army utilizes a number of different bases of varying size and fortification. There is always the **principal base** in a theatre of operation, such as Kandahar Airfield in southern Afghanistan. There are also small sub-bases. The larger ones in remote regions, housing a company of 150 soldiers or more, are termed **forward operating bases**. These bases are closer to the enemy. If the base is within the confines of an urban area it can be referred to as a **camp**. These are usually well-fortified locations where troops can rest and get hot showers and meals. Smaller bases, which are even closer to enemy positions, are described as **patrol bases**. The army often names its forward and patrol bases: **Camp Nathan Smith** or **Forward Operating Base Mas'um Ghar**, both in Afghanistan, for instance. Depending upon the security situation, the army may sometimes demand, as part of an embedding agreement, that forward bases be identified in generic terms, such as **a forward operating base in Panjwaii district**.

Units

1. To help readers evaluate a military action, put the numbers and types of troops and their support high in the story. Because **battalion, brigade, army** and other formations vary in size and makeup from country to country, the terms mean little unless qualified.

2. These are some Canadian land units and their approximate sizes: **section**, 10 soldiers; **platoon**, three sections totalling 35;

company, three platoons totalling 125-150; **battalion**, three or four companies totalling 375-600. A **brigade** consists of three battalions. A **battle group** numbers about 1,000 to 1,800 and includes representatives from various branches of the military such as infantry and armour.

Note: The figures do not add up because, in addition to fighting personnel, each unit includes a varying number of commanders, signallers, etc.

3. A **regiment** is a unit with a proper name. Canada's Armed Forces has three infantry regiments (each with three battalions), three armoured regiments and three artillery regiments, in addition to dozens of reserve units.

The infantry regiments (in order of seniority): **Royal Canadian Regiment, Princess Patricia's Canadian Light Infantry, Royal 22e Regiment.**

Armour: **Royal Canadian Dragoons, Lord Strathcona's Horse (Royal Canadians), 12me regiment blinde du Canada.**

Artillery: **1 Royal Canadian Horse Artillery, 2 Canadian Horse Artillery, 5 regiment d'artillerie legere du Canada.**

4. The Air Command is divided into four operational groups: **Fighter Group; Air Transport Group; Maritime Air Group** and **10 Tactical Air Group.** The entire formation is routinely called the **1st Canadian Air Division.**

5. The main combat army of the air force is the **fighter group**, which currently uses the dual-role CF-18 fighter-bombers. Unlike the United States, Canada does not have dedicated bombers, such as the B-1s or the older B-52s.

Capitalization

➤ See chapter **Capitalization**, page 278.

Ranks

1. The Canadian Forces modify British tradition in the use of ranks and appointment titles, particularly for land forces. In an artillery regiment, for example, a private is a gunner, and a corporal is a bombardier. In an engineer regiment, a private is a sapper; in an armoured unit, a trooper; in a communications unit, a signalman; in a guards regiment, a guardsman; in a rifle regiment, a rifleman.

2. Plurals of military ranks and appointments add *s* to the principal rank category, not to the qualifying word: **major-generals, lieutenant-colonels, sergeants major.**

3. A person with at least four years of service who has achieved certain technical qualifications holds the rank of **corporal**. In effect, it is equivalent to a senior private rather than a rank

indicating leadership responsibility. The first level requiring leadership and special qualifications is the rank of **master corporal**.

4. Sometimes **commissioned** and **non-commissioned** officers are confused. Non-commissioned officers — master corporals, sergeants and warrant officers — have leadership functions, but do not hold formal commissions; the documents signed by the Queen that formally "commission" officers (from 2nd lieutenant to general) to do their jobs. **Warrant officers** actually have a "warrant" — a sort of lesser-grade commission.

Titles

The Canadian Forces use such titles as guardsman and master seaman for both males and females. Following are listed by descending order of rank.

Note: For clarity for a non-military audience, The Canadian Press does not use abbreviations used by the Forces.

Use these titles for army and air force personnel:

Rank	Before a name
general	Gen.
lieutenant-general	Lt.-Gen.
major-general	Maj.-Gen.
brigadier-general	Brig.-Gen.
colonel	Col.
lieutenant-colonel	Lt.-Col.
major	Maj.
captain	Capt.
lieutenant	Lt.
second lieutenant	2nd Lt.
officer cadet	Officer Cadet
chief warrant officer	Chief Warrant Officer
master warrant officer	Master Warrant Officer
warrant officer	Warrant Officer
sergeant	Sgt.
master corporal	Master Cpl.
corporal	Cpl.
bombardier	Bombardier
private	Pte.
guardsman	Guardsman
gunner	Gunner
rifleman	Rifleman
sapper	Sapper
signalman	Signalman
trooper	Trooper

Use these titles for navy personnel:

Rank	Before a name
admiral	Admiral
vice-admiral	Vice-Admiral
rear admiral	Rear Admiral
commodore	Commodore
captain	navy Capt.*
commander	Cmdr.
lieutenant-commander	Lt.-Cmdr.
lieutenant	navy Lt.*
sub-lieutenant	Sub-Lt.
acting sub-lieutenant	Acting Sub-Lt.
chief petty officer	Chief Petty Officer
first class, second class	1st Class, 2nd Class
master seaman	Master Seaman
leading seaman	Leading Seaman
able seaman	Able Seaman
ordinary seaman	Ordinary Seaman

* The word **navy**, lowercase, should be used before these titles to differentiate them from the army and air force titles of captain and lieutenant, which are ranked lower.

Usage for some foreign ranks and old Canadian ranks that may appear in copy periodically. They are listed alphabetically, not by descending order of rank:

Rank	Before a name
air commodore	Air Commodore
aircraftman first class	Aircraftman 1st Class
airman	Airman
airman first class	Airman 1st Class
air marshal	Air Marshal
air vice-marshal	Air Vice-Marshal
chief master sergeant	Chief Master Sgt.
commissioned warrant officer	Commissioned Warrant Officer
craftman	Craftman
ensign	Ensign
field marshal	Field Marshal
first lieutenant	1st Lt.
first sergeant	1st Sgt.
flying officer	Flying Officer
fusilier	Fusilier
group captain	Group Capt.
gunnery sergeant	Gunnery Sgt.
lance-corporal	Lance-Cpl.
leading aircraftman	Leading Aircraftman
master chief petty officer	Master Chief Petty Officer
master gunnery sergeant	Master Gunnery Sgt.
master sergeant	Master Sgt.
midshipman	Midshipman
pilot officer	Pilot Officer
platoon sergeant	Platoon Sgt.

private first class	Pte. 1st Class
regimental sergeant major	Regimental Sgt. Maj.
seaman apprentice	Seaman Apprentice
seaman recruit	Seaman Recruit
senior chief petty officer	Senior Chief Petty Officer
sergeant first class	Sgt. 1st Class
sergeant major of the army	Army Sgt. Maj.
technical sergeant	Tech. Sgt.
wing commander	Wing Cmdr.

Retired officers

1. In certain circumstances, a military rank may be used in first reference before the name of an officer who has retired. Do not use the abbreviation **Ret.** but put **retired** before the lowercase rank: **retired brigadier Pat Turner**.

2. In stories involving military activities, former majors, lieutenant-commanders, squadron leaders and other high officers may be referred to by their old rank.

3. Even in stories involving purely civilian matters, brigadiers and higher may be referred to by rank, if the officers prefer.

4. When rank is used, decorations may at times be added. In civilian stories, decorations need not be mentioned except for the Victoria Cross, Cross of Valour or other outstanding awards normally pertinent to the story.

Military justice

1. Members of the Canadian Forces are covered at all times by a separate justice system known as the **Code of Service Discipline** under the National Defence Act. It is also possible for a member of the military to face charges separately under the Canadian Criminal Code, but he or she would also face concurrent charges and penalties under the military justice system.

2. Whenever a member of the Canadian Forces is killed on duty a military police investigation is launched as a matter of routine to formally determine the circumstances. This does not mean that the military suspects criminal behaviour in the death. It is only after the findings of the preliminary investigation that a determination of criminality is made.

3. If the military believes there is some systemic or procedural flaw that has contributed to the death, the commanding officer of a unit or branch has the authority to convene a board of inquiry, which is an entirely separate investigation. The inquiry looks at the circumstances, the procedures and training. The boards are empowered to make wide-ranging recommendations. Military police investigations can produce evidence that form part of the inquiry. Depending on the circumstances, boards can recommend military police investigations.

Courts martial

1. Military courts martial are properly open to the media, though in many instances the media are not advised they are in progress. Their decisions are privileged.

2. A court martial's decision may be overruled by the federal cabinet or the Court Martial Appeal Court upon the person aggrieved presenting a petition. In either case the further ruling merits equal prominence.

Ceremonies

Guards

a) A **royal guard** is paraded for visiting royalty, governors general and lieutenant-governors. It consists of 100 men and women with arms, a band and colours (regimental flags). A **guard of honour** is turned out for any other dignitary: 50 troops with arms and usually a band. A **mounted escort** accompanies the dignitary's vehicle, the riders armed, often with lances, and drawn from the RCMP or a regiment.

b) In Canada, a dignitary **inspects** the guard by walking up and down the ranks. In the United States, a dignitary **reviews** it.

Colours

a) In Canada, the colours are carried by a **colour party**, an officer bearer escorted by non-commissioned officers. The American equivalent is called a **colour guard**.

b) Regimental colours are dipped only to the sovereign or a member of the Royal Family. In the ceremony of **trooping the colour** — carrying the regimental flag along ranks of soldiers — only one colour is trooped, hence the name.

c) Flags are always raised to the top of the mast or pole. Then, if required, they are **lowered to half-mast**. If tangled with the rope, they are **fouled**.

Military funerals

a) A **gun carriage** consists of a towed gun, with a platform fixed above the barrel, on which the coffin is fastened. The six who carry the coffin are the **bearer party**; the 12 who fire volleys at the graveside are the **firing party**.

b) Wreaths are **laid** or **placed**, trumpets **sounded** and bugles **blown** or **sounded**.

Military honours

a) Canadian Forces members are awarded two types of medals. **Valour medals** recognize specific acts of bravery on the battlefield. **Service medals** recognize a series of outstanding career achievements, a specific operation or time spent in a particular theatre of operation.

b) Canada's highest decoaration for valour is the **Canadian Victoria Cross**, inspired by the Victoria Cross, which was handed out to Commonwealth soldiers in the First and Second World Wars and the Korean War.

c) The next highest decoration for bravery is the **Star of Military Valour** followed by the **Medal of Military Valour.**

Warfare

1. There are generally two types of warfare.

Conventional warfare is typically fought as state-to-state conflicts, involving large, heavily armed opposing forces in large battles. They are sometimes, but not always, preceded by formal declarations of war and are supposed to be fought under recognized international conventions, such as the Geneva Conventions, which spell out a code of conduct and guidelines for the treatment of prisoners and civilians in occupied territories.

Irregular warfare, usually called insurgency or guerilla conflicts, generally involve armed resistance to a government within a country by one faction; civil wars; and cross-border incursions with insurgent forces using international boundaries as safe haven. This warfare is generally fought by small bands of lightly armed forces, although some have escalated into full-blown conflicts involving modern armies. Although the Geneva Conventions apply to these conflicts, insurgency campaigns are characterized by their indiscriminate killing of civilians and their use of roadside bombs and booby traps to wear down the opposing side.

2. Both types of warfare are governed by **strategy,** the overall aim of the war or individual campaignand tactics; and **tactics,** the methods used to achieve the goals.

Miscellaneous

1. Write **promoted major-general,** not **promoted to major-general.** But **promoted to the rank of major-general** is correct.

2. Distinguish between **rank** (position within the military hierarchy) and **appointment** (specific duty). A person with the **rank** of master warrant officer may be given the **duties** of regimental quartermaster sergeant, a non-commissioned officer in charge of a regiment's quarters, supplies, etc.

Master Warrant Officer Pat Smith has been named regimental quartermaster sergeant.

Regimental Quartermaster Sergeant John Smith holds the rank of master warrant officer.

3. When locating a Canadian regiment, be sure to use the *official* hometown or towns.

4. Do not refer to the Princess Patricia's Canadian Light Infantry as **the Pats**, a term disliked by its members. But **the Patricias** (no apostrophe) is acceptable for the unit or a group of individuals.

5. The nickname of Quebec's Royal 22e Regiment is **the Van Doo** (from vingt-deux). Personnel of the regiment may be referred to as **the Van Doos** and one of them as **a Van Doo**.

6. The term **Snowbirds** is officially used to designate the Canadian Forces aerobatic team. The full complement including support personnel is designated 431 Air Demonstration Squadron.

7. The **Skyhawks** parachuting performers are formally known as the Canadian Forces Parachute Team.

8. **CF-18** is the designation for the Canadian version of the U.S. fighter aircraft F-18.

9. Avoid Americanisms. Canadian usage is **Last Post, guard of honour** and **AWL** (absent without leave). American usage is **Taps, honour guard** and **AWOL**. Canadians take **basic military training**; they do not attend **boot camp**. And they fly flags at **half-mast**, not **half-staff**.

10. Do not refer to the Royal Military College at Kingston, Ont., as the **West Point of Canada** or **Canada's Sandhurst** in stories for Canadian consumption.

11. A **volley** is one shot from each of several weapons fired simultaneously; a **fusillade** is several shots fired from one weapon sequentially. One gunman can fire a fusillade but not a volley. Artillery fires in **salvos**.

12. A **sniper** fires shots from hiding, usually at long range, into the enemy's camp or at individuals.

13. In flying, a **sortie** is one mission by one plane.

14. While the term **troops** can be used to refer to a body of soldiers — **100 troops advanced** — it should not be used in the singular as a substitute for **soldier**. A troop is a military unit.

15. Be aware of the distinction between **wounds** and **injuries**. Wounds are usually the results of a battle, such as damage from a firearm or shrapnel. Injuries, such as broken bones, are also possible on the battlefield and where possible should be described as such.

16. Be careful with the language of war. Many terms often used are not neutral and have been sanitized to hide their true meaning. Soldiers are **killed** or **dead**, not **fallen**. Rather than **peacemaking, detainees** and **collateral damage**, make it **war, prisoners** and **civilian casualties**. In irregular wars, the enemy is not a **soldier** but an **insurgent** or **militant**.

17. Similarly, military culture is rich in jargon and acronyms. Avoid them as much as possible.

18. **Veterans** are those who survived the wars they served in. Do not describe soldiers killed in action as veterans.

➤ See **Aircraft, ships, guns**, page 262.

Three Canadian snipers watch over Canadian troops in a valley in Afghanistan in March 2002. To help readers evaluate a military action, put the numbers and types of troops high in a story.

THE CANADIAN PRESS/Stephen Thorne

Names, nicknames, initials

1. In general, the names of people should be given in the spelling and form they normally use: **Bob Rae**; **Joe Clark**; **John F. Kennedy** or **J.F. Kennedy**; **P.G. Wodehouse**.

2. Follow personal preference for lowercased names: **k.d. lang** (not **K.D. Lang**), **bp Nichol** (not **B.P. Nichol**) except at the start of a sentence.

➤ For the names of organizations, see **Capitalization**, page 280.

3. In obituaries, try to spell out initials at some point but not in the lead where the unfamiliar name might confuse readers: **Pelham Grenville Wodehouse**.

4. A given name reads better than a single initial: **Robin Hood**, not **R. Hood**.

5. First and middle initials are used if that is a person's preference: **W.O. Mitchell, George W. Bush**. And they are important in identifying a person charged with a crime and in listing accident victims.

6. Occasionally a public figure becomes known by initials without periods: **GBS, PET**. But most of the time, use periods after initials.

7. Use **Sr.** and **Jr.** only with the full name and do not set them off with commas: **Galen Weston Sr.**

Note: In general, reserve **Sr.** and **Jr.** for cases where father and son are alive and known and there is possibility for confusion.

8. Retain the designation **II** or **2nd** and the like if it is a person's preference: **Henry Ford III, Eric Van Husen 2nd**.

9. When necessary to distinguish between father and son in second reference, write **the elder** or **the younger Talbot**.

10. If confusion with another person is possible, include clarifying information: **O'Brien is not related to the businessman of the same name.**

11. When common names like **Mary Smith** and **Jean Dupont** get into the news, ages and occupations are needed to ensure proper identification, especially in police stories and if middle initials are not known.

12. People with first names applicable to either sex — **Beverley, Chris, Jean, Lee, Leslie, Terry, Tony** — should be identified as man or woman. Not **the accused, Pat O'Brien**, but **the woman accused, Pat O'Brien**. Often a pronoun introduced quickly — **he** or **she, him** or **her** — suffices.

13. A nickname is essential if it helps identify the subject: **Joseph (Joey) Smallwood**. Use a nickname instead of a given name only when a person is best known by the nickname: **Magic Johnson** (given name Earvin).

➤ See **Sports**, page 152.

14. To enclose nicknames, use parentheses, not quotation marks: **Mike (Pinball) Clemons**, not Mike "Pinball" Clemons.

15. In non-English names, **de, di, la, ter, van, von** and the like are usually lowercase except at the start of a sentence: **Charles de Gaulle, the de Gaulle era**. But: **She said, "De Gaulle lived to retire."** And respect an individual's preference: **Bill Vander Zalm**. If a building or some other memorial is named after the person, capitalize it: **Van Gogh Museum**.

16. In transliterating a Russian name, use the English phonetic equivalent where one exists: **Alexander Solzhenitsyn**, not **Aleksandr**. Prefer -ov and -ev endings: **Khrushchev**, not **Khrushchyov**. But with Russian émigré names, follow the individual's preference: **Ignatieff, Rachmaninoff**.

17. In Chinese, Korean and many other Asian names, the family name comes first: **Roh in Roh Tae-Woo**. But westernized people often put the given name first: **Morris Lee**.

18. For Spanish and Portuguese names, the only safe guide is the way the individuals use them.

19. For Arabic names, use an English spelling that approximates the way a name sounds in Arabic. If an individual has a preferred spelling in English, use it. If usage has established a particular spelling, use it. (Many inconsistencies in the transliteration of Arabic names are the result of pronunciations that vary from region to region.) Arabs are usually known by two or three names, with the final name being used on second reference. The articles **al-** or **el-** may be dropped or not depending on the person's preference. The Arabic word for son (**ibn** or **bin**) is sometimes part of a name: **Osama bin Laden** (**bin Laden** on second reference). Some Arabs are known only by title and a given name on first reference: **King Hussein**. Others use both the title and their full name (**Sheik Sabah Salem Sabah**). Follow common usage on first reference. On second reference, use the last name in the sequence (**Hussein, Sabah**).

20. After first reference, it is often useful to include in important stories the pronunciation of unfamiliar, difficult names of people and places breaking into the news, especially if the item is also moving on broadcast services: **Former Supreme Court justice Frank Iacobucci (yak-a-BOOCH-ee)**.

21. If a person goes by one name only, mention this so the reader doesn't think part of the name is missing: **Abdullah, who goes by one name**.

22. First names may be used on second reference for children and youths under 18, except in sports stories; they may also be used for adults for deliberate informality.

23. Plurals of proper names are usually formed by adding *s* or *es:* **Alexes, Burnses, Charleses, Henrys, Joneses, Marys, Perrys, Rubys**. But **Tommies, Johnnies**.

➤ See **Capitalization**, page 280; **Government**, page 310; **Plurals of nouns**, page 356; and **Titles**, page 410.

Canadian singer k.d. lang. Follow the preference of the person on the capitalization of their name.

(AP Photo)

Numbers

General

1. In general, spell out whole numbers below 10 and use figures for 10 and above.

three batters, the fifth inning, nine minutes, 10 guests, the 16th hole, the 22nd day, the sixth Earl of Hodderston, a woman in her 50s

2. In a series there will often be a mixture.

There are 27 trees: two beeches, 10 chestnuts, three elms and 12 maples. The dealer sold 10 four-cylinder cars, three sixes and 12 eights.

3. For numbers in official names, follow the organization's spelling style even when it is at odds with Canadian Press practice.

7Up, the film 7 Fathers, 360networks Inc.

4. Use arabic numerals unless roman numerals are specified below.

5. Do not use commas with dimensions, measurements and weights consisting of two or more elements.

a woman five feet 11 inches tall; the baby weighs seven pounds six ounces; a trip of six months three weeks two days; in two hours 21 minutes 45 seconds (but the six-foot-three, 250-pound tackle)

6. To avoid ambiguity, write increased to 15 per cent from 10 (not increased from 10 to 15 per cent).

7. To be meaningful, a percentage loss or gain should normally be accompanied by a dollar or some other amount.

Sales fell 10 per cent to $10,000. Sophie Dukakis, a hairdresser, said she now has 10 customers, a 20 per cent increase.

When to use figures

1. In addresses:

2 Newgate St., 3A Western Ave.

Note: Spell out **First** through **Ninth** as street names.

37 Fifth Ave., 23 59th St.

2. In ages standing alone after a name:

Melanie, 2, has two brothers, eight and nine. Tim, two months old, had typhoid.

Note: When the context does not require **years** or **years old**, the reader presumes the number is years: He **was 21**. One girl is **five**.

3. In dates and years:

3 BC, AD 5; Dec. 8, 8th of December; 1983, '83; the 1920s, the '20s; the Dirty '30s; the mid-1940s, the mid-'40s; he's in his late 50s.

Note: Write **the second century, the 20th century, the fifth century BC**.

4. In decimals, and in numbers larger than 1 with fractions, and in uncommon fractions:

0.15 of a percentage point, 0.25 centimetre, a .30-calibre rifle, pressures of 0.45 and 3.25, 2½ days, 15/16ths, 99 44/100ths, 3½-year-old

But two-fifths, two-thirds finished

Note 1: Unless precision is essential, keep decimals to two places: **12.25 metres** (not **12.254 metres**).

Note 2: If there is no unit before a decimal point, use a cipher: **0.25**. But write **.30 calibre** and the like in keeping with common practice.

5. In decisions, rulings, scores, votes and odds:

The court ruled 6-3, a 6-3 ruling. Montreal beat Vancouver 3-1 (but a two-goal margin). The bill was passed by a vote of 35-6, with one abstention; or a 35-6 vote. Of the 35 ballots, two were spoiled. It was a majority of nine.

odds of 5-2, a 10-1 longshot

6. In heights expressed informally:

He stands 6-11.

7. In highlights at the start of an item:

— 156 tanks and armoured personnel carriers.

— $1.8 billion for new aircraft engines.

8. In military and paramilitary terms:

2nd Lt. Esther White (but White is a second lieutenant), U.S. Petty Officer 3rd Class Mike Kenny (but prefer Mike Kenny, a U.S. petty officer third class), a 6-pounder, 8 mm, M-16 rifle, 8th Army, 6th Fleet, 1st Canadian Division

9.   In monetary units preceded by a symbol:

$2 (not **$2.00**), two dollars; two euros, 2.5 euros; **$1 million** (but **one million people**); **$2 billion, the $2-billion project**

10. In designations of aircraft, ships, spacecraft and vehicles:

Dash 7, A-4 Skyhawk, the liner Queen Elizabeth 2, QE2, the yachts Australia II and Canada 1, Apollo 8, Alouette 2

Note: Use a hyphen before the numeral but not after it: **DC-8B**.

11. In sequential designations:

Act 1 (but **the first act**), **Article 3, Channel 2, Chapter 9, Grade 7, Highway 6, in No. 2 position, Room 4, RR 2, Section 5, back to Square 1**

Note: The common nouns **line, page, paragraph** and **size** followed by figures are not capitalized: **page 3, line 9, size 8 shoes**.

12. In temperatures:

5 C, -6 C (use a hyphen)

But when Celsius or Fahrenheit is not specified spell out: **five degrees**.

13. In times:

1 a.m. (not **1:00 a.m.**), **9 at night, 2 o'clock, 10:15 p.m., a 2:09 run, 3:20:15** but **a time of three hours 20 minutes 15 seconds**

14. In lists of figures that include both whole numbers and ones with decimals:

The interest rates are 7.35 per cent for six years, 7.25 per cent for five years and 7.00 per cent for four years.

15. For latitude and longitude:

59 degrees 30 minutes north

When to spell out

1. At the start of a sentence, if you must start with a number:

Twenty to 30 escaped unharmed, as well as 10 horses.

Note 1: Do not spell out the year at the start, but avoid: **1972 was a leap year.**

Note 2: Do not spell out a street address at the start: **221 had a discreet sign: Oceano Palms.**

Note 3: When numbers from 21 through 99 must be written out, use a hyphen: **Thirty-five or 36 may have died.**

2. In informal or casual usage:

Letters poured in by hundreds and thousands. Damage was in the millions. a thousand and one delights

3. In figures of speech and the like:

Twelve Apostles, Ten Commandments, Big Ten, wouldn't touch it with a ten-foot pole, a ten-gallon hat

Note: Write the Dirty '30s, the Roaring '20s, the No. 1 or number 1 choice.

4. In common fractions below 1 standing alone:

one-half, one-quarter inch, five-eighths

Note: In casual use, write a half, half a loaf, a quarter share.

Roman numerals

Use roman numerals to indicate sequence for people and animals and in proper names where that is the widely accepted style. Otherwise avoid them as hard to grasp.

Queen Elizabeth II (rarely needed); Pope John XXIII; Henry Ford III; Nijinsky II; Bluenose II (but Canada 1); The Godfather, Part II; Superman III.

In particular, paraphrase large numbers: the 36th Super Bowl, not Superbowl XXXVI.

Note 1: For the ship, write Queen Elizabeth 2 or QE2.

Note 2: Write SALT II, Vatican II and the like to conform to widespread practice.

Large numbers

1. Round numbers in the thousands are usually given in figures.

They took 2,000 prisoners. $3,500, 375,000 francs

Note: Spell out for casual usage: There were thousands of mosquitoes.

2. Express large numbers in millions and billions instead of the less familiar trillion, quadrillion and the like.

a million billion (instead of quadrillion), a billion billion (instead of quintillion)

Note: In Canada and the United States, a billion is a thousand million; in the United Kingdom and some other places, it is a million million.

3. Except for monetary units preceded by a symbol, round numbers in the millions and billions generally follow the rule of spelling out below 10.

two million bushels, 2.5 million bushels, 10 billion cubic metres, five billion marks, $1 billion

Note: Spell out for casual usage: **What's a billion? I've told you a million times. a billion and a half**

4. In expressing a range, repeat **million** or **billion**.

25 million to 30 million

Note: The adjectival form may be written **a $2- to $3-million loss**, but prefer **a loss of $2 million to $3 million**.

5. Hyphenate adjectival forms before nouns.

a two-million-bushel crop, a $10-billion gap, the 2.2-million-member Canadian Labour Congress

6. Use commas to set off numbers of four or more figures except house, telephone, page, year and other serial numbers.

2,500; 100,000 billion; 1265 Yonge St.; 1-800-268-9237; p. 1025; 2000 (year)

7. Use figures for numbers up to 999,999. Above that, switch to words if absolute precision is not required.

a loss of $100,000, a $1.2-million project

People, places

The following countries and territories can be used in placelines. (Numbers refer to notes at end, page 346.)

Country/Region	Noun	Adjective	Capital	Currency
Afghanistan	Afghan(s)	Afghan	Kabul	afghani
Albania	Albanian(s)	Albanian	Tirana	lek
Algeria	Algerian(s)	Algerian	Algiers	dinar
American Samoa	American Samoan(s)	American Samoan	Pago Pago	dollar
Andorra	Andorran(s)	Andorran	Andorra La Vella	euro
Angola	Angolan(s)	Angolan	Luanda	kwanza
Antigua	Antiguan(s)	Antiguan	St. John's	dollar
Argentina	Argentine(s)	Argentine	Buenos Aires	peso
Armenia	Armenian(s)	Armenian	Yerevan	dram
Aruba	Aruban(s)	Aruban	Oranjestad	guilder
Australia	Australian(s)	Australian	Canberra	dollar
Austria	Austrian(s)	Austrian	Vienna	euro
Azerbaijan	Azerbaijani(s)	Azerbaijani	Baku	manat
Azores	Azorean(s)	Azorean	Ponta Delgada	escudo
Bahamas	Bahamian(s)	Bahamian	Nassau	dollar
Bahrain	Bahraini(s)	Bahraini	Manama	dinar
Bangladesh	Bangladeshi(s)	Bangladesh	Dhaka	taka
Barbados	Barbadian(s)	Barbadian	Bridgetown	dollar
Belarus	Belarusian(s)	Belarus	Minsk	ruble
Belgium	Belgian(s)	Belgian	Brussels	euro
Belize	Belizean(s)	Belizean	Belmopan	dollar
Benin	Beninese (sing., pl.)	Beninese	Porto-Novo	franc
Bermuda	Bermudian(s)	Bermudian	Hamilton	dollar
Bhutan	Bhutanese (sing., pl.)	Bhutanese	Thimphu	ngultrum/rupee
Bolivia	Bolivian(s)	Bolivian	La Paz	boliviano
Bosnia-Herzegovina	Bosnian(s)	Bosnian	Sarajevo	marka
Botswana	Motswana (sing.) Batswana (pl.)	Botswana	Gaborone	pula
Brazil	Brazilian(s)	Brazilian	Brasilia	real
Brunei	Bruneian(s)	Bruneian	Bandar Seri Begawan	dollar
Bulgaria	Bulgarian(s)	Bulgarian	Sofia	lev
Burkina Faso	Burkinabe (sing., pl.)	Burkina Fasan	Ouagadougou	franc
Burundi	Burundian(s)	Burundi	Bujumbura	franc
Cambodia	Cambodian(s)	Cambodian	Phnom Penh	riel
Cameroon	Cameroonian(s)	Cameroonian	Yaounde	franc

Country/Region	Noun	Adjective	Capital	Currency
Canary Islands	Canary Islander(s)	Canary Island	Las Palmas	peseta
Cape Verde	Cape Verdean(s)	Cape Verdean	Praia	escudo
Cayman Islands	Cayman Islander(s)	Cayman	Georgetown	dollar
Central African Republic	Central African(s)	Central African	Bangui	franc
Chad	Chadian(s)	Chadian	N'djamena	franc
Chile	Chilean(s)	Chilean	Santiago	peso
China	Chinese (sing., pl.)	Chinese	Beijing	renminbi/yuan
Colombia	Colombian(s)	Colombian	Bogota	peso
Comoros	Comoran(s)	Comoran	Moroni	franc
Congo, Democratic Republic of ❶ (formerly Zaire)	Congolese (sing., pl.)	Congolese	Kinshasa	franc
Congo, Republic of ❶	Congolese (sing., pl.)	Congolese	Brazzaville	franc
Cook Islands	Cook Islander(s)	Cook Islands	Avarua	dollar
Costa Rica	Costa Rican(s)	Costa Rican	San Jose	colon
Croatia	Croat(s)	Croatian	Zagreb	kuna
Cuba	Cuban(s)	Cuban	Havana	peso
Cyprus	Cypriot(s)	Cypriot	Nicosia	pound/lira
Czech Republic	Czech(s)	Czech	Prague	koruna
Denmark	Dane(s)	Danish	Copenhagen	krone
Djibouti	Djiboutian(s)	Afar, Issa	Djibouti	franc
Dominica	Dominican(s)	Dominican	Roseau	dollar
Dominican Republic	Dominican(s)	Dominican	Santo Domingo	peso
East Timor	Timorese	Timorese	Dili	U.S. dollar
Ecuador	Ecuadorian(s)	Ecuadorian	Quito	U.S. dollar
Egypt	Egyptian(s)	Egyptian	Cairo	pound
El Salvador	Salvadoran(s)	Salvadoran	San Salvador	colon
Equatorial Guinea	Equatorial Guinean(s)	Equatorial Guinean	Malabo	franc
Eritrea	Eritrean(s)	Eritrean	Asmara	nakfa
Estonia	Estonian(s)	Estonian	Tallinn	kroon
Ethiopia	Ethiopian(s)	Ethiopian	Addis Ababa	birr
Falkland Islands	Falkland Islander(s)	Falkland	Stanley Island	pound
Faroe Islands	Faroe Islander(s)	Faroe Islands	Thorshavn	krone
Fiji	Fijian(s)	Fijian	Suva	dollar
Finland	Finn(s)	Finnish	Helsinki	euro
France	French(wo)man	French	Paris	euro
French Guiana	French Guianese (sing., pl.)	French Guianese	Cayenne	euro
French Polynesia	French Polynesian(s)	French Polynesian	Papeete	franc

Country/ Region	Noun	Adjective	Capital	Currency
Gabon	Gabonese (sing., pl.)	Gabonese	Libreville	franc
Gambia	Gambian(s)	Gambian	Banjul	dalasi
Georgia	Georgian(s)	Georgian	Tbilisi	lari
Germany	German(s)	German	Berlin	euro
Ghana	Ghanaian(s)	Ghanaian	Accra	cedi
Gibraltar	Gibraltan(s)	Gibraltan	Gibraltar	pound
Greece	Greek(s)	Greek	Athens	euro
Greenland	Greenlander(s)	Greenlandic	Godthab	krone
Grenada	Grenadian(s)	Grenadian	St. George's	dollar
Guadeloupe	Guadeloupian(s)	Guadeloupe	Basse-Terre	euro
Guam	Guamanian(s)	Guamanian	Agana	dollar
Guatemala	Guatemalan(s)	Guatemalan	Guatemala	quetzal
Guinea	Guinean(s)	Guinea	Conakry	franc
Guinea-Bissau	Guinean(s)	Guinean	Bissau	franc
Guyana	Guyanese (sing., pl.)	Guyanese	Georgetown	dollar
Haiti	Haitian(s)	Haitian	Port-au-Prince	gourde
Honduras	Honduran(s)	Honduran	Tegucigalpa	lempira
Hong Kong		Hong Kong	(part of China)	dollar
Hungary	Hungarian(s)	Hungarian	Budapest	forint
Iceland	Icelander(s)	Icelandic	Reykjavik	krona
India	Indian(s)	Indian	New Delhi	rupee
Indonesia	Indonesian(s)	Indonesian	Jakarta	rupiah
Iran	Iranian(s)	Iranian	Tehran	rial
Iraq	Iraqi(s)	Iraqi	Baghdad	dinar
Ireland	Irish(wo)man	Irish	Dublin	euro
Israel	Israeli(s)	Israeli	Jerusalem ❷	shekel
Italy	Italian(s)	Italian	Rome	euro
Ivory Coast	Ivorian(s)	Ivorian	Abidjan	franc
Jamaica	Jamaican(s)	Jamaican	Kingston	dollar
Japan	Japanese (sing., pl.)	Japanese	Tokyo	yen
Jordan	Jordanian(s)	Jordanian	Amman	dinar
Kazakhstan	Kazakhstani(s)	Kazakhstani	Astana	tenge
Kenya	Kenyan(s)	Kenyan	Nairobi	shilling
Kiribati	Kiribatan(s)	Kiribatan	Tarawa	dollar
Kosovo ❸	Kosovar	Kosovo	Pristina	euro
Kuwait	Kuwaiti(s)	Kuwaiti	Kuwait	dinar
Kyrgyzstan	Kyrgstani(s)	Kyrgstani	Bishkek	som
Laos	Laotian(s)	Laotian	Vientiane	kip
Latvia	Latvian(s)	Latvian	Riga	lat
Lebanon	Lebanese (sing., pl.)	Lebanese	Beirut	pound
Lesotho	Masotho (sing.) Basotho (pl.)	Basotho	Maseru	maloti
Liberia	Liberian(s)	Liberian	Monrovia	dollar
Libya	Libyan(s)	Libyan	Tripoli	dinar
Liechtenstein	Liechtensteiner(s)	Liechtenstein	Vaduz	franc
Lithuania	Lithuanian(s)	Lithuanian	Vilnius	litas

Country/ Region	Noun	Adjective	Capital	Currency
Luxembourg	Luxembourger(s)	Luxembourg	Luxembourg	euro
Macedonia, Former Yugoslav Republic of ❹	Macedonian(s)	Macedonian	Skopje	dinar
Madagascar	Malagasy (sing., pl.)	Malagasy	Antananarivo	franc
Malawi	Malawian(s)	Malawian	Lilongwe	kwacha
Malaysia	Malaysian(s)	Malaysian	Kuala Lumpur	ringgit
Maldives	Maldivian(s)	Maldivian	Male	rufiyaa
Mali	Malian(s)	Malian	Bamako	franc
Malta	Maltese (sing., pl.)	Maltese	Valletta	lira
Martinique	Martinican(s)	Martinican	Fort-de-France	euro
Mauritania	Mauritanian(s)	Mauritanian	Nouakchott	ouguiya
Mauritius	Mauritian(s)	Mauritian	Port Louis	rupee
Mexico	Mexican(s)	Mexican	Mexico City	peso
Micronesia, Federated States of	Micronesian(s)	Micronesian	Palikir	dollar
Moldova	Moldovan(s)	Moldovan	Chisinau	leu
Monaco	Monegasque	Monegasque	Monaco	euro
Mongolia	Mongolian(s)	Mongolian	Ulan Bator	tugrik
Montenegro ❺	Montenegrin	Montenegrin	Podgorica	euro
Montserrat	Montserratan(s)	Montserratan	Plymouth	dollar
Morocco	Moroccan(s)	Moroccan	Rabat	dirham
Mozambique	Mozambican(s)	Mozambican	Maputo	metical
Myanmar	Myanmarese	Myanmar	Yangon	kyat
Namibia	Namibian(s)	Namibian	Windhoek	dollar
Nauru	Nauruan(s)	Nauruan	Yaren	dollar
Nepal	Nepalese (sing., pl.)	Nepalese	Kathmandu	rupee
Netherlands ❻	Netherlander(s)/ Dutch(wo)man	Netherlander/ Dutch	Amsterdam ❻	euro
Netherlands Antilles	Netherlands Antillean(s)	Netherlands Antillean	Willemstad	guilder
New Caledonia	New Caledonian(s)	New Caledonian	Noumea	franc
New Zealand	New Zealander(s)	New Zealand	Wellington	dollar
Nicaragua	Nicaraguan(s)	Nicaraguan	Managua	cordoba
Niger	Nigerois (sing., pl.)	Niger	Niamey	franc
Nigeria	Nigerian(s)	Nigerian	Abuja	naira
Niue	Niuean(s)	Niuean	Alofi	dollar
Norfolk Island	Norfolk Islander(s)	Norfolk Island	Kingston	dollar
North Korea	North Korean(s)	North Korean	Pyongyang	won
Norway	Norwegian(s)	Norwegian	Oslo	krone
Oman	Omani(s)	Omani	Muscat	rial

Country/ Region	Noun	Adjective	Capital	Currency
Pakistan	Pakistani(s)	Pakistani	Islamabad	rupee
Panama	Panamanian(s)	Panamanian	Panama City	
balboaPapua New Guinea	Papua New Guinean(s)	Papua New Guinean	Port Moresby	kina
Paraguay	Paraguayan(s)	Paraguayan	Asuncion	guarani
Peru	Peruvian(s)	Peruvian	Lima	sol
Philippines	Filipino(s) (male) Filipina(s) (female)	Philippine	Manila	peso
Pitcairn Island	Pitcairn Islander(s)	Pitcairn Island	Adamstown	dollar
Poland	Pole(s)	Polish	Warsaw	zloty
Portugal	Portuguese (sing., pl.)	Portuguese	Lisbon	euro
Puerto Rico	Puerto Rican(s)	Puerto Rican	San Juan	dollar
Qatar	Qatari(s)	Qatari	Doha	rial
Reunion	Reunionese (sing., pl.)	Reunionese	Saint-Denis	euro
Romania	Romanian(s)	Romanian	Bucharest	leu
Russia	Russian(s)	Russian	Moscow	ruble
Rwanda	Rwandan(s)	Rwandan	Kigali	franc
St. Helena	St. Helenan(s)	St. Helenan	Jamestown	pound
St. Kitts-Nevis	Kittsian(s), Nevisian(s)	Kittsian, Nevisian	Basseterre	dollar
St. Lucia	St. Lucian(s)	St. Lucian	Castries	dollar
St-Pierre-Miquelon	St-Pierrais (sing., pl.)	St-Pierrais	St-Pierre	euro
St. Vincent, Grenadines	Vincentian(s), Grenadinian(s)	St. Vincentian, Grenadinian	Kingstown	dollar
Samoa	Samoan(s)	Samoan	Apia	tala
San Marino	San Marinese (sing., pl.)	San Marinese	San Marino	euro
Sao Tome and Principe	Sao Tomean(s), Principian(s)	Sao Tomean, Principian	Sao Tome	dobra
Saudi Arabia	Saudi(s)	Saudi Arabian, Saudi	Riyadh	riyal
Senegal	Senegalese (sing., pl.)	Senegalese	Dakar	franc
Serbia ❸	Serb	Serbian	Belgrade	dinar
Seychelles	Seychellois (sing., pl.)	Seychellois	Victoria	rupee
Sierra Leone	Sierra Leonean(s)	Sierra Leonean	Freetown	leone
Sikkim	Sikkimese (sing., pl.)	Sikkimese	Gangtok	rupee
Singapore	Singaporean(s)	Singaporean	Singapore	dollar
Slovakia	Slovak(s)	Slovak	Bratislava	koruna
Slovenia	Slovene(s)	Slovenian	Ljubljana	tolar
Solomon Islands	Solomon Islander(s)	Solomon Island	Honiara	dollar
Somalia	Somali(s)	Somali	Mogadishu	shilling

Country/ Region	Noun	Adjective	Capital	Currency
South Africa	South African(s)	South African	Pretoria ❼	rand
South Korea	South Korean(s)	South Korean	Seoul	won
Spain	Spaniard(s)	Spanish	Madrid	euro
Sri Lanka	Sri Lankan(s)	Sri Lankan	Colombo	rupee
Sudan	Sudanese (sing., pl.)	Sudanese	Khartoum	dinar
Suriname	Surinamer(s)	Surinamese	Paramaribo	dollar
Swaziland	Swazi(s)	Swazi	Mbabane	lilageni (emalangeni, pl.)
Sweden	Swede(s)	Swedish	Stockholm	krona
Switzerland	Swiss (sing., pl.)	Swiss	Bern	franc
Syria	Syrian(s)	Syrian	Damascus	pound
Taiwan	Taiwanese (sing., pl.)	Taiwanese	Taipei	dollar
Tajikistan	Tajik(s)	Tajik	Dushanbe	ruble
Tanzania	Tanzanian(s)	Tanzanian	Dar es Salaam	shilling
Thailand	Thai(s)	Thai	Bangkok	baht
Togo	Togolese (sing., pl.)	Togolese	Lome	franc
Tokelau Islands	Tokelau Islander(s)	Tokelau Islands	Fakaofo	dollar
Tonga	Tongan(s)	Tongan	Nuku'alofa	pa'anga
Trinidad and Tobago	Trinidadian(s), Tobagan(s)	Trinidadian, Tobagan	Port-of-Spain	dollar
Tunisia	Tunisian(s)	Tunisian	Tunis	dinar
Turkey	Turk(s)	Turkish	Ankara	lira
Turkmenistan	Turkmen (sing., pl.)	Turkmen	Ashkhabad	manat
Turks and Caicos Is.	Turks/Caicos Islander(s)	Turks/Caicos Islands	Grand Turk	dollar
Tuvalu	Tuvaluan(s)	Tuvaluan	Funafuti ❽	dollar
Uganda	Ugandan(s)	Ugandan	Kampala	shilling
Ukraine (not *the*)	Ukrainian(s)	Ukrainian	Kyiv	hryvnya
United Arab Emirates	Emirati(s)	Emirati	Abu Dhabi	dirham
United Kingdom	Briton(s)	British	London	pound
United States	American(s)	American/U.S.	Washington	dollar
Uruguay	Uruguayan(s)	Uruguayan	Montevideo	peso
Uzbekistan	Uzbek(s)	Uzbek	Tashkent	soum
Vanuatu	Vanuatuan(s)	Vanuatuan	Port Vila	vatu
Vatican City		Vatican	Vatican City	lira
Venezuela	Venezuelan(s)	Venezuelan	Caracas	bolivar
Vietnam	Vietnamese (sing., pl.)	Vietnamese	Hanoi	dong
Virgin Islands (Br.)	Virgin Islander(s)	Virgin Island	Road Town	dollar

Country/Region	Noun	Adjective	Capital	Currency
Virgin Islands (U.S.)	Virgin Islander(s)	Virgin Island	Charlotte Amalie	dollar
Yemen	Yemeni(s)	Yemeni	Sanaa	rial
Zambia	Zambian(s)	Zambian	Lusaka	kwacha
Zimbabwe	Zimbabwean(s)	Zimbabwean	Harare	dollar

❶ Congo can be used in second reference for both countries unless confusion is likely.

❷ Recognition withheld by many countries over the Palestinian question. Tel Aviv is the administrative capital.

❸ Kosovo has declared independence from Serbia; use as placeline when appropriate.

❹ Macedonia can be used in most references.

❺ Montenegro's independence from Serbia was formalized in 2006.

❻ Holland may be used in casual contexts. The seat of government is The Hague.

❼ Pretoria is the executive capital, site of the president's office and of foreign embassies. The legislature sits in Cape Town.

❽ Funafuti is capital, but administrative offices are on Fongafale island.

U.S. state descriptive terms

Alabamian
Alaskan
Arizonan
Arkansan
Californian
Coloradan
Connecticuter
Delawarean
Floridian
Georgian
Hawaiian
Idahoan
Illinoisan
Indianian
Iowan
Kansan
Kentuckian

Louisianian
Mainer
Marylander
Massachusettsan
Michiganite
Minnesotan
Mississippian
Missourian
Montanan
Nebraskan
Nevadan
New Hampshirite
New Jerseyite
New Mexican
New Yorker
North Carolinian
North Dakotan

Ohioan
Oklahoman
Oregonian
Pennsylvanian
Rhode Islander
South Carolinian
South Dakotan
Tennessean
Texan
Utahn (Utahan, adj.)
Vermonter
Virginian
Washingtonian
West Virginian
Wisconsinite
Wyomingite

Provincial descriptive terms

Albertan
British Columbian
Manitoban
New Brunswicker
Newfoundlander, Labradorian

Nova Scotian
Ontarian
Prince Edward Islander, Islander
Quebecer
Saskatchewanian (rare; prefer *a resident of Saskatchewan*)

Placelines

Readers are interested in knowing exactly where the news is happening, both in Canada and abroad. If it is in their community, they have an obvious interest. But it could also be happening somewhere where they know people or they have been. Few Canadians live their full lives in the area in which they were born and brought up. Career moves take them from one part of the country to another and sometimes to still another. And, of course, thousands of Canadians have come here from other parts of the world.

Internet and wireless technology also make it possible to map or select news items that have been geotagged based on their placeline and other communities mentioned. These geotags, which usually consist of latitude and longitude co-ordinates, place news and photos to a specific intersection, street address or building. Readers with a wireless device featuring GPS technology can then search for news happening around their specific location.

Most stories carry a placeline as their first piece of information. The placeline tells a reader where most of the story took place. Whenever possible, place stories where the main event occurred. Usually, the placeline consists of the name of the community, followed by the province or state, if in Canada or the United States, or the country, if located elsewhere.

Locating the news

1. Don't assume the placeline itself is enough of a locator. Name well-known streets or areas in stories about major fires and the like. In Halifax it might be: **a block from Barrington Street in the restored Historic Properties district of the waterfront beneath Citadel Hill.** In Hong Kong: **in the heart of the Central District within sight of the Bank of China Tower and just three blocks from the Star Ferry Pier. This also helps in the geotagging process.**

2. Readers interested in entertainment and celebrities want to know where events are held. In a review of a show or coverage of an event involving a big-name star, try to set the scene for the reader: **the cast met for an after-show dinner at the Bayshore Inn, on Burrard Inlet facing the mountains of West Vancouver.**

3. But keep in mind as well those readers who are unfamiliar with even the biggest cities. Pause early in the story to set the scene: **highrises on the Toronto harbourfront with a view over boat-dotted Lake Ontario and out to the greenery of the Toronto Islands; the shooting at the University of Montreal, whose Art Deco administration tower atop Mount Royal can be seen from all over the city.**

4. Don't assume readers know precisely where familiar mid-size cities are. Give places like Moncton, Kitchener, Prince Albert and Kelowna a physical presence and geographical location when that would help readers picture an event.

5. Pinpoint the location of news in remote areas, as well: **The two tankers collided at the tiny community of Purple Springs on Alberta Highway 3 just east of Taber and about a 40-minute drive from Lethbridge; The power station is near Gillam in a rugged area of northeastern Manitoba inland from Hudson Bay and about 14 hours by road from Winnipeg.**

6. Sometimes referring back to the story's placeline helps: (Glenwood, N.L.) — **this central Newfoundland logging town about 300 kilometres west of St. John's**; (Mahim, India) — **this seaside town just outside Mumbai.**

7. Don't assume the placeline is going to give the reader a clear geographic sense of where the news has happened. For example, a story from Edmonton that says a force of specially trained police officers has been set up to give immediate emotional support to battered women must make clear where the force will function. In Edmonton alone? In all major Alberta centres? Or throughout Alberta? Watch phrases like *city police* and *the provincial department* which may be adequate for local media but rarely for a national news service. Usually it is better to name the city and province in first references.

8. Avoid **here** in copy, since it may force the reader to check the placeline a second time. Do the reader a favour by repeating the name of the community at appropriate times in the story (**the mayor of Ste. Agathe, south of Winnipeg**).

9. Although the placeline normally tells the reader where the event occurred, there are exceptions. On an exclusive picked up from other media, the placeline is usually the city where the newspaper or station is based, even if the event took place elsewhere. Such pickups are usually under 300 words and the fact that the exclusive is being reported is as much a part of the story as the news itself.

WINNIPEG — The Conservatives plan a leadership convention in March, the Winnipeg Free Press said today in a report from Ottawa.

But use the placeline given by a newspaper to a story when the material is not exclusive or is readily available, and the newspaper has granted permission for it to be used.

MONTREAL — As much as 20 per cent of Canada's 10 million tonnes of annual newsprint capacity could disappear over the next two years as producers close aging and unproductive mills.

"It's a disaster out there," consultant Jim Rowland told the
Globe and Mail in an interview.

Note: It is often necessary to obtain permission from the
newspaper to pick up a story from outside the paper's Return
News district. If the story is voluntarily filed to The Canadian
Press, that implies permission for it to be picked up.

10. A story that rounds up events or developments in several
centres does not have a placeline. It can carry a **Roundup** slug:
FedBudget-Rxn-Rdp.

Note: A placeline is preferred whenever possible. The **Roundup**
slug should be reserved for those stories that are true roundups,
not stories with most of the elements from one centre and a
couple of elements from another. In that case, placeline the story
in the first centre and specify in the body of the story where the
secondary material came from.

11. Other items that don't carry a placeline include stories,
Quicks and other such items that don't have or need a geographic
focus, and columns for sports, entertainment and other specific
topics.

12. A byline is used on a placelined story only when the reporter
has been in the community to collect information. On rare
occasions, it is permissible to drop the placeline from a specific
community where the reporter deserves a byline, but was not in
the community.

➤ See **Bylines**, page 462; **Credit lines**, page 464.

13. In a story obtained by phone but carrying the placeline of the
event, it is sometimes worth explaining how the information was
gathered.

**The masked gunman disrupted the meeting just as city
council was to vote on the firearms ban, Mayor Shirley
Millson said in a phone interview.**

14. For stories from websites, use the placeline where the website
originates if the story is an exclusive. For stories that The
Canadian Press has been granted permission to carry, use the
placeline where the story occurred or was written.

15. Stories from conference calls or teleconferences should be
placelined where those holding the conference are located.
However, if the reporter has added major elements to the story, it
can be placelined from the location of the reporter and a byline
added.

16. Stories based on news releases in Canada reporting outside
the country should be placelined where the release is issued.

17. Avoid contrived novelty placelines, for example: **IN THE
CAB OF A SEMI-TRAILER TRUCK SOMEWHERE ON
HIGHWAY 97.** Unconventional placelines are occasionally
legitimate when copy is written and filed from that point, for

example: **HMCS ATHABASKAN** (not **ON BOARD HMCS ATHABASKAN**). Ensure the approximate position of the ship is described early in the text.

18. Stories that take place on Canadian Forces bases can carry the short form CFB — for example, **CFB TRENTON, Ont.** Or they can be placelined in a nearby civilian community — for example, **HALIFAX** — with an explanation in the body of the story that the event took place on a Forces base.

19. Prefer placelines that would fit in one line of body type in a newspaper column. Most domestic and foreign news is reported from capitals or major cities; those listed in this chapter under Canadian, U.S. and foreign placelines require no other identification in the placeline.

Canadian placelines

1. The community is followed by the province or territory with the exceptions of these well-known cities:

CALGARY	MONTREAL	VANCOUVER
CHARLOTTETOWN	OTTAWA	VICTORIA
EDMONTON	QUEBEC	WHITEHORSE
FREDERICTON	REGINA	WINNIPEG
HALIFAX	SASKATOON	YELLOWKNIFE
HAMILTON	TORONTO	

Note 1: WHITEHORSE and YELLOWKNIFE stand alone as placelines, but the *Northwest Territories* or *Yukon* should be mentioned in the opening paragraph.

Note 2: QUEBEC stands alone as a placeline; use *Quebec City* in the body of a story.

Note 3: Write **ST. JOHN'S, N.L.**, and **SAINT JOHN, N.B.**, to avoid confusion.

2. **Nunavut** should be written out in all placelines, including stories from its capital: **IQALUIT, Nunavut.**

3. The former municipalities of *Scarborough, Etobicoke, York, East York* and *North York* are all part of Toronto and should be identified as such in placelines and copy. All other Greater Toronto Area communities carry their own placelines.

The municipalities on the Island of Montreal carry a **MONTREAL** placeline. Communities off the island carry their own placelines.

Vancouver does not have a regional government, so communities such as *West Vancouver* and *North Vancouver* carry their own placelines.

4. For reserves and First Nations communities, use the name favoured by the community: **GRASSY NARROW FIRST NATION, Ont.**

U.S. placelines

1. The community is followed by the state abbreviation with these exceptions:

➤ For state abbreviations, see **Abbreviations**, page 257.

ATLANTA	HOUSTON	PHILADELPHIA
BALTIMORE	INDIANAPOLIS	PHOENIX
BOSTON	LAS VEGAS	PITTSBURGH
CHICAGO	LOS ANGELES	ST. LOUIS
CINCINNATI	MIAMI	SALT LAKE CITY
CLEVELAND	MILWAUKEE	SAN ANTONIO
DALLAS	MINNEAPOLIS	SAN DIEGO
DENVER	NEW ORLEANS	SAN FRANCISCO
DETROIT	NEW YORK	SEATTLE
HONOLULU	OKLAHOMA CITY	WASHINGTON

2. Use the commonly accepted **United States**, not United States of America.

Other foreign placelines

1. The community is followed by the country in the placeline with these exceptions:

Note: Write HAMILTON, Bermuda, SYDNEY, Australia and

AMSTERDAM	HONG KONG	PARIS
BAGHDAD	ISLAMABAD	PRAGUE
BANGKOK	JERUSALEM	RIO DE JANEIRO
BEIJING	JOHANNESBURG	ROME
BEIRUT	KUWAIT CITY	SAN MARINO
BERLIN	LONDON	SAO PAULO
BRUSSELS	LUXEMBOURG	SHANGHAI
CAIRO	MACAU	SINGAPORE
DJIBOUTI	MADRID	STOCKHOLM
DUBLIN	MEXICO CITY	TOKYO
GENEVA	MILAN	VATICAN CITY
GIBRALTER	MONACO	VIENNA
GUATEMALA CITY	MUNICH	ZURICH
HAVANA	NEW DELHI	
HELSINKI	PANAMA CITY	

ST. PETERSBURG, Russia, to avoid confusion with the Canadian cities and St. Petersburg, Fla. MONTE CARLO is used for racing stories; MONACO for all others.

2. Use the commonly accepted short version of a country's or region's name.

Argentina, not Republic of Argentina
Bahamas, not Commonwealth of the Bahamas
China, not People's Republic of China
Hong Kong, not Special Administrative Region of Hong Kong
Kuwait, not State of Kuwait
Sikkim, not Kingdom of Sikkim
Taiwan, not Republic of China

3.   Do not use *The* with the name of a country in placelines.

Bahamas	Gambia	Philippines
Congo	Netherlands	

Note: It is always **Ukraine**, never the Ukraine.

Note: Do use El Salvador.

4.   Use **UNITED NATIONS** alone in placelines.

Place names

General

1. The style authority for Canadian place names is the *Canadian Oxford Dictionary*, with some exceptions. Those exceptions are listed in *Caps and Spelling*. If the place name is not in Oxford, editors should turn to the Secretariat of the Canadian Permanent Committee on Geographical Names (http://geonames.nrcan.gc.ca/). So check Caps first, then Oxford, then the website.

2. In Quebec place names, retain hyphens and shorten *saint* and *sainte* to *St* and *Ste* (no periods): **Ste-Anne-des-Monts**. When technically possible, retain accents except in the case of **Montreal** and **Quebec,** which have long-standing English versions of their names. Do not hyphenate English place names in Quebec: **East Broughton, Otterburn Park.** Names preceded by the definite article do not need a hyphen after the article: **La Malbaie.**

➤ See **French**, page 304.

3. Use the full name of Canada's easternmost province, **Newfoundland and Labrador,** whenever space permits. **Newfoundland**, alone, can be used in more casual references or when the island only is being described.

4. *The National Geographic Atlas of the World* is The Canadian Press's authority for place names outside Canada with exceptions listed below.

5. The umlaut in German names is indicated by placing the letter *e* after the vowel affected. *Düsseldorf* becomes *Duesseldorf.*

6. Use the Ukrainian, not the Russian, transliteration for Ukrainian place names. This means it is **Kyiv** (not Kiev) and **Chornobyl** (not Chernobyl). Other Ukrainian transliterations: **Kharkiv, Lviv, Odesa** (cities); **Crimea** (southern region of Ukraine); and **Carpathy** and **Zacarpatia** (mountains).

Exceptions

These are the exceptions to *National Geographic* spellings:

Algiers	Copenhagen	Genoa
Antwerp	Corfu	Havana
Athens	Corinth	Ithaca
Bangkok	Damascus	Kabul
Belgrade	Dardanelles	Kandahar
Blue Nile River	Doha, Qatar	Kingstown (Ireland)
Brunswick	Dubai	Lisbon
Brussels	Dunkirk	Lucerne
Bucharest	Florence	Milan
Cologne	Geneva	Moscow

Munich	Sinai, Mount	Turin
Naples	Sofia	Tyre
Nuremberg	Sparta	Venice
Olympus	Taipei	Vesuvius, Mount
Prague	The Hague	Vienna
Rhodes	Tiber River	Warsaw
Rome	Tibet	

Regions

1. In the broadest sense, *America* refers to North and South America, and *American* to any resident of the continents. But the narrower meanings of the words — the United States and its citizens — are more commonly the ones intended and are acceptable in unambiguous contexts.

2. **North America**: Canada, the United States, Mexico, Greenland, Central America, the tiny .French islands of St-Pierre-Miquelon and, in broad contexts, the islands of the Caribbean.

Central America: Belize, Costa Rica, El Salvador, Guatemala, Honduras, Nicaragua and Panama.

3. **South America**: Argentina, Bolivia, Brazil, Chile, Colombia, Ecuador, Paraguay, Peru, Uruguay, Venezuela, plus French Guiana, Guyana and Suriname on the northeastern coast which regard themselves as Caribbean countries.

4. **Latin America**: the parts of Central and South America where Spanish or Portuguese is the dominant language. Most countries south of the United States are included. Exceptions are French Guiana, Suriname and areas with a British background: the Bahamas, Barbados, Belize, Grenada, Guyana, Jamaica, Trinidad and Tobago and the smaller islands in the West Indies.

5. **British Isles**: Britain and all Ireland and the islands near their coasts.

United Kingdom: England, Scotland, Wales and Northern Ireland.

Britain: England, Scotland and Wales, but *British* encompasses the United Kingdom.

Ireland: The island is divided into Northern Ireland (part of the United Kingdom) and the independent republic of Ireland.

6. **Scandinavia:** Geographically, the peninsula occupied by Norway and Sweden. Culturally, the countries of Norway, Sweden and Denmark and sometimes Iceland, Finland and the Faroe Islands.

7. **Middle East** or, less desirably, **Mideast**: usually taken to include Bahrain, Egypt, Iran, Iraq, Israel, Jordan, Kuwait, Lebanon, Oman, Qatar, Sudan, Saudi Arabia, Syria, Turkey, the United Arab Emirates and Yemen. Do not use *Near East*.

8. **Far East**: China, Japan, North and South Korea, Taiwan and the eastern Soviet Union. **Note:** Hong Kong and Macau are now part of China.

9. **Southeast Asia**: Cambodia, Indonesia, Laos, Malaysia, Myanmar, New Guinea, the Philippines, Singapore, Thailand and Vietnam.

10. **South Asia**: India, Pakistan, Bangladesh, Sri Lanka, Nepal and the Maldives. **Note:** Natives of these countries are South Asian, not East Indian.

People and places

1. Shorten *Great Britain* to *Britain* in news stories. Write *Briton*, not *Britisher*.

2. Refer to the British capital, both in placelines and the body of a story, simply as *London*. Use *London, England,* only if ambiguity would otherwise result; for example, if two Londons appear in the same story.

3. For the people, prefer *Scot, Scots(wo)man,* not *Scotch(wo)man*. Use *Scottish* as the usual adjective, meaning pertaining to Scotland: **Scottish Highlands, Scottish descent**. Use *Scotch* of food, drink, plants, animals and things originating in Scotland: **Scotch broth, Scotch tweed, Scotch thistle, Scotch terrier**. But **scotch** (whisky).

4. Where necessary, specify *the republic of Ireland* or *Northern Ireland*.

5. Israel declared Jerusalem its capital in 1950 despite Arab protest. Many countries, including Canada, do not recognize it as such. They maintain their ambassadors in Tel Aviv, which may be referred to as the administrative capital.

➤ See **Placelines**, page 347; **People, places**, page 340.

Plurals of nouns

In general, form the plural of a noun by adding *s* to the singular; add *es* if the singular ends in *s, x, ch, sh* or *z*.

taxis, lenses, complexes, stitches, lashes, topazes

The plurals of the following words often cause problems.

Nouns ending in *f, fe* and *ff*

1. Most nouns in this category have a plural in *s*.

beliefs, briefs, chiefs, griefs, mischiefs, roofs, safes, skiffs, tariffs, tiffs

2. Some have a plural in *ves*.

calves, elves, halves, knives, leaves, loaves, selves, shelves, thieves, wives, wolves

3. A few have two plurals; Canadian Press style is shown.

dwarfs, handkerchiefs, hoofs, scarves, still lifes, wharfs

Write **staffs** (poles), **staves** (music).

Nouns ending in *o*

1. Nouns ending with an *o* preceded by another vowel usually have a plural in *s* (not *es*).

cameos, folios, kangaroos, patios, portfolios, radios, ratios, rodeos, studios, tattoos, zoos

2. Nouns ending in *o* preceded by a consonant have a variety of plurals.

a) Some end in *es*.

dominoes, echoes, embargoes, heroes, mementoes, mosquitoes, mottoes, Negroes, noes, potatoes, tomatoes, tornadoes, volcanoes

b) Some end in *s*.

albinos, avocados, cantos, contraltos, dittos, dynamos, Filipinos, gauchos, ghettos, gigolos, octavos, pianos, piccolos, provisos, quartos, silos, solos, tangelos, tobaccos, twos, tyros, zeros

c) Some have two forms; Canadian Press style is shown.

banjos, buffaloes, cargoes, concertos, Eskimos, frescoes, innuendoes, lassos, salvoes, sopranos

Nouns ending in *y*

1. Nouns ending in *y* preceded by a vowel have a plural in *s*.

alloys, attorneys, chimneys, days, forays, keys, monkeys, storeys

But **soliloquies**; prefer **moneys** to **monies**.

2. Nouns ending in *y* preceded by a consonant have a plural in *ies*.

armies, authorities, beauties, bodies, caddies, categories, cherries, cities, communities, companies, cries, flies, ladies, parodies, skies

But **drys** (prohibitionists), **standbys**

Nouns ending in *ics*

Nouns of this type are singular or plural depending on use. They are singular when denoting the science or a course of study, plural when denoting an activity or quality.

Classics means Latin and Greek. The classics are neglected nowadays. Ethics is defined as a moral philosophy. His ethics are questionable.

➤ See **Singular or plural**, page 395.

Proper nouns

1. Proper nouns usually form the plural by adding *s*.

Drapeaus, Elizabeths, Germanys, Kansas Citys, Kennedys, Little Italys, Marys

Note: Some follow the *ies* rule: **Johnnies, Tommies, the Alleghenies (Allegheny Mountains), the Rockies (Rocky Mountains)**

2. Proper nouns ending in *ch, s, x* and *z* have a plural in *es*.

Finches, Joneses, Foxes, Heinzes

Compound words

1. Most compounds form the plural by changing the principal word to its plural form.

ambassadors at large, assistant surgeons general, attorneys general, chiefs of staff, commanders-in-chief, consuls general, courts martial, editors-in-chief, fathers-in-law, goings-on, governors general, lieutenant-governors, ministers-designate, ministers without portfolio, notaries public, secretaries general, solicitors general, trade unions

But **Trades Union Congress**

2. If both nouns are of about equal weight, both take the plural.

men employees, menservants, women writers

3. If no word is significant, the final word usually takes *s* or *es*.

forget-me-nots, hand-me-downs, no man's lands, pick-me-ups, will-o'-the-wisps, Johnny-come-latelies

4. Compounds ending in *ful* add *s*.

armfuls, cupfuls, handfuls, spoonfuls

Nouns with the same singular and plural

aircraft, alms, amends, bellows, bison, chassis, corps, counsel, deer, fish, forceps, goods, grouse, head (of cattle, etc.), **headquarters, insignia, means, moose, off-spring, pains, precis, proceeds, rendezvous, remains, series, salmon, shambles, sheep, species, sweepstakes, swine, trout, United States, wheat, whereabouts**

Note: But when more than one kind or species is referred to, a regularly formed plural is sometimes used.

Many fishes, ranging from salmon to eel, are netted. New wheats — crosses of Thatcher and Selkirk — continue to be develop

Nouns plural in form, singular in meaning

checkers, dominoes, measles, mews, mumps, news, rickets, shingles (disease), **works** (factory)

Abbreviations, acronyms, numbers as nouns

Form the plural by adding an *s*.

UFOs, URLs, PhDs, CD-ROMs, 1960s

Dos and don'ts

Such expressions form their plurals normally.

no ifs, ands or buts; yeses and noes; all the ins and outs

But words being discussed as words form the plural by adding *'s*.

Some writers mistakenly leave out the the's. He filled his speech with like's and you know's.

➤ See **Punctuation**, page 378.

Foreign nouns

Nouns of this type sometimes have an English as well as a foreign plural. Canadian Press style is shown.

addendum, addenda
adieu, adieus
alga, algae
alumna, alumnae (fem.)
alumnus, alumni (masc.)
analysis, analyses
antenna, antennas (aerials),
antennae (feelers)
apparatus, apparatuses
appendix, appendices
aquarium, aquariums
automaton, automatons
axis, axes
bacterium, bacteria
basis, bases
beau, beaus
bureau, bureaus
cactus, cactuses, cacti
catharsis, catharses
census, censuses
coccus, cocci
crisis, crises
criterion, criteria
cul-de-sac, cul-de-sacs
curriculum, curricula
datum, data
dilettante, dilettantes
dogma, dogmas
ellipsis, ellipses
erratum, errata
formula, formulas
fungus, fungi
genius, geniuses
genus, genera
gladiolus, gladioli
helix, helixes
honorarium, honorariums
hypothesis, hypotheses
impetus, impetuses

index, indexes
larva, larvae
larynx, larynxes
madam, mesdames (madams
for brothel-keepers)
matrix, matrixes
maximum, maximums
medium, media (mediums in
spiritualism)
memorandum, memorandums
millennium, millenniums
minimum, minimums
minutia, minutiae
monsieur, messieurs
nucleus, nuclei
oasis, oases
opus, opuses
parenthesis, parentheses
phenomenon, phenomena
plateau, plateaus
prospectus, prospectuses
radius, radii
referendum, referendums
sanatorium, sanatoriums
seraph, seraphs
sinus, sinuses
stadium, stadiums
stimulus, stimuli
stratum, strata
syllabus, syllabuses
symposium, symposiums
tableau, tableaus
terminus, terminuses
thesis, theses
vertebra, vertebrae
virtuoso, virtuosos

Possessives

1. Singular and plural nouns not ending in s take an apostrophe and s to form the possessive case.

father's pipe, women's lib, people's food, the kibbutzim's leaders, alumni's donations

Note: It looks careless to err on words like **children's (not childrens') shoes, women's (not womens') issues, men's (not mens') salaries.**

2. Plural nouns ending in s take an apostrophe alone.

teachers' apples, the two peoples' history, the Joneses' daughter

Apply the same rule when the name of a place or organization is plural and ends in an s, even though it is treated as a singular term.

United States' policy, Marvin Gardens' property, Halton Hills' mayor

3. **Singular nouns and names ending in s (or an s sound) normally take an 's.**

Chris's sandwich, Burgess's novel, Butz's statement, the witness's testimony, Strauss's opera

But names of two or more syllables that end with an *-eez* sound often take only an apostrophe.

Lansens' foot, Moses' tablets, Mars' laws, Socrates' plays

4. Names ending in a silent s or x take an apostrophe and s.

Duplessis's cabinet, Delibes's Coppelia, Malraux's paintings, Francaix's symphony

Note: A few French names end in an s sound and follow normal rules for the possessive.

Saint-Saens' music, de Lesseps' canal

5. For company and institutional names, follow the organization's preference.

Professional Golfers' Association, Canadian Forces Headquarters

6. Where the usage is more descriptive than possessive, omit the apostrophe.

an autoworkers spokesman, a board of directors meeting, the carpenters union, citizens band radio, a Leafs defenceman, a 1940s car, the UN website

7. Use a single apostrophe for joint possession, separate apostrophes for separate possession.

Smith and Cusak's pharmacy, Pierre and Marie's children, Pierre's and Marie's shoes

8. A group of words used to express a single idea takes an apostrophe on the last word only, although many such phrasings can and should be avoided.

the mayor of Calgary's speech; the government of Canada's policy; her mother-in-law's car; Dodd, Mead's latest books

➤ For plurals of compound words, see **Plurals of nouns**, page 356.

9. In general, inanimate objects take an *of* phrase rather than an apostrophe.

the colour of the coat, not **the coat's colour**

the incidence of flu, not **the flu's incidence**

Note 1: But many idioms, particularly expressions of time and measure, take an apostrophe even though there is no actual ownership.

a stone's throw, the law's delay, a couple of dollars' worth

Note 2: To test whether an apostrophe is needed in such expressions as **two weeks(') pay** and **six months(') pregnant**, mentally substitute the singular and the correct answer will appear: **a week's pay, one month pregnant.**

10. Compound nouns with built-in apostrophes are generally singular.

arm's length, baker's dozen, confectioner's sugar, cow's milk, debtor's prison, farmer's market, fool's paradise, fuller's earth, printer's ink, traveller's cheques, writer's cramp

11. Most pronouns are written without an apostrophe.

hers, its, ours, yours, theirs, whose

But **anyone's guess, another's hopes, others' feelings, each other's view, no-body's fool, anyone else's house, no one else's**

Note: Beware the careless confusion of **its** and **it's** (it is), **theirs** and **there's** (there is), **your** and **you're** (you are), **whose** and **who's** (who is).

Pronunciation guide

In all its endeavours, The Canadian Press is expected to get it right. No less important is its pronunciation of places, especially Canadian ones. The following is not a definitive list, but a selection of Canadian place names whose pronunciation may trap the unwary.

Legend:

An attempt has been made to simplify this guide, sacrificing nuance for expedience in using it, in the assumption that any subtle inaccuracy will not be heard by the listener.

1. Hard vowels are represented as: ay, ee, eye, oh, yew.

2. Soft vowels are represented by the letter itself. For clarity, an "h" is sometimes added to a soft "a", "i" and "u."

3. The sound "oo" as in "cool" is represented by "oo"; "oo" as in "cook" is represented by "uh."

4. A hard "g" is represented as "gh."

5. The sound "ow" as in "now" is represented by "ow"; "ow" as in "low" is represented by "oh."

6. Capitalized syllables denote the emphasis.

A

Abinger, Ont.	AB - in - gher
Abitibi, Que.	AB - ih - TIBB - ee
Abougoggin, N.B.	ab - oo - JOG - in
Acaciaville, N.S.	a - KAY - shuh - vil
Acadieville, N.B.	a - KAYD - ya - vil
Actinolite, Ont.	ak - TIN - oh - leyet
Adeyton, N.L.	AY - dih - tun
Agassiz, B.C.	AG - a - see
Agincourt, Ont.	AY - jin - kort
Ahousat, B.C.	a - HOO - zat
Ailik, N.L.	EYE - lik
Akwesasne, Que.	ak - wuh - SAS - nay
Aldouane, N.B.	ALD - wayn
Alida, Sask.	a - LEE - da
Alpena, N.S.	al - PEE - na
Amherst, N.S.	AM - erst
Anahim Lake, B.C.	AN - a - him
Annieopssquotch, N.L.	ah - nee - OP - skwotch
Anse Bleue, N.B.	anz BUL - uh
Antigonish, N.S.	ann - tee - gon - ISH
Apohaqui, N.B.	app - oh - HAH - kwee
Ardoise, N.S.	AR - doyz
Argentia, N.L.	arr - JEN - cha
Arisaig, N.S.	AR - ih - sag
Aroostook, N.B.	a - ROOS - tuhk

Arras, B.C.	A - rass
Arvida, Que.	arv - EYE - da
Ashaunipi, N.L.	ash - a - ON - a - pee
Aspotogan, N.B.	as - po - TOH - gan
Aspy (Bay), N.S.	ass - pee
Assiginack, Ont.	a - SIG - in - ak
Athalmer, B.C.	ATH - al - mer
Attawapiskat, Ont.	a - ta - WA - piss - kat
Awenge, Ont.	a - WEN - ghe

B

Babine, B.C.	ba - BEEN
Bacalhoo, Nfld. (or Baccalieu)	bak - a - LOO
Baccaro, N.S.	BAK - a - roh
Baddeck, N.S.	ba - DEK
Baden, Ont.	BAY - den
(Badger's) Quay, N.L.	kee
Bagot, Que.	BAG - ott
Baie Verte, N.L., N.B.	bay - VERT
Balcarres, Sask.	bal - CAR - ess
Baleine, N.S.	bay - LEEN
Barachois, N.B., N.L.	BA - ra - shwaw
Baraneed, N.L.	BAR - need
Barriere, B.C.	ba - RIH - ayr
Bartibog, N.B.	BAR - tih - bohg
Bas Caraquet, N.B.	ba ka - ra - KET
Bastarache, N.B.	BASS - tar - ash
Bauline, N.L.	ba - LEEN
Bay d'Espoir, N.L.	bay dess - PAYR
Bay D'Est, N.L.	bay - dih - EEST
Bay L'Argent, N.L.	bay LAR - jent
Bayonne, B.C.	bay - YON
Beauce, Que.	bohss
Beauharnois, Que.	boh - HARN - wah
Beausejour, Ont., N.B., Man.	boh - ze - zhoor
Becaguimec, N.B.	bek - a - GWIM - ek
Becancour, Que.	BAY - kan - koor
Bedeque, P.E.I.	ba - DEK
Beinn Breagh, N.S.	ben - BREE - a
Belle Cote, N.S.	bel - KOH - tee
Belle Riviere, Ont.	BEL - riv - er
Belleisle, N.B.	bel - il
Belleoram, N.L.	bel - AW - ram
Beloeil, Que.	bel - EYEL
Ben Eoin, N.S.	ben - YAWN
Benacadie, N.S.	ben - AK - a - dee
Bengough, Sask.	BEN - goff
Benoits (Cove), N.L.	BEN - was
Berthierville, Que.	BAYR - tyay - vil
Bethune, Sask.	BETH - yoon
Betsiamites, Que.	BET - see - a - mit
Bienfait, Sask.	BEEN - fayt

Bindloss, Alta.	BIHND - los
Biscayan (Cove), N.L.	BIS - kay - un
Blenheim, Ont.	BLEN - um
Bloedel, B.C.	bloh - DEL
Blomidon, N.S.	BLOM - ih - don
Bluesky, Alta.	bloo - skeye
Boiestown, N.B.	BOIZ - town
Boisbriand, Que.	BWA - bree - awn
Boisdale, N.S.	BOIZ - dayl
Boishebert, N.B.	BWAH - hay - bayr
Boissevain, Man.	BOIZ - eh - vayn
Bonne Bay, N.L.	bon bay
Bosanquet, Ont.	boh - SAN - kwet
Bouctouche, N.B.	BUHK - toosh
Boughton Island, P.E.I.	BOH - ton
Boularderie, N.S.	BOO - lar - DREE
Boutiliers (Point), N.S.	BOOT - il - eers
Bowser, B.C.	BOW - zer
Bralorne, B.C.	BRAY - lorn
Bras D'Or, N.S.	bra - DOR
Breadalbane, P.E.I.	bra - DAWL - ban
Brechin, Ont.	BREK - in
Brochet, Man.	bro - SHAY
Brosseau, Alta.	BROO - soh
Brougham, Ont.	brohm
Brudenell, P.E.I.	BROO - de - nel
Brule, Cape Breton, N.S., N.B.	BROO - lay
Brule, Pictou County, N.S., N.L.	BROOL
B-Say-Tah, Sask.	bee - SAY - tah
Buchans, N.L.	BUCK - ans
Buffet (also Harbour), N.L.	BUFF - it
Bulyea, Sask.	BULL - yay
Burgeo, N.L.	BER - joh
Burin (Peninsula), N.L.	B-YEW -rin
Butte View, Sask.	BUT vyew

C

Caissie (Cape), N.B.	KAY - see
Calabogie, Ont.	kal - a - BOH - ghee
Calais, (Maine)	KAL - as
Canobie, N.B.	KAN - oh - bee
Cap Pele, N.B.	kap pe - LAY
(Cape) Anguille, N.L.	an - GWIL
(Cape) Espoir, N.L.	es - PAYR
(Cape) Fourchu, N.S.	for - SHOO
(Cape) Traverse, P.E.I.	TRAV - ers
(Cape) Wolstenholme, Que.	WOH - sten - hohm
Caplin, N.L.	KAY - plin
Capreol, Ont.	KAYP - re - ol
Caraquet, N.B.	KAR - a - ket
Carmangay, Alta.	KAR - man - gay
Carmi, B.C.	KAR - meye

Cascumpeque, P.E.I.	KAS - cum - pek
Catalina, N.L.	kat - a - LEYE - na
Caughnawaga, Que.	kog - na - WAH - ga
Cayuga, Ont.	kay - YEW - ga
Ceepeecee, B.C.	see - pee - see
Centre, N.S.	SEN - tree
Chamcook, N.B.	sham - KUHK
Charlevoix, Que.	SHAR - luh - vwah
Charlo, N.B.	SHAR - loh
Chateauguay, Que.	SHA - toh - gay
Chauvin, Alta.	SHOH - vin
Cheakamus, B.C.	chee - AK - a - mus
Chebogue, N.B.	she - BOH - guh
Cheticamp, N.S.	SHET - ih - kamp
Chezzetcook, N.S.	CHEZ - a - kuhk
Chiganois, N.S.	SHEEG - a - noy
Chilcotin, B.C.	chil - COH - ten
Chimo, Que.	CHEYE - moh
Chiputneticock, N.B.	ship - oot - net - ih -kook
Choate, B.C.	choht
Ciboux, N.S.	see - BOO
Clayoquot, B.C.	KLAK - wut
Coaticook, Que.	koh - AT - ih - kuhk
Cocagne, N.B.	ko - KAN
Coderre, Sask.	koh - DAYR
Coeur D'Alene, B.C.	kur - da - LAYN
Cogmagun, N.S.	KOG - ma - gun
Coghlan, B.C.	KOG - lan
Colonsay, Sask.	ko - LON - zee
Comox, B.C.	KOH - moks
Concession, N.S.	kon - SESS - ee - ohn
Conche, N.L.	konch
Coquihalla, B.C.	ko - kih - hal - a
Coquitlam, B.C.	ko - KWIT - lam
Cottrell's Cove, N.L.	KOT - rels
Coulonge, Que.	koo - LONJ
Courtenay, B.C.	KORT - nee
Cowichan, B.C.	KOW - ih - chan
Crapaud, P.E.I.	kra - POHD
Crichton, Sask.	KRAY - ton
Cuckholds (Cove), N.L.	KUK - holds
Cumshewa, B.C.	KUM - shoo - a
Cupar, Sask.	KOO - par

D

Dalhousie, N.B.	dal - HOW - zee
Daveluyville, Que.	da - va - LUH - ee - vil
Debert, N.S.	di - BURT
DeGrau, N.L.	dee - GRAW
Delhi, Ont.	DEL - heye
Des Joachims, Ont.	da - SWISH - em
D'Escousse, N.S.	des - KOOS

Dochet, N.B.	DOH - shay
Domremy, Sask.	DAW - ra - mee
Dufresne, Man.	du - FRAYN
Dunedin, P.E.I.	dun - EE - din
Dunvegan, Alta., N.S.	dun - VAY - gan
Duricle, N.L.	DYEW - rikl
Duvar, P.E.I.	doo - VAR

E

Ecum Secum, N.S.	EE - kum SEE - kum
Egremont, Ont.	EE - gre - mont
Eholt, B.C.	EE - hohlt
Elie, Man.	EE - leye
Embarras, Alta.	EM - be - raw
Emo, Ont.	EE - moh
Engen, B.C.	EN - ghen
Englee, N.L.	ON - glee
Erieau, Ont.	EER - ih - oh
Escuminac, N.B.	es - KOOM - in - AK
Esdraelon, N.B.	ez - DRAY - lon
Esquimalt, B.C.	es - KWEYE - malt
Etobicoke, Ont.	e - TOH - bi - koh
Eutsuk (Lake), B.C.	OOT - suk

F

Falher, Alta.	fa - LAYR
Falmouth, N.S.	FOL - muth
Fauquier, B.C.	foh - keer
Fauquier, Ont.	FOH - kee - ay (FOH - keer)
Faust, Alta.	fost
Fermeuse, N.L.	furm - YOOZ
Fermont, N.L.	FAYR - moh
Fleur de Lys, N.L.	flur - da - LEE
Forget, Sask.	FOR - zhay
Fourchu, N.S.	FOR - shoo
Framboise, N.S.	fram - buh - WAZ

G

Gabarus, N.S.	gab - a - ROOS
Gaetz (Brook), N.S.	gayts
Gaff Topsail, N.L.	gaf - TOP - sl
Gambier Harbour, B.C.	GAM - beer
Gananoque, Ont.	gan - an - OK - wih
Gaskiers, N.L.	GAS - kers
Gaspe, Que.	GAS - pay
Gatineau, Que.	GA - tee - no
Gaultois, N.L.	GAWL - tus
Giffard, Que.	ZHEE - far
Giscombe, B.C.	GHI - scum
Gitsegukla, B.C.	ghit - si - GUHK - la
Glace Bay, N.S.	GLAYSS - bay
Gleichen, Alta.	GLEE - shen

Glenavon, Sask.	glen - AV - on
Glendyer, N.S.	glen - DEE - yer
Gloucester, Ont.	GLAW - ster
Goderich, Ont.	GOD - rich
Govan, Sask.	GOH - van
Grand Aldoune, N.B.	grand al - doo - AYN
Grand Bruit, N.L.	grand brit
Grand Digue, N.B.	grawn dig
Grand Etang, N.S.	grand ee - TANG
Grand Manan, N.B.	grand ma - NAN
Grand Pre, N.S.	gran pray
Grandigue, N.B.	GRAW - deegh
Grandigue, N.S.	GRAN - dig
Grandois, N.L.	GRAN - doys
Greenwich, N.S.	GREN - itch
Griquet, N.L.	GRIH - ket
Groais (Island), N.L.	gray
Gros Mourne, N.L.	grohs morn
Grosses Coques, N.S.	GROHS - kok
Guy, Alta.	ghee

H

Hagensborg, B.C.	HAG - ens - burg
Hagerman's Corners, Ont.	HAYG - er - mans
Haida, B.C.	HEYE - da
Haldimand, Ont.	HAWL - di - mand
(Harbour) Buffet, N.L.	BUFF - it
Havre Boucher, N.S.	HAH - ver BOO - shee
Hawarden, Sask.	hay - WAR - den
Hebert, N.B.	hay - BER
Hebert (River), N.S.	HIB - ert
Hecate (Straits), B.C.	HEK - ut
Hilliers, B.C.	HIL - yerz
Hockley, Ont.	HUK - lee
Hondu, Alta.	HON - doo
Hulatt, B.C.	HUL - it

I

Igloolik, N.W.T.	ig - LOO - lik
Ignace, Ont.	IG - nas
Illecillewaet, B.C.	il - ih - sil - ih - wit
Ingonish, N.S.	ing - oh - NISH
Iona, P.E.I.	eye - OH - na
Iosegun, Alta.	eye - OHS - e - gun
Iqualuit, Nunavut	ee - KAL - oo - eet
Islay, Alta.	EYE - lee
Isle aux Morts, N.L.	eyel - oh - MORT
Isle Madame, N.S.	eyel ma - DAM
Isleville, N.S.	EYESS - vil

J

Jacquet (River), N.B.	JAK - et

Jervis (Inlet), B.C.	JAR - vis
Jervois, N.L.	JER - vis
Jeune (Landing), B.C.	joon
Jonquiere, Que.	zhawn - KEE - ayr
Journois, N.L.	JUHRN - wah
Juan de Fuca, B.C.	whon - da - FYEW - ka
Judique, N.S.	JOO - dik

K

Kahlnawake, Que.	ga - na - WA - gay
Kaien (Island), B.C.	KAY - en
Kakawis, B.C.	KA- ka - wis
Kaleden, B.C.	ka - LEE - den
Kalum (Lake), B.C.	KAY - lum
Kaministiquia, Ont.	kam - ah - NIST - ih - kwa
Kangiqsualujjuaq, Que.	kan - djik - soo - AL - loo - joo - ak
Kaniapiskau, Que.	kan - ee - a - PISS - koh
Kapasiwin, Alta.	ka - PASS - ih -win
Katepwa, Sask.	ka - TEP - wa
Keirsteadville, N.B.	KEYER - sted - vil
Kejimkujik, N.S.	keg - JIM - koo - jik
Kennebecasis, N.B.	ken - e - be - KAY - sis
Kennetcook, N.S.	ken - et - KUHK
Keppoch, N.S., P.E.I.	kep - IK
Khutzeymateen, B.C.	KOOTZ - a - ma - teen
Kikkertaksoak, Que.	kik - er - TAK - soh - ak
Killaby, Sask.	KIL - a - bee
Kimmirut, N.W.T.	KIM - ee - root
Kincardine, N.B., Ont.	kin - KAR - din
Kitchuses, N.L.	ki - CHOO - siz
Kitsumgallum, B.C.	kit - sum - GAY - lum
Kitwanga, B.C.	kit - wun - GAH
Klappan, B.C.	kle - PAN
Kleecoot, B.C.	KLEE - kut
Koksilah, B.C.	kohk - SEYE - la
Kouchibougwack, N.B.	KOOSH - ih - buh - kwak
Kronau, Sask.	KROH - noh
Ksituan, Alta.	SIT - wan
Kugaruak, N.W.T.	KUG - a - ROO - ak
Kugluktuk, N.W.T.	kug - LUK - tuk
Kushonook, B.C.	KUSH - nuhk
Kuujjuaq, Que.	KOO - joo - ak
Kyuquot, B.C.	kih - OO - kut

L

Lac du Bonnet, Man.	lac doo - BON - ee
Lac la Biche, Alta.	layk la BISH
Lac la Hache, B.C.	lac la HASH
Lacolle, Que.	la kuhl
Lacombe, Alta.	la - KOHM
LaHave, N.S.	la HAYV
L'ange-Gardien, Que.	lawn gar - dee - EN

L'Anse a Diable, N.L.	lanz ah DEE - ah - BLA
La Pocatier, Que.	la pok - a - tee - AYR
La Riviere, Man.	la rih - VEER
La Scie, N.L.	la see
La Vallee, Ont.	la VAL - ee
LaPoile, N.L.	la - POYL
L'Ardoise, N.S.	LORD - wayz
Lasqueti, B.C.	la - SKEE - tee
Le Gaulet, N.B.	le goo - LAY
Lebret, Sask.	la - BRET
Legal, Alta.	lih - GAL
Leitches (Creek), N.S.	LEE - chez
Lejac, B.C.	le - ZHAK
Lemieux, Ont.	le - MYEW
L'Equille, N.S.	la - KEEL
Les Eboulements, Que.	lays E - bool - maw
Les Escoumins, Que.	lays ESS - koo - meh
Letellier, Man.	le - tel - YAY
Letete, N.B.	le - teet
Levis, Que.	lay - VEE
Lilloet, B.C.	lil - oh - WET
Limoges, Ont.	lee - MOHJ
Lindell, B.C.	lin - DELL
Liskeard, Sask.	LISS - kurd
Listuguj, Que.	LIS - ta - goosh
Lochaber, N.S.	lok - AH - ber
Lochiel, Ont.	lok - EEL
Loggieville, N.B.	LOH - ghi - vil
Longueuil, Que.	lon - GOY
L'Original, Ont.	lor - NEL
Losier (Settlement), N.B.	LOH - zee - ay
Lougheed, Alta.	lah - HEED
Louis (Creek), B.C.	LOO - iss
Louisbourg, N.S.	LOO - iss - burg
Louisdale, N.S.	LOO - iz - dayl
Lucknow, Ont.	LUK - noh
Luseland, Sask.	LOOS - land
Lutselk'e, N.W.T.	LOOT- sel - KAY
Lynedoch, Ont.	LIN - dok

M

Macdame (Creek), B.C.	mac - DAYM
Machar, Ont.	MAK - ar
Machin, Ont.	MAY - chin
Mactaquac, N.B.	MAK - ta - kwak
Madoc, Ont.	MAY - doc
Magaguadavic, N.B.	MAG - a - DAY - vic
Magog, Que.	MAY - gog
Mainadieu, N.S.	man - a - doo
Makaroff, Man.	MAK - a - roff
Makaroff, Sask.	ma - KAR - ov
Makkovik, N.L.	ma - KOO - vik

Malagawatch, N.S.	MAL - a - gah - wotsh
Malakwa, B.C.	MAL - a - kwah
Malpeque, P.E.I.	MAHL - pek
Maltempeque, N.B.	mal - TOM - pek
Manawagonish, N.B.	man - a - WAH - gon - ish
Manigotagan, Man.	ma - nih - ga - TAW - gan
Margaree (Valley), N.S.	mar - ga - REE
Mascouche, Que.	mas - KOOSH
Maskinonge, Que.	mas - kee - no - ZHAY
Matane, Que.	ma - TAN
Matapedia, Que., N.B.	ma - ta - PEED - ya
Matsqui, B.C.	MAT - skwee
Mattawa, Ont.	MAT - a - waw
Maugerville, N.B.	MAY - jer - vil
Mazenod, Sask.	MAY - zen - odd
Meagher's (Grant), N.S.	mahrz
Medonte, Ont.	meh - DON - tay
Memramcook, N.B.	MEM - ram - kuhk
Merasheen, N.L.	mee - ra - SHEEN
Mercier, Que.	MAYR - see - yay
Merigomish, N.S.	meh - rih - goh - MISH
Mersea, Ont.	mer - SEE - a
Metchosin, B.C.	meh - CHOH - sin
Meteghan, N.S.	muh - TAY - gun
Michel, B.C.	mih - SHEL
Mille Roches, Ont.	MIL - rush
Miminigash, P.E.I.	mim - in - ee - GASH
Minas (Basin), N.S.	MEYE - nas
Minudie, N.S.	meye - NOO - dee
Mira, N.S.	MEYE - ra
Miramichi, N.B.	mih - ra - mih - SHEE
Miscou, N.B.	MIS - koo
Miscouche, P.E.I.	mis - KOOSH
Mississauga, Ont.	miss - iss - AW - ga
Mistassini, Que.	mis - TASS - ee - nee
Mortier, N.L.	MOR - tih - er
Moulin-Morneau, N.B.	MOO - lin - morn - NOH
(Mount) Uniacke, N.S.	YEW - nih - ak
Moyie, B.C.	MOY - ay
Muchalat, B.C.	MUSH - a - lat
Musquodoboit, N.S.	muss - kuh - DOB - it

N

Nachvak (Fiord), N.L.	NA - vak
Nackawic, N.B.	NA - ka - wik
Nagogami (River), Ont.	na - GOG - a - mee
Naicam, Sask.	NAY - k'm
Nakina, Ont.	na - KEE - na
Nakina (River), B.C.	nak - in - aw
Nakusp, B.C.	na - KUSP
Namao, Alta.	na - MAY - oh
Namu, B.C.	na - MOO

Nanaimo, B.C.	na - NEYE - moh
Napadogan, N.B.	na - pa - DOG - in
Napan, N.B.	na - PAN
Napierville, Que.	NA - pee - ayr - vil
Nasagaweya, Ont.	NAS - a - ga - way - a
Nashwaaksis, N.B.	nash - wawk - SISS
Natal, B.C.	na - TAL
Natashquan, Que.	na - tash - KWAN
Nauwigewaak, N.B.	na - WIJ - e - wawk
Nazko, B.C.	NADZ - koh
Necum Teuch, N.S.	NEE - kum taw
Neepawa, Man., Sask.	NEE - pa - waw
Neguac, Que.	NIG - a - wak
Nemiskau, Que.	ne - MIS - kaw
Nepean, Ont.	ne - PEE - an
Nepisiguit, N.B.	ne - PIZ - ih - gwit
Neultin, Man.	nyew - EL - tin
Neustadt, Ont.	NYEW - stat
New Aiyansh, B.C.	NYEW eye - ANCH
Newfoundland	nyew - fnd - LAND
(Nicholas) Denys, N.B., N.S.	DEN - is
Nicola, B.C.	NIK - oh - la
Nictau, N.B.	nik - taw
Nictaux, N.S.	nik - taw
Nikomen, B.C.	ni - KOH - men
Nimpkish, B.C.	NIM - kish
Nipawin, Sask.	NIP - a - win
Nipigon, Ont.	NIP - ih - gon
Nipissing, Ont.	NIP - ih - sing
Nitchequoin, Que.	NICH - e - kwon
Noel, N.S.	nohl
Nokomis, Sask.	no - KOH - miss
Nordin, N.B.	nor - DEEN
(North) Gower, Ont.	gor
Notikewin, Alta.	not - e - KEE - win
Nottawasaga, Ont.	NOT - a - was - SAW - ga
Nunavut	NOON - a - voot

O

Ochiltree, B.C.	OKL - tree
Oderin, N.L.	oh - DEER - in
(Offer) Wadhams, N.L.	WOD - umz
Ogema, Sask.	OH - guh - ma
Ohaton, Alta.	oh - HAT - on
Opasatika, Ont.	OH - pa - SAT - ih - ka
Opeepseway, Ont.	oh - PEEP - se - way
Opinipiwan, N.B.	oh - pin - ih - pi - won
Oromocto, N.B.	or - oh - MUK - toh
Orono, Ont.	OH - ron - oh
Oso, Ont.	OH - so
Osoyoos, B.C.	oh - SOY - yus
Outaouais, Que.	OO - ta - way
Outremont, Que.	OOT - re - moh

P

Pacofi, B.C.	pa - KOH - fee
Paincourt, Ont.	PAN - kor
Painsec, N.B.	PAN - sek
Pangnirtung, N.W.T.	PANG - ner - tung
Passamaquoddy, N.B.	pas - a - ma - KWOD - ee
Passchendaele, N.S.	PASH- en - dayl
Passekeag, N.B.	PASS - a - keg
Pelee (Island), Ont.	PEE - lee
Pembina, Man.	PEM - bih - na
Pembroke, Ont.	PEM - bruhk
Pen D'Oreille, B.C.	PON - do - ray
Penetanguishine, Ont.	pen - e - TANG - gwih - sheen
(also Penetang for short)	PEN - ih - TANG
Pequaquet, N.B.	pe - KWA - ket
Perce, Que.	PAYR - say
Pereau, N.S.	pe - ROH
Petit de Grat, N.S.	pe - TEE da graw
Petit Forte, N.L.	PET - ih fort
Petitcodiac, N.B.	pet - ih - KOH - dee - ak
Petite Riviere, N.S.	pa - TEET re - VEER
Petites, N.L.	pa - TEETS
Petpeswick, N.S.	pet - PES - wik
Piapot, Sask.	PEYE - a - pot
Pictou, N.S.	PIC - toh
Piedmont, Que.	PEED - moh
Pikwitonei, Man.	pik - ih - tuh - NAY
Pinantan, B.C.	pin - AN - tan
Pisquid, P.E.I	PIZ - kid
Placentia, N.L.	pla - SEN - cha
Point Amour, N.L.	point a - MOR
Point-Au-Baril, Ont.	point a - BA - rel
Point Au Gaul, N.L.	point oh - GAWL
Point Enragee, N.L.	point on -ra - ZHAY
Point Leamington, N.L.	point LEM - ing - ton
Pointe Claire, Que.	point klayr
Pointe du Chene, N.B.	point duh - SHEEN
Pokeshaw, N.B.	pohk - ee - SHAW
Pokesudie, N.B.	PUK - shoo
Pomquet, N.S.	POM - ket
Ponteix, Sask.	PON - tex
Port aux Choix, N.L.	PORT o -SHWAH
(Port) Dalhousie, Ont.	dal - HOO - zee
Port de Grave, N.L.	POR da GRAYV
Port Joli, N.S.	port joh - LEE
Port Mouton, N.S.	port - ma - TOON
Port Ryerse, Ont.	port REYE - er -see
Portage, P.E.I.	POR - tij
Portage la Prairie, Man.	POR - tij la prayr - ee
Pouce Coupe, Alta.	poos KOH - pay
Pouce Coupe, B.C.	poos KOH - pee
Pouch (Cove), N.L.	pooch

Povungnituk, Que.	poh - VUNG - ni - tuk
Powassan, Ont.	poh - WOS - an
Pownal, P.E.I.	pon - EL
Presque, N.L.	presk
Presque Isle, ME	presk eyel
Prevost, Que.	PREE - voh
Provost, Alta.	PROH - vohst
Punnichy, Sask.	PUN - ih - cheye
Purdue, Sask.	pur - DOO

Q

Qikqtarjuag, N.W.T.	kih - kik - TAR - zhoo - ak
Quamichan, B.C.	KWOM - ih - chan
Qu'Appelle, Sask.	kwa - PEL
Quathiaski (Cove), B.C.	kwoth - ih - AS - kee
Quesnel, B.C.	kwih - NEL
Quidi Vidi, N.L.	KID - ee VID - ee
Quirpon, N.L.	KAR - poon
Quispamsis, N.B.	kwis - pam - sis
Quyon, Que.	KWEE - on

R

Ramea, N.L.	ram - ee - a
Rayleigh (Mount), B.C.	RAY - lih
Read (Island), B.C.	reed
Remac, B.C.	REE - mak
Remo, B.C.	REE - moh
Rencontre, N.L.	ron - KON - ter
Renews, N.L.	re - N-YEW-Z
Renous, N.B.	re - NOOS
Repentigny, Que.	ruh - PAWN - tih - nyee
Restigouche, N.B.	RES - ti - goosh
Reykjavik, Sask.	ree - KYA - vik
Richibucto, N.B.	rish - a - BUK - toh
Rigolet, N.L.	rig - o - LET
Riondel, B.C.	REE - on - del
Riske (Creek), B.C.	RIS - kee
Roche Percee, Sask.	ross PER - see
Rossignol, N.S.	ROSS - ig - nol
Rothesay, N.B.	ROTH - say
Rouleau, Sask.	ROH - loh
Rouyn, Ont.	ROO - on
Rouyn-Noranda, Que.	roo - EN no - RAN - da
Rusagonis, N.B.	roosh - a - GAW - nish
Ruthilda, Sask.	roo - thil - da

S

Saanich, B.C.	SAN - ich
Saguenay, Que.	SA - ga - nay
St. Basile, N.B.	saynt BA - zeel
St. Chrysostome, P.E.I.	saynt kris - OSS - tom
St. Croix, N.B.	saynt kroy
St. Eustache, Que.	saynt OO - stash

St. Foy, Que.	saynt fwah
St. Francois (River), Que.	saynt fran - SWAH
St. Henri, Que.	saynt HEN - ree
St. Hubert, Que.	saynt hyew – BAYR
St. Hyacinthe, Que.	saynt heye - a - sinth
St. Kyrans, N.L.	saynt KEER - ans
St. Laurent, Man.	sant law - RENT
St. Louis, Sask.	sint LOO - ee
St. Norbert, N.B.	saynt nor - BAYR
St. Marthe, Ont.	sant mart
St. Vital, Man.	saynt vi - TAL
Salisbury, N.B.	SAHLS - bur - ee
Salmon Arm, B.C.	sam - on arm
Salmonier, N.L.	sam - o - NEER
Salvage, N.L.	sal - VIJ
Sardis, B.C.	SAR - dis
Saugeen, Ont.	saw - gheen
Saulnierville, N.S.	son - YAY - vil
Saumarez, N.B.	SUM - a - rez
Savary (Island), B.C.	SAY - va - ree
Scaterie (Island), N.S.	SKAT - a - ree
Schepeler, Ont.	SHEP - ler
Schreiber, Ont.	SKREYE - ber
Scoudouc, N.B.	skuh - DOOK
Sechelt, B.C.	SEE - shelt
Semans, Sask.	SEE - mans
Semiahmoo, B.C.	sem - ih- A - moo
Sept-Iles, Que.	set - TILL
Sesekinika, Ont.	se - se - kin - EE - ka
Shaunavon, Sask.	SHAW - na - vin
Sheguindah, Ont.	she - GWIN - da
Shemogue, N.B.	shem - oh - goo - EE
Shenacadie, N.S.	she - NAK - a - dee
Shepody, N.B.	SHEP - o - dee
Sheshatsheit, N.L.	SHESH - a - shee
Shinemacas, N.S.	SHIN - e - ma - kas
Shube, N.S.	SHOO - bee
Shubenacadie, N.S.	shoo - ben - AK - a - dee
Shule, N.S.	shoo - LEE
Shunacadie, N.S.	shuh - NAK - a - dee
Shuswap, B.C.	SHOO - swap
Sicamous, B.C.	sik - a - moos
Sigas, N.B.	seye - gas
Siglunes, Man.	SIG - luh - nes
Similkameen, B.C.	si - MIL - ka - meen
Simpsian, B.C.	TSIM - shee - an
Sintaluta, Sask.	SIN - ta - loo - ta
Skagit, B.C.	SKA - jit
Skidegate, B.C.	SKID - e - ghet
Skir Duh, N.S.	sker doo
Skookumchuck, B.C.	SKOO - kum - chuk
Sointula, B.C.	swon - TYEW - la

Somenos, B.C.	SOM - en - ohs
Sooke, B.C.	sook
Sorel, Que.	so - REL
Souris, P.E.I.	SOO - ree
Souris, Alta., Man.	soo - ris
Spallumcheen, B.C.	spal - um - CHEEN
Spillimacheen, B.C.	spil - a - ma - SHEEN
Squamish, B.C.	SKWA - mish
Squilax, B.C.	SKWEE - laks
Steinbach, Man.	steye'n - bak
Stewiacke, N.S.	ST'YEW - ee - ak
Stikine, B.C.	stik - EEN
Stouffville, Ont.	STOH - vil
Stoughton, Sask.	STOW - t'n
Strathnaver, B.C.	strath - NAY - ver

T

Tabusintac, N.B.	TAB - oo - sin - TAK
Taghum, B.C.	TAY - gum
Tagish, Yukon	TAG - ish
Tahsis, B.C.	TAH - sis
Tahtsa, B.C.	TAT - sa
Takysie (Lake), B.C.	ta - KEYE - zee
Taltson (River, Bay, Lake), N.W.T.	TAWL - son
Tantallon, N.S.	tan - TAL - on
Tantramar, N.B.	TAN - tra - mar
Tarentorus, Ont.	ta - ren - TOR - us
Tasu, B.C.	ta - SOO
Tatalrose, B.C.	TAT - al - rohz
Tatasenshini, B.C.	tat - sen - SHEE - nee
Tatlayoko, B.C.	tat - lay - OH - ko
Tavane, N.W.T.	TAV - a - nee
Tazin (Lake), Sask.	TAZ - n
Tecumseh, Ont.	te - CUM - see
Tehkummah, Ont.	TEK - uh - ma
Temiscouata, Que.	te - mis - KWA - ta
Temiskaming, Ont., Que.	te - MIS - ka - ming
The Pas, Man.	the pah
Thetis (Island), B.C.	THEE - tiss
Thlewdiaza, Man.	thloo - dee - AH - za
Tignish, P.E.I.	tig - NISH
Timagami, Ont.	tim - OG - a - mee
Tintagel, B.C.	tin - TAY - jel
Tobeatic, N.S.	toh - be - AT - ik
Tobique, N.B.	TOH - bik
Topsail, N.L.	TOP - sl
Tossorontio, Ont.	tos - o - RON - tshoh
Tracadie-Sheila, N.B.	TRA - ka - dee SHEYE - la
Tranquille, B.C.	trong - KEEL
Trepanier, B.C.	tri - PAN - ee - er
Trepassey, N.L.	tra - PA - see
Trois-Rivieres, Que.	TRWAW - reev - yayr

Tsawwassen, B.C.	ta - WASS - en
Tsechincut (Lake), B.C.	che - SING - kut
Tugaske, Sask.	ta - GAS - kee
Tulameen, B.C.	TUL - a - meen
Tulsequah, B.C.	TUL - se - kwa
Tuvalik, Que.	too - VAL - ik
Tyendinaga, Ont.	teye - en - dih - NAY - ga
Tzouhalem, B.C.	tsoo - HAY - lem

U

Ucluelet, B.C.	yew - KLOO - let
Uigg, P.E.I.	OO - igh
Upsalquitch, N.B.	UP - sal - kwitch
Usk, B.C.	usk

V

Valligan, B.C.	VAL - ih - can
Vanacher, Ont.	va - NAK - er
Varennes, Que.	va - REN
Vars, Ont.	vars
Vegreville, Alta.	VEG - ra - vil
Verdun, Que.	vur - DUN
Villemarie, N.L.	vil - a - ma - REE

W

Wabamun, Alta.	WOB - a mun
Wabiskaw, Alta.	wah - BIS - kaw
Wadena, Sask.	wah - DEE - na
Wagmatcook, N.S.	WAG - mut - kuhk
Wakaw, Sask.	wah - kaw
Walhachin, B.C.	wol - a - SHEEN
Wapske, N.B.	WOP - skee
Wasagaming, Man.	wa - SAW - ga - ming
Washademoak, N.B.	WOSH - a - de - MOH -ik
Waskatenau, Alta.	wah - SET - naw
Waskesiu, Sask.	wos - ke - SOO
Watagheistic (Island), Que.	wot - a - ghee - IS - tik
Wauchope, Sask.	WAW - kup
Waweig, N.B.	WAH - wig
Wawota, Sask.	wa - WO - ta
Wetaskiwin, Alta.	we - TAS - kih - win
Whycogomagh, N.S.	weye - KOHG - o - ma
Wiarton, Ont.	WEYE - ar - ton
Wirral, N.B.	WEER - al
Wollaston, Ont.	WUHL - as - ton
Wycocomagh, N.S.	weye - KAW- guh - maw
Wyndell, B.C.	WIN - del

X

Xena, Sask.	ZEE - na

Y

Yahk, B.C.	yak
Yamachiche, Que.	yam - a - SHEESH
Ymir, B.C.	WEYE - mir
Yoho, B.C.	YOH - hoh
Youbou, B.C.	YOO - boh
Youghall, N.B.	yawl

Z

Zeballos, B.C.	ze - BAL - us

Punctuation

General

Punctuation brings order to writing. It helps make the message of a sentence immediately clear. But don't overdo it. A sentence littered with clauses set off by commas, dashes and semicolons can look like a word jungle and chase the reader away.

Apostrophe

1. Use an apostrophe to denote possession.

Davis's car, the Davises' house, Marx's Capital, children's toys, the media's problem, Jesus' name

➤ See **Possessives**, page 360.

2. Use an apostrophe to indicate the omission of letters or figures.

she'd, it's (for it is), couldn't, rock 'n' roll, Where E'er You Walk, "Give 'em hell!", the early '30s, the class of '80, "We'll 'elp 'im for 'is mother, an' 'e'll 'elp us by-an'-by." — *Rudyard Kipling*

Note: Contractions are acceptable, but avoid such forced contractions as **it'd, should've, Tom'll go**; use only readily recognized forms: **won't, shouldn't, he'd.**

3. Use an apostrophe with verbs formed from capitals. **OK's, OK'ing, KO'd, MC'ing, X'd out**

4. Use an apostrophe in plurals of lowercase letters.

Mind your p's and q's. Dot your i's and cross your t's.

5. In general, do not use an apostrophe with plurals of capital letters or numbers.

She graduated with straight As, the three Rs, the ABCs, two VIPs, a formation of F-18s, the Dirty '30s

Note 1: Use an apostrophe with plurals of capital letters if necessary to avoid ambiguity.

A's in math and physics are hard to come by.

Note 2: Whether to write a single letter as a capital or lowercase in a particular context depends somewhat on personal taste; logic favours **with a capital S and with a small** *s*.

6. Do not use an apostrophe to form the plurals in expressions like **the whys and wherefores.**

Here are a few dos, don'ts and maybes. I don't want any ifs, ands or buts. Just give us straight yeses or noes.

Note: Use the apostrophe to form the plurals of words being discussed as words.

three as's, too many is's, not enough the's

7. Do not use an apostrophe with shortened forms that have become accepted as complete words.

cello, copter, flu, gym, phone

Brackets (parentheses)

1. In general, try to use brackets sparingly, when other punctuation won't do the job.

Their biggest difficulties were the heat (temperatures were in the high 20s) and clouds of blackflies.

2. Use brackets to insert fuller identification in proper names, direct quotation and such.

the Moose Jaw (Sask.) Times-Herald. Use commas when no proper name is involved: the Moose Jaw, Sask., daily. But prefer the daily in Moose Jaw, Sask., or some such.

"When you ask how (Finance Minister Ellen) McFadden can survive, you are asking the wrong question."

3. Use brackets to enclose a nickname within a name.

William (Bible Bill) Aberhart

➤ See **Names, nicknames, initials**, page 332.

4. Use full brackets in numbering or lettering a series within a sentence.

The union pressed for (a) more pay, (b) a shorter work week and (c) better pensions.

➤ See **Period**, paragraph 6 note, below.

5. Use brackets to enclose political affiliations.

Sen. Iva Villman (Lib-Man.)

6. Use brackets to enclose equivalents and translations.

"We can expect two more inches (five centimetres) of rain." The measure now goes to the Bundestag (the lower house of parliament).

7. If a punctuation mark applies to the whole sentence, put the mark after the closing bracket.

Words must be reputable (not socially frowned on). "I tell you this" (turning to the jury): "I am innocent."

8. If a punctuation mark applies only to the words inside the parenthetical section, put the mark inside the closing bracket.

Most employees learned the new system quickly. (It helped to have supervisors on hand.)

"After I gave the alarm (by shouting 'Fire!'), I slid down the rope."

9. In general, a parenthetical sentence takes a capital only if it is a direct quotation.

"We couldn't meet today (she had an appointment), but arranged to have lunch tomorrow."

His comment ("Wow, you're not exactly tall") had annoyed her.

Colon

1. Use a colon, rather than a comma, to introduce a direct quotation longer than a short sentence.

Winston Churchill said in 1942: "This is not the end. It is not even the beginning of the end. But it is, perhaps, the end of the beginning."

2. Use a colon in lines introducing lists, texts and tables.

> VICTORIA — Highlights of the throne speech:
> — The creation of 10,000 jobs . . .

3. Use a colon to introduce an amplification, an example or a formal question or quotation. It takes the place of **for example, namely, that is.**

It was a mixed cargo: iron ore, wheat and coal. Various solutions were possible: sell the herd, try to renew the loan, take a partner.

4. Generally do not capitalize the first letter of a sentence that follows a colon; but a capital may be used if emphasis is desirable.

Their learning is like bread in a besieged city: every man gets a little, but no man gets a full meal. — *Samuel Johnson.* This is the rule: Write in easy, conversational English. Verdict: Not guilty.

Note: Capitalize the first word of a quoted sentence: **The prince cried: "Too late! Help came too late."**

5. Use a colon to mark a strong contrast.

Man proposes: God disposes. Eating isn't just a necessity: it's a pleasure.

6. Use colons in question-and-answer formats and for interviews. Quotation marks are not used.

Q: When do you expect an agreement?

A: Before Christmas.

Tatje: Why are you a critic?
Papadakos: One must live.

7. Use a colon to separate hours, minutes and seconds in clock and elapsed times, and periods before fractions of a second.

7:30 p.m. a record time of 1:25:15.4

Note: Write **8 a.m.**, not **8:00 a.m.**

8. Use a colon after a formal salutation.

Madam Speaker: Gentlemen: Dear Mrs. Odisho:

Note: Informal salutations may take a comma.

Dear Jack, My dear Puran,

9. Use a colon to indicate chapter and verse, act and scene and other citations.

A soft answer turneth away wrath. — *Proverbs 15:1*

There's daggers in men's smiles. — *Macbeth 2:3.147*

10. Use colons to separate titles and subtitles unless the author's or publisher's form differs.

The Chinese: Portrait of a People

11. Put colons outside closing quotation marks.

Paisley said of the charge of "bigot": "It's a lie."

She was referring to "the most serious of all charges": murder.

Comma

1. Put commas between the elements of a series but not before the final **and, or** or **nor** unless that avoids confusion.

men, women, children and pets

The major decided he must either attack at once, await fresh troops or withdraw.

Breakfast consisted of oatmeal, fried eggs, and bread and butter.

2. Use commas before clauses introduced by the conjunctions **and, but, for, or, nor** or **yet** if the subject changes.

We are all in the gutter, but some of us are looking at the stars. — *Oscar Wilde*

Note: The comma may be omitted when the clauses are short or the subject of both is the same.

The gun boomed and the race was on. The twins shouted and waved and finally managed to attract the driver's attention.

3. Use commas to set off an introductory clause or long phrase that precedes the main clause.

If God did not exist, it would be necessary to invent Him. — *Voltaire*

Note: Even if the introductory clause or phrase is short, a comma may be used for emphasis: **Even so, the vote was close.**

4. Put a comma after the main clause only if the clause that follows is parenthetical.

I'm selling you this gold brick because I like your face. The doctor bought a ticket, though she didn't expect to win.

5. Use commas to separate adjectives before a noun when the commas represent **and.**

a frank, open face; a vigorous, genial, popular man; well-meaning, enthusiastic, immature novices

6. Omit commas if the adjectives could not be separated by **and** and still make sense.

a cold marble floor; Tom's new 10-speed racing bike; her old brown winter coat; an aristocratic French family

Note 1: As another rule of thumb, if the order of the adjectives could not be changed (as in these examples), omit the commas.

Note 2: When in doubt, err on the side of too few commas.

7. Do not put commas around an identifying word, phrase or clause if it is essential to the meaning of the sentence. Do use them if the phrase could be omitted without changing the meaning of the sentence.

The Queen was accompanied by her son Prince Edward.
But: The Queen was accompanied by her youngest son, Prince Edward.

The girl who is singing is my daughter.
But: The girl, who was alone, got into the cab.

They drove to a village where they had seen bandits.
But: They drove to a village, where they bought bread.

8. Use a comma to separate an introductory clause from a short, complete sentence in quotations.

The prime minister replied, "I have nothing to add to what I said in the House."

Note: Do not use a comma if a quotation is extremely short or is an integral part of the clause.

Stop saying "I told you so."

She heard a voice yelling "Baby needs new shoes!" and there was her husband shooting craps.

"A guy comes up to me and says 'Oh, yeah?' and I say 'Oh, yeah?' and slap his face."

9. Use a comma to set off a paraphrased question or statement.

The question is, How can it be done? She said, No, she hadn't seen the boy.

But: She said no.

10. Use commas to set off parenthetical expressions, direct address and the like.

**That's right, isn't it? Come into the garden, Maud.
Madam Speaker, I deny that.**

Note: Commas are used with transition words like **besides, meanwhile, indeed, of course, too, in fact, as a result** and **consequently** if the sentence reads better with a pause.

11. Use a comma to separate words and numbers when confusion might otherwise result.

He who can, does. He who cannot, teaches. — *G.B. Shaw.*
Ralph waxed the floor, and his sister dusted. All day, workers had been preparing the field. Some time before, the Plateans had surrendered. Instead of 20, 50 came.

12. When words readily understood are omitted for brevity, use commas to mark the omission, unless the sentence reads smoothly without them.

**To Rolf he gave $5; to Mohammed, $2; to Darrin, nothing.
One child received $5, another $2 but the third nothing.
Let your yea be yea and your nay, nay.**

13. Use commas to separate geographical elements.

The tour bus runs from Basel, Switzerland, to Milan, Italy, with frequent stops.

Note 1: Do not omit the second comma.

The runner left St. John's, N.L., last week.

Note 2: Do not put a comma before **of**, indicating place.

Tom Stoddard of Mission, B.C., was first.

Note 3: Avoid this clumsy construction: **a Prince George, B.C., lawyer.**

Prefer: A lawyer in Prince George, B.C.

14. Use commas to set off the year from the month plus day.

March 31, 1949, was the date that Newfoundland joined Confederation.

Note: Do not use commas when the day is not included.

January 1998 was mild in Victoria. Clark died at Easter 1835.

15. In general, use commas to set off thousands but not in years, street addresses or page, phone or serial numbers.

13,250 kilometres	$1,450,250	page 1235
2000 (year)	1530 Rose St.	serial 76543
416-364-0321		

16. Use commas to set off a person's age, degrees, awards and affiliations.

Jean Tateyama, 48, Brandon, Man.; René Tremblay, PhD, faced Alex Dodd, VC, in the debate.

17. Do not use commas with Sr. or Jr., or with numerals that can similarly be regarded as an integral part of a name.

Maurice Leblanc Sr. spoke first. Pope John XXIII was popular. Albatross II finally reached port.

18. Do not use commas with multi-unit dimensions, measures, weights or times.

two feet four inches by three feet 10 inches, 10 pounds 12 ounces, two hours 30 minutes 25 seconds

But: a four-foot-11, 90-pound youngster

19. Put commas inside closing quotation marks.

Barb said, "I don't want any," but the pedlar only smiled. The clue consisted of four words: "spinner," "blackbird," "watchman" and "maple." "It sounded like 'gorp,'" he said.

Note: Occasionally, such punctuation is not needed. **More than 1,600 protesters chanting "We're anti-violent people" marched along Portage Avenue.**

20. A comma follows a bracket if sentence structure requires it.

The speech was long, hard to hear (people were coughing), uninspired and uninspiring.

21. Use a comma or a dash but not both.

Not: Wilfred was, — like all the Clutterbucks, — a man of striking personal charm.

Dash

1. The dash is an effective tool but can easily be overused. Many times it can be avoided by breaking a long sentence into two shorter ones.

2. Use dashes to set off mid-sentence lists punctuated by commas.

The ministers will discuss common problems — trade, tourism, immigration and defence — before going to the summit talks.

3. Use dashes when commas (generally preferable) would create confusion.

The pies — meat and fruit — were cheap.

4. Use a tight dash to introduce sections of a list.

Highlights of the federal budget Tuesday:
  —About 12,500 homeowners are expected to qualify for mortgage assistance.
  —Employee benefits . . .

5. Use a dash to mark a sharp break in a word or sentence.

"I've been laughed at, ignored — but I'm boring you."

Note 1: When a sentence breaks off, no period is used after the dash.

"Really, Madam Speaker, I must —"

"Order!" the Speaker shouted.

Note 2: When a quotation simply trails away, use three periods.

"Maybe if I had tried harder ... "

6. Use dashes to mark off interpolations.

"Besides" — he tapped me on the knee — "you're wrong."

7. Use a dash to introduce a phrase or clause that summarizes, emphasizes or contrasts what has gone before.

Quiet, respectful, deferential, even obsequious — those were Mulliner's chief characteristics.

Our army is composed of the scum of the earth — the mere scum of the earth. — *Duke of Wellington*

The English country gentleman galloping after a fox — the unspeakable in full pursuit of the uneatable. — *Oscar Wilde*

8. Use a dash to attribute a quotation.

Pedantry is a misplaced attention to trifles which then prides itself on its poor judgment. — *Jacques Barzun*

9. Do not use dashes with colons, semicolons and commas.

10. Write dashes with spaces before and after but not with agate sports summaries and the exceptions noted above.

Ellipsis

1. Use three periods to indicate an omission from a text or quotation.

The decision ... rests solely with your elected representatives, not with pollsters or the news media.

Note: Put spaces before and after the periods.

2. In condensing a text, use an ellipsis at the beginning, inside or at the end of a sentence. If it is at the end, put the punctuation before the ellipsis. Hence four periods end a sentence.

The decision...rests solely with your elected representatives....

... But the government won't ignore thoughtful suggestions, no matter what their origin.

Similarly: **What is the answer?... We must strive harder,...**

Note: Guard against distortion that might result from putting together statements that were not together in the original. The solution may be to interrupt the sequence by starting a new paragraph or renewing the attribution.

3. In news stories, use an ellipsis only inside a sentence, not at the beginning or end.

"The decision ... rests solely with your elected representatives," the prime minister said.

After a reference to comments of delegates, he added, "But the government won't ignore thoughtful suggestions."

➤But see Dash, No. 5, above for one exception.

4. Ellipses may be used to separate entries in the *Notes* section at the bottom of sports game copy.

Notes: It was Drew's first regular season slam with Boston. He had one in Game 6 of last season's ALCs.... Red Sox manager Terry Francona rested catcher Jason Varitek after the club played a night game Wednesday. He's expected to get two straight days, with backup Kevin Cash scheduled to make his usual start catching knuckleballer Tim Wakefield on Friday.... The Royals' season-high 11-game trip concludes with four gamed in Toronto beginning Friday

Exclamation mark

1. Do not overuse this strong mark of punctuation. Use it to denote great surprise, a command, deep emotion, emphasis and sarcasm.

We won!   "Take aim! Fire!"   Ouch!   Never!   Oh, sure!

Note: If a one-word exclamation rates heavy emphasis, put it in a separate sentence; otherwise treat it as part of another sentence.

"Oh! She almost fell."   "Oh! you frightened me!"   or   "Oh, you frightened me!"

2. Use an exclamation mark with questions that are exclamatory in form.

"You mean we won!"

"How could she do that to him!"

3. Do not use an exclamation mark to end a mildly exclamatory sentence.

Hurry along, please. Have your tickets ready.

4. Do not use a comma or period after an exclamation mark.

"Fire! Fire!" the janitor shouted.

Someone cried "She's drowning!"

5. Put an exclamation mark inside quotation marks when it is part of the quoted material, outside when it is not.

"That's a lie!" a backbencher shouted.

Imagine calling a cabinet minister a "liar"!

Hyphen

1. Compound words may be written solid (**sweatshirt**), open (**oil rig**) or hyphenated (**white-haired**).

➤ See **Compound Words**, page 302.

2. Write words as compounds to ease reading, to avoid ambiguity and to join words that when used together form a separate concept.

a once-in-a-lifetime chance, a hit-and-run driver, voice-over-Internet-protocol technology, a used-car dealer, a small-business tax, an extra-high collar, light-year, first-fruits, man-hour, blackbird, streetcar, airbrush

3. In general, hyphenate compound modifiers preceding a noun, but not if the meaning is instantly clear because of common usage of the term.

the third-period goal, three-under-par 69, a 5-4 vote, multimillion-dollar projects, 40-cent coffee

But **the acid rain threat, the United States dollar, a savings bank deposit, a sales tax increase, the task force landing**

4. Adverbs ending in *-ly* are not followed by a hyphen. The *-ly* alerts readers that the word that follows is modified: **a brightly lit room, an eagerly awaited speech.**

5. Hyphens are seldom needed with proper nouns (**a United Kingdom custom**), established foreign terms (**a 10 per cent drop**) or established compound nouns (**a high school principal**).

6. Certain word combinations are often hyphenated even when standing alone.

noun plus adjective (**fire-resistant, fancy-free**), noun plus participle (**blood-stained, thought-provoking**), adjective plus participle (**sweet-smelling, hard-earned**), adjective plus noun plus -*ed* (**open-handed, red-faced**)

7. Use a hyphen to indicate joint titles and to join conflicting or repetitive elements.

secretary-treasurer, writer-editor, musician-painter, comedy-tragedy, drip-drop, walkie-talkie

8. Hyphenate most well-known compounds of three or more words.

happy-go-lucky, good-for-nothing, Johnny-come-lately, forget-me-not, mother-in-law, a two-year-old

But **coat of arms, next of kin, no man's land**

9. Use a hyphen with certain compounds containing an apostrophe.

bull's-eye, mare's-nest, cat's-paw

10. Use a hyphen to avoid doubling a vowel, tripling a consonant or duplicating a prefix.

co-operate, re-emerge, anti-intellectual, doll-like, brass-smith, re-redesign, sub-subcommittee

But **readjust, reaffirm, reinstate, reopen,** etc.

11. Use a hyphen to join prefixes to proper names.

anti-Trudeau, pro-Communist

But **transatlantic, transpacific**

12. Use a hyphen to join an initial capital with a word.

T-shirt, V-necked, X-ray, S-bend, H-bomb

13. Use a hyphen with fractions standing alone and with the written numbers 21 to 99.

two-thirds, three-quarters, fifty-five, ninety-nine

14. Use hyphens with a successive compound adjective (note spacing).

18th- and 19th-century fashions; 10-, 20- and 30-second intervals

15. Use a hyphen in aircraft identification and such, between the symbols for make or type and model number, but not after the number.

DC-10, DC-8L, MiG-25

But **Boeing 767**

16. Use a hyphen to connect dates except when preceded by **from** or **between.**

the 1982-83 tax year, from January to May (not from January-May), between 1970 and 1976 (not between 1970-76)

Note: Don't drop the first two digits if the numbers are not the same: **1998-99**, but **1998-2002**.

17. Use a hyphen to differentiate between words of different meanings but the same or similar spellings.

correspondent (letter writer), **co-respondent** (in divorce); **resign** (quit), **re-sign** (sign again); **recover** (regain health), **re-cover** (cover again)

18. Use a hyphen to avoid awkward combinations of letters.

cave-in, not **cavein**; **co-star**, not **costar**; **de-ice**, not **deice**; **non-native**, not **nonnative**; **re-ink**, not **reink**; **set-to**, not **setto**; **sit-in**, not **sitin**

19. Use a hyphen for the minus sign in temperatures, with bracketed political affiliations and in the names of compound ridings.

-10 degrees, Joan Singh (Con-Man.), Ajax-Pickering

20. Hyphens are commonly used in broadcast copy to connect numbers and ease readabilitiy.

25-to-50-thousand people, 12-hundred rats, the vote was 157-13

Parentheses ➤ See **Brackets**, page 379.

Period

1. Use a period to end a declarative or a mildly imperative sentence.

The wind blew and the ground began to dry. Give me the book. Let them have their say.

Note: For greater emphasis, use an exclamation mark, advisedly.

"Stick 'em up!"

2. Use a period to end an indirect question, a request phrased as a question, or a rhetorical question.

The reporter asked how many were killed. Would someone answer my question. What do I care.

3. Use a period with decimals, including decimal currencies.

3.25 $9.50

4. Use a period after certain abbreviations.

➤ See **Abbreviations and acronyms**, page 253.

5. Put periods inside quotation marks.

The writer said, "This is the end." Her brother said, "I don't know why she said 'This is the end.'"

6. Omit periods after headings, figures, roman numerals, single letters (except initials) and scientific and metric symbols.

Pope, unionist meet; $52; Chapter 2; Albatross II; E flat; Au (for gold); 15 cm; 20 C

Note: But use periods, as an alternative to brackets, after a letter or number denoting a series.

To improve readability: 1. Don't be too formal. 2. Organize before you start to write. 3. Be active, positive, concrete.

7. Omit periods after letters used as names without specific designation.

Suppose A takes B to court for damages.

➤ For the use of periods to indicate omission, see **Ellipsis** above.

8. One space after a period at the end of a sentence is usually sufficient in most uses.

Question mark

1. Use a question mark after a direct question, but not after an indirect one.

What day is this? The nurse asked what he wanted.

Note: When a question occurs within a question, both ending at the same time, use only one question mark.

Who asked "Why?"

2. Use question marks to express more than one query in the same sentence.

Reporters must ask themselves, How does it look? sound? feel? taste? smell?

Note: If a question is not complete until the end of the sentence, use a question mark there.

Do you want coffee, tea or milk

3. Use a question mark to express doubt or uncertainty.

The dates of the English dramatist John Heywood are given as 1497(?)-1580(?).

4. Do not use a question mark if the person addressed is expected to act rather than answer.

Would you mind spelling the second name.

5. Question marks go inside or outside quotation marks, depending on meaning.

The Speaker asked, "What was the question?" Did the prime minister say "fuddle-duddle"? He asked, "Did the prime minister say 'fuddle-duddle'?"

6. A question mark supersedes the comma or period that usually ends a quotation.

"Who goes there?" the sentry shouted.

Quotation marks

1. In general, always use double quotation marks except for headlines and quotes within a quote.

2. Use quotation marks to enclose direct quotations.

The lawyer said, "I don't think the police should be paying suspects for information."

3. Use quotation marks to begin and end each part of an interrupted quotation.

"We can't hear you," the girl said. "The radio is on."

Note: Capitalize the first word of the second part of an interrupted quotation only if the second part begins a new sentence.

4. Alternate double and single marks in quotes within quotes.

"I heard her say, 'I only hit him when he sneered and said "Never."'"

5. Capitalize the first word of any mid-sentence quote that constitutes a sentence.

The woman said, "He sneered and said 'Never.'"

This has the same effect as the brush-off used in theatrical circles of "Don't call us. We'll call you."

The trainmaster gave the order to "Get the hell out!"

6. Put each speaker's words in a separate paragraph to make it immediately clear that the speaker has changed.

Vilmik laughed. "Who gave him the quarter?"
"Not me," said his wife. "I'm broke."
"I know," said Vilmik. "Let's ask your mother."

7. When a quote by a single speaker extends more than one paragraph, put quotation marks at the beginning of each paragraph but at the end of only the last.

"As I said earlier, my father was always reasonable about things like that.

"But when it came to money, he could be totally unreasonable. An out-and-out miser.

"Still, on the whole, he was fair-minded."

However, if the quote in the first paragraph is a partial one, use quotation marks at the beginning and end of the partial quote.

He said the argument was "remarkably bitter."

"I didn't know two people could hate each other so much."

8. Provide the speaker's identity quickly if a quotation is unusually long. It should either precede the quotation, follow the first sentence (or the second if it is short and closely linked to the first), or be interpolated.

"This is the best time to call an election," Lumie said.

"There is a tremendous momentum going to us. Waiting can only cost us votes. It's now or never."

"We've lost. We've lost," wailed another bystander. "The British have won. Our army has been lying to us."

"The Puritan hated bear-baiting," Macaulay adds, "not because it gave pain to the bear, but because it gave pleasure to the spectators."

9. Use quotation marks to set off a pungent or significant word or phrase but not around routine words or phrases.

His first ship was an old "rustbucket."

Not: The minister replied that the economy is "improving."

Note: Fragmented quotes are justifiable only when the words are controversial, add colour or give the flavour of an event or the style of a speaker.

10. Use quotation marks around unfamiliar terms on first reference.

The fluid was named "protoplasm" by a Czechoslovak.

10. Put quotation marks around words used ironically.

The "friendly" soccer game ended with two players booked.

11. In partial quotes, do not put quotation marks around words the speaker could not have used.

Not: Ali boasted "he was rarin' to go."

12. The Canadian Press cannot deliver material in italics to all its customers for technical reasons. Instead, for clarity, it puts quotation marks around the titles of compositions, including books, computer games, movies, operas, plays, TV programs and songs. (If technically possible, italics are recommended instead.)

Random House will publish "How to Get Rich" in April, to coincide with the show's live season finale.

The Cowsills recorded a series of hits between 1967 and 1970, including *The Rain, the Park and Other Things* and *Hair*.

It is not usually necessary, for clarity, to put quotation marks around the names of reference books, catalogues, newspapers and magazines, the Bible or O Canada. Italics can be used for books, newspapers and magazines for consistency if desired.

The Bible is a bestseller throughout the country.

Every year we sing O Canada on July 1.

Maclean's magazine publishes its university guide every year.

➤ See **Capitalization**, sections **Compositions**, page 271, **Music**, page 279, **Quotations**, page 283.

13. Do not use quotation marks to enclose slogans and headlines.

The pickets carried signs that read Cut Taxes, Not Jobs and Cut Government Spending. The article was headed Drug Squad Flouts Gun Rules.

14. Do not use quotation marks in question-and-answer formats.

**Q: Do you recognize this man?
A: Yes.**

15. Do not use quotation marks on texts, transcripts or editorial excerpts in symposiums.

**OTTAWA — Text of Gov. Gen. Rhoda Mann's New Year's message:
The mood at the dawn of a new year . . .**

St. John's (N.L.) Telegram: The real needs of Canadians . . .

Note: In editorial symposiums, the name of the paper is in boldface, followed by a colon, not a dash.

16. Do not use quotation marks around single letters.

She got a B on the test. He wore the captain's C on his shirt.

17. Periods and commas always go inside closing quote marks; colons and semicolons outside. The question mark and exclamation mark go inside the quote marks when they apply to the quoted matter only; outside when they apply to the entire sentence.

18. When a sentence ends with single and double quotation marks, separate them by a space.

19. Use single marks for quotations in headlines.

Semicolon

1. Use a semicolon to separate statements too closely related to stand as separate sentences.

"I never read a book before reviewing it; it prejudices a man so."— *Sidney Smith*

2. Use a semicolon to separate phrases that contain commas.

Best actor, Daniel Day-Lewis, *There Will Be Blood*; best actress, Marion Cotillard, *La Vie en Rose*; best film, *No Country for Old Men*.

3. Use a semicolon to precede explanatory phrases introduced by for example, namely, that is and the like when a comma seems too weak.

Some pleasures cost next to nothing; for example, reading.

4. Semicolons go outside quotation marks.

Police finally cornered the "bear"; it was a poodle.

Slash

1. Use a slash mark to separate alternatives.

and/or, either/or

But use a hyphen for joint titles and to join conflicting elements.

secretary-treasurer, comedy-tragedy

2. Use a slash mark to replace per in measurements.

80 km/h (80 kilometres per hour)

3. A slash is also used to separate the numerator and denominator of a fraction.

3 5/8, 1 7/8, 17 2/3

Singular or plural?

1. In general, a subject singular in form takes a singular verb; a subject plural in form takes a plural verb.

An outbreak of bombing and shelling was heard. On each side of the road were drifts of trilliums.

2. A collective noun (a group of people or things) takes a singular verb if it is seen as a unit, a plural verb if thought of more as a collection of individuals. The singular is more common.

The audience was silent. The audience were stamping their feet. Her family is sending money. Her family are all ill.

This also applies to proper collective nouns, such as the names of sports teams and performing groups.

The Jazz is the first western team to win the championship. The Clash say the key to their songs is complex harmony.

It is important to be consistent once the decision is made.

Not: The Clash are playing its greatest hit.

But: The Clash is playing its greatest hit.

3. When two parts of a compound subject are separated by **with, together with, including, besides, no less than, in addition to, plus, as well as** or **likewise**, the verb agrees with the first part.

The ship with all its crew was lost. Gray as well as his wife and son was in the car. The meat plus packaging weighs about a kilogram.

4. **All, a lot, any, half, majority, more, most, per cent, remainder, rest** and **some** take either a singular or plural verb depending on whether the noun is singular or plural.

Is all the money accounted for? All the cars are new. The government's majority makes it safe from defeat. A majority of Canadians favour wage control.

5. **Anybody, anyone, another, anything, each, either, every, everybody, everyone, many a, neither, no one, nobody, somebody** and **someone** take a singular verb.

Everyone wants his money back. No one knows the future. Neither of the teams stands a chance. Each of the three students comes from a different country.

6. When a sentence contains **not only . . . but also, either . . . or** or **neither . . . nor**, the verb agrees with the nearer subject.

Either the sergeant or the troops are out of step. Either the troops or the sergeant is out of step. Not only the children but also the babysitter was asleep.

7. **None** takes a plural verb when it stands for *not any;* it takes a singular verb when it is followed by a singular noun or when the idea of *not one* is to be emphasized.

None of the passengers were Canadian. None of the furniture was dusted. Ten climbers have tried but none (preferably **not one) has succeeded.**

8. In general, **acoustics, economics, gymnastics, politics, mathematics** and other words ending in *-ics* are singular when they are referred to as a science or course of study and plural when referred to as a practical activity or a quality.

The acoustics are bad. Acoustics is on the curriculum. Her politics are left wing. Politics is a dirty business. My mathematics are weak. Mathematics, rightly viewed, possesses not only truth, but also supreme beauty. — *Bertrand Russell*

Note: When in doubt, use the singular.

9. When **number, total** and **variety** are preceded by *the,* they take a singular verb. Preceded by *a,* they take a plural verb.

The number of unemployed rises monthly. A number of unemployed have found jobs. The total stolen has topped $1 million. A total of 21 people were involved.

10. When **couple** is used in the sense of two persons, it almost always takes a plural verb and plural pronouns.

The couple were hurt when their car crashed.

Note: Couple in this sense is singular on the rare occasion when it is treated as a unit.

A couple pays $10 a ticket.

11. A numerical statement may be singular or plural depending on whether the number is thought of as a unit or as a collection of items.

Three weeks is a long time. Six feet of earth is enough for any man. There was two minutes left in the game. Two days of spring make winter seem almost worthwhile.

12. Subjects plural in form but singular in effect take a singular verb.

Great Expectations has been made into a movie. Jarndyce and Jarndyce is literature's most famous lawsuit.

13. When two subjects form one idea, the verb is singular.

Bread and butter is included. The tumult and the shouting dies. — *Rudyard Kipling*

14. **Data** is plural in scientific writing but usually singular in other uses. **Media is** plural, although singular uses are increasingly accepted. Treat **agenda** as singular.

The media were blamed. The data supports this theory. The agenda was short.

15. When a sentence begins with an introductory **there**, the number of the verb is determined by the delayed subject.

There is much to be seen. **There are** many beautiful sights.

16. **One of those** takes a plural verb when the phrase introduces a clause.

The clerk **is one of those people who are** always right. It **must be one of the longest sentences that have** ever been written.

Note: To confirm that the verb must be plural, reverse the sentence: **Of the longest sentences that have** (not has) **ever been written, it must be one.**

Slang and jargon

Slang and its cousins, jargon and buzzwords, riddle our spoken language and often make the leap onto the page. They can enliven stories, giving them colour and flavour in a brief word or phrase. Slang can also help express emotions effectively. But too much or unfamiliar terms can also make copy impenetrable to all those readers not familiar with it. Or it can offend those who regard it as too informal or even improper.

Adding to the challenge is the fact that it is virtually impossible to define slang. Many words in the English language started out as so-called slang and now are respectable nouns and verbs. It has been a sizable part of our language for a good 400 years, commonly used by all ages and social groups. The problem is that by definition it derives from a particular subgroup and as such may not be familiar to everyone.

The subgroup may be as small as the TV audience of a show such as *Seinfeld*, whose members will immediately understand the meaning of such phrases as **shrinkage** or **low talker**. Others will just scratch their heads in confusion. Slang is also by nature faddish — what is understood today may not be next week. And it can get stale very easily. Yesterday's **groovy** and **yuppie** seem very dated today.

Some tips

1. Slang, as long as it is not vulgar or otherwise offensive, works well in quotes if the context helps define its meaning.

Thousands of teen girls crowded around singer Justin Bieber as he made an appearance at MuchMusic in downtown Toronto on Thursday. "Ohmigod, he's so hot," screamed one, tears running down her face.

2. To confirm whether slang is widely known or considered offensive, check the *Canadian Oxford Dictionary*. Be cautious of using slang that is not in the dictionary.

3. Use when appropriate. Sometimes it is not.

Not: The children's dad was led away in handcuffs after their blood-spattered bodies were found in the basement.

Better: The father of the three children was led away in handcuffs after their blood-spattered bodies were found in the basement.

Not: Police are finding 12-year-old hookers working on the streets of Vancouver.

Better: Police have found girls as young as 12 working as prostitutes on Vancouver streets.

4. There is a great temptation to use truncated words in today's

English: **veggies or veg** (vegetables); **photo op** (photo opportunity); **PR** (public relations); **porn** (pornography). Again, it can be appropriate in the proper context or if a particular casual effect is desired. Otherwise, avoid.

5. Some writers are particularly fond of turning nouns into verbs: **Klein gaffed while trying to defend his plans to reform health care.** Avoid unless the word has made the jump into common usage as a verb.

6. Don't use quote marks around slang unless it is likely to be a new term for most readers.

Not: She "texted" her after she won the golf tournament.

Jargon

Inside language of a profession or any other specialist group should be translated into understandable English. But the translation needs care.

Not: "The bullet lodged in the cerebrum," the doctor said.

But: The bullet lodged in the upper front part of the brain, the doctor indicated.

Not: There was "a severe loss of separation" between the two aircraft, the air traffic controller said.

But: The two planes nearly collided, the air traffic controller suggested, explaining that is what he meant when he used the term "a severe loss of separation" in his report.

Not: Police withheld his identity pending notification of next-of-kin.

But: Police withheld his name.

Abstract nouns, especially ones ending in *-ion* and strung together with prepositions, often signal foggy writing. Passive verbs can be culprits as well.

Short words tend to be concrete, standing for people, places, objects and acts.

Not: Medically speaking, the inhalation of the toxic substance is considered capable of the creation of psychological compulsions resulting in his criminal behavior.

But: Doctors said breathing the poison may have affected his mind and driven him to kill.

➤ See **Government jargon**, page 313.

Spelling

General

Is there any subject more controversial for editors than Canadian spelling? Spelling issues bring more mail to The Canadian Press style editor than anything else.

Many Canadians are passionate about spelling words "Canadian" — but there are many opinions on what exactly is Canadian. That's because the Canadian style has been to borrow from both Britain and the United States. For some words Canadians opt for a spelling that may have originated in the United States (or more accurately, North America). For other words we follow the British style. On some words, we never use the British variant (**tyre** for **tire, gaol** for **jail**); on others we never use the American version (**check** for **cheque, maneuver** for **manoeuvre**).

The Canadian Press's general philosophy is to use the spelling most commonly found across the country. Our authority for spelling is the *Canadian Oxford Dictionary*. Exceptions are listed in *Caps and Spelling*.

Despite the hybrid nature of our spelling roots, there are some general spelling rules that Canadians seem to accept. Like Americans, we prefer ize/yze endings for words such as **criticize** and **rationalize**. Like the British, we prefer -**ce** endings instead of -**se** endings on nouns like **defence** and **offence**; we double the l at the ends of words when adding a suffix: **travelled, rivalled, medallist**; and most Canadians use -**our** endings for words such as **honour** and **favour**.

Some specifics

1. Where Oxford gives alternative spellings — **amok/amuck, judgment/judgement** — use the spelling listed first, unless shown otherwise in *Caps and Spelling*.

2. When a verb has two forms for the past tense — **kneeled/ knelt, leaped/leapt** — The Canadian Press uses either one without preference.

3. Canadian Press style prefers the *sh-* spelling for Yiddish words: **shlemiel, shlock, shmatte**.

4. Unless Oxford shows otherwise, the plural of a noun is formed normally, by adding -*s* or -*es*: **shaman/shamans, box/boxes**. If the plural is irregular, it is given in parentheses: **man (men)**. Where there is a choice — **mango (-es** or **-s), virtuoso (-i** or -**os)** — use the first spelling: **mangoes**, except when *Caps and Spelling* says otherwise: **virtuosos**.

5. For words in common use, Canadian Press style is **e** rather

than the diphthongs **ae** and **oe**. So it is **archeologist, encyclopedia, fetus, gynecologist, hemorrhage, medieval** and **pediatrician**. Generally, proper names retain the diphthong: **Caesar, Oedipus, Phoebe**.

➤ See **Plurals of nouns**, page 356; see also *Caps and Spelling*.

When not to use Canadian Press spelling

When the spelling of the common-noun element of a proper name differs from our style, The Canadian Press uses the spelling favoured by the subject. This applies to all geographical places and the titles of books, movies and so on.

Thus it is **Lincoln Center** (not Lincoln Centre); **Bar Harbor, Me.** (not Bar Harbour); **Color Your World** paint store (not Colour Your World); the book or movie **The Color Purple** (not The Colour Purple).

One exception is names of government departments and agencies. Use the **U.S. Defence** (not Defense) **Department**, for example, and the **U.S. Labour** (not Labor) **Department**. In such stories, references to the U.S. labour secretary and the defence minister, or defence spending and labour rates are also likely to be found. This exception will avoid having these words spelled two ways in similar usages in the same story. Otherwise, it would be **The defence secretary said the Defense Department would increase spending.**

➤ For further details on spelling and an alphabetical listing of words, see *Caps and Spelling*.

Beyond spelling

Given the proximity of the United States and the convergence of American and Canadian media, many American expressions can creep into Canadian writing. Below is only a partial list of terms that differ in the two countries. An editor would be wise to look out for these expressions, and change them, to avoid complaints from readers or misunderstandings.

American	*Canadian*
attorney	lawyer, counsel or Crown attorney
AWOL	AWL
bound over for trial	committed for trial
charges are filed	charges are laid
college	community college, CEGEP, university
five-star general	Canadian generals wear Maple Leafs
8th grade	Grade 8

American	Canadian
honor guard	guard of honour
railroad	railway
Indian reservation	aboriginal (First Nations) reserve
freshmen	Grade 9
sophomores	Grade 10
juniors	Grade 11
seniors	Grade 12

➤ See also **Military,** page 329.

Technical terms

General

1. Avoid unfamiliar scientific, medical, technological and technical terms. When they must be used, give a simple, accurate explanation.

She acted oddly because she had Tourette's syndrome, a nervous disorder characterized by involuntary movements and vocal sounds.

2. Explain the unfamiliar in terms of the familiar.

A centrifuge acts like a cake mixer or merry-go-round, forcing objects outward from the centre.

Keratin is the main protein in fingernails, tiger claws, alligator scales, rhinoceros horns and feather quills.

3. Technical language can be less intimidating if the explanation is given first.

The medical team said a study of the mammoths' white blood cells, called leucocytes, shows them to be perfectly preserved.

4. An everyday term is generally preferable to a scientific one. For example, use **evergreen** instead of **coniferous, marijuana** instead of **cannabis.**

5. Because of the rapid pace of change, it can be difficult to know where to draw the line with terms in communications technology stories. One useful general rule is to avoid abbreviations and acronyms that are used only by industry insiders. If in doubt, err on the side of caution by including an explanation: **Wi-Fi, a wireless network.**

Scientific names

1. The name of a family or genus is capitalized: **Branta.** Use lower case for the species, even when derived from a proper name like Canada: **Branta canadensis** (Canada goose). Use lowercase for conditions caused by the genus: **listeriosis.**

2. The genus may be shortened if the reference is a common one:

Brucella abortus (aborts cows, causes undulant fever in people)	Br. abortus
Escherichia coli (intestinal bacterium)	E. coli
Staphylococcus aureus (causes boils)	S. aureus

Drugs

1. In general, refer to a drug by its generic name, not its brand name: **a tranquillizer, diazepam; a pain reliever, ASA.**

2. If an unfamiliar brand name has to be used, follow it with the generic name and a description: **Antabuse, a brand of disulfiram used to discourage the drinking of alcohol.**

When allied news agencies use the term **aspirin**, change it to **ASA** in most cases. In Canada, Aspirin is a trademark and it must be capitalized.

➤ See **Capitalization**, page 291; **Trade names**, page 415.

Medical

1. Prefer a common term to a medical one:

bleed to hemorrhage	chickenpox to varicella
broke to fractured	whooping cough to pertussis
clot to embolism	German measles to rubella
indigestion to dyspepsia	bad breath to halitosis
cut to laceration	scarlet fever to scarlatina
scrape to abrasion	shingles to herpes zoster
injury to lesion	stitch to suture

2. In general, don't capitalize diseases, conditions, symptoms, tests and treatments:

legionnaires' disease, scarlet fever, infarction, barium X-ray, cobalt therapy, severe acute respiratory syndrome (SARS)

But capitalize proper names that are part of the term:

Alzheimer's disease, German measles, Parkinson's disease, Down syndrome, Lassa fever, Pap smear, Heimlich manoeuvre.

3. Unless there's a compelling reason to give the precise cause of death, it's usually enough to say a person died, say, of **a stroke, a heart attack** or in childbirth, rather than of **cerebral hemorrhage, coronary thrombosis** or **puerperal fever.**

4. Similarly, say **Belfour sprained his right thumb,** instead of **Stress X-rays taken on Belfour, under local anesthetic, showed a tear of the ulnar collateral ligament of the metacarpal-phalangeal joint of the right thumb.**

5. Widespread interest justifies giving more details in reporting the illness or death of a prime minister, president, pope, movie star or other major figure.

➤ See **Obituaries**, page 91.

Condition

1. Descriptions used by hospitals to report a patient's condition are often vague. It helps if a story explains that a patient is **conscious, allowed to sit up** or **receive visitors, is being fed intravenously**, and so on.

2. Here are four common descriptions of conditions, with the meanings some hospitals attach to them:

Good: The pulse, breathing and other vital signs are normal and stable. The patient is comfortable and conscious, and the outlook for recovery is good.

Fair: The pulse, breathing and other vital signs are near normal and the patient is conscious, but he or she is uncomfortable or may have minor complications. The outlook for recovery is favourable.

Serious: The patient is acutely ill and the chance of recovery is uncertain. The pulse, breathing and other vital signs may be abnormal or unstable.

Critical: Death may be imminent. The pulse, breathing and other vital signs are abnormal and unstable and there are major complications.

Burns

There are four degrees of burns, but most hospitals refer to only three: *first, second* and *third* — the third being the most severe.

First degree means the skin is red; *second*, it's blistering; *third*, skin has been destroyed along with underlying tissue and won't heal without grafting.

In a *fourth*-degree burn, muscle and bone have also been damaged.

Hospitals may also refer to partial and full burns. Ask specifically about the extent of tissue damage and the need for skin grafts and other measures.

AIDS

Acquired immune deficiency syndrome (or acquired immunodeficiency syndrome) is a breakdown of a person's immunological system, the body's natural defences against disease. Someone is said to have AIDS if a life-threatening infection or cancer results from failure of the defence system.

It's inaccurate to say someone has died of AIDS. Give the actual cause of death — pneumonia, perhaps — and add that it was complicated by AIDS or was AIDS-related.

AIDS is believed to be spread through the exchange of bodily fluids in the following ways: through sexual activity; use of HIV-infected syringes; transfusion of HIV-infected blood; and from an infected mother to her fetus.

Researchers generally agree that HIV, the human immunodeficiency virus, must be present for AIDS to develop. Therefore, it is permissible to say that **HIV causes AIDS**. However, since HIV can cause several infections or diseases, not just AIDS, don't call it **the AIDS virus**.

➤ See **Obituaries**, page 92.

Influenza

Influenza, often called by its nickname flu, is a highly contagious viral infection that attacks the respiratory tract. Rapid onset of symptoms is characteristic of influenza. They include severe cold-like symptoms, muscle aches, fever and lethargy. Because it is caused by a virus, influenza is not treatable with antibiotics.

Flu does not target the gastrointestinal tract and does not cause vomiting and diarrhea, except occasionally in young children. The often-seen term "stomach flu" is a misnomer and should not be used.

Richter scale

The Richter scale is an open-ended gauge of ground motion recorded on a seismograph during an earthquake. Every increase of one number means that the ground motion is 10 times greater.

However, science has refined the art of comparing earthquakes since 1935 when Charles Richter helped develop a scale that measured quakes in southern California. Modern seismology equipment is more sensitive and can measure a wider range of quakes than the original Richter scale, although newer scales have been designed to meld with Richter's model. Don't automatically use the phrase **on the Richter scale** when writing about earthquake magnitudes. General references, such as **a quake of 5.2 magnitude**, are usually sufficient.

A quake with a magnitude of 2 is the smallest normally felt by humans. One of magnitude 4 can cause moderate damage in a populated area, one of 5 considerable damage, one of 6 severe damage, and one of 7 widespread heavy damage. A quake of magnitude 8, a "great" earthquake, is capable of tremendous damage.

Time

What day is it?

1. The Canadian Press doesn't use **yesterday** or **tomorrow** in stories for print use and only uses **today** if needed in QuickHits — urgent copy intended for broadcast and online use. (These items are updated later, with the day of the week added, for newspaper and other print media.) Otherwise, to avoid confusion, the day is always named.

2. Name the day if it falls within seven days of the current date: **on Tuesday** or **next Sunday** or **last Friday.**

3. For more distant dates, use the date: **May 5.**

4. For significant events and in sports schedules, give the day and the date: **The budget will be presented Friday, Nov. 4;** or **Saturday, May 13: Toronto at Montreal.**

5. Place the day in a sentence where it would fall normally in conversation: not **The premier Thursday announced** but **The premier announced Thursday.**

6. Use **on** when it helps readability or to break up a series of capitalized words:

The measure passed in the House of Commons on Monday. The Edmonton Oilers defeated the Vancouver Canucks on Friday.

7. Don't wrench a lead out of shape trying for a weak or phoney current-day angle. Bury the time element if necessary, and get the news in the lead.

8. Avoid putting an obsolescent angle in a lead: **The vote was expected Tuesday.** The event may have occurred by the time the story is read. Instead, concentrate on getting the latest information in the lead and bury the time element so it can be dumped if necessary. Get a new Writethru out as soon as possible after events overtake the story.

9. Don't write that an event has taken place if the story is written beforehand in anticipation of the event.

➤ See **Advances,** page 443.

What time is it?

1. The exact time of an event is usually unnecessary. Instead, give the reader a sense of the time by describing the scene.

Not: A spectacular collision between two commuter trains occurred at 9 a.m. today.

But: A spectacular collision between two commuter trains caused chaos in downtown Montreal during the morning rush hour.

2. But give a specific time for important announcements, key votes, space launches, ransom deadlines or other events in which the time is a vital component. Give the time in the placelined community, with the equivalent in eastern time in brackets if necessary: **The volcano erupted at 8 a.m. local time (4 p.m. EDT).**

3. Specify the time zone in undated stories.

4. Specify time zones in stories involving the time of live radio and TV programs broadcast nationally. In cases of recorded or delayed broadcasts, provide the eastern time. Each newspaper can provide information on local broadcasts if need be.

5. Time is written in figures. However, write **noon** or **midnight,** not **12 noon** or **12 midnight.**

6. Write **5 a.m.,** not **5:00 a.m.**

7. A colon separates hours, minutes and seconds when figures are used. A period separates seconds from tenths of seconds: **7:32 p.m.** or **Her time was 3:45:20.6.** When written out it would be: **Her time was three hours 45 minutes 20.6 seconds.**

What zone is it?

1. Use abbreviations for time zones with a clock reading: **11 a.m. MST** or **midnight Sunday night PST.** Spell out time zones when they are not accompanied by a clock reading: **Newfoundland daylight time.**

2. Capitalize Newfoundland, Atlantic and Pacific time zones when spelled out. Other time zones — eastern, mountain and central — are lowercase: **Atlantic daylight time** but **eastern standard time.**

3. Greenwich mean time is five hours ahead of eastern standard time and four hours ahead of eastern daylight time. From around the beginning of April through October, when Britain is on **summer time** — their equivalent of **daylight time** — London is one hour ahead of GMT.

➤ See **Abbreviations and acronyms,** page 255.

Canadian time zones

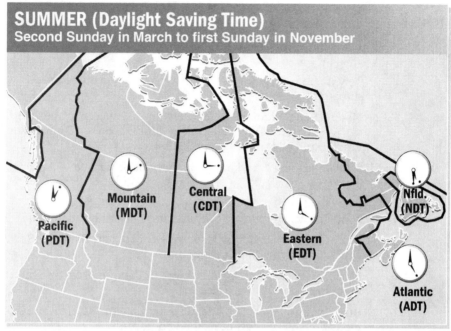

SUMMER (Daylight Saving Time)
Second Sunday in March to first Sunday in November

Pacific
(PDT)

Mountain
(MDT)

Central
(CDT)

Eastern
(EDT)

Nfld.
(NDT)

Atlantic
(ADT)

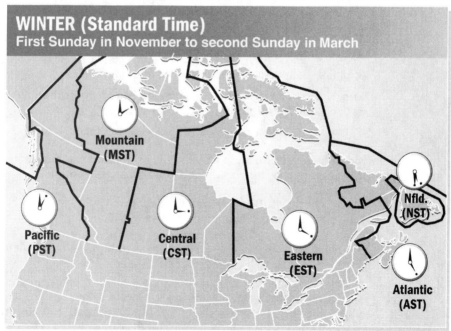

WINTER (Standard Time)
First Sunday in November to second Sunday in March

Mountain
(MST)

Pacific
(PST)

Central
(CST)

Eastern
(EST)

Nfld.
(NST)

Atlantic
(AST)

Source: National Research Council Canada   THE CANADIAN PRESS

Titles

General

1. For rules on capitalization of titles, ➤ see Capitalization, page 288.

2. With few exceptions, a person's given name is used with surname on first reference.

Note: Famous authors, composers and the like may be referred to by surname only: **Dickens's Bleak House, Beethoven's Fifth, Darwin's theory of evolution.**

3. Front-loading — piling nouns in front of a name — is hard on the reader. Instead, use *of*, *the* and *a*, and set off long titles with commas.

Not: Groovy Records of Canada president Sheryl Jones . . .

But: The president of Groovy Records of Canada, Sheryl Jones, attended the news conference.

Not: Deputy foreign affairs minister Jacques Martin was the main architect of the program.

But: Jacques Martin, the deputy foreign affairs minister, was the main architect of the program.

4. False titles are best avoided.

U.S. modern dance innovator Margaret Mason, retired Yukon judge Roger Kimmerly

A phrase in apposition, preceded by *the*, is proper English.

the U.S. modern dance innovator Margaret Mason, the retired Yukon judge Roger Kimmerly

5. Use titles on first reference but seldom after that.

Collins (not **Archbishop Collins**) **also attended the mass.**
The size of the deficit startled Charest (not **Premier Charest**).
Berger (not **Sgt. Berger**) **was first ashore.**
The next in line is William (not **Prince William**).

But when a story is long or filled with names, repeat a title rather than risk losing a reader.

6. Use such titles as **Dr.** and **Rev.** only when those named are dealing with their speciality. A doctor in the Commons speaking about the environment is simply **Martha Singer, the Regina Conservative.** Speaking about medicare, she becomes **Dr. Martha Singer, the Regina pediatrician and Conservative.**

7. Use **chairman** or **chairwoman**, **spokesman** or **spokeswoman** as appropriate. **Chairperson** and **spokesperson**

can be used if the sex of the person is not known. But use substitutes for awkward constructions (**councillor instead of alderperson**) whenever possible.

Courtesy titles

1. In general, do not use the courtesy titles **Mr., Mrs., Miss** or **Ms.**

Justice (not Mr. Justice) Ian Binnie wrote the ruling. Murray said she enjoys singing. Campbell said abortion should be illegal.

When it is necessary to use **Mrs., Miss** or **Ms.**, follow the woman's preference.

2. If appropriate, refer to a couple on first reference by their first names and their common last name: **William and Jane Levinski.** If their relationship is not that of husband and wife, explain: **Wayne Gretzky and his sister, Kim.**

3. When married people do not use a common surname, an explanation can be added for clarity.

Adrienne Clarkson and her husband, John Ralston Saul

4. To distinguish between persons of the same last name on second reference, repeat first names.

Professional titles

1. In general, use **Dr.** for licensed health care professionals. Where pertinent specify.

Dr. John Lucyk; Lucyk, an orthodontist. Dr. Sonya Chong; Chong, a chiropractor. Dr. Bert Clifford; Clifford, a veterinarian. Dr. Catherine Clarke; Clarke, a psychologist.

Note: Each province decides which of its health care practitioners may use **Dr.** (In Ontario, that includes chiropractors, physicians, psychologists, dentists, optometrists and podiatrists.) If in doubt, check.

2. Do not use **Dr.** for people with doctorates outside the health-care field. If pertinent, say a person has an earned or an honorary degree and give the discipline.

Lynch, a doctor of divinity. Callaghan received an honorary doctorate of letters from the University of Moncton.

Religious titles

1. Use a religious title before a person's name on first reference. Subsequently use either the surname alone (in most instances), the title preceded by *the*, or a general description.

Archbishop Hugo Dood; Dood, the archbishop. Rabbi David Silverstein; Silverstein, the rabbi. Rev. Keith Wallace; Wallace, the priest

Note: Write **Rev.**, not **the Rev.** Never write **Rev. Wallace.**

2. All popes and some Eastern Orthodox archbishops and bishops, as well as some Roman Catholic and Anglican nuns and brothers, are known by a title and given name only. In such instances, the title is usually retained in subsequent use of the name.

Pope Benedict, Metropolitan Andrew, Archbishop Volodymyr, Mother Mary, Sister Agatha, Brother Jude

Note: It is not necessary to include **XVI** in first references to **Pope Benedict.** It is also acceptable to refer in subsequent references to **Benedict** rather than **Pope Benedict** in subsequent references.

3. The name of the office (**Bishop, Canon, Deacon,** etc.) is preferred as the title before the name: **Archbishop John Somers.** But such forms as **Most Rev. John Somers, Archbishop of New Westminster, B.C.,** are acceptable on occasion.

4. Write **John Cardinal Brown,** not **Cardinal John Brown.**

5. Some of the more common identifying titles that apply to various levels of Christian religious office include:

Roman Catholic:
The Pope - **His Holiness**
Cardinal - **His Eminence**
Archbishop - **Most Rev.**
Bishop - **Most Rev.**
Monsignor - **Right Rev.** (but usually **Msgr.**)

Anglican:
Primate - **Most Rev.**
Archbishop - **Most Rev.**
Bishop - **Right Rev.**
Dean - **Very Rev.**
Canon - **Rev.** (**Rev. Terry Scott** or **Canon Scott**)

United Church:
Moderator - **Right Rev.**
Ex-moderator - **Very Rev.**

Presbyterian:
Moderator - **Rev.**

6. Some religions lack a formal hierarchy, with leaders chosen by the congregation or community. In such cases use descriptive terms such as **holy man** or **priest**, as in **Hindu priest Sharad Rao** or **Sikh priest Satinder Singh.**

7. Forms of address familiar to the clergy but not to others should be avoided except when in direct quotation:

His Holiness, His Eminence, His Grace, Lord Bishop, His Lordship, His Excellency

8. Unfamiliar titles should be explained.

Primate Michael Peers, the head of the Anglican Church of Canada; Imam Muhammad Nasim, minister of the Jami Mosque; Kazi Muhammad Abdul, a Muslim religious judge.

9. **Rev.** precedes the full name of most ministers and priests, including Buddhists. It is not used by Christian Scientists, Mormons, Jehovah's Witnesses or Seventh-day Adventists, among others. Muslims use the title **Imam** for leaders of their mosques.

Note: Do not use **Rev.** as a noun meaning clergyman: **The reverend reads murder mysteries.**

10. Unless it is immediately obvious from the context, do not use **Catholic Church** on first mention for the **Roman Catholic Church.** Several other communions maintain the Catholic tradition in varying degrees while rejecting papal infallibility and other dogmas. These include Eastern Orthodox, Anglican, Old Catholic, Polish National Catholic, Lusitanian (Portugal), Spanish Reformed Episcopal and Philippine Independent Catholic.

Hereditary, honorary titles

1. The honorary titles **right honourable** and **honourable** are used only when they appear in direct quotation.

2. **Right Hon.** applies for life to the Governor General, prime minister, chief justice of Canada, and members of the British Privy Council.

3. **Hon.** is applied for life to members of the Canadian Privy Council and lieutenant-governors. With royal assent, it may be used **for life** by retired judges of superior courts and some others. It is applied **during office** to senators, Speakers of the Commons and legislatures, judges of the Supreme and Federal courts of Canada and corresponding courts in the provinces, and members of provincial cabinets. Also applied to most peers' children.

4. The rules regarding the use of hereditary titles are complex and vary from country to country. In general, use the title as it is commonly used in the country of origin.

5. In Britain, the order of rank begins with the Royal Family. Use **King, Queen, Prince** and **Princess** before first names: **Princess Anne, Prince William, Queen Victoria.** It is usually sufficient to refer to the reigning monarch as simply **the Queen** or **the King.** After the Royal Family are these (usually) hereditary titles, in descending order (females or wives in brackets): **duke (duchess); marquess (marchioness); earl (countess); viscount (viscountess); baron (baroness); baronet (baronetess).**

6. Dukes are referred to by their full title in first reference: **Arthur, Duke of Wellington**, the **Duke of Wellington**.

7. Although the full titles of marquesses, earls, viscounts and barons and their female counterparts can serve as alternative names (**Marquess of Bath**), they are more commonly identified as lords: **Lord Bath, Lady Bath**.

8. **Lady** is used before the first names of the daughters of dukes, marquesses and earls: **Lady Jane**. **Lord** is used before the first name of the son of a duke, marquess or earl, although this person may also hold his own title.

9. A baronetcy is similar to a hereditary knighthood and holders of the title are called sirs, not lords: **Sir Jeffrey Allen**. A baroness is **Lady Allen**, not **Lady Jane**.

10. There are also life peerages granted by the Crown, with the most common being a life baron. A life peerage offers all the privileges of a hereditary title except it cannot be passed on to the recipient's descendants. If the title is relevant, use it as granted: **Lord Black of Crossharbour**. But if the person is better known by his birth name, use it: **Conrad Black**.

11. The titles of knight and dame are honorary and do not make a person a member of the nobility. In these cases, make it **Paul McCartney**, not **Sir Paul McCartney**; **Taylor**, not **Dame Elizabeth**.

Trade names

1. Capitalize trademarks: names (and symbols) used by organizations and protected by law.

Frigidaire, Skor bars, Tamiflu

Note: Brand name is a non-legal term for **trademark** or **service mark**.

2. Variety names and names of market grades are capitalized.

Golden Delicious apples, Choice lamb, Grade A beef

3. Common-noun elements of trademarks are generally lowercased.

Dove soap, Harris tweed, Lipton soup, Mott's Clamato juice, Spic and Span cleaner

4. In general, follow an organization's capitalization.

eBay, iPod, TVOntario, Toys "R" Us

Exception No. 1: For all-caps promotional names, capitalize only the first letters: **Scrabble** (not **SCRABBLE**), **Via Rail** (not **VIA Rail**)

Exception No. 2: For all-lowercase promotional names, capitalize the first letter for clarity: **Adidas** (not **adidas**) **sportswear**, **Smart** (not **smart**) **car**

5. The use of a trademark is easily avoided by substituting a general term.

soft drink/pop for Coke, adhesive bandage for Band-Aid, flying disc for Frisbee

6. Use a brand name when it gives point, colour or impact to a story.

She wore Jimmy Choo shoes that had seen better days.

The children were playing a board game using Smarties as counters.

The robbers escaped in a Volkswagen Beetle.

➤ See **Capitalization**, page 291.

7. **Aspirin** is a trademark in Canada. Generic alternatives include **acetylsalicylic acid, ASA pills** and **a painkiller**.

8. Trademarks not guarded by their owners from being used as generics may lose the protection of the law.

cellophane, corn flakes, dry ice, escalator, kerosene, raisin bran, nylon, laundromat, linoleum, shredded wheat, trampoline, yo-yo

10. Sources of information about trademarks include the Canadian Intellectual Property Office, part of Industry Canada, which maintains an online database. Do not follow the capitalization in the *Canadian Oxford Dictionary*.

11. Here are trademarks often encountered in news stories, with generic alternatives.

Baggies plastic bags
Band-Aid adhesive bandage
Bic ballpoint pen
Caterpillar tractor
Chiclets chewing gum
Coca-Cola, Coke cola drink
Cream of Wheat cereal
Crisco shortening
EpiPen epinephrine injector
Fiberglas glass fibre, fibreglass
Fig Newton cookies
Frigidaire appliances
Frisbee flying disc
Fritos corn chips
Fudgsicle ice cream on a stick
Gravol travel-sickness medicine
Hush Puppies casual shoes
Javex bleach
Jaws of Life extraction equipment
Jeep vehicles, but **jeep** for the military vehicle
Jell-O gelatin dessert
Jet Ski personal watercraft
Kleenex tissues
Levi's jeans
Lycra spandex fibre
Lysol disinfectant
Miracle Whip salad dressing

Mott's Clamato tomato-clam cocktail
Muzak background music
Novocain anesthetic, but **no-vocaine**
Pablum baby cereal, but **pabulum**
Pepsi-Cola, Pepsi cola drink
Plexiglas acrylic plastic
Polaroid camera, sunglasses
Popsicle flavoured ice on a stick
Pyrex oven glassware
Q-Tips cotton swabs
Realtor (a member of the National Association of Realtors, prefer **real estate agent**)
Scotch tape adhesive tape
Stetson hat
Styrofoam plastic foam
Tabasco pepper sauce
Taser stun gun
Technicolor coloured movies
Teflon non-stick coating
TelePrompTer cueing device
TV Dinner frozen dinner
Vaseline petroleum jelly
Velcro tape fasteners
Xerox photocopier

Weather

Introduction

Weather affects everyone. It's almost impossible to write too much about the weather. But write about it in human terms.

The heavy snowfall that is commonplace in northern Ontario during the winter months — closing schools, stranding motorists, generally disrupting life — is news to Vancouver residents basking in 20 degree sunshine. It is certainly news to anyone planning to travel through the region.

Endless rainfall on the Prairies while farmers are trying to bring in their fall harvest not only causes the farmers major concern but affects the commodity markets as well.

Write about weather in terms of its effects on people. Numbers help but prefer descriptions: **ankle-deep puddles, knee-deep snow, winds turning umbrellas inside out and bending small trees, a downpour causing wading pools to overflow and soaking through clothing.**

Weather knows no boundaries. A hurricane that forms off the coast of Cuba may eventually find its way to Halifax after causing havoc in the Carolinas. Is Newfoundland next in its path? A good weather story does not leave readers thinking a storm stopped at a national or provincial border.

Add Canadian content to any story about weather problems in the northern United States.

Where warranted, use comparisons of other recent storms or those that caused major damage.

Consider a regional weather roundup to provide a proper perspective of what the weather pattern has done.

National weather stories should be considered whenever there is a thread to tie everything together.

Weather in metric

Temperatures are expressed in degrees Celsius, with **0 C** the freezing point of water and **100 C** the boiling point. Do not use **below zero**; use **-5 C** (minus five degrees C). **C** is commonplace; it is not necessary to write out Celsius each time.

For everyday comparison: **30 C is swimming weather, 20 C room temperature, -10 C skating weather.**

Wind speed is measured in kilometres an hour: **light**, up to 20 km/h; **moderate**, 21-40 km/h; **strong**, 41-60 km/h; **gale**, 61-90 km/h; **whole gale**, 91-116 km/h; **hurricane**, over 117 km/h.

Rainfall is given in millimetres and **snowfall** in centimetres. A centimetre of snow equals a millimetre of rain.

Light shower   2.5 mm/h rainfall.

Heavy downpour   25 mm/h rainfall.

Good base for skiing   100 cm of snow

Atmospheric (barometric) pressure is measured in kilopascals. Normal pressure ranges from 98 to 103 kPa.

Terminology

Following are terms that may appear in weather forecasts from Environment Canada. Temperatures are Celsius.

acid rain: Rain mixed with sulphur dioxide, nitrogen oxide and other industrial and automobile pollutants to form acids, at times as strong as lemon juice or vinegar.

air mass: A large body of air with uniform temperature and moisture in a horizontal plane. The transition zone between different air masses is called a **front**. In a **cold front**, cold air is replacing warm; in a **warm front**, warm air is replacing cold.

atmospheric (or **barometric**) **pressure**: The pressure exerted by the atmosphere as a result of gravity. A rapidly falling barometer generally heralds a storm; when the barometer is rising, fair weather can usually be expected.

blizzard: A fierce storm with winds of more than 40 kilometres an hour, temperatures of less than —10, visibility less than half a kilometre.

chinook: A warm, dry wind which mainly affects the foothills of the Rockies. Can raise temperatures 20 degrees within minutes.

cyclone: A wind system rotating counterclockwise around a calm central area. In North America the term is sometimes used for a tornado or storm, in the Indian Ocean region for a hurricane.

flash flood: A sudden flood caused by heavy rain or the rapid melting of snow. A **flood crest** is the highest level reached before the water recedes.

freezing rain, freezing drizzle, ice storm: Rain or drizzle that freezes on impact with objects.

gale warning: Issued when winds are expected to be 34 to 48 knots (about 63 to 89 km/h) over water.

heavy snow: The definition varies from region to region. Heavy snow in Vancouver may be five centimetres, in Montreal 15.

high: An area of high pressure with winds moving clockwise, which often brings fine weather. Used interchangeably with anticyclone (a term not widely understood, however).

humidex: An index that combines the effects of summer temperatures and humidities:

Humidex	Degree of comfort
20-29	Comfortable
30-39	Varying degrees of discomfort
40-45	Most people uncomfortable
46 and over	Some outdoor work must be restricted

humidity, relative: The amount of water vapour in the air expressed as a percentage of the maximum amount the air can hold at that temperature and pressure.

hurricane or **typhoon:** A tropical storm with wind speeds of over 117 kilometres an hour. The hurricane eye is the relatively calm centre. Hurricanes develop east of the international date line. Typhoons develop west of the line; in the Indian Ocean they are called cyclones.

inversion: Instead of decreasing with height as is normal, the temperature remains constant or increases.

knot: A unit of speed: one nautical mile (6,080 feet) an hour is about 1.85 km/h.

low: An area of low atmospheric pressure that has an air circulation counter-clockwise in the Northern Hemisphere.

marine warning: Alerts mariners and shoreline residents of dangerous winds or freezing spray.

nearshore waters, coastal waters: Within five to 10 kilometres of shore.

offshore waters: Up to 400 kilometres from shore.

probability of precipitation: The chance of rain, snow and so on for a specified period, expressed in increments of 10 per cent, from zero (none expected) to 100 (a certainty).

ridge: An elongated area of relatively high pressure extending from the centre of a high-pressure region.

severe thunderstorm: Damaging winds usually with gusts to more than 60-80 kilometres an hour, heavy rain and possibly hailstones, frequent lightning and occasionally a tornado.

small craft warning: A warning issued for pleasure boaters when winds are expected to maintain speeds of 20-35 knots (37-63 km/h).

snow pellets: Tiny balls of snow that rebound on striking hard ground.

thundershower: Rain lasting 10-15 minutes, associated with a thunderstorm.

tornado: A destructive rotating column of air with a funnel shape touching the ground and accompanied by a loud roar. Sometimes called a twister.

tropical storm: A weather system one step below a hurricane; winds from 62 to 117 km/h.

trough: An elongated area of relatively low pressure extending from the centre of a low-pressure region.

typhoon: ➤ See **hurricane**.

UV index: A measure of the intensity of ultraviolet rays. The index ranges from 9.0 or higher, which is considered extreme (takes less than 15 minutes to get sunburn), to less than 4.0 (takes an hour or more).

weather advisory: Alerts the public that weather conditions, though not dangerous, may cause general inconvenience.

weather warning: Alerts the public to conditions that may endanger life, property and the public welfare.

whiteout: Dense blizzard and total obscurity of physical features. Commonest in the Arctic and on the Prairies.

wind chill index: An index of the effects of wind velocity and low temperature that measures how cold it feels. For instance, if the temperature is -10 but the wind chill is -20, the winds make it feel as cold as -20 on a calm day.

wind direction: The direction from which the wind blows: an east wind blows toward the west.

wind shear: A swirling current of air produced at the junction of two horizontal air streams of greatly differing speed or direction. A possible hazard to aircraft landing or taking off.

Words

This chapter is designed to demonstrate some tricky distinctions in the meanings of words and some rulings on correct or preferred usage.

according to	Avoid in attributions if it seems to cast doubt on the source's credibility.
adventuresome **adventurous**	ready to take risks fond of adventure
adverse **averse**	unfavourable opposed
affect (verb) **effect** (noun or verb)	influence, have an effect on a result; bring about, accomplish
aggravate **irritate**	make worse annoy, exasperate
allude to **refer to**	suggest without naming name
allusion **illusion**	a casual or indirect reference a false impression
altercation	a noisy dispute or quarrel (not a fistfight)
alternate(ly)	in turns, first one and then the other: **The raiders lay alternately watching and sleeping.**
alternative(ly)	providing a choice (usually the word wanted): **an alternative route.**
ambiguous	having two or more meanings: **The large lady's hat** is ambiguous.
ambivalent	having mixed feelings: **He was ambivalent about arms spending, recognizing the need for defence but wishing the money better spent.**
amiable **amicable**	friendly, of people friendly, of situations and agreements
amount **number**	How much? (weight and money) How many? (individual items)
antagonist	➤ See **protagonist**.

apparent	Write He died apparently of a heart attack, not He died of an apparent heart attack.
apparently **obviously**	seemingly, presumably plainly, unmistakably
apt **liable** **likely**	customarily inclined; naturally fit open to something unpleasant probable, expected
arbitrate **mediate**	render a binding decision in a dispute help settle a dispute
as	meaning *since* or *because* should be used with care. It can sometimes be mistaken for *while* or *during the time that*: As he was going out, she asked him to buy a paper.
as **like**	introduces clauses: It tastes good as a cigarette should. introduces a noun or pronoun not directly followed by a verb: He smokes like a chimney.
as if, as though	may be used interchangeably to connect clauses.
assume **presume**	accept for the sake of argument take for granted
assure	➤ See ensure.
at present	➤ See presently.
audience **spectators**	watches or listens. watch.
avenge **revenge**	retaliate for another retaliate for oneself
averse	➤ See adverse.
avocation **vocation**	a hobby, diversion a career, occupation
awhile	➤ See while.
bait **bate**	lure (a baited hook); torment hold in (bated breath)

barely	➤ See **hardly**.
beg the question	assume the truth, usually unjustifiably, of the thing to be proved: **The worthless Senate should be abolished.** Beg the question doesn't mean evade a straight answer.
beside **besides**	at the side of in addition to
bi-	is ambiguous in **biweekly, bimonthly, biennial,** etc. Prefer **twice a week, every two weeks, semi-weekly, semi-annual, half-yearly,** etc.
blatant **flagrant**	offensively noisy, obtrusive shameless, brazen
bloc **block**	a combination of people, countries or organizations to foster a shared interest a group of things: shares, seats, tickets
blond (adjective) **blond** (noun)	She has blond hair. a male or female

boat
 	
  ship
  vessel
	a small craft propelled by oars, sails or motor; also a submarine, motor torpedo boat, ferry
	a large craft with sails or engine
	a ship or a boat bigger than a rowboat

born **borne**	come into being by birth carried, endured
breach **broach**	break a contract or a wall open a barrel or a topic
breech birth	baby born buttocks first
can (could) **may (might)**	denotes ability or power to do something. suggests doubt; also expresses permission to do something.
cannon **canon**	a gun a church decree; a clergyman
canvas **canvass**	coarse cloth solicit
catch-22	a dilemma from which there is no escape. Note the lowercase.

celebrator	one who celebrates, a partygoer
celebrant	an officiating priest
cement	powder used in making concrete
concrete	rocklike material for roads, buildings, etc.
centre (verb)	is followed by **on** or **in**.
revolve (verb)	is followed by **round** or **around**.
childish	silly, puerile
childlike	innocent, confiding
chord	used in musical and mathematical senses: **The name struck a chord.**
cord	used in anatomical senses: **spinal cord, vocal cord, umbilical cord**; also: **nylon cord, cord of wood.**
client	uses the services of a professional person other than a doctor, or of a business.
customer	buys goods from a shop or a business.
climactic	of a climax
climatic	of climate
climax	➤ See **crescendo**.
commence	➤ See **begin**.
communique	Use for official communications, not for terrorists' threatening notes and the like.
compare to	liken to: **The staff compared (likened) him to Hitler.**
compare with	show similarities and differences (the term usually wanted): **He cannot compare with Ruth Rendell as a writer of mysteries.**
contrast with	show differences
complementary	completing; supplying needs
complimentary	praising; free
composed of	made up of
comprise (no of)	contain all the parts
include	contain some of the parts
concrete	➤ See **cement**.
connotation	➤ See **denotation**.

consensus	agreement, majority view (**general consensus of opinion** is redundant)
contagious **infectious**	passed on by contact passed on by contact or some other means
contemptible **contemptuous**	despicable scornful, insolent
continual **continuous**	frequently repeated (a dripping tap) uninterrupted (Niagara Falls)
controversial	is not needed when it is clear from the context that the subject is contentious: **The Opposition let the legislature bells ring for three hours Monday in its fight against a (controversial) housing bill.**
convict	➤ See inmate.
convince **persuade**	is followed by **of** or **that**, but not **to**. is followed by **of**, **that** or **to**.
cord	➤ See chord.
council (noun) **counsel** (n. or v.)	an assembly advice, a legal adviser; to advise
country	➤ See nation.
couple	almost invariably plural in reference to people: **The couple were hurt when their plane crashed. But A couple pays $5.**
credible **creditable** **credulous**	believable praiseworthy gullible
crescendo **climax**	increasing in strength or loudness highest point, top of a crescendo
customer	➤ See client.
defective **deficient**	faulty lacking, incomplete
definite **definitive**	firm, clear final, absolute

defuse (verb)	to render harmless
diffuse (adjective)	scattered
demolish, destroy	**completely** is redundant. (Avoid as synonym for **defeat** in sports stories.)
denotation	what a word specifically means: **Pig denotes a swine.**
connotation	what a word suggests: **Pig connotes dirt, greed, the little pig who went to market and other storybook characters.**
deny	➤ See **rebut, refute.**
dependant (noun)	one who depends on another
dependent (adj.)	depending on
deprecate	express disapproval of
depreciate	lose in value; belittle
desert	barren; something deserved; to abandon
dessert	a sweet
different from	is used with a noun or pronoun.
different than	introduces a clause.
dilemma	a choice between two equally pleasant or unpleasant things (not a synonym for difficulty)
disc	in such references as **a compact disc, a disc jockey, a slipped disc**
disk	of computers only: **disk drive, a floppy disk**
discomfort	make uncomfortable, uneasy
discomfit	embarrass, thwart
disinterested	impartial
uninterested	not interested
dissatisfied	➤ See **unsatisfied.**
draft	current of air, sum of money, rough plan, military service, hauling, beer drawn from a barrel (never **draught**)
due to	Use only if *caused by* or *ascribed to* could be substituted: **The crash was due to ice.** Not: **Due to ice, the plane crashed.** Try **because of, owing to.**

eatable	can be eaten because not revolting
edible	can be safely eaten
economic	relating to economics
economical	thrifty
-ee, -er	In general, *-ee* denotes the recipient of an action: **employee, examinee, trainee**; *-er* denotes the doer of the action: **employer, examiner, trainer.** But *-ee* sometimes applies to a person who behaves in a certain way: **absentee, debauchee, escapee, refugee.**
effect	➤ See **affect**.
effective	having an effect; coming into operation
effectual	answering its purpose
elicit (verb)	to draw out, evoke
illicit (adjective)	not legal
emigrant	leaves the country.
immigrant	enters the country.
migrant	moves from one place to another.
eminent	prominent
imminent	near at hand
ended	Use of past: **week ended (last) Jan. 1.**
ending	Use of future: **week ending (next) May 1.**
enormity	monstrous wickedness, serious error
enormousness	great size
ensure	to make sure
insure	to provide insurance
assure	to remove worry or uncertainty
especially	➤ See **specially**.
exhausting	causing exhaustion
exhaustive	complete
expedient	suitable for a particular purpose; advantageous
expeditious	quick
extradite	hand person to another country; obtain such person for trial
extricate	disentangle, release

farther	denotes physical distance: **farther down the road.**
further	everything else: **to slip further into debt.**
female	refers to sex of human beings, animals or plants: **female servants.**
feminine	applies to qualities said to be characteristic of girls and women: **feminine charm.**
fewer	Use with plurals: **fewer bills.**
less	Use with singulars: **less sugar, a man less.**
figuratively	means in an allied but not exact sense: **She (figuratively) broke his heart.**
literally	means exactly as stated. Wrong: **She literally broke his heart.**
find	➤ See **locate.**
first, firstly	Write either **first, second, third** or **firstly, secondly, thirdly,** but not a mixture.
flagrant	➤ See **blatant.**
flair	aptitude, knack
flare	a flame; a widening
flaunt	show off
flout	mock, scoff at
flounder	move clumsily
founder	fill with water and sink; fail
following	Prefer **after** as a preposition.
foot, feet	In compounds before a noun, use **foot: a six-foot pass.** In more formal and precise contexts, use **feet: six feet three inches.** In informal usage, **inches** is omitted and **foot** is usual: **six foot three.**
forbid	is followed by **to: The captain forbade them to go ashore.**
prohibit	is followed by **from: Government workers were prohibited from striking.**

forego	precede
forgo	abstain from
fortuitous	by chance
fortunate	lucky
fulsome	disgusting, loathsome, excessive
gambit	a chess opening in which a player sacrifices a piece to secure an advantage; any opening move
gamut	a whole series or scope of anything
gas	may be used for **gasoline** if there is no confusion with manufactured or natural gas.
generation	about 30 years
genius	➤ See **talent**.
gibe	➤ See **jibe**.
Gothic	of architecture: **a Gothic cathedral**
gothic	all other uses: **a gothic novel**
gourmand	a heavy eater
gourmet	a connoisseur of food
greeted by	used with people
greeted with	used with things
grill	a metal frame for cooking; question closely
grille	grating, screen
grisly	gruesome, horrible
grizzly	greyish, of bears and beards
hail	greet, call to
hale	take forcibly (as to court). But avoid.
hanged	killed by hanging
hung	suspended
happen	➤ See **transpire**.
hardly, barely, scarcely	1. These are used without a negative: I can (not **can't**) hardly read the small print.
	2. They are followed by **when**, not **than**: Scarcely had they got home when (not **than**) the phone rang.

historic	important or famous in history
historical	about or based on history
hoard	an amassed store (often of money)
horde	large group, pack
human (adjective)	used for both good and bad traits of humanity
humane	merciful, kind
humans	used in contrast to animals. In other cases, **human beings** is more appropriate.
hurting	normally requires object. **Poor sales hurt the company** (not **The company was hurting**); **Guy Carbonneau has been playing with knee problems** (not **Guy Carbonneau has been hurting**).
if and when	Use one, not both.
if, whether	are interchangeable when they make sense and are not ambiguous.
illusion	➤ See **allusion**.
immigrant	➤ See **emigrant**.
imminent	➤ See **eminent**.
imply	suggest or hint at; speakers or writers imply.
infer	deduce or conclude; hearers or readers infer.
inapt	unsuitable
inept	clumsy
infectious	➤ See **contagious**.
inflammable	Used interchangeably to mean capable of being set on fire. Prefer **flammable**.
inmate	occupant of a hospital, home, prison or other institution
prisoner, convict	occupant of a prison
insure	➤ See **ensure**.
irritate	➤ See **aggravate**.
it's	abbreviation for **it is** (or **it has**)
its	belonging to it (**held its own**)

jibe	agree or be in accord with
gibe	jeer, mock
judicial	of a judge or law court
judicious	sound of judgment
jurist	a person versed in law (not necessarily a lawyer or a judge)
laden	**a truck laden with melons** implies it is weighed down.
loaded	**a truck loaded with melons** is simply carrying melons.
lay (laying, laid, laid)	to lay something down (takes a direct object): **The boy laid the towel on the sand.**
lie (lying, lay, lain)	to recline (does not take a direct object): **Then he lay on the towel.**
lead (noun and verb)	metal; present tense of **to lead**
led (verb)	past tense of **to lead**
lectern	➤ See **podium.**
lend (lent,	Use as the verb: **Lend me your ears. Lend**
not **loaned)**	**me $10.**
loan	Use as the noun: **a $100 loan**
less	➤ See **fewer.**
lighted, lit	Used interchangeably in the past tense, though **lit** is more common: **The lamps were lighted/ lit.** As an adjective before a noun, **lighted** is preferable: **a lighted cigarette**; except when the adjective is preceded by an adverb: **a brightly lit room.**
like	Normal usage for examples is **Mother Teresa helped rescue people like the poor, the sick and the abandoned.**
such as	is often used to introduce examples set off with commas: **Several famous composers, such as Mozart and Schubert, died young.**
like - as	➤ See **as - like.**
likely, liable	➤ See **apt.**
linage	number of lines
lineage	ancestry, descent

lit	➤ See lighted.
literally	➤ See figuratively.
loaded	➤ See laden.
loath **loathe**	reluctant to detest
locate **find**	fix the position of (a downed aircraft) discover without reference to a particular setting (a missing child)
luxuriant **luxurious**	lush costly, rich
madam **madame**	a polite form of address: "No, madam"; a brothel-keeper a French title of respect: Madame Jules Benoit
male **masculine**	refers to sex of humans, animals or plants: a male lion. applies to qualities said to be characteristic of boys and men: masculine vigour. ➤ See gender.
masterful **masterly**	domineering expert, skilful
may (might)	➤ See can (could).
me, I	To, with, from and other prepositions are followed by me, him, her, us and them, not I, he, she, we or they: Mother gave it to Jack and me (not I). Put your trust in him (not he) who knows best. Many of us (not we) voters are tired of promises.
mediate **meter** **metre**	➤ See arbitrate. a measuring machine a measure of distance; a verse rhythm
meticulous **scrupulous**	careful about small details conscientious, thorough
migrant	➤ See emigrant.
momentarily	➤ See presently.
momentary **momentous**	short-lived, for a moment important

moral	virtuous; a lesson from a story
morale	mental attitude
more than	is followed by a singular verb when the noun is singular: **More than one tank was hit.**
	➤ See **over**.
myself	is properly used to intensify: **I myself wouldn't have gone.** Do not use it instead of **I** or **me**: **Gord and myself (I) weren't invited. The bride didn't invite Gord or myself (me).**
naked	the general word meaning without clothing or covering
nude	often a synonym for **naked**; otherwise usually restricted to artistic or pornographic contexts
nation	the people of a country
country	a nation's territory
nauseous	causing nausea, feeling nausea, nauseated
noxious	harmful, unpleasant
negligent	careless
negligible	small, unimportant
noisome	harmful, foul-smelling
no sooner	is followed by **than**, not **when**.
notable	worth noting
noticeable	easy to see, prominent
nude	➤ See **naked**.
number	➤ See **amount**.
O	is usually restricted to invocations: **O God, help me.** It is always capitalized and is written without a comma.
oh	is an exclamation: **Oh God, he's back. Oh, did he?** It is capitalized only at the start of a sentence. Write **oh-oh**, not **oh, oh**.
observance	obeying, paying heed to
observation	noting, looking at
obsolete	no longer in use
obsolescent	becoming obsolete

obviously	➤ See apparently.
official **officious**	connected with an office; authorized meddlesome, bossy
oh	➤ See O.
one another	➤ See each other.
one of those who **oral** **verbal**	is followed by a plural verb. spoken spoken or written
over	In the sense of *in excess of,* used interchangeably with **more than**: **Creasey and Simenon have each published over (more than) 500 books.**
pair	generally plural: **The pair were seen with their son. But A pair receives a smaller pension.**
paramount **tantamount**	supreme equal to
parliamentarian	an expert in parliamentary procedure; a skilled debater; not a synonym for MP
peddle **pedal**	sell; a **pedlar** sells. cycle; a **pedaller** pushes pedals; to **softpedal** is to play music with the soft pedal down.
people **persons**	In general, use **people**, even if the number is small or precise: **Two people died.** Better: **A man and a woman died.** Use for formality or occasional variety: **Persons over 21 are eligible.**
perquisite **prerequisite**	special privilege, advantage (a perk) a necessary condition
persuade	➤ See convince.
podium **lectern**	the platform a speaker stands on the reading desk a speaker stands behind
practicable **practical**	able to be done useful, sensible, functional

precede	to go before
proceed	to go along, continue
prerequisite	➤ See **perquisite**.
presently	soon, in a moment (**avoid:** usually misunderstood)
at present	now
momentarily	for a moment
presume	➤ See **assume**.
principal	chief, most important; capital sum; school head
principle	basic truth or rule; code of conduct
prior to	Use **before**.
prisoner	➤ See **inmate**.
prohibit	➤ See **forbid**.
prone	➤ See **supine**.
protagonist	chief actor, champion of a cause
antagonist	opponent
punctilious	attentive to detail
punctual	prompt
quartet	➤ See **trio**.
rack (noun)	framework: **hat-rack**
rack (verb)	to trouble, torture, destroy: **nerve-racking**
wrack (noun)	wreckage, seaweed
rampage	➤ See **spree**.
rankle	A thing **rankles**; it does not **rankle** someone. Right: **The insult rankled.** Wrong: **The insult rankled Joe.**
ravage	damage badly, devastate
ravish	delight, enrapture; rape
reason	is followed by **that** or **why**, not because: **The reason for the loss was that taxes rose.**
rebut, refute	prove to be false: **She refuted the charge of theft by producing a sales receipt.**
deny	declare to be false: **He denied the charge but had no alibi.**

regretful full of regret
  regrettable the cause of regret

reign monarch's rule
  rein harness

reluctant unwilling, grudging
  reticent sparing of words, reserved

repetitive characterized by repetition: **a repetitive beat**

  repetitious characterized by unnecessary or tedious repetition: **repetitious arguments**

revenge ➤ See avenge.

revolve ➤ See centre.

rob A person or place is robbed, not the thing stolen: **A company was robbed of a payroll.** Not: **A company's payroll was robbed.**

rush Do not use when the idea of speed is implicit, as in stories involving ambulances, fire trucks and police cruisers. Not: **She was rushed to hospital.** Write **taken** or some such.

scarce of things normally available
  rare of things seldom found at any time

scarcely ➤ See hardly.

scrupulous ➤ See meticulous.

seasonable suitable to the occasion or season
  seasonal occurring at a particular season

sensual arousing or satisfying bodily appetites or sexual desire: **the sensual pleasures of eating; a sensual striptease**

  sensuous appealing to the senses, sometimes the mind: **a ballet dancer's sensuous movements; a sensuous passage of Mozart**

ship ➤ See boat.

shot Use the specific **shot and wounded** or **shot and killed** as appropriate.

situation	Avoid the practice of putting other nouns or phrases before **situation**: a crisis situation, a classroom situation, a bad-debt situation.
some	meaning *about* is proper: some 20 years later, some 500 troops.
spare	scanty, frugal; thin: a spare diet, a spare style of writing; a spare man
sparse	thinly scattered, not thick: a sparse population, a sparse beard
specially	for a particular purpose
especially	to a great degree, outstanding
spectators	➤ See audience.
stationary	unmoving
stationery	writing material
stimulant	drug, etc. (not alcohol, a depressant)
stimulus	incentive, spur
strait	narrow, confined (**straitjacket**, Davis Strait)
straight	unbent, direct
strategy	refers to the overall campaign.
tactics	the art of moving forces; adroit management
such as	➤ See like.
supine	face upward (but **avoid**)
prone	face downward
tack	course of action or policy
tact	ability to deal sensitively with others; sensitivity
tactics	➤ See strategy.
talent	special ability
genius	exceptionally great talent
tantamount	➤ See paramount.

that

As a conjunction, *that* may be omitted if no confusion results: **King said (that) she would go.** It is often needed after such verbs as **assert, declare, estimate, make clear, point out, propose, state, warn: She warned** that **the committee would oppose the plan.** It may be needed with time elements (**White said** that **in 1950 he was destitute**) and before such conjunctions as **after, although, as, because, before, in addition to, when: Green said** that **when she heard the shot, she was asleep.**

that

often introduces an essential clause — one that defines the noun it is attached to and cannot be omitted: **The house that is painted white is mine.**

which

introduces a non-essential or parenthetical clause — one that adds information that could be omitted without changing meaning: **The house, which was built in 1940, is white.**

that-who

➤ See **which-who-that**.

the

Do not drop *the* from the beginning of sentences or wherever idiom or grammar demands it. Not: **Terms of the contract were secret; Police would not reveal names of the injured.**

then

Avoid putting *then* as an adjective before a noun if it sounds equally well or better in its normal position. Not: **the then prime minister, Lester Pearson.** But: **the prime minister then, Lester Pearson.**

transpire
happen

become known
occur

trio, quartet

Use only in the musical sense, not of any casual grouping of three or four.

troops

In general, **troops** describes a body of soldiers: **The troops were flown in by helicopter.** It is not used of small numbers of individuals: **30 troops.** But idiom permits its use with large numbers, say in the hundreds: **Some 250 troops surrounded the prison.**

try to	try to (not and) understand
uninterested	➤ See **disinterested**.
unsatisfied **dissatisfied**	falling short of satisfaction discontented
upcoming	Write **coming, approaching** or **forthcoming** if an adjective is needed.
urban **urbane**	of a town or city well-bred, suave
verbal	➤ See **oral**.
vessel	➤ See **boat**.
veteran	one who served in the military; person of long experience. Avoid such descriptions as **five-year police veteran** and **a veteran of four NHL seasons**.
vocation	➤ See **avocation**.
waive **waver**	give up, forgo falter, move to and fro
-ward, -wards	Americans prefer the **-ward** form: **toward, backward, afterward**; Britons prefer **-wards: towards, backwards, afterwards**; Canadians use both forms.
was **were**	simple past tense Use **were** when expressing a wish or a condition contrary to fact, and after **as if** and **as though**: I wish I were you. She spoke to him as if he were a fool.
whether, if	➤ See **if, whether**.
whether or not	Retain the *or not* when an alternative is emphasized: **I will go whether you like it or not**.
which-that	➤ See **that-which**.

which normally refers to things but may be used of people in a body: **She spoke to the crowd, which grew silent.**

who usually refers to people but sometimes to animals, especially those with names: **Snip, who is 14, is a toy poodle.**

that refers to people or things: **It was the pilot that (or who) spoke.**

while (noun) They had to wait for a while. (note the for).

awhile (adverb) They had to wait awhile. (no preposition).

who-whom Who stands for **he-she-they, whom** for **him-her-them.** When in doubt, break the sentence in two: **She met a man who she thought was her brother.** (She thought **he** was her brother, so **who** is correct.) **She met a man** whom **she took for her brother.** (She took **him** for her brother, so **whom** is correct.)

wove the normal past tense of **weave: His daughter wove him a scarf.**

weaved the past tense of **weave** means to avoid hitting something: **The forward weaved through the defence**; or to tell an involved story: **The old man weaved a chilling plot.**

wrack ➤ See rack.

yoke wooden crosspiece
yolk yellow of an egg

The news report

Advances

General

Reports based on scientific and medical studies, speeches and other material are routinely provided to the media in advance of their delivery to the public. That allows reporters to treat the material more carefully and organize background or explanations as needed.

Reporters on regular health beats often sign agreements with medical journals that allow them to see embargoed studies in advance. Accidental embargo breaks can result in sanctions and loss of access for a period of time, which puts a news organization at a disadvantage.

Some of this material can be distributed early by a news agency, embargoed for release at a time set by the source of the study or speech. Through coding, The Canadian Press usually limits the relay of advance copy to its newspaper and broadcast clients only, so they can process the material in time for their next deadline or newscast. Advance material is not sent to online and database services, since this would mean instant publication. Once the embargo has passed, such stories move to online and database services.

Keep in mind that items such as advisories are sent to databases so the content of an embargoed story should not be revealed in an advisory before release time. If the story originates with a medical journal, it's advisable to keep the wording in the advisory vague.

TORONTO — A new study will be released on cancer care. EMBARGOED until 5 p.m. EDT.

Broken embargoes

1. Canadian Press editors should tell the source of embargoed material that we will abide by the release time only as long as others do. In virtually all cases, we will release the material immediately if someone else is found to have broken the embargo.

2. However, if it appears that the embargo was broken in a very limited way, perhaps accidentally, by one media outlet, check with a supervisor before releasing the story onto all Canadian Press services. If the original report was limited in play, it may not justify releasing it into the wide sweep of the agency's network.

3. Send an advisory if an embargo has been broken.

> **Royal, Release Advisory**
> **EDs:** Toronto Royal-Bank on the Royal Bank of Canada's annual report, moved in advance for release at 10 a.m. EDT, is now available for publication. The embargo has been broken by other media.
> **THE CANADIAN PRESS TORONTO**

Speeches

1. Stories about speeches distributed before the speech is delivered need a phrase such as **in a speech prepared for delivery to.** A separate paragraph can say **A text of the governor's address was provided to the news media before delivery.** The paragraph should be easy to drop if a newspaper or website wants to do so after the speech is delivered.

2. Writethrus to correct or update a story moved in advance must be transmitted promptly. An important addition by the speaker is indicated by saying **Madhani digressed from her prepared speech and . . .** If there is an important omission, say so and indicate in the story the wording of the original text.

3. When a speech has been delivered and the advance stands, move it again with the paragraph referring to the advance text deleted. Advise editors in a note at the top of the Writethru.

Removes reference to text being provided in advance. Speech was delivered as written.

4. When a text contains controversial or spectacular statements, every effort should be made to confirm the statements were indeed made. If The Canadian Press cannot staff the speech, arrangements should be made for a fast check with an assigned newspaper or broadcast reporter.

5. When a speaker drops a controversial statement from a speech, this is sometimes more important than the speech itself if it indicates a change in policy or a moderation of tone. The speaker must always be questioned about the reason for the omission. Seek reaction from others involved in the issue.

Advance slugs

1. Advance items carry cautionary slugs. Style examples follow.

2. Embargo times should normally be in eastern time. Specific times in the body of a story, however, are not changed to their eastern equivalent.

3. To avoid misunderstanding, explain to sources issuing important releases that newspapers need lead time in order to print the story; a release time of 6:30 p.m., for instance, means the article won't be published in a newspaper until the next day.

Sometimes sources will set off-hour embargo times, such as 3 a.m. They want it picked up in that day's newspapers but are trying to avoid it from being used in a previous-night newscast or online before the morning. On such embargoes, be clear in an Editors note that the item is not to be used online or on-air before then. (See examples below.)

Style for slugs

Follow these styles for advances.

1. On copy for a specific time for all services:

> **Prisons, Advance**
> **EDs: HOLD FOR RELEASE UNTIL 3 A.M. EDT WEDNESDAY, MAY 28. DO NOT POST ONLINE, BROADCAST OR PUBLISH BEFORE 3 A.M. EDT WEDNESDAY.**

Once the embargo is lifted, retransmit the story on all services, adding the following note in the slugging: **Eds: Repeat of earlier embargoed story.**

2. On feature copy where the embargo applies only to online use:

> **Prisons, Advance**
> **Eds: HOLD FOR RELEASE ONLINE UNTIL 3 A.M. WEDNESDAY, MAY 28.**

Advisories

"Extra! Extra! Triple murder!" Like an old-time newsboy hawking papers on the corner, The Canadian Press knows that to move news, you have to get the paying customers' attention.

The media organizations that The Canadian Press serves want to know:

• About the news that's coming 10 minutes from now, and in the day ahead.

• What's happening tomorrow? Next week? Next month?

• Will there be pictures, video and graphics?

• Anything special in the report that will be worth planning for?

These questions and others are answered by means of *advisories* — notes to editors transmitted along with the news copy.

Some are improvised, pounded out as a hot story breaks and develops. Some are routine — **Top News** advisories, which move several times a day; daily **Calendars** of news events and the weekly **Look-Ahead List**. Others are issued in advance of major events such as elections to detail Canadian Press coverage plans. Still others commend editors' attention to special projects the agency is undertaking.

All are driven by the same rationale: customers expect information from an information company.

Advisories

Editors say the most helpful thing The Canadian Press can do is keep them fully and quickly informed. Not only when big news breaks but as it develops, situations change and deadlines approach.

If a story expected at 9:30 a.m. is going to be delayed, send an advisory. Explain the delay if possible.

But editors also need to know about what's happening beyond the day's top news. They want advisories as early as possible on major long-range plans for enterprise series, foreign assignments, advance stories leading up to a political leadership convention and the like.

And make no mistake: these advisories translate directly into play.

Spot breaks

1. The phone rings. A major break seems to be in the making. But there is no immediate official confirmation. Remember: editors somewhere are waiting for the story — either on air, online or in a newspaper. They want a message like this:

> **Tornado, Advisory**
> **CP checking report of major tornado near Olds, Alta.**
>   Eds: The Canadian Press is checking a report that a major tornado has touched down near Olds, Alta., about a 40-minute drive north of Calgary. Official word is expected from police shortly. There are no confirmed reports of injuries or damage at the moment.
>   **THE CANADIAN PRESS EDMONTON**

2. Always put confirmed facts into a publishable story, not an advisory. But keep editors up to the minute as coverage plans take shape. Don't wait until an eyewitness account or other strong sidebar is fully written before sending a tip. Send fast word on the timing of a news conference or official police statement. Move an immediate advisory if a scheduled briefing is delayed or cancelled. Advisories take seconds to write and send. One advisory may save a dozen phone calls, crucial during a major breaking story.

> **Tornado, 1st Writethru Advisory**
> **Media briefing in Olds, Alta., on tornado damage**
>   Eds: The town clerk of Olds, Alta., will brief reporters on the tornado that struck today, killing at least seven people and causing severe damage throughout the area north of Calgary. The briefing will be held in the town office at 4911 51st Ave. at 11:45 a.m. The Canadian Press is staffing.
>   **THE CANADIAN PRESS EDMONTON**

3. Give editors and producers as full a rundown as possible on plans for copy, photos, graphics, audio and video. This can be done in either a Top News advisory or a separate advisory:

>   Eds: Besides the budgeted stories **Tornado**, **Tornado-Victims** and **Tornado-Rebuild**, there will be separates on past tornadoes in the West (**Undated—Tornado-Past**) and how tornadoes are formed (**Undated—Tornado-Profile**), a first-person account, including video, by a man who saw the tornado strike (**Tornado-Eyewitness**), a QuickSketch, QuickQuotes, Graphics and Photos.
>   **THE CANADIAN PRESS EDMONTON**

Co-ordinate advisory handling with Head Office or another bureau when appropriate:

> Eds: A list of major Canadian disasters this century will move shortly.
> **THE CANADIAN PRESS TORONTO**
>
> Eds: The prime minister is expected to comment on today's tornado in southern Alberta at 3:45 p.m. EDT. John Ward of The Canadian Press is covering.
> **THE CANADIAN PRESS OTTAWA**

➤ See **Big Breaking News**, page 146.

Planned events

1. Expected timing of copy on staged events is vitally important as well. Editors want to know whether copy will move in time for final deadlines. Tell them:

> **CRIME-Girls-Frozen, Advisory**
> **RCMP hold media availability on freezing death of two young sisters**
> Editors: The RCMP are holding a media availability at 11:45 a.m. CST at F Division headquarters in Regina about charges being laid in the deaths of two young girls who froze on the Yellow Quill First Nation in January. Jennifer Graham of The Canadian Press is staffing.
> **THE CANADIAN PRESS EDMONTON**

2. Send an advisory if something unexpected happens at a scheduled event:

> **French-Open, Advisory**
> **French Open rain advisory**
> Eds: Play at the French Open has been called off for the day because of rain.
> **THE CANADIAN PRESS**

Publishable and non-publishable notes

Advisories carried on the top of stories fall into two general categories: publishable and non-publishable. The former are aimed at the reader. The latter are for editors' information.

Publishable:

NHL Preview: Detroit Red Wings offer "new look"
The following story is one in a series by Canadian Press sports writers previewing the new National Hockey League season. Neil Stevens of Toronto reports on the "new-look" Detroit Red Wings and their chances of improving their strong finish in the Central Division last season.
By Neil Stevens
THE CANADIAN PRESS
DETROIT — Gordie Howe may have put it best . . .

And at the end of the story:

. . . nowhere to go but up."
Next: Jim Morris of Vancouver looks at the Vancouver Canucks.

Non-publishable:

Eds: Petr (not Peter) in the following is correct. Macdonald is lowercase "d."

Top News advisories

The Canadian Press moves advisories throughout the daily news cycle from each department (such as Sports or Entertainment) and each regional news bureau that showcase the top news stories and give editors a head's up on what is coming up. The very top news items from each of those advisories is compiled into an overall Top News Advisory that also moves throughout the day.

Friday, July 9, 2010
12:30 noon.
TOP NEWS ADVISORY
Here are the latest Top News stories from The Canadian Press. All times are Eastern unless otherwise stated. Coverage plans are included when available. Entries are subject to change as news develops. This advisory replaces The Canadian Press News Budget.
Contact the National Desk at 416-555-5555.

TOP STORIES THIS HOUR
Big month for employment: 93,200 new jobs in June
Jobs
OTTAWA — Canada pumped out jobs at a spectacular pace in June, outstripping the United States and most other advanced economies and reducing the unemployment rate to its lowest level since early last year. Statistics Canada said the economy had created a whopping 93,200 new jobs last month — almost all in Ontario and Quebec and all in the services sector. AUDIO.

B.C.'s 2010 Olympic bill nears $1 billion; $160 million over budget
OLY-BC-Bills
VANCOUVER — The province of British Columbia says it spent $925 million to host the 2010 Winter Olympic and Paralympic Games. That's $160 million more than the official Olympic budget of $765 million. Will be updated.

Petraeus makes quick visit to Kandahar
Afghan-Cda-Petraeus
KANDAHAR, Afghanistan — New NATO commander Gen. David Petraeus touched down in Kandahar briefly today on his first visit to the area where the bulk of U.S. troops will be battling the Taliban. Petraeus arrived via a Blackhawk helicopter and landed at one of a dozen security checkpoints set up on major routes around Kandahar city. AUDIO.

Cold War redux: US, Russia swap 14 spies in Vienna
Russia-Spy Arrests
MOSCOW — The U.S. and Russia orchestrated the largest spy swap since the Cold War, exchanging 10 spies arrested in the United States for four convicted in Russia in a tightly choreographed diplomatic dance today at Vienna's airport. Two planes — one from New York and another from Moscow — arrived in Vienna within minutes of each other, parked nose-to-tail at a remote section on the tarmac, then spent about an hour and a half before departing. A small bus was seen moving between the two planes. British media later said the U.S. plane landed at a military base in England. AUDIO. PHOTO. BUZZ

Giddy-up! Calgary Stampede kicks off with parade
Stampede-Parade
CALGARY — Thousands of people packed downtown Calgary to watch the so-called greatest outdoor show on Earth kick off with a bang. Prime Minister Stephen Harper launched the Calgary Stampede parade by setting off a series of fireworks that flew high above the crowd. PHOTO. Will be updated; Harper attends reception at 5:45 p.m. local time.

Queen to become great-grandmother, palace says
EU-Britain-Royal-Great-Grandchild
LONDON — The Queen will soon become a great-grandmother for the first time. Buckingham Palace says Peter Phillips, the son of Princess Anne, and his wife, Montreal-born Autumn, are expecting their first child in December.

COMING LATER TODAY
TORONTO — Lloyd Robertson, chief anchor of CTV News who will retire in 2011, will greet his successor. 2 p.m.
CALGARY _ Prime Minister Stephen Harper attends a reception after a parade kicks off the Calgary Stampede. 7:45 p.m. ET.

COMING THIS WEEKEND
Sunday
KANESATAKE, Que. — A peace march is held to commemorate the 20th anniversary of the beginning of the Oka Crisis. 10 a.m.

Long-range advisories

1. Advance billing on special projects, foreign travel and other major assignments means better play. Editors will look for the copy and use the advance notice to block out space days ahead of time. An advance advisory also gives papers a chance to plan local follows, often a key selling point. An example:

Food-Fear, Advisory
The Canadian Press begins a series this week on world food crisis and its impact on Canada

In the Philippines, "rice access cards" are being issued. In Ethiopia, subsidized wheat is being distributed in urban centres. Brazil and many other countries have banned rice exports.

Around the world, governments are using every means at their disposal to stave off riots in the face of burgeoning costs and shortages of food staples.

What is behind this food crisis and what will Canadians face?

Over the next two weeks, The Canadian Press will move a multi-part series that looks at these issues. Stories will carry the common slug Food-Fear and be accompanied by photos, graphics, including a logo, and video. Each story stands on its own and can be used separately, although the series is also designed to be used together in a weekend section.

The series will include the following stories:

Moved Monday, May 12:
FOOD-File-Fears

TORONTO — The spectre of rising world food prices could force Canadians used to buying whatever foods strike their fancy to change their habits — and use the careful spending example set by their parents and grandparents. Home economists who remember the days when shopping was all about economy and not about gourmet products offer advice on how to cut down the weekly grocery bill. 700 words. By Judy Creighton. PHOTOS, Recipes, QuickTips.

Moving Tuesday, May 13:
Food-Fear-Prices

UNDATED — Take a wealthier China, add a dash of biofuel, stir in some profit-seeking investors and you've got the recipe for what some are calling a global food crisis. It isn't clear which of these ingredients is most responsible for a spike in crop prices that have panicked many of the world's most populated countries. By Lauren Krugel. VIDEO, GRAPHIC.

Food-Fear-Consumers

TORONTO — The two-bag limit did little to curb the recent run on rice at Hong Tai Supermarket, an Asian supermarket in the city's east end — but store manager Ann Luong said the $4 increase did. Some Canadian consumers may be feeling anxious about the ripple effect rising costs could have on their supply as well as their wallets. By Lauren La Rose. PHOTO.

Moving Wednesday, May 14:

Food-Fear-Canada

OTTAWA — Canadians can be excused for wondering at the turmoil around the world over exploding food prices that threaten to starve some of the poorer parts of the developing world. But our good luck with relatively tame food prices is likely to run out in 2009. 800 words. By Julian Beltrame.

Food-Fear-Farmers

VEGREVILLE, Alta. — The vanity plate on Ken Farion's pickup in the driveway of his Alberta farmhouse reads DRTPOR. Given the way wheat prices have sprouted lately, he may have to change that. "The optimism is so great this year," he says. "I'm going to seed the maximum possible acreage." By Bob Weber. VIDEO, PHOTOS.

Moving Friday, May 19:

FOOD-Fear-Restaurants

TORONTO — Restaurants face a double whammy with rising food and fuel prices. First they must deal with paying more for their ingredients. Then they have to hope their customers still feel rich enough to eat out regularly. 500 words. By Judy Creighton. PHOTOS, VIDEO.

If you have any questions, please call Senior Supervising Editor Patti Tasko at 416-555-5555.

THE CANADIAN PRESS TORONTO

Other advisories

The range of potential advisories is unbounded.

There is a simple test: If an editor was on deadline or planning ahead, would an advisory help?

Here are some examples of useful advisories:

High-Skydiver, Advisory

French adventurer Michel Fournier holds news conference at 4 p.m.

Eds: French adventurer Michel Fournier and his organizers are holding a news conference at 4 p.m. CST about what went wrong today as he tried to launch into the stratosphere to attempt a high skydiving record. Jennifer Graham of The Canadian Press is staffing.

THE CANADIAN PRESS EDMONTON

Brownwich, Advisory

Trial of former P.E.I. cabinet minister resumes at 10 a.m. AST Monday

Eds: The trial of former P.E.I. cabinet minister Ethel Brownwich resumes at 10 a.m. AST Monday with testimony from her secretary. Alison Auld of The Canadian Press is staffing and expects to file a story by noon AST, depending on the testimony.

THE CANADIAN PRESS HALIFAX

Aboriginal-Occupation, Advisory
First Nations news conference in Maycroft, Alta., cancelled
Eds: The Maycroft, Alta., budget item Aboriginal Occupation will not be available. A news conference scheduled for 2 p.m. MDT Thursday was cancelled. An unbudgeted 250-word story will move by 5 p.m. MDT, and if there are further developments later in the day an advisory will be sent outlining coverage plans.
THE CANADIAN PRESS EDMONTON

Calendar and Look-Ahead

Few features of journalism can match the exhilaration of covering a sudden, fast-breaking story. Few frustrations can match trying to catch up with a major story that could have been foreseen and planned for if it hadn't been for neglected datebooking.

Every Canadian Press bureau and department seeks out hints of news to come in the reams of news releases, newsletters, emails, press kits and other material that are directed its way.

The agency keeps track of coming events for its own coverage planning and to inform its newspaper and broadcast customers. There are two main advisories focused on scheduled news events, the weekly **Look-Ahead** list and the daily **Calendar**.

The **Look-Ahead** is assembled in Toronto from a central electronic datebook maintained by bureaus and departments. It moves each Thursday afternoon and covers events, by date, from the Sunday of the following weekend through two weeks down the road.

The **Calendar**, also prepared in Toronto, lists events for the following day and is transmitted at about 3 p.m., 6 p.m. and 1 a.m. The Calendar sent Fridays covers events through Monday.

The format for contributions to both these lists is the same: a brief description of the event, time, place and any other information useful to regional newspapers or broadcasters who may plan to cover. An **x-** in front of the placeline denotes that The Canadian Press is staffing the event; a **y-** denotes picture coverage; and a **z-** denotes graphics coverage.

Examples:

HALIFAX — Nova Scotia standing committee on human resources to discuss appointments to agencies, boards and commissions. (9 a.m. at Room 1, 3rd floor, Dennis building, 1740 Granville St.)

xy-OTTAWA — Daily question period. (2:15 p.m. at House of Commons, Centre Block, Parliament Hill.)

> CALGARY — Barbara Kingsolver and husband Steven Hopp talk about their novel "Animal, Vegetable, Miracle," their search for an alternative way to eat and live. (7:30 p.m. at Knox United Church, 444 Seventh Ave.)

- Specify when times, places are unavailable. But such detail, or an explanation for its absence, is essential when the event carries an **x-**.

- Description of the event should be brief but still spell out its news interest.

Not: Joe Saxon appears in court.

But: Joe Saxon, accused of attacking a neighbour with an electric weed trimmer, stands trial for first-degree murder.

- Entries into the datebook database should be in full — no in-house abbreviations such as newser for news conference. Full names and titles are required, as they would be in a news story.

Calendar updates and changes

When it is necessary to update, correct, delete or add a Calendar item, include a word specific to the topic in the slug. It should be **Calendar-Inuit** so editors can easily pinpoint what is being changed:

> **Calendar-Inuit**
> **Inuit meeting postponed until May 13**
>   Eds: Please note that the Calendar item from IQALUIT, Nunavut, on the meeting of Inuit leaders is incorrect. The meeting has been postponed until May 13.
>   **THE CANADIAN PRESS EDMONTON**

Online news advisories

Another type of advisory that The Canadian Press produces regularly are ones advising editors what websites are reporting. These advisories also include the note (CVD) to indicate whether The Canadian Press wire is covered on the story.

> **Web-Fronts-Globe**
> The top news stories on the Globe and Mail's website for June 6, 2010:
> Gulf oil spill's threat to wildlife turns real (CVD) B.C. voters must stop 'dreaded HST', NDP urge (CVD) Canadians protest response to Israel flotilla action (CVD) Peter MacKay, fiancee split up (CVD) Stephen Hawking ready to get to work in Canada (CVD)

Broadcast formats

Although most stories break on the print and broadcast wires together, either as NewsAlerts or QuickHits, formatted items designed specifically for broadcast use usually follow.

Separates

For broadcasters, the **separate** is the building block of the data service. Not only do they provide up-to-date news, they include details, colour, and background, which are useful for rewrites over several news cycles. Separates run to a maximum of 150 words.

Each separate is identified with a slug that should convey as much about a story as possible in as few words as possible. Regardless of developments, a story will bear the same slug for its duration as news.

Separates also carry a placeline. Well-known cities, such as provincial capitals, are not further identified. Lesser-known cities are followed by their province, state or country.

When significant new developments occur, a new separate is sent, with the word "Update" added to the slug. This is followed by a few words in brackets outlining what's new.

> Federal-Budget
> Federal-Budget-Update (details of tax cuts)
> Federal Budget-Update (finance minister's comments)
> Federal Budget-Update (opposition reaction)

The source of the story is included in brackets at the end of the separate. This indicates whether the material originated with The Canadian Press, Associated Press or a client news station.

Roundups

Sometimes it takes more than a 150-word separate to adequately cover a story and its developments and complications. In these cases, different but related stories are combined into a roundup, which contains from two to eight separate angles. The slug is followed by the word **Roundup**.

Each item in a roundup is identified by a separate slug, helping newscasters choose what to read. Items are generally written tighter and provide less background than separates.

> --**Terror Roundup**--
>
> (Canadians-Afghanistan)
> A small group of Canadian soldiers has arrived in Kandahar, and is looking for a place to establish a camp.

Over a dozen troops are touring the area where a 750-member Canadian battle group will operate within a month.

The Canadians will help the Americans root out die-hard Taliban and al-Qaida fighters, guard the Kandahar airport, remove mines and protect aid convoys and workers. (The Canadian Press)

(U-N-Afghanistan)

The U-N Security Council has imposed sanctions against Osama bin Laden, his al-Qaida network and remnants of the Taliban.

The resolution, adopted unanimously, requires all countries to impose an arms embargo and a travel ban on individuals and groups associated with them, while freezing their financial assets.

An American official says it will help accomplish the U-S administration's goal of going after the Taliban and al-Qaida wherever they may be hiding and operating. (The Associated Press)

(Terror-Canadian Passport)

Intelligence sources say one of the ringleaders of an al-Qaida cell accused of plotting to blow up U-S soldiers, ships and several embassies in Singapore, was carrying a Canadian passport.

The Arab man, who called himself "Sammy," was allegedly the director of a cell, who picked targets in Singapore and conducted video surveillance of them beginning in October, 2001.

He was carrying a Canadian passport in the name of Jabarah Mohd Mansur. (The Canadian Press)

Packaging the news

Top stories are told over and over during the course of a day or several days, as the story develops. These stories have often been sent already as separates, but packaged items are more tightly written, containing only the most interesting facts.

NewsWatches

National **NewsWatches** are a summary of the six top national and international stories, presented in order of importance.

The lead item in the NewsWatch can change frequently or stay the same depending on the story. If the top story remains the same, the item is rewritten for each individual NewsWatch. For example, a federal budget may be the top story for several hours, even into the next morning. One NewsWatch item could focus on tax cuts, the next on new government spending, another on deficits, and so on. Morning copy could cover reaction.

Information on matching audio is provided for at least two stories.

NewsWatches usually end with a lighter item, such as a lifestyles, health, entertainment or a humorous story known as a kicker.

Stories in all NewsWatches are identified with the same slug as the matching wire separate. That slug is found at the top of each story, in brackets, at the far left.

While NewsWatches are designed to form the basis of a complete national newscast, each story is written to stand alone.

To allow subscribers to easily identify the latest NewsWatch in their computer directory, the files are numbered from one through 20, and the number is included in the slug. The number of the NewsWatch is also in brackets at the end of each story.

--Tenth NewsWatch--

(New Defence-Chief) (Audio: P01)

Defence Minister Peter MacKay calls him a gentleman general.

Lieutenant-General Walter Natynczyk (nuh-TIN'-chuck) has been named the new chief of defence staff.

The Winnipeg native currently serves as vice-chief.

His rank will be upgraded to general when he replaces outgoing General Rick Hillier, who is stepping down Canada Day.

Natynczyk says he's honoured to have been appointed as Canada's top military officer.

He says one of his first priorities will be to visit the troops in Afghanistan. (10)

(BIZ-GM-Cuts) (Audio: 113)

General Motors says a plant in Oshawa, Ontario will close as planned.

The head of the Canadian Auto Workers union emerged from a one-hour meeting in Detroit with G-M brass angry and disappointed.

Hargrove says the union is currently evaluating its options.

He hasn't ruled out a full-scale walkout.

C-A-W members are protesting for a third day at G-M's Canadian headquarters in Oshawa and local union officials say that protest will continue. (10)

(TSX Record-Oil) (Audio: 099)

The soaring price of oil is pushing the market's main index in Toronto to new highs.

The S&P/T-S-X hit an inter-day record of 15,154.77 points this morning before falling back.

It came as oil surpassed 134-dollars a barrel.

The R-B-C's John Johnston says he sees a correction in oil prices coming over the summer months -- but he predicts prices will stay at current levels over the long term. (10)

(RCMP-Class-Action)

A disabled ex-Mountie hopes to take Ottawa to court.

The proposed suit alleges the federal government clawed back money from his disability award.

Fifty-year-old Gary Buote of Summerside, P-E-I claims he was forced out of the service in 1993 after being injured on the job four years earlier.

He's seeking compensation for himself -- and possibly thousands of others -- who are also having "pain-and-suffering" payments deducted from their pensions. (10)

(US-Democrats)

Hillary Clinton will officially end her presidential campaign at an event in Washington tomorrow.

Her campaign says she will thank supporters and formally endorse Barack Obama in a speech at noon (eastern time).

The New York senator is expected to urge Democrats to unite behind Obama to help him defeat Republican John McCain in November. (10)

(Japan-Company-Diets)

It pays to be fit in Japan.

Under new laws that kicked in April 1st, companies can be penalized by the government if their workers aren't healthy.

Workers aged 40 to 74 are now required to have their waist measured at health checkups.

If waistlines don't improve in five years' time, companies will be forced to pay higher premiums that feed into national health care insurance for people 75 and older. (10)

(NewsWatch by Rose Smith)

Packaged rewrites in the NewsWatch format are also moved in categories such as regional news, business and entertainment.

Sports packages

The **Sports Summary**, which moves in the morning, is an in-depth look at all the major events in the sports world and is intended for longer morning sportscasts. The **Sportsbreak** is made up of six to eight items that are shorter in length and is designed to provide a quick overview of the sports world. **Sportsminutes** move at night to provide a snapshot of the top events. Each item is a maximum of two sentences, written to allow as many stories as possible to be delivered in 60 seconds.

Audio skeds

An audio sked is a wrap-around script that first introduces the newsmaker being quoted in the accompanying audio clip, then finishes off the story. The intro and extro must be written clearly and concisely so that it's the newsmaker who delivers the news.

Audio cuts are streamed into national, parliamentary, regional, and sports categories. A slug identifies where the audio is coming from and what time it is sent.

NATIONAL Audio 1:15 p.m. ET

128 - (Bernier-Fallout)

OTTAWA. x--16s. The Harper government continues to dismiss security concerns over the Bernier-Couillard affair despite new media reports that raise fresh questions. The C-B-C is reporting Julie Couillard met with a man closely tied to criminal bikers in 2006 -- less than a year before she began dating then-foreign affairs minister Maxime Bernier. The Globe and Mail newspaper reported today Couillard's house was under R-C-M-P surveillance in 1998. In the Commons today, Liberal M-P Bob Rae asked how much the government knew about Couillard's past.

("...Madame Couillard.") (SOURCE:The Canadian Press) (115p)

TAG: The Tories maintain it is a private matter and refuse to discuss it.

129 - (BIZ-Jobs)

TORONTO. x--17s. The national unemployment rate was unchanged in May at 6.1 per cent as the economy created only 84-hundred new jobs. Thirty-two-thousand-200 full-time jobs were lost -- replaced by the creation of 40-thousand-600 part-time jobs. Bank of Montreal analyst Doug Porter says it's not good news -- but it doesn't indicate a recession.

("...in the U-S." (SOURCE:The Canadian Press) (115p)

TAG: Porter predicts the Bank of Canada will cut its key rate again at Tuesday's setting following today's jobs report.

The subject of the audio is identified in brackets after the cut number. The skeds include a placeline, the length of the cut, and the source. The same slug is used for both audio and wire stories.

Correcting mistakes

The general guidelines for correcting mistakes, found in Corrections and Correctives (page 466), apply to the broadcast service. There are some specifics that apply to broadcast items only.

Errors on the broadcast wire are identified by the word **CORRECTION**, followed by the slug of the original story and time of its transmission. The reason for the correction is outlined in brackets on a separate line. The entire story is then repeated, with the correct information. Important corrections — for example when a story may be legally dangerous — are also sent with an urgent slug.

Slugs for Corrections on NewsWatches and other packaged rewrites not only indicate which package is being corrected, but also which item is being corrected. The corrected story, not the entire package, is repeated.

For an error in a Separate:

CORRECTION-NBA Jordan Divorce

Please replace the item NBA-Jordan-Divorce, which moved around 11:10 p-m E-T.

(Fixes first paragraph to show couple married for 12 years, not 13)

CHICAGO -- The Chicago Tribune says Michael Jordan's wife has filed for divorce, seeking to dissolve her 12-year marriage to the world's most famous basketball player.

The newspaper says Juanita Jordan cited irreconcilable differences in seeking a dissolution of her marriage to Jordan.

She seeks permanent custody of the couple's three children, the 25-thousand-square-foot marital residence in suburban Chicago, and half the couple's property.

Jordan cited a desire to spend more time with his family when he retired from the Bulls the first time in October 1994, and again in January 1999.

He maintained his Chicago-area residence when he returned to basketball as a front-office executive with the Washington Wizards last season.

Jordan's decision to resume his playing career has kept him in Washington full-time.

For an error in a NewsWatch:

CORRECTION-Fifteenth NewsWatch (Telemarketing Fraud)

In the Fifteenth NewsWatch that just moved, substitute the following for the item Telemarketing-Fraud:

(Corrects lead line to include new information from police that the three Montreal-area residents are the first non-bikers in Quebec to be charged under the anti-gang law.)

(Telemarketing-Fraud)

Three Montreal-area residents have become the first non-bikers in Quebec to be charged under the federal anti-gang law.

The three are accused of masterminding a telemarketing scam.

If there is an error in an audio skedline, a correction is sent using the same format used for a wire story. If there is a mistake in the audio itself, an advisory tells stations not to use it, explaining what is wrong and saying whether it will be replaced. When available, a replacement is sent, with the audio sked identifying the report as a substitute.

ADVISORY-Atlantic Audio 3:35 p.m.

NETWORK ADVISORY

Make no further use of cut AT08. It contains an incorrect name of the terror operation. A sub will move on the 4:20 p.m. Atlantic feed

Atlantic Audio 4:20 p.m. AT

The following cut is a sub for AT08. It fixes the name of the operation against terrorists to Operation Enduring Freedom.

AT09 -- (Terror-Canada-Sailors)

HALIFAX (Melanie Patten-The Canadian Press) 32s. Sailors at Atlantic Canada's main navy base in Halifax are busy preparing to set sail for the Middle East. (SOURCE: The Canadian Press) (420p)

Audio cuts are killed when erroneous information is legally dangerous or the story is so off-base it is beyond a simple correction.

BULLETIN-KILL-National Audio 5:45 p.m. EST

Stations: For LEGAL reasons, make no use of cut 158 on the 5:45 p.m. EST feed. The voicer will not be subbed.

Bylines and credit lines

General

General

Bylines recognize a reporter's original contribution and diligence on a story. When a Canadian Press byline is preserved by one of our clients in their newspaper or on their website, it sends a public signal of a job well done.

Bylines shouldn't be misused. They aren't normally warranted for a rewrite of someone's news release, the monitoring of a telecast or other task involving minimal imagination and enterprise. Solid original reporting and bright writing rate a byline.

Canadian Press staff with full-time specialist beats should let editors and readers know about their expertise. Such identifications are used whenever department heads or specialist writers are reporting about their areas of speciality.

Multiple bylines can look awkward. Consult supervisors before sending a story with more than two bylines.

Basic guidelines

1. Bylines are used on top stories, outstanding features and stories by specialist writers.

2. A byline may be removed at the request of a writer if extensive changes are made to the story. In the case of Analyses or first-person material, which should not be distributed without a byline, the writer may request that the story be ditched if a dispute over editing changes cannot be resolved.

3. Desk editors may remove the byline when a story requires exceptionally heavy editing and the writer's approval is not available for the changes.

4. Bylines are not used from placelines where the writer has not been to collect the information reported. Where a reporter's diligence with the phone and other resources has helped produce a story that deserves recognition, or if the story has been gathered from a variety of locations, consider moving the story without a placeline. Or a credit line can be used.

5. Department heads and specialist writers drop their titles when their position or speciality is irrelevant; for instance, if the Canadian Press Business Editor covers an axe murder next door.

6. Aside from columns, first-person writing is normally reserved for a vivid, dramatic experience involving the writer: **As I watched, the avalanche roared down on the village, flinging trees and rocks aside.** The first person is also justified when a

staffer is an expert on the subject in the news: as a former Olympic rower commenting on a world record in the event, for instance.

7. Always obtain consent (written consent on major events) before using any non-staffer's byline on a first-person descriptive story.

8. Bylines are set uppercase and lowercase. No other slug intervenes between them and the story.

Style

For Canadian Press and Associated Press staff:

1. On most stories with or without a placeline:

> By Nick Patch

> By Jim Bronskill and Mike Blanchfield

Note: For double bylines, both writers must be in the location of the placeline.

2. For department heads and specialist writers with job titles:

> By Helen Branswell, Medical Reporter

3. For reviews by staffers without job titles but with special knowledge of a particular field, use the byline and add a note at the end of the review under three dashes:

> Canadian Press reporter Lauren Krugel studies the flute.

4. For Notes packages and other collections of material from a variety of sources, put together with originality, add a note at the end under three dashes:

> Compiled by Shi Davidi.

For non-staffers:

1. For string correspondents, use only the byline on stories with or without a placeline:

> By Arpon Basu

2. For stories picked up with few if any changes from member newspapers and used with the byline:

> By Walter Smith, Hamilton Spectator

3. For experts writing about their speciality, or for material that is carried unedited on the wire from other publications or organization, use the byline alone and add the credentials in a boldface note, usually at the end of the story under three dashes
.

> David Suzuki is a scientist, broadcaster, author and chair of the David Suzuki Foundation.

Note: If necessary, clarify the source of the item in an Editors Note:

> Eds: The following opinion column is provided by the David Suzuki Foundation and distributed unedited by The Canadian Press. It is intended for use on op-ed pages.

4. For arts reviews from papers or freelance writers, use the byline alone and add the identification in a boldface note at the end of the review under three dashes:

> Michelle Walsh is a theatre critic for the Halifax Chronicle-Herald.

> Barbara Dumont, a graduate of the National Ballet School, is a freelance dance critic.

5. Similarly for travel stories and other material by freelances:

> Joan Hanright is a freelance writer based in Darmouth, N.S.

> Bill Brioux is a freelance TV columnist based in Brampton, Ont.

6. For stories written especially for the agency, such as a first-person account by an eyewitness, precede with a publishable editors note:

> Jim Anderson was working in the fields of his 100-hectare farm Friday when a twin-engine jet crashed less than a kilometre away, killing 10 people. Here is his eyewitness account.
>
> **By Jim Anderson**
> **THE CANADIAN PRESS**
> BRADFORD, Ont. — It was the high-pitched whine of the engine that first caught my attention . . .

For unbylined stories:

1. For stories without placelines, usually the normal credit line (**THE CANADIAN PRESS, THE ASSOCIATED PRESS**) is enough.

2. From two or more services, byline the prominent service and put a credit line for the other at the bottom:

With files from The Canadian Press

Credit lines

1. On *rare* occasions, a credit line is appropriate for a reporter who has written or made a significant contribution to a story, but is not in the location of the placeline. Credit lines should not be

used for routine contributions; they should meet the same criteria that would be required for a byline:

—By Steve Lambert in Winnipeg.

—With files from Steve Lambert in Winnipeg.

2. On roundups, the byline goes to the writer. A notable contribution from another writer can be acknowledged with a credit line. A notable contribution in a roundup would be material that is used in the lead or that makes up a significant chunk of the story.

Newspapers and broadcaster credit

1. All stories picked up from newspaper or broadcast clients, even if they carry a byline, should carry a bracketed credit at the bottom of the story.

(Toronto Star)

(CTV)

2. If the story was combined from items from more than one client, list them according to the amount of material contributed:

(Toronto Star, Globe and Mail)

Note: These types of items are usually only made available to traditional print and broadcast clients, not online users. Code accordingly.

Corrections and Correctives

Mistakes happen. Misinformation gets reported. When it does, the first priority is always to get it fixed, quickly and properly.

Canadian Press stories exist in continuous publication online for at least 24 hours, though some types of items can be online much longer. Although there are contractual limits on how long websites can archive Canadian Press content, often these stories are kept online much longer. Unlike a newspaper version, online stories aren't frozen in one form. They can be changed at any time in their life as current online news. This means the window for doing a Writethru to correct a mistake is much larger than the traditional deadline cycle for newspapers.

The Canadian Press uses the following forms to deal with problems or potential problems with stories:

Writethru Correction — makes a change in fact or wording.

Kill — eliminates a story that is wrong, legally dangerous or damaging.

Writethru Correction Sub — replaces a story that has been killed.

Corrective — used to catch up with an error that has probably already been published. It is specifically designed to face the error head on and set the record straight frankly. It deals only with information shown to be in error.

Writethru Corrections

If a story that has been filed within the previous 24 hours or so is discovered to have an error, a **Writethru Correction** fixing the story should be sent immediately. This is the best way to correct erroneous details for all clients, including online services where the story is still being carried.

Precise details on where and what the error was should be detailed in a **Correction note** that is included with the story, either at the bottom (for online readers) or at the top (for newspaper or broadcast editors). It should be written in a readable style (no journalistic shorthand) that clearly but briefly explains what was wrong with the previous story.

This is a corrected story. A previous version misspelled Raphael Bruhwiler's last name.

The only circumstance where a **Writethru Correction** would not automatically move a day after a story originally moved would be if a story with the same slug was developing afresh. A **Corrective** would then likely be the best option. Discuss with supervisors.

If a story is a standup item with a long shelf life, the time period for filing a Writethru Correction could be extended well beyond 24 hours. Thursday-for-weekend stories and stories sent to wire with advance publication dates could have Writethru Corrections several days after being filed. In these cases, include when the story originally moved:

This is a corrected version of a story originally published Sept. 17. The earlier story erroneously reported the coldest spot on Pluto was 297 degrees below zero.

Legal considerations

When a story is corrected because it could pose a legal risk, don't include this information in the publishable Correction note. Instead, use a non-publishable Editors note on the story to alert editors that there is a legal issue involved. To avoid compromising the agency's legal position through use of casual language that may be trying to explain a complex situation in few words, keep the explanation basic and factual.

LEGAL: Edited for legal reasons to remove identity of driver of pickup truck.

As well, put the usual publishable Correction note on the story to tell online readers what has changed, but leave out any reference to legal issues:

This is a corrected story. An earlier version included an incorrect name.

Other considerations

1. Writethru Corrections should be sent with exactly the same coding as the story they are correcting so they are delivered to the same clients who received the incorrect version.

2. An additional tool for making clients aware that an important Correction has moved is to send an advisory, on the regular wires for newspaper and broadcast clients, and by email for web clients:

> **EDITORS: Please note the important correction in Dog-Jumps-Fox, 2nd Writethru, moved at 17:15 ET. It corrects earlier copy that erroneously said the fox jumped the dog. In fact it was the dog that jumped the fox.**

Such an advisory should move with the same coding and index categories as the original story did, as well with an Advisories index.

3. Never try to fudge a mistake in a developing story by overtaking it with a Writethru that includes a clarifying statement or skates around the original error completely. All mistakes should be acknowledged with a note in the Correction box that specifies a previous mistake is being fixed.

4. After a Correction is moved, discuss with supervisors on whether a **Corrective** (page 468) is also needed.

Kills, Subs

Sometimes the mistake is of such a serious nature that a Correction Writethru alone is inadequate. In that case The Canadian Press moves a Kill advisory on the wire to newspaper and broadcast clients, and by email to online clients.

Kills identify the story by placeline and slug, specify the reason and say whether a substitute story is planned. They should be moved with the same rankings and other metadata as the original story to ensure they reach the same online clients. (For newspaper and broadcast feeds, Kills will automatically be upgraded to urgent, with bells.)

> **Bus-Crash-Inquest, Kill**
>
> Editors: KILL Toronto Bus-Crash-Inquest for LEGAL reasons. Story names 17-year-old juvenile and says he is charged with auto theft. Will be sub.

Note: If there is reason to believe a story might be seriously wrong or legally dangerous, do an immediate Writethru Correction, removing the problematic details, while checks are made. This removes the dangerous material from online services until the facts are known. If the material later turns out to be accurate, another Writethru adding it back in can be moved.

Once a story is killed, a substitute Writethru Correction should move immediately. It is flagged at the top with a non-publishable Editors note explaining the reason for the correction. It must move with the same rankings and codings as the original story. (Newspapers and broadcasters will receive it on an automatically upgraded urgent priority.)

> **Bus-Crash-Inquest, 1st Writethru Correction**
>
> Eds: Subs for Toronto Bus-Crash-Inquest previously killed. It eliminates for LEGAL reasons the name of the 17-year-old juvenile.
>
> TORONTO — A 17-year-old driver . . .

Correctives

Is it likely that newspapers have already published the erroneous story? If so, a Writethru Correction will not work for them. They will need a brief publishable item fixing the error.

Always go back to the original story when writing a Corrective. Focus on the precise words that are wrong and deal only with the erroneous information. But deal with it fully and openly. Never try to *interpret* the original. If it is wrong, it is wrong.

Here is a sample Corrective when the mistake is CP's alone:

> **Hockey-Pond-Championship, CCTV**
> **CORRECTIVE**
> **THE CANADIAN PRESS**
> HUNTSVILLE, Ont. — The Canadian Press erroneously reported Jan. 29 that the Shoot for the Cure campaign raises money for cancer research. In fact, the program raises money for spinal cord awareness, prevention and research.

When the mistake originates with a story from another media organization, the Corrective should say that The Canadian Press *distributed* an erroneous report. In all but extreme cases (see No. 6 in the *General guidelines* below), consult the media organization before carrying a Corrective based on a pickup. Advise a supervisor so that further steps may be taken to reach the newspaper or broadcaster.

The Canadian Press believes that readers should be given both the correct version and the erroneous version together, to make clear what was wrong. It is not enough to present the correct information while acknowledging only that *erroneous information was reported previously*.

When an error originates with a government announcement, a company news release or some other official source, a followup story should be done if there is a legitimate news angle. For example, a followup to a story based on erroneous mortgage rates released by a bank might be tied to the angle that bank branches were flooded with calls.

If there is no legitimate news angle, then a Corrective should be moved. Do not state that The Canadian Press *erroneously reported* or *distributed an erroneous report* , but do explain how the error originated.

> Correction to Jan. 29 story on Shoot for the Cure campaign
> DARTMOUTH, N.S. — A Canadian Press story March 19 that was based on a police release said that a Nova Scotia man was facing charges after an assault involving a Taser. However, police later said the assault involved a stun gun, but not one manufactured by Taser International Inc.

General guidelines

1. Make sure the Corrective fully corrects what was wrong in the original. Also include the date of the error.

2. When facts and figures are involved, simply admit the error and give the correct information.

3. Consult a supervisor or counsel if there is a chance libel or contempt may be involved. Seek advice also if a Corrective might hurt The Canadian Press's legal position or aggravate the damage caused to a potential complainant.

➤ See **Corrections**, page 466.

4. Add regrets or an apology where there has been obvious damage to the reputation of a person or corporation. Such a story should be approved by counsel. It must carry an Editors Note asking media that published the original error to give equal prominence to the Corrective. See Style No. 5, page 470.

5. If a member of the public with a vested interest disputes a story, and if The Canadian Press itself or an originating media organization stands by it, carry the person's denial along with the statement that the agency or the organization stands by its report. Main Desk may need to check counsel on the appropriate wording.

6. Consider an immediate Corrective if the weight of evidence suggests the original was wrong, even when the originating media organization cannot be reached. But keep pushing to reach staff. Consult supervisors.

7. Correctives must be sent to all services that carried the original item, using the same coding. Also consider the services that may have used the erroneous material in another format. A faulty Quick may have been turned into a graphic. An incorrect spelling of a name may be in a photo cutline. An erroneous fact may be in audio skeds. A story sent on more than one wire initially may have been corrected only on one service. Alert all desks that may have used the material.

Style

1. Correctives carry a headline that specifies the date and a brief description of the content of the original story.

Correction to June 23 Caribou protection plan story

2. Correctives have a placeline, almost invariably that of the original story.

3. Be specific in descriptions of the incorrect material.

Not: The Canadian Press erroneously reported Nov. 28 that oil exports increased in 2007.

But: The Canadian Press erroneously reported Nov. 28 that oil exports increased during the first eight months of 2007 declined by 17 per cent. In fact, oil exports fell by 27 per cent.

4. Add an Editors Note on the Corrective and move a separate advisory for serious or legally dangerous errors:

Eds: Papers that published the St. John's, N.L., Elwood Hatcher slaying story of Sunday, June 1, dealing with the arrest of two suspects, are asked to give equal prominence to the following CORRECTIVE.

5. If an apology has been deemed necessary, use this style:

The Canadian Press regrets its error and apologizes for any embarrassment or inconvenience caused John Doe or Margaret Roe.

Clarifications

1. A Clarification is carried when a story is not essentially wrong but is incomplete or may have left room for a possible misunderstanding. It is a brief placelined item that carries the slug **CLARIFICATION** in the version field. Follow the handling steps set out for Correctives.

2. A Clarification should make clear that the original story — or in the case of a pickup, the story distributed by The Canadian Press — left out important information or could be misinterpreted. The Clarification would then provide a fuller version or straighten out the possible misunderstanding.

3. A Clarification would be appropriate, for example, if a story gave only one side of an issue, or if the wording could be read two ways, or if someone felt unfairly treated, even though there were no errors of fact.

> **Suspensions, Clarification**
> **CLARIFICATION**
> WINNIPEG — The Canadian Press reported July 15 that Winnipeg city council had ordered two municipal employees suspended from their jobs for going fishing when they should have been inspecting sewage lines.
> The story may have left the impression that the suspended workers had not disputed council's action. In fact, both workers have been supported by their union and are contesting the suspensions.
> They maintain they were on accumulated leave when they were spotted with fishing equipment on the banks of the Red River just outside Winnipeg.

➤ See **Broadcast formats**, page 459.

Newspage copy

1. Newspage copy or *the newspager* is most often tied to a major break in sports or business, sometimes entertainment. They are intended for use on the front page of a newspaper or a general news section of a website. They may be read by many people who may not have specific knowledge of sports or business. These stories fall into two main categories:

a) Short items that capture the key elements of the event and their impact. These items are written to whet the appetite for fuller coverage on sectional pages: for example, a story on the Toronto Maple Leafs winning the Stanley Cup. The top of the newspage story should be complete enough to flag fuller treatment inside.

b) Longer stories that take a non-specialist approach to a specialist event: how Edmonton celebrates a Grey Cup win; how employees in a small town react to a big-city decision by their only employer to go out of business after 80 years; how consumers will be affected by the merger of two meat-packing plants that have long been competitors. Strong human elements are essential in looking behind the game score, job-loss statistics and other hard-news angles.

2. In either case, plain English and the absence of jargon are essential. Sports-page copy on the Leafs winning the Cup can talk about goals-against average but newspage stories must go back to basics. Technical terms should be explained, issues presented in terms of their impact on the public or readers and leading figures in the story seen in human terms.

Slugs and coding

Every item moved by The Canadian Press carries with it an elaborate system of slugs and coding to identify it and ensure it is delivered into the newsrooms, websites and databases that should receive it. The delivery options can range from a large metropolitcan newspaper that receives virtually everything to a specifically focused website that only receives, for example, environmental stories and photos from Eastern Canada.

Much of this routing is accomplished via computer intelligence that reads the item and how it has been identified by an editor and figures out where to send it. Humans, however, must properly label items so the computer can do its work.

This section provides only an overview of this arcane world of "metadata." Specific details change regularly.

Rankings

The Canadian Press assigns every text story a ranking based on its content and importance. This controls where the story is delivered and how fast it moves. There are eight rankings:

News Urgent: For NewsAlerts, Urgents, important QuickHits. Will be automatically slugged as urgent, with bells, and moves ahead of other content on an urgent priority.

News Need to know: Major stories of the day that will appear in a nightly newscast or in the first three pages of a newspaper or the top of the queue in a web directory.

News Good to know: Back-page or secondary material that wouldn't make a national newscast.

News Buzz: These includes oddities, brites and kickers, but should also embrace those watercooler stories that everyone is talking about: the big lottery draw, the tax hike on liquor, the Hollywood star who just got sentenced to jail.

News Valued Added (also called News Optional): Situational stories, newsfeatures, sidebars to spot news stories that add a deeper or different perspective.

Feature Regular: Staff-written features such as food and health columns, film reviews, basic AP feature content.

Feature Premium: Editorials, columns, sidebars to regular features, theatre and book reviews, enterprise and other value-added AP feature material.

Routine: Advisories, budget lines, other non-publishable or non-news items.

Departmental designators

Before computers were smart enough to know that a story with the word Hollywood in it should be categorized as entertainment news, editors assigned departmental designators help sort copy into categories and into different queues in computer systems.

Today, newsfeeds can be auto-indexed into thousands of narrow categories. But they also still deliver content into wider basic categories to traditional newspaper wires. In this system, the filename received from The Canadian Press news network begins with a specific letter that indicates the type of content: Canadian general news, world news, sports and so on.

These are the departmental designators still in use:

A — Atlantic regional general news
B — Business
C — Quebec-Ontario regional general news
D — Western regional general news
E — Entertainment
F — Financial routine
G — National general news
J — Travel
L — Lifestyles
M — Service messages and advisories
P — Press releases
Q — Audio schedules
R — Sport scores, summaries and other tabular sports copy
S — Sports in general
W — World general news
X — Spare category for sport, such as Olympics
Y — Spare category for news, such as elections
Z — Spare category

Slugs

The slugline of an item contains one or more words that describe the contents of the story. All elements are separated by hyphens. The exact same keyword(s) is used any time the story is changed by later developments, or when other stories are related to the same topic: **Avalanche; Avalanche, 1st Writethru; Avalanche-Survivors.**

Keep slugs tight, yet descriptive. International news agency standards limit the slug length to 24 characters, although they may appear longer in receiving databases.

An all-caps word is sometimes used to designate copy intended for specific parts of a newspaper or website. This word appears at the beginning of the slugline: **BOOKS-John-Irving; NHL-Trade.**

All-caps slugs include: **ART; BOOKS; BRITE** (for amusing or lighter stories); **CRAFT** (media industry news); **CRIME; FASHION; FILM; FOOD; GAMES** (computer and video games); **GARDEN; HEALTH; HOMES; MUSIC; OBIT** (for obituaries);

ODDITY; RELIGION; SCIENCE; THEATRE; TRAVEL; TV; WEA (for weather items). The sports report also has an extensive list of all-caps slugs to designate specific sports; check deskbooks for up-to-date lists.

Uniqueness in slugging is important to avoid confusing two or more stories: **OBIT-Maureen-Forrester,** not **Died**. Consistent slugging using keywords helps databases autoroute items into specific directories: **NHL-Accident** ensures a customer who subscribes to NHL stories will receive a story that takes place far from the rink.

Version field

The version field provides more detailed information on the story. It is used by both editors and computers to search for and link and update related copy. Some examples:

NAC-Yashin, Urgent 1st Writethru

NAC-Yashin, 2nd Writethru Correction

Clandestine, Advance

ELXN-Ont,Rdp

In The Canadian Press editorial system, editors select any appropriate version field labels and proper slugging is applied to the story on output.

Specific slugs

This section outlines the main story slugs and the forms in which they are written by Canadian Press editors and writers. To save space, not all the coding and slugging lines are included in all examples.

NewsAlert — Used for most newsbreaks — important government announcements, court decisions and the like. In one sentence, it alerts editors that an Urgent is on its way.

It carries the headline **Canadian Press NewsAlert** and is flagged with bells. The item has a placeline and can be headline style or one sentence. It moves on an urgent priority.

Afghan-Cda-Death, NewsAlert
Canadian Press NewsAlert
  KANDAHAR — Military officials say a Canadian foot soldier has been killed while on patrol outside Kandahar city.

QuickHit — Used on an urgent story that is being filed to all services (print, broadcast and online). It is usually the next step for a breaking story where the goal is to get the news out to all subscribers as quickly as possible. When developments slow down, the broadcast and print streams separate so copy can be written with the specific needs of each service a priority. However, the QuickHit format can be resurrected should events start happening quickly again.

A **QuickHit** is a combination of print and broadcast styles. (For details, see page 147.) It carries the basic slugging of a print story, including a headline, and is automatically reformatted in broadcast style upon transmission for radio clients.

> **Myanmar-Cyclone**
> **Myanmar state radio reports cyclone death toll has soared past 22,000**
> **THE CANADIAN PRESS**
>   YANGON, Myanmar — Myanmar state radio says the death toll from the cyclone that hit last weekend has soared above 22,000.
>   A broadcast on the government-run radio station says 22,464 people are now confirmed dead in cyclone Nargis.
>   Thousands more are missing.
>   The cyclone tore through the country's heartland and its biggest city of Yangon early Saturday.
>
>   Relief efforts for the stricken area, mostly in the low-lying Irrawaddy River delta, have been difficult, in large part because of the destruction of roads and communications.
>   The first assistance from abroad arrived today from neighbouring Thailand. Canada has said it is setting aside up to $2 million in humanitarian assistance for storm victims.

1st Writethru — Used on a story that replaces a previous story in the same cycle. When warranted, it is followed by **2nd Writethru**, **3rd Writethru** and so on.

A Writethru repeats the story in its entirety, with any changes incorporated and described in a detailed Update note at the top of the item. Update notes always begin **Update:** and should explain changes that are being made. Include paragraph numbers so editors do not have to read through the story looking for the changes. Update notes should be considered publishable, as they appear on some databases available to the public. Do not use unfamiliar abbreviations or newsroom lingo.

When the story is being updated with new material, be specific about what is new. Use an urgent slug if the material significantly changes the story.

> **Plane-Crash, Urgent 1st Writethru**
> **URGENT**
> **Update: Coast Guard confirms in paras 2-4 that wreck of the jet has been found**
> **Swissair jetliner crashes off coast of Nova Scotia; 229 aboard**
> **THE CANADIAN PRESS**
> **By Steve MacLeod**
>   BLANDFORD, N.S. — The wreckage of a Swissair jet that crashed with 229 people aboard has been located in the dark ocean waters off the coast of Nova Scotia.

If the story is being corrected, the mistake that is being fixed must be explained in the **Correction** box of the metadata in a way that both general readers and editors can understand. This Correction note may appear at the bottom of stories filed to the web as well as at the top of stories filed to newspapers and broadcasters. Material in the Correction box will automatically generate a **Correction** slug in the version field of a file.

> **Plane-Crash, 2nd Writethru**
> **Update: CORRECTS number aboard plane to 229 from 227;**
> **fixes destination to Geneva in para 2.**
> **Swissair jet crashes into ocean off Nova Scotia with 229**
> **people aboard**
> **THE CANADIAN PRESS**
> **By Steve MacLeod**
>   BLANDFORD, N.S. — Ships and aircraft were searching the ocean early today for a Swissair jet carrying 229 passengers and crew that crashed near this tiny fishing village.
>   The MD-11 jet, en route from New York to Geneva, was attempting an emergency landing at Halifax airport, said Andrew Ereau of search and rescue in Halifax.

➤ See **Corrections**, page 466.

Headlines

All items on Canadian Press print wires need two headlines, a short one used for online and wireless applications; and a longer one used for newspapers and databases. Headlines may be the traditional news headline: **Nine killed when bomb explodes on London subway during rush hour**; or a line that identifies the content of the item: **Friday's Probable Pitchers.**

➤ See **Headlines,** page 80.

Index categories

Canadian Press editors assign subject index categories to text items. These can be as broad as the traditional groupings used by newspapers —**Entertainment, Sports, National** — or as narrow as **Your Money** (personal finance items) or **Beverage** (stories about the beverage industry). Each story must be assigned one of the traditional newspaper categories but other index codes used depend on the content of the item. Software can then further categorize content into even narrower grouping, using the broader categories as guidance. Index codes change regularly; see deskbooks for current lists.

Public relations and the media

Just about every news report you read or newscast you hear or see bears the stamp of public relations people. They haven't written, collected or read the news — but their influence is decidedly there.

The power of the media is a given, and companies, organizations and individuals want to use it to look and sound good. That's where the public relations worker comes in.

Anyone who speaks for the local food bank, the fire department, or works in the communications arm of a company is in a form of public relations. Fielding media inquiries for some is just one more in a long list of responsibilities. Others work full-time at it.

PR professionals know that few stories on the local newscast are the result of weeks of investigative work by legions of producers and reporters. Even if the stories are the result of lots of legwork, they know the stories usually need someone to react to them to provide context and to keep the story alive.

People in public relations (or media relations) organize news conferences and briefings and issue news releases. They write speeches, crafting phrases they hope will be used as sound bites by the electronic media. They book media interviews for their clients and coach them on what to say.

Because PR people obviously wish to shape information, the relationship between them and journalists can be uneasy. Reporters often describe those in PR as spin doctors and flacks, viewing their work as attempts to manipulate, erect roadblocks and sugarcoat reality. PR personnel worry the media may get the facts wrong or ignore their message altogether.

However the fields of journalism and PR remain intertwined.

For the PR practitioner, an understanding of how journalism works is essential. For the journalist, an understanding of how to use PR professionals as a helpful resource — without letting them hijack the story — is also a valuable asset.

For PR professionals

Is what you have to say news? That's not easy to determine. The jury is still out on what news is.

News is usually defined as information about important or interesting recent events. However, what constitutes important and what constitutes interesting?

An event that personally affects the most listeners and viewers is usually a top story. It can affect their hearts, their minds, their health, their families, or their wallets. Your information must matter to people. Ask yourself, "Would this interest me if I weren't doing this job?"

Timing is everything

If you want the media's attention, you've got to time it right. News is hot only when it's current, and new only for a few hours. That leaves a narrow window of opportunity. For instance, if you want your client to comment on an election, she must be available within hours — not a week later.

One way to get your story on the news is to come up with a sidebar idea. A sidebar is a story that dovetails nicely with another story, usually a major news item. For instance, if the big story is a record hailstorm, a story about a local restaurateur serving free meals to residents without electricity would be a sidebar.

A myriad of factors decides what makes it into a newscast or newspaper. Such things as what else is happening, where things are happening, the interests of the editor or reporter, and who will be hearing or seeing the news all come into play. Since those factors are out of your hands, make sure your information is relevant and timely.

For more featurish stories, assignment editors need a big lead time. If your client has a new style of backpack designed to help teens' tired backs, don't send the news release out the week before Labour Day. Get it out by the end of July, when back-to-school news packages are being planned.

News releases

Newsrooms are inundated with news releases every day. Most of them go straight into the garbage. But a few will become the basis of a news story, especially if they are announcing genuine news. A well-written news release, like a well-written news story, can help that process by grabbing an editor's attention.

What makes a good news release? Accurate information, clearly presented, that answers all the basic questions a reporter or reader might have. Although the purpose of a news release is quite different from that of a news story, many of the same writing principles apply.

Content

1. Write in everyday English. Forget the bureaucratic or scientific jargon. Explain unfamiliar terms. Prefer **begin** to inaugurate, **best** to optimum, **less than ideal** to sub-optimal, **carry out** to implement, **final result** to bottom line.

2. Don't hide bad news under fancy words. The layoff of 150 workers is just that; it's not consolidation or downsizing. Be specific and save the reporter a phone call.

3. If you must use unusual technical terms, explain them.

4. Try to answer the questions all readers ask: *Who? What? When? Where? Why? How?* What is happening? Who says? Who is involved? When will it happen? And where? How or why is it happening?

5. Don't try to answer all six questions in the first sentence. Put what you consider the most important news in the first paragraph.

Not: At a news conference today, Atlas Mines president John W. Merryweather said he was "happy to announce that the company has signed a $100-million, five-year agreement" with Karasawa Industries of Tokyo to produce coal for the Japanese metallurgical company, which would "necessitate the reopening of the Dovetail mine and the creation of 250 jobs at the coal face and in surface installations."

But: The Dovetail coal mine, which has been closed for 20 years, is to be reopened as part of a $100-million, five-year contract with a Japanese company. Some 250 miners and surface workers will be hired.

The details can be added in subsequent paragraphs.

6. How much detail? That's a matter of judgment. Put yourself in the reader's place and try to answer all pertinent questions. What network will the show be on and when? How soon will the new vaccine be in drugstores? What prize did your prize-winning author win? The Pulitzer? Or the Grade 10 English award? The union is pressing for $1 an hour more. What is the current rate?

7. Give some background on the organization or company involved in the news. Make sure it is factual and doesn't give the wrong impression. Resist hyperbole. Don't say the company had its highest revenues ever in the last year without also mentioning that profits were down.

8. Include the source of the news. The person quoted should be someone in authority — the company president, the coach, the chief fundraiser, the researcher who made the discovery. Include phone numbers. Reporters like to get their own quotes; broadcast reporters will need quotes on tape.

9. Make sure time elements are clearly presented. Specify when the book is going to be released. If it is a tour, provide specific details. If the ballet company is going to Europe, include cities, dates, theatres and hotels so news coverage can be arranged.

10. Include the person's age and birthplace in biographical material. Tracking down such small but important facts can consume a lot of a reporter's time. If people from across the country are involved in a news event, include hometowns.

Format

Certain conventions should be followed, no matter if the release is being delivered by fax, regular mail or electronic mail:

1. Put a date at the top of the release. Specify at the top if the news item can be used at once. If it is to be released at a specific time, add that information: For release at 8 p.m. EST Monday, Dec. 23.

2. Headlines can be useful, especially in lengthy announcements. They don't need to be fanciful — just a clear summary of the main news is fine.

Not: Royal Bank president speaks to Canadian Club

But: Royal Bank president predicts interest rates will increase by the second quarter

3. At the top or bottom of the release, give the names and titles of people who can be contacted for more information, their phone numbers and the name of the organization and address. Make sure they will be at those numbers when the release is distributed.

4. Gimmicks might get an editor's attention for a minute or two, but they are no substitute for solid information tied to a genuine news event. Samples or other free material are not usually wanted. Exceptions would be cases where the product is needed to write a story — a new book or video, for instance.

Pictures and video

Illustrations, including video, are usually a welcome addition to a news release. Like the written information, they should be new or in some way unusual, or relate to a live news topic. They attract attention because of human interest and appeal to the emotions, or they can relate to some important person, event or place.

The best photos have a sharp, sparkling quality. Avoid busy backgrounds and low, "artsy" lighting. Captions should identify everyone in the picture.

Video is most useful if it illustrates the content of the story, not the people promoting the story. Thirty seconds of the assembly line that is producing the new video game or a few minutes of game play caught on tape are preferrable to a PR person extolling its virtues.

Who gets a news release?

1. Keep a contacts list up to date. It is always best to direct a release to the beat reporter, but make sure that person is not on holidays or out of town. Next best is the appropriate editor, such as the entertainment editor for an announcement on music awards. An urgent release during off-hours should be directed to the news desk.

2. The president, publisher or other top executives of a news organization rarely attend news conferences or assign staff to cover them, so nothing is gained by sending them a copy of a news release.

3. Don't blanket news organizations with the same release. It is only going to get reported once. The bank president may be taking his speech on a cross-country tour, but a national news organization is only going to carry one story, preferably the first time he makes it.

News conferences

News conferences are a good way to get your message out to several media outlets at once — a time saver for everyone. They also usually provide good quality sound and opportunities for film clips. However, staging a successful news conference is not just setting a date and sending out a news release. It takes planning.

Technical setup

Radio and TV reporters require a certain amount of equipment and space. Some hotels and conference centres provide everything you need, including technical expertise. If this is not available, consider hiring someone who is able to set up sound and lighting systems.

If you have more than one speaker, set up a single sound feed that goes to all microphones on the table. This avoids interruptions from reporters trying to move their microphones in front of the speaker. This is especially important since many news conferences are broadcast live.

Find a way to record the journalists' questions onto the sound feed. This helps keep your client's responses in context when reporters go back over their tape, and it helps viewers and listeners of a live broadcast make sense of what's being said.

Be sure there is enough room for media personnel to set up and operate their equipment. Radio reporters like to be next to their recording equipment so they can keep tabs on the machines' counters, which speeds up the editing process. Each TV tripod takes up about as much space as two office chairs. Risers come in handy at events where there will be a lot of cameras and people. Remember camera operators often roam around to get their shots.

TV cameras require proper lighting. If you aren't providing lighting, make sure there's a place for one of the camera operators to plug in her unit.

How your client looks on video is almost as important as what he's saying. The best colours for a backdrop are blue and green, particularly if the speakers are wearing suits. Never use a window as a backdrop. It makes everyone on camera appear to be silhouettes.

Telephone news conference calls are popular in business and sports, but don't work for the electronic media. The sound quality is awful, and there are no pictures.

Content

Ever notice how often California fires lead the evening news in Canada? Events that provide good audio and video footage often get more attention because they play higher in a broadcast newscast than a more "important" news story. It will be tough to match the drama of a fire, but think about how to produce compelling audio and video.

Your event isn't news unless it affects somebody. For TV particularly, find people who are affected and will share their stories. These people will look more natural and less like mouthpieces for the company if they are filmed in their homes or in relevant locations other than the news conference room. For example, if your client runs a program that helps people improve their job skills, persuade some people who've found better jobs as a result of the program to speak to reporters. Allow reporters to film them at work. Let radio reporters record one of the job skills classes. It is best to provide these visuals and recording opportunities the same day as your news conference, allowing plenty of time for reporters to assemble and file their stories.

Additional information is often required to put the story in perspective, such as the history of the company or background that led to the announcement. Have these facts ready, or be prepared to get them quickly if asked.

Refrain from calling your conference a major news story unless it really is. Crying wolf will hurt you in the long run because journalists will stop going to your events.

Keep on top of the news. For instance, don't hold your news conference on a government budget day. Likely no one will show up.

Naturally, you will want to know how many media personnel will be attending your news conference. But don't bank on finding out much ahead of time. Decisions on assignments are generally made the morning of the news conference.

Remember news does have busy and slow seasons. Traditional slow times are around Christmas and in the summer. This can be your chance to get the media's attention, especially if you have a seasonal tie-in. But don't forget you still need a news hook.

One final note: make sure there's adequate parking. You might even suggest where in your news release. News vehicles seldom have special parking status.

Breaking news

Sometimes a company or service finds itself smack in the middle of a publicity storm. The switchboard is swamped, your voice-mailbox is full, and TV crews are waiting outside your office door. It's a tense time to be in public relations. You may be tempted to run and hide. But the best thing to do is to face the crisis head-on.

First, gather what information you can and phone the reporters who've called. Bring them up to date and let them know when a company representative will be available for an interview.

If your superiors can't — or won't — tell you what's going on, explain to the reporters that you don't have anything now but will contact them when you do. And keep your word.

Once there is something to say, find an articulate spokesperson who will go on radio and TV, either live or in a taped interview. If company management is too busy or is media-shy, do the interview yourself. It's the fastest and best way to ensure the media hear your side of the story.

If your firm decides to hold a news conference, notify all media that contacted you about the story. Telling only a few will generate bad feelings. Allow enough time for news crews to get to the news conference.

The demand for fresh sound and pictures is insatiable during an ongoing top story, even if the situation has not changed in hours. The same old clips just won't do newscast after newscast. If the chief players are busy or unwilling to take questions, it's up to you, the PR person, to address the media on a regular basis, even if you end up saying the same thing over and over.

Coaching your client

Many corporate leaders may be fearless in the boardroom but timid when it comes to facing a microphone. Here are a few basic rules for appearing on TV or radio.

1. Give concise answers to reporters' questions, and keep each answer to no more than 20 seconds. Eight to 14 seconds is ideal. Your recorded response is called a "sound bite," "clip," or "actuality." The catchier the clip, the better. But don't give one- or two-word answers. They're usually as useless as long-winded replies.

2. You don't have to have been to acting school to provide decent clips, but the person who speaks colourfully and clearly and with a bit of timbre in her voice makes it to air more often than the monotone mumbler. You should know your message and not be afraid to be passionate about it.

3. Simpler is better. Your interviewer is unlikely to be an expert in your field and neither is the viewing and listening public.

Make the point in plain language. Avoid industry jargon. Explain yourself as though you were speaking to a friend outside the business. If possible, make analogies with everyday things. Anticipate the questions and have ready answers. You can't predict all the curveballs, but you can usually make a good guess. If you don't know the answer, admit it. If you don't want to answer a particular question, simply say so.

4. If the interview is being conducted over the telephone, don't use a speakerphone; it results in poor sound. Cellphones can cut out, although sometimes their use is unavoidable.

5. If a TV interview is being held at a news conference, dress appropriately. Inappropriate clothes can be a distraction on television, and people do tend to make judgments based on appearance. If you're in a chair, sit up straight. Don't hover over the microphones and don't lean back. Don't tap the table — microphones pick up the sound. Don't fidget. Keep your hands out of your pockets. Don't look into the camera if the interviewer is present; look at the interviewer. Treat the camera and technical crew with as much courtesy as you do the journalist. That can make a big difference in how you appear on TV.

Bibliography

These works were consulted in the preparation and shaping of the *Canadian Press Stylebook:*

Barber, Katherine (ed.). *The Canadian Oxford Dictionary.* Oxford University Press. Toronto, 2005.

Barzun, Jacques. *Simple & Direct: A Rhetoric for Writers.* Harper & Row. New York, 1975.

Bernstein, Theodore M. *The Careful Writer: A Modern Guide to English Usage.* Atheneum. New York, 1973.

Burchfield, R.W. (ed.). *The New Fowler's Modern English Usage.* Oxford University Press. Oxford, 1996.

Chicago Manual of Style. University of Chicago Press, Chicago, 2003.

Collins-Robert French-English English-French Dictionary. William Collins Sons & Co. (Glasgow) and Dictionnaires Le Robert (Paris), 1987.

Copperud, Roy H. *American Usage and Style: The Consensus.* Van Nostrand Reinhold. New York, 1980.

Evans, Harold. *Editing and Design; Newsman's English.* Heinemann. London, 1973.

Fee, Margery and McAlpine, Janice. *Guide to Canadian English Usage.* Oxford University Press. Toronto, 2007.

Christian, Darrell, Jacobsen, Sally and Minthorn, David (eds.). *Stylebook (online edition).* The Associated Press. New York.

Hale, Constance and Scanlon, Jessie. *Wired Style: Principles of English Usage in the Digital Age.* Broadway Books, New York, 1999.

Jacobi, Ernst. *Writing at Work: Dos, Don'ts and How Tos.* Hayden Book Co. Rochelle Park, N.J., 1976.

Manser, Martin H. *Good Word Guide.* Bloomsbury Publishing. London, 1988.

Manual of Style. U.S. Government Printing Office. Gramercy Publishing. New York, 1986.

McFarlane, J.A. and Clements, Warren. *The Globe and Mail Style Book.* McClelland and Stewart. Toronto, 1998.

Messenger, William E., de Bruyn, Jan, Brown, Judy and Montagnes, Ramona. *The Canadian Writer's Handbook.* Oxford, 2005.

Metric Press Guide. Metric Commission Canada. Ottawa, 1981.

Nickles, Harry G. *Dictionary of Do's and Don'ts.* McGraw-Hill. New York, 1975.

Robertson, Stuart M. *Robertson's Newsroom Legal Crisis Management.* Hallion Press. Dunedin, Ont., 1991.

Rose, Turner. *Stylebook for Writers and Editors*. U.S. News and World Report. Washington, 1984.

Ross-Larson, Bruce. *Edit Yourself*. W.W. Norton. New York, 1982.

Sabin, William. *A Reference Manual*. McGraw-Hill Ryerson. Toronto, 1978.

Shaw, Harry. *Dictionary of Problem Words and Expressions*. McGraw-Hill. New York, 1975.

Shewchuk, Blair and Mietkiewicz, Mark. *Online News Fundamentals: An Introduction to Journalism on CBCNews.ca*. Canadian Broadcasting Corporation, 2009.

Skilling, Marjorie E. and Gay, Robert M. *Words Into Type*. Meredith Publishing. New York, 1964.

Strunk, William Jr. and White, E.B. *The Elements of Style*. Macmillan Publishing Co. New York, 1979.

Timmons, Christine and Gibney, Frank (eds.). *Britannica Book of English Usage*. Doubleday. Garden City, N.Y., 1980.

Walsh, Bill. *Lapsing Into a Comma*. Contemporary Books, 2000.

Worth, Sylvia (ed.). *Rules of the Game*. St. Martin's Press. New York, 1990.

Acknowledgments

The greatest debt for any edition of the *Canadian Press Stylebook* is undoubtedly to the past. The earliest workers and managers at The Canadian Press established the traditions of quality, integrity and consistency for the news agency and gathered them into book form. Senior managers of the past put their various personal — and sometimes eccentric — stamps on Canadian Press style. Later, Bob Taylor contributed an enviable knowledge and a distinctly human touch to regular updatings of the stylebook. Peter Buckley co-ordinated a major revision and his sensible voice on style and ethics issues continues to reverberate throughout the book. In 2008, we integrated the contents of our broadcast style guide into this book, adding the work of Georgette McCulloch, Mike Omelus, Jerry Fairbridge and Keith Leslie to the mix.

Canadian Press staff across the country have traditionally shared in the updating and revising of this book. For many, it is work fitted around their regular workload. People from every bureau and desk toss in ideas for improvements. All recognize the importance of making the *Stylebook* as authoritative and helpful as possible.

For this edition, the following agency journalists contributed material or acted as a sounding board for style decisions: Andrea Baillie, Dean Beeby, Heather Boyd, Helen Branswell, Neil Davidson, Mike Fuhrmann, Tammy Hoy, Ellen Huebert, Rose Kingdon, James McCarten, Angela Pacienza, Graeme Roy, Anne-Marie Tobin, Sheryl Ubelacker and Scott White.

Senior Main Desk Editor Malcolm McNeil again provided his frontline expertise on dealing with legal considerations. Graphic artist Sean Vokey gave us a dynamic update on our cover and helped update the chapter on graphics.

Thuy Anh Nguyen of our marketing department kept the production process flowing, while Chris Cohick of Satchmo Publishing, who helps manage our online stylebooks, was invaluable in turning our content into an old-fashioned book.

A solid thanks goes to these people and all the reporters and editors at the national news agency, whose daily attention to the craft of journalism gives the *Stylebook* an unmatched resource to draw upon. Thanks also to our loyal stylebook readers from outside The Canadian Press who keep us on our toes with regular suggestions for improvements, additions and changes. The editor salutes them all.

Index

The Canadian Press is
Canada's trusted news leader

NEWS & INFORMATION

Whether you need desktop access to real-time breaking news stories and audio reports, or content for your website in text, images, video and multimedia graphics, The Canadian Press is your source.

Monitor The Canadian Press Wire in real time – The only service that alerts you to Canadian Press stories before they may be carried by print or broadcast media.

Online Financial Tools – Financial data, charts and stocks.

Online News and Video – Continuously updated feed of top news stories and online video from across Canada and around the world or a custom feed of niche news based on your search criteria.

Mobile – Mobile access to breaking news headlines. On the move, but never out of touch.

Sports data from STATS Inc. – Up-to-date scores, news and stats data by sport, league, team or player, available in Canada from The Canadian Press.

IMAGES

More than just the best pictures at your fingertips. An array of photo assignment services, video netcasting and Canada's largest online image database for editorial, corporate communications, commercial and government clients.

Images Archive – Choose from more than two million news, current event and historical images.

Images Assignments – News, studio and specialty photographers across Canada and beyond.

Images and Video Distribution – Reliable distribution of your PR images and commercial video directly to the media

Netcasting – Broadcast multimedia events live on the Internet.

BROADCAST NEWS & DISTRIBUTION

Canada's largest satellite distribution network delivers live and taped programming – features, concerts, specials, remote broadcasts and play-by-play sports. Extreme Reach Canada provides advertisers a direct digital pipeline from production to air, ensuring delivery that is faster, more reliable, efficient and affordable.

Broadcast Wire and Audio – Regional, national and international news and programming for Canadian radio/TV.

Satellite – State-of-the-art distribution of audio to more than 400 radio stations across Canada.

Extreme Reach Canada – Pure-digital radio and TV ad delivery gives you the peace of mind of knowing what it's going to cost, how it's going to look, and that there won't be any surprises along the way.

CONTACT US

sales@thecanadianpress.com   416-507-2129   www.thecanadianpress.com